Culture
and Its Creators

Culture

Contributors:
Raymond Aron
Saul Bellow
Joseph Ben-David
Reinhard Bendix
Priscilla P. Clark
Terry Nichols Clark
S. N. Eisenstadt
Clifford Geertz
Jack Goody
Morris Janowitz
Harry G. Johnson
Seymour Martin Lipset
Talcott Parsons

Edited by
Joseph Ben-David and Terry Nichols Clark

and Its Creators

Creators

Essays in honor of Edward Shils

The University of Chicago Press
Chicago and London

THE UNIVERSITY OF CHICAGO PRESS, CHICAGO 60637
THE UNIVERSITY OF CHICAGO PRESS, LTD., LONDON
© 1977 by The University of Chicago
All rights reserved. Published 1977
Printed in the United States of America
81 80 79 78 77   9 8 7 6 5 4 3 2 1

An earlier version of "Writers and Literature in
American Society," by Saul Bellow, was first published under the title "A World Too Much with Us"
in *Critical Inquiry,* vol. 2, no. 1
© 1975 by Saul Bellow

LIBRARY OF CONGRESS CATALOGING IN PUBLICATION DATA
Main entry under title:

Culture and its creators.

  Includes bibliographical references.
  CONTENTS: Aron, R. On the proper use of ideologies.
—Lipset, S. M. The end of ideology and the ideology of
the intellectuals.—Eisenstadt, S. N. The sociological
tradition. [etc.]
  1. Sociology—Addresses, essays, lectures.
2. Ideology—Addresses, essays, lectures. 3. Intellectual life—Addresses, essays, lectures. 4. Shils,
Edward Albert, 1911-   I. Shils, Edward Albert,
1911-   II. Aron, Raymond, 1905-   III. Ben-David,
Joseph.   IV. Clark, Terry N.

HM213.C85   301   76-610
ISBN: 0-226-04222-7

Contents

Joseph Ben-David and
Terry Nichols Clark

Preface

Societies have a tradition that defines their boundaries in space and time, defines their relations to other societies, explicates the relationships among individuals, subgroups, and society as a whole, and gives to all this some unity and meaning. In modern societies conditions of life are constantly and rapidly changing, and the meaning of relationships among individuals, groups, and societies requires continual efforts of reinterpretation. These efforts are represented in ideology and literature. But in order to be accepted, interpretations require authority. In the past this authority was derived from revealed or traditional religion that contained an account of man's and society's place on earth and in the cosmos. Today this authority has been transferred to science, the only source of universally accepted beliefs about man's place in the universe but a source that generates constant revisions of those beliefs and also contributes to changing the physical environment of human society. Hence the centrality of ideology, literature, social science, and science in general in the culture of modern societies.

The present book is structured around these themes. The first group of essays deals with the relationships between social science and ideology. Social science attempts to interpret social events in a logically coherent and empirically verifiable way and to understand the regularities underlying social action. Ideology, in the broadest and loosest sense, includes a variety of attempts to foster social cohesion and guide collective action by means of appropriate terms and effective rhetorics and to interpret the changing situations of groups and societies. Since this rhetoric must be or must claim to be consistent with the only source of generally accepted knowledge, namely, scientific knowledge, there is inevitably much overlap between these two intellectual endeavors, and the frequent mutual incursions at the very least engender intellectual confusion and misguided policies.[1]

These incursions, their causes and consequences, are examined in the first five essays. Raymond Aron and S. M. Lipset deal with the end-of-ideology debate—triggered in the 1950s by the encroachment of social science upon ideology—and with the reaction in recent years against the very notion that ideology has ended. Aron clarifies the conceptual confusion responsible for much of the argument, while Lipset describes the history of the debate, noting how an inquiry which began as a consensual enterprise in scientific sociology subsequently turned in part into an ideological debate.

In the following three essays, also concerned with the relations between social science and ideology, S. N. Eisenstadt, Morris Janowitz, and Harry Johnson deal with the reverse process, the incursion of ideology upon sociology, journalism, and economics. Eisenstadt relates this problem to the structure of the sociological tradition and stresses its continuity in the history of sociology. Janowitz and Johnson analyze the impact on professional journalism and economics of ideas and practices introduced into American intellectual life by the student rebellions of 1968-70.

The next two essays—those by Bendix and Geertz—look beyond the mutual relations between social science and ideology to a primary source of social cohesion and collective identity, a "center" which holds societies together. Bendix explores the cultural components of the emergent national identity among the middle classes in eighteenth-century Germany, the consequent self-assertion against French cultural hegemony, and the eventual creation of an independent cultural and political center in Germany. Geertz deals with the structural characteristics of political centers by applying a broad comparative framework to study the means by which three such centers in traditional societies transmitted their values to the periphery. These two papers illustrate very well the much greater importance writers and scholars have in the creation of modern as opposed to traditional centers.

Where these first seven essays deal with the influence of culture—namely, sociology, ideology, and the symbolical representation of the "center"—upon society, the remaining group of articles reverses the relationship and examines the effect of society and social structure on the creation of literary and scientific culture. Modern so-called "mass societies" are distinguished from traditional societies by a closer integration of the entire population into their central institutions and value systems. Consequently the status of authority has diminished in political as well as cultural matters, and this diminution has been accompanied by an insistence on equality, on consensual standards, and on public accountability for all actions; moreover, privacy is not respected and is constantly transgressed.[2]

For writers in particular, very much aware of the personal and private quality of creativity, such societies create both difficulties and opportunities, some of which are explored by Saul Bellow and by Priscilla and Terry Clark. Bellow suggests the deleterious effects on literature which follow from the absence of a "significant space" around the writer to protect him from the "noise" of mass society. The Clarks look primarily at France to determine how economic opportunities and institutional arrangements there have created conditions and motivations to engage in writing as a quasi-profession.

The final essays deal with another creative occupation, science and scholarship. Jack Goody explores the interrelationship between the evolution of communication and systems of thought and draws attention to hitherto unnoticed continuities between earlier modes of thought and modern scientific thinking. The volume closes with the papers of Joseph Ben-David and Talcott Parsons on the social structure of science and aspects of the problem of the institutionalization of individual creativity in mass society. Ben-David delineates the normative control exercised informally by the scientific community through certain elite organizations. Parsons treats the implantation and institutionalization of science in American society as an end in itself.

These articles illustrate the influence of Edward Shils's work on the sociology of culture. It is a measure of his contribution to the field that, without any deliberate design on the part of the authors or the editors, every part of the book deals with problems related to his work and uses concepts derived from it. We shall not attempt to review this work but only to indicate the relationships between some of it and the issues dealt with in this volume. Shils has been a pioneer in clearing up the logical confusion attending the concept of ideology and its relation to other types of social thought[3] and in exploring the role of intellectuals in present-day society;[4] his work on the institutionalization of sociology as a profession and as an academic discipline has been fundamental to all discussion of these questions;[5] his interpretation of charisma and his concepts "center and periphery" have been indispensable in the analysis of political and cultural leadership and societal cohesion;[6] his trenchant criticism and revision of the term "mass society" as it evolved in the first decades of this century have been crucial to a balanced treatment of the place of literature (and, potentially, of art) in the modern world;[7] and he introduced into sociology the concept of "scientific community," now central to the sociology of science.[8] Last, but by no means least, as founder and editor of *Minerva* and frequent contributor, both to it and to countless symposia, colloquia, and meetings large and small, Edward Shils has commented on and analyzed virtually every aspect of higher education and learning in every major country of the world.[9]

His own work tells but part of the story, for he has given unstintingly of his time, his acumen, and his erudition to many authors whose work bears his imprint. The essays collected in the present volume are a tribute not only to the sociologist but also to the colleague, teacher, and friend whose penetrating criticism and invaluable suggestions have helped to refine many an argument and to elaborate many a new hypothesis. For all the participants in this volume—and for many others who could not participate—he has been an example of clarity of expression, rigor and originality of thought, immense erudition, uncompromising and constructive criticism, and unfailing generosity in sharing ideas with others. This book is offered to him in gratitude and admiration.

JOSEPH BEN-DAVID
TERRY NICHOLS CLARK

Raymond Aron

 On the Proper Use of Ideologies

Twenty years ago Edward Shils gave the title "The End of Ideology" to his review of the Milan conference organized by the Congress for Cultural Freedom. Some months earlier I had chosen the title "End of the Ideological Age?" (with a question mark) for the conclusion to *The Opium of the Intellectuals*. And a few years later a collection of articles by Daniel Bell appeared with the title *The End of Ideology*. It was an idea—a theme or phrase—whose time had clearly come, for the debate went on for a dozen years or so, prompting tracts and texts from advocates and adversaries alike.[1]

Closer to politics than to science, a controversy of this sort thrives on ambiguity. What, for instance, did "ideology" mean to parties on either side of the fence? Without stirring up polemics that belong to the past, I wish to make a few remarks—retrospective, no doubt —more as an exercise in self-criticism than in self-justification.

What then did I mean in 1955 by the possibility of the "end of the ideological age"? I was thinking of the 1930s, of my own experience of the Weimar Republic, and the shock at seeing every party brandish a flag, a uniform, a symbol, an ideology. At that time and place "ideology" designated a more or less systematic conception of political and historical reality and a program of action derived from a mixture of facts and values. Systematization was the keynote. The radical break between the present regime and the promised land, the opposition between the corrupt world of today and the transfigured one of tomorrow, could only lead, as they did, to millenarianism and fanaticism.

Translated by Priscilla P. Clark

1

The Second World War considerably simplified the ideological map: there remained only Marxist-Leninism on the one hand and its opponents on the other. These anatagonists of Marxist-Leninism could scarcely be called unified, running as they did from social democrats at one extreme to traditionalists and even ex-fascists at the other. Still, to my mind they were alike because none was capable of constructing an ideology or an ideological system in the strict sense of the term. Condemned to submit to history, the once great nations of Europe no longer aroused any nationalistic fervor. Freed from regrets for paradises lost after the defeat of the right, the bourgeoisie accepted modern industrial society and indeed explicitly took as its goal the growth of production and a less inequitable distribution of the fruits of economic progress.

It goes without saying that I expected neither a meeting of minds nor irenic policies. Even if the right lost its hostility to parliaments and to factories, even if the millenarian left ceased to mistake authoritarian planning under a single party for the final realization of human destiny, more than enough room remained for sociopolitical conflicts, both actual and intellectual. The dual allegiance of democratic nations to liberalism and egalitarianism creates an inevitable and immense disparity between what democracy is and what it is supposed to be. Only ideology, in the strict and specific meaning I used, purports to bridge this gap between the real and the ideal. The end of ideology meant not the end of ideas but the end of the pseudo-rational or rationalistic millenarianism of which Marxist-Leninism furnished the most recent example.

Coming before the Khrushchev report, this analysis seemed confirmed by the events of the ensuing years as, one after another, the European powers experienced "economic miracles" and as the West heard, from the Soviet leaders themselves, irrefutable testimony to the ravages of Stalinism. However, the student disorders and the leftist violence of the 1960s seemed to refute these predictions of things to come, which some regarded as too optimistic, others as too discouraging. My own analysis had stressed two elements: the *systematization* of ideas, the hope for the kingdom of God on earth, and the potential for *fanaticism*. If utopia is defined less by a vision of the future than by the unconditional rejection of the present, then utopia can do perfectly well without Marxist-Leninism or any other conceptual framework. Furthermore, pure fanaticism thrives more on hate than on hope. If ever Marxist-Leninism ceases to attract and contain fanatics, they will express their rejection of the present through violence instead of supplying disciplined troops to a party which stands for order—an order imposed on the faithful in the short run and on everyone in the more or less long run.

What, then, has happened in Europe during these past twenty years? No one has refuted the diagnosis—that there is no ideological system extant to replace Marxist-Leninism if and when it dies out. What events have contradicted is the apparent if not explicit confusion among doctrinal systematization of ideology, fanaticism, and chiliasm. At the same time, themes of social protest forgotten during the cold war or overshadowed by the economic success of the West have acquired new currency. Thus, the weakening of the last great ideological system did not promote a pragmatic approach to problems but, quite to the contrary, encouraged widespread social protest.

In part the error or misinterpretation resulted from a lack of a sense of history. Like Marxism itself, insofar as it is an ideological system rather than a scientific theory, Marxist-Leninism represents only *one* possible response to *one* great debate in contemporary society: the joint debate over property and the market. Is private property to blame if the stupendous increase in productivity has failed to eliminate poverty? Incrimination of property is a leitmotif in social thought. In the first stage of industrialism, when the means of production were often concentrated in the hands of a single individual, industry itself revived the arguments of the accusing chorus. The cycles, apparent overproduction, and anarchy of the free market left it vulnerable to socialist criticism, which was already common coin in the first half of the nineteenth century. Marxism and, subsequently, Marxist-Leninism have played on these themes with incomparable talent and to great effect; and since their popularity fluctuates with the economy, any real depression assures the at least fleeting success of these familiar tunes.

If debate over the organization of the economy dominated discussion it was because labor unions, at least in Europe, as well as certain parties on the left, adhered to antiliberal doctrines (collective ownership of the means of production, a planned economy). To be sure, some unions and leftist parties were more Marxist than others. The English labor movement for one has always been allergic to the Marxism which had such an impact on all the socialist parties on the Continent. Still, because it was more concerned with distribution of rewards than with the mode of production, the English labor movement was defined above all by its platform of socioeconomic reforms. We had all largely forgotten that these polemics between liberalism and socialism were preceded by an ideological debate which dealt with the very foundations of modern society, certain characteristic features of which had already been indicted by two men, one before, one during, the French Revolution: Jean-Jacques Rousseau, who opposed the *philosophes* of the *Encyclopédie*, and Edmund Burke, who denounced the Jacobins of the Revolution. The first taught that scientific and artistic progress did not bring moral progress; the second wrote that the time of sophists, economists, and calculators had come and that the glory of Europe was forever extinguished.

In the nineteenth century the man on the left declared his allegiance to the rationalism of the Enlightenment, believing, as he did, in human progress through science. But Marxism had assimilated a number of the themes of rejection and expectation which were part of those philosophies clearly hostile to modernism. While Marx himself condemned romantic nostalgia, he considered it inextricably tied to capitalism; socialism alone would fulfill men's desires for communion, socialism alone would reconcile men with one another and with nature. Saint-Simon's industrialism as the means, Rousseau's vision as the end—the idea translates an aspect of the thought of Marx, and perhaps of Marxists even more.

If we keep this in mind, the success of neo-Marxists like Herbert Marcuse and the virulence of the leftists at the end of the 1960s become understandable and even logical. The Soviet experience had deprived Marxist-Leninism of a good share of its utopian potential. Some of the evils of industrial society suddenly seemed all the more apparent because others seemed on the verge of disappearing. The alienation of the individual in the anonymity of rationally organized enterprises, the destruction of nature, the pollution of air and water, and all the classic accusations, once considered reactionary, against the Prometheanism of modern society—these became a substitute for, or complement to, Marxist polemics against capitalism: a substitute in the eyes of doctrinaire defenders of ecology or the environment, who distrusted governmental and economic planners no less than the managers of private corporations; a complement in the view of a Herbert Marcuse, who is so little bothered by consistency that he retains his belief in collective ownership of the means of production even though the Soviet experience has shown that collective ownership enslaves one-dimensional man still further.

For the first time since 1917, Marxist-Leninists are being attacked from the left, and these attacks strike a sympathetic chord among those of a revolutionary temperament. Yet none of the groups or splinter groups of the far left has elaborated a new ideological system; none has been able to supply a theoretical framework for a mass party. Some wave the Trotskyite banner, convinced that another 1917 must come, this time to lead to neither Stalin nor Brezhnev. Others graft onto a more or less Marxist interpretation of capitalism a program of action that is closer to anarchism. Still others simply reject industrial society without proposing any alternatives.

In brief, it is clear that the end of the great ideological systems had brought neither reasonable discussion nor pragmatic action but instead a proliferation of sects and a retrieval by the left of themes which used to belong to the right. Confusion reigns. The French weekly that regularly proclaims unity on the left as the highest priority also publishes a magazine which advocates a return to nature and the simple life. Twenty years ago such writings would have been condemned out of hand by proper (i.e., leftist) intellectuals as a reactionary crime. The Western obsession with growth, denounced by certain factions of the left, comes straight out of the Soviet five-year plans, in the sense that it is the Western response to the statistics thrown out by Marxist-Leninist propaganda. Currently a good many critics on the left incriminate the very notion of growth, while the Communists remain faithful to the productivist gospel.

Ideological discussions are incomparably richer now than during the cold war, when we had dogmatic assertions from one side and, from the other, apologias for the democratic-Keynesian-liberal synthesis. Today the very foundations of contemporary society are subject to debate. At the same time, no ideological system has emerged which will withstand comparison with those of the past. The search for moderate growth, for nonpolluting industries, for a market economy without depressions, for the reduction of inequalities—these are not easily condensed into slogans. The way we define ideology—whether we stress conceptual systematization or diversity of themes or, again, the passions which these themes engender—will determine the way we speak of ideologies and whether we talk about their collapse or their resurgence.

Even though it was begun in Europe, or by American intellectuals with European roots, the debate over the end of ideologies (or ideology) took place mostly in the United States, where it necessarily acquired a distinctive coloring. Even in the early 1950s and even on the far left, American intellectuals, unlike Jean-Paul Sarte or Maurice Merleau-Ponty, rarely evinced much interest in ideological systems. Even before the disorders of the 1960s, those who subscribed to the end-of-ideology position were subjected to a barrage of criticism from all sides, accused at one and the same time of conservatism, skepticism, and pragmatism. Only if "conservative" is taken to mean anyone who is not a revolutionary can Daniel Bell and S. M. Lipset be called conservative. Both basically accepted the American political as well as economic system, but then so did most of their opponents. Nor were they necessarily more hostile to reforms. At most it could be said that because they measured the American against the Soviet system, Bell and Lipset were inclined to judge America less harshly than those who measured it against an ideal. Whatever the popularity of Bell's argument, and it was limited, it belongs to a period of transition, to a time when the West was still defining itself in terms of the Soviet enemy and, while doing so, was feeling both superior and victorious. But however proud they were when they measured themselves against the Stalinists, these Westerners became quite morose when they considered what they themselves really were.

On a higher level of abstraction, the affirmation that ideology was ending, or might end, struck a different note in the United States than in Europe, where the dialectic between Marxism and anti-Marxism is fairly much taken for granted and is understood immediately by intellectuals of every persuasion. In the United States, where even today, but especially twenty years ago, Marxism remained marginal, the rejection of ideology signaled not so much confrontation of reality and ideas as antagonism to ideas themselves, acceptance of reality and pragmatism, and the ordering of human affairs as best as possible, with no utopian vision, no desire to transform the socioeconomic system.

Whether or not this pragmatism had anything to do with the anti-ideology thesis, it clearly continued an American tradition. At the same time, it seemed to break with the tradition of idealism. Ever since 1776, every party, not excepting radical or populist movements, has claimed descent from the Founding Fathers and their ideas. Liberty and equality will inspire revolutionaries as long as the economy renews inequalities and as long as various social controls restrict civil liberties. Such ideas, once directed at unbridled capitalism, like the capitalism of trusts at the end of the nineteenth century, serve now, in the late twentieth century, to censure the capitalism of conglomerates or even the capitalism of the welfare state. The adaptability of these criticisms betrays their utopian component, but one far removed from the utopias of former Marxist-Leninist Europeans like Herbert Marcuse and Ernst Bloch; for not only do the ideas of the Enlightenment not constitute a system, they exclude the very idea of system. The notion of equality is expressed in many ways which are not always compatible; all are imperfectly realized and realizable. Equality before the law is resisted by custom and habit; legal measures are able to challenge custom only by infringing upon those personal freedoms once held inviolable. And then, to what extent is equality of opportunity possible when, thanks to their different social backgrounds, members of even the same age group start from very different points in the race for success? Finally, even supposing it were to be attained, equality of opportunity logically engenders inequality of condition. To what extent should society intervene in this race to achieve the egalitarian ideal?

In the past, as befitted a pioneer society which was not reacting against a feudal or aristocratic order, America insisted on equality of opportunity: equality before the law, the juridical basis of universal citizenship; equality of opportunity, the guiding principle of social justice. Never fully realized, these two notions may be called utopian; but, unlike a millenarian utopia, whether Marxist or leftist, they activate the never-ending task of reform.

Bell and Lipset would surely have agreed with these remarks. They opposed "revolutionism," the myth of salvation through a break with historical tradition; they opposed the Soviet model and all the utopias condemned to exist in a vacuum by their failure to specify ways and means. But since for the most part Bell's and Lipset's adversaries were not revolutionaries either, or Marxists or even socialists, they did not make the mistakes denounced by the American critics of ideology. The result was that these critics of ideology ended up looking like pragmatists bereft of idealistic fervor, either resigned to the impossibility of achieving the American dream or frankly satisfied with the status quo. Theirs was, moreover, a pragmatism difficult to distinguish from skepticism.

The accusation is unfair if this supposed skepticism means simply a reluctance to convert to a faith or a recognition that the gap between principles and institutions will never be bridged. Still and all, the charge is understandable in a situation where the diagnosis appeared to announce an era of calm or resignation—not the end of reform but the end of great passions and great debates. Now there is no doubt that the expectation (or fear) of consensus has in fact collapsed (or was dispelled). More than that, by combining certain elements drawn from the Marxist-Leninist theory of imperialism with the typically American polemic against the concentration of power and wealth in trusts and conglomerates, adversaries of the "Establishment" came closer than ever before to elaborating a theoretical system. The Vietnam war did not just unsettle American youth; it helped open up the young to ideology in the European sense. Never had intellectuals seemed so inclined toward ideology as ten years after some of them had announced its demise. We would do well to renounce the "end of ideology" as a proposition, or at least as a phrase, and find some other way to express whatever truths it contained.

Fanaticism and millenarianism come and go, wax and wane, subside without disappearing. One utopia seems to be refuted by events, to die; another appears, or the same one reappears in a different guise.

Anyone old enough to take in at a single glance the systole and diastole, the alternation, of faith and skepticism, cannot but marvel that the same hopes, however often trampled, can still launch assaults on the same Bastilles—or the old Bastilles wearing a new coat of paint. The same fate is shared by those who have so often feared the end of utopia and of transcendent idealism and those who have so often wished for or even foreseen reasonable discussion of means and ends. Men, or in any case the citizens of secular societies, dispel their common illusions and, to use Pareto's terms, demonstrate the constancy of residues and the variability of derivations.

In Marxist terms we would say that Western pluralistic societies always contain groups which reject the existing social order. In the forefront among such groups today are the intellectuals in the Soviet sense—meaning all those with academic degrees and more or less skilled, nonmanual occupations. Their education and their perspective on social and political issues incline these intellectuals to be severe. I can scarcely think of any society today which lives up to its principles. The technical-administrative structures imposed by complex economic techniques maintain inequality of power and prestige even where men determine to reduce earning differentials. Widespread secondary education and the expansion of higher education multiply competitors in the race for success, which inevitably leaves, behind the winners, reveling in their glory, the losers, embittered by ambitions unfulfilled.

Today in France the hue and cry is raised against the educational and social system for not preventing the transmission of privileges from one generation to the next ("privilege" taken to include any advantage, merited or not, which redounds to the benefit of any occupant of a high social or professional position). Sociology is coming to understand how this transmission of privilege takes place and also the fact that it does not foreclose either the transformation of the social structure between one generation and the next or a certain incidence of social mobility, in either direction, within each generation. This phenomenon is more characteristic of society in general than of any particular political system, but in either case it is generally condemned by contemporary egalitarians. In this sense it could be said that modern societies claim as their own the very ideas (or ideals) by which they are condemned, whereas, in the past, myth and religion helped stabilize the existing order instead of undermining it (although it is true that myths and religions have always exercised negative as well as positive functions).

In lieu of a transcendent ideal, secular societies are today founded on ideas—on systems of ideas, on principles—derived from fact and from values, all of which presume both institutions and ideals. While ideology can be defined broadly enough to include religious doctrine and myths, I prefer to define it by this particular historical situation: modern societies are based on a certain idea of what they want to be, or what they think they are, or what they ought to be. Political discussions inevitably become ideological, because to understand reality and to set goals one must refer to political or social ideas.

Marx usually set ideology against science or objective truth because, in his view, the liberal economy ignored or altered the facts in order to justify capitalism. Not that economists necessarily intended to camouflage surplus value or exploitation. But, given their position and interests, they were naturally inclined to take an optimistic view of the situation and to impute that view to science. Did Marx consider this tendency irresistible, or did he believe that even members of the bourgeoisie or capitalists, taken individually, might rise above class interests and vision? I do not doubt that Marx believed in the universality of truth—and that included economic or historical truth. For him *Capital* and its ideas of surplus value and exploitation constituted a true interpretation of capitalism. Was it a scientific truth (as in physics or biology) or a philosophical truth (as in Hegel)? A moot question surely. But I consider it beyond dispute that Marx himself did not go as far as Mannheim's radical perspectivism. Because of its interests and historical consciousness the bourgeoisie as a social class could not accede to the Marxist vision. But individual bourgeois could. Perspectivism and the grounding of sociopolitical thought in the social being, to follow Mannheim, are facts, hence a concern of the sociology of knowledge. They are not constraints, which concern the theory of knowledge and which would eliminate even the idea of truth (including, perhaps, the truth of perspectivism itself).

By their very nature the principles of contemporary societies—principles derived not from belief in some transcendent source but from the social order—provoke a distinctive ideology or ideological discussion because of the propensity of every social group to invoke ideas and then to identify with them the institutions they recommend. These ideas, or clusters of ideas, range from abstract, indeterminate ideas—like liberty and equality at one extreme, or Marxism at the other—which explain, judge, and prophesy all at once. Marxism explains exploitation and poverty, condemns capitalism, and prophesies the advent of socialism, which, following a resounding catastrophe, will realize the abstract ideals of the Enlightenment. Originally defined by the rejection of utopia, Marxism appears a century later as the prototype of a certain utopia, more utopian than avowed utopias because it claims to be scientific.

If ideology is taken, in a sense close to that of Pareto's "derivations," to mean all the ideas or clusters of ideas tied to a given social group, whose sociohistorical consciousness they reflect and whose claims they justify, then any discussion, even a theological one, can be ideological. More strictly construed, however, ideologies and ideological controversies characterize those societies which themselves set their responsibilities and objectives, having no recourse to models in either the universe or religious doctrine. Such societies must measure themselves against their own principles or ideals.

As Scheler noted, such principles or ideals are permanently available in the universe of Ideas, whence historical circumstances or material factors bring one or another to the fore. Ideological discussions in the broadest sense never cease, because man expresses his feelings in a pseudo-rational form; this tendency is even less likely to cease in modern societies, because every social group expresses its aspirations in overtly socioeconomic terms, borrowed from the so-called scientific disciplines.

Whether the definition of ideology is taken from Pareto or from Marx, it seems to me that modern societies evidence an extreme and irresistible penchant for ideological controversy. (Some say that it even replaces theological controversy, since debates in any society concern whatever domain, real or not, is considered essential; in the past, this domain was occupied by religion or the place of man in the universe; today, it is the socioeconomic system or the organization of society around human ends.)

Why this movement toward ideology? First the great explorations of new lands, and later the momentum of the French and Industrial revolutions, made European countries conscious of their distinctive nature. The place of European culture among other cultures, the conquest and costs of industrialism, the destruction of social hierarchies inherited from the past, and the concomitant irresistible movement toward democracy—all these themes from the past, however disfigured or dissimulated, turn up in contemporary political theories. Liberalism and socialism are only two forms of industrialism, but each repels counterrevolutionaries, those who yearn for the state of nature or at least for nature undefiled by man. For two, perhaps three, centuries European-American culture has thought of itself, not as an order, but as a movement; and this perspective accounts for two characteristic attitudes: either one bows, in hope or with resignation, before the irresistible movement toward democracy or socialism, or else one judges this movement with reference to an ideal.

In each case, the European mind joins a Promethean optimism to a sense of history. That God is dead means not just "Everything is permitted" but also, and especially, "Everything is possible." If, thanks to science and technology, man is able to land on the moon, is it not absurd to judge him incapable of organizing the social order to attain his view of the good society? One of the reasons for the intellectuals' fondness for socialism has to do with socialism's generally optimistic view; at least it seems to be more optimistic than reliance on the half-blind working of the free market. Men today ask more of that vague entity they call society than ever before, and for that reason they are all the more disappointed and indignant when no more is forthcoming than in the past.

Social scientists are today no more successful than they were yesterday at answering the major questions which generate politics:

How flexible is the organization of complex societies? To what extent can it be modified to effect a substantial reduction in inequalities—inequalities in the earnings and, even more, in the prestige and power of legally equal citizens? To what extent does legislation for equality protect the personal liberties characteristic of the West? We tend to settle all these incertitudes by fiat, though we generally think our decisions both probable and reasonable. The revolutionary, on the other hand, persists, never despairing that the tenth attempt will succeed where nine have failed, while the nihilist rejects the weakness of hope and is generally content to assert that the existing social order should not survive at all.

As I have said, party doctrines retain elements of a philosophy of history, and this explains why the decline of Marxist-Leninism has stirred up themes temporarily neglected: the nostalgia for community, distress over the industrial pollution of nature, etc. It nevertheless remains true that no system has succeeded Marxist-Leninism. Why not? Because it is irreplaceable. Because it contains virtually all the criticisms of modern culture, wrapped up in the denunciation of capitalism and the promise of a new tomorrow. With the help of dialectical argument, economic planning and collective ownership of the means of production are able to retain the positive and suppress the negative aspects of present reality. Who would not endorse such a system—even though to do so requires sacrificing reason and ignoring experience? Half mixed in with the realities of the Soviet system, Marxist-Leninism works no miracles. Its merits and demerits, in the wealthier countries at any rate, are openly discussed and compared to those of Western regimes.

Henceforth, conformism on the left will oscillate between ecology—the fight against pollution and for the quality of life—and denunciation of conglomerates, imperialism, and inequality. Sects proliferate because each one harps on a single theme. All together, in their separate ways, they call into question the framework of Western societies, the democratic-liberal-Keynesian synthesis. Economic crises diffuse this protest to social strata barely touched by previous waves.

To be sure, it is awkward to apply a single label to the Stalinist catechism and to the socioeconomic analysis of both free-market economies and authoritarian economies planned to realize equality (in its various meanings), efficiency (growth rate and technical progress), personal liberties, and quality of life. The Marxist side believes that the entire history of mankind, if not of the universe, ends in socialism and that socialism creates a society without contradictions, or at least without contradictory contradictions (make sense of that if you can!). The other side starts from the problems common to all modern economies and works from models and experience to determine the probable consequences of proposed solutions. Union of reality and values, prophecy, for the one; dualism of what is and what ought to be and patient amelioration, for the other. So opposed did these two attitudes once seem to me that it never occurred to me to give them the same name.

My change of vocabulary today is due, first, to the multitude of intermediate cases between the two ideal types; second, to the existence of orthodoxies derived from doctrines hostile to Marxist-Leninism but just as crude and imperialistic; and, finally, to the similarity of the themes used by the social sciences and by propagandists, the continual interchange between the self-consciousness that modern societies draw from social conflict and the consciousness they derive from supposedly scientific disciplines. This interchange sometimes leads to a quasi identity of the two, as in so-called socialist countries, where an ideocracy is based on the truth of Marxist-Leninism. Western societies have no equivalent of Marxist-Leninism, either as a basis for a regime or as a foundation for intellectual synthesis or pseudo-synthesis. No theory to date, whether economic or sociological, has escaped suspicion of ideology, a term designating a perspective which, while claiming to be neutral and objective, is, on the contrary, found to be rife with moral or political biases and practical implications.

Nevertheless, the difference between the attitudes expressed in Marxist-Leninism and in democratic-liberal thought is a real one, and it perhaps stands out with even greater clarity against a common background. For this conflict opposes pride and modesty. Where the believer affirms a universal truth and refuses to distinguish between what he knows and what he wants, the critic, well aware of the traps set by passion and the ambiguities inherent in reality, continually questions his propositions, his models, his conclusions.

In one of his last letters, written from Posen on 23 June 1831, Karl von Clausewitz recounts to his wife that they must often have irritated the Marschall von Gneisenau by their reluctance to accept anything on faith. "The Marschall," writes von Clausewitz,

> is absolutely unable to get used to looking at things critically, at least not right away and not when they are presented with wit.

Yesterday I found my name written in red in the margin of the following passage in the *Journal des Débats* [French parliamentary record] (I immediately erased it): "It is a fact that the most serious and most enlightened minds are those which doubt the most and that those who doubt the most are those with the firmest convictions."[2]

Do those who doubt today have the firmest convictions? I would scarcely dare affirm so much. Aside from the core of regulars and professionals, the Communist Party renews its clientele faster or more often than other parties. The authentic liberal doubts everything and patiently searches for truth. But he will never doubt his firmest moral and intellectual convictions. I was not wrong in opposing this attitude to that of true believers, the faithful of secular religions. I was wrong to call one ideological and the other not. We would do better to look to Pascal and speak of "the proper use of ideologies."

Seymour Martin Lipset

2

The End of Ideology and the Ideology of the Intellectuals

The proposition that advanced industrial or postindustrial society would be characterized by a "decline" in—or even the "end" of—ideology was asserted by many writers during the 1950s and early 1960s and has come under sharp criticism in recent years. Seemingly, the reemergence of left-wing politics in the form of assorted "New Lefts" and the growth of mass movements based on excluded elements (ethnic minorities, women students) constitute *prima facie* evidence that the "end-of-ideology" writers were wrong. A whole host of left-wing intellectuals have emphasized this "error" in order to discredit "pluralistic" political analysis. They argue that its basic inadequacy has been demonstrated by the fact that some of its more prominent spokesmen, particularly Raymond Aron, Daniel Bell, Edward Shils, and myself, mistakenly predicted "the end of ideology."[1] Typical of such attacks were comments made in a review in the *Times Literary Supplement* of a book dealing with ideologies:

> Not so very long ago Raymond Aron, Daniel Bell and Seymour Martin Lipset, among others, were confidently predicting the decline of ideological fervour in the Western industrialized countries. . . . The fact was, of course, that this itself was an ideology; a tacit one, no doubt, but one, nevertheless, that rationalized and supported the existing

This paper was written with support from a grant by the National Endowment for the Humanities for a study of the role of the intellectuals in modern society. An earlier preliminary version was published as "Ideology and No End," *Encounter* 39 (December 1972): 17–22.

system. . . . In effect what the proponents of the idea of the
decline of ideology were saying was that, in Mannheim's terms,
utopia was dead. . . . This was wrong . . . ; the past two decades
have been characterized by a growth and proliferation of total
ideologies.[2]

Kenneth Keniston, an American faculty supporter of the student
activism of the 1960s, also criticized the writings of "Daniel Bell,
Seymour Martin Lipset, and Edward Shils that the age of ideology
was over" as patently wrong. He argued that their "historically
parochial" liberal orientation prevented them "from anticipating,
much less understanding, what was increasingly to happen among a
growing minority of the young during the 1960s."[3]

A Russian scholar, L. N. Moskvichov, the deputy head of the
Chair of Marxist-Leninist Philosophy of the Academy of Social
Sciences of the Central Committee of the Communist Party of the
Soviet Union, also singled out the writings on the subject by
Raymond Aron, Edward Shils, Daniel Bell, and Lipset. He noted
that the theory of the end of ideology "is particularly popular among
right-wing social democrats and modern revisionists and serves in
some degree to substantiate their ideas of 'liberal' socialism, 'socialism with a human face' or various 'models' of socialist society."[4]

Although this paper will focus on left-wing critics, it should be
recognized that, as Moskvichov notes, "There are a number of
authors who take a right-wing ideological stand for whom the theory
is nothing more than irresponsible 'gobbledygook' which leads to the
West being disarmed ideologically in the face of world communism."[5]

The implicit assumption in the leftist criticism is that an alternative and more accurate estimate was presented by radical thinkers,
who anticipated a revival of revolutionary politics in the West.
Generally, most of these polemicists make their point by ridiculing a
variant of the "end of ideology" that was never stated by any of those
attacked.[6] More significant, however, as a phenomenon to be
studied by those interested in the sociology of knowledge—or the
ethics of controversy, or indeed the selective ideological character of
memory—is the way in which these critics conveniently ignore the
varying ideological background of discussions of the decline of
ideology and political conflict in the years preceding the rise of the
New Left. It may be worthwhile recalling some of that history for the
record.

As with many other "politically relevant" concepts, the famous phrase first appeared in a Marxist classic, Friedrich Engels' essay on Feuerbach. Engels argued that "there would be an *end to all ideology*" unless the material interests underlying all ideologies remained "of necessity unknown to these persons."[7] That is, insofar as true consciousness existed, as men became aware of their real interests, ideology—i.e., the elaboration of false consciousness— would disappear. As Lewis Feuer pointed out: "The obsolescence of ethical ideology is a corollary of historical materialism as applied to the superstructure of a socialist society."[8]

Another fountainhead of ideas in political sociology, Max Weber, pointed to a secular decline in total ideologies as a consequence of the inherent shift over time within societies from an emphasis on *Wertrationalität*, or substantive rationality, involving orientations toward ultimate values, to *Zweckrationalität*, or "functional rationality," referring to an emphasis on efficient means to attain goals.[9] Inherently a passionate commitment to absolute ends must break down. As William Delany has noted, "That continuous rationalization, demythicization and associated disillusionment are characteristic of Western religious institutions, capitalism, music, bureaucracy and political ideologies is, of course, the major theme in the life work of 'the sage of Heidelberg.' "[10]

With specific reference to contemporary politics, however, Weber, drawing on the work of the Russian scholar, Moisei Ostrogorski, contended that a blurring of ideological differences is inherent in the situation of political parties operating under conditions of universal suffrage. In a letter to Robert Michels in 1906, discussing the German Social Democratic party, Weber predicted that, although the party still had "something like a *Weltanschauung*," the fact that it accepted the logic of a political democracy would lead to a decline in its ideological commitments in favor of a more pragmatic orientation.[11]

The first explicit formulation of the end- or decline-of-ideology thesis also came from Germany. Writing from his office in the Frankfurt Institute for Social Research in the late 1920s, Karl Mannheim, in the very book, *Ideology and Utopia*, which established the study of ideology as a major topic for sociology, discussed the conditions which were producing a "decline of ideology" and the "relinquishment of utopias," since total doctrines (*Weltanschauungen*) were being reduced to partial pragmatic ones.[12] The underlying logic of Mannheim's analysis reiterated the main points of Weber's assumptions concerning a shift from substantive to functional rationality as inherent in the development of bureaucratic industrial society. Mannheim also emphasized the way in which the logic of politics reduces ideological commitments, noting that, as a movement associated with utopian doctrines gains governmental or state power, "the more it gives up its original utopian impulses and with it its broad perspective...."[13]

Following up the implications, but not the politics, of Engels' assumption that ideology would decline with the resolution of the oppression of the masses, Mannheim suggested that such a change could occur without the triumph of socialism, since he anticipated that the impulses of the lower "strata whose aspirations are not yet fulfilled, and who are [therefore] striving towards communism and socialism" would decline as society is able

> to reach a somewhat superior form of industrialism, which will be sufficiently elastic and which will give the lower strata a degree of relative well-being.... (From this point of view it makes no difference whether this superior form of social organization of industrialism, through the arrival at a position of power on the part of the lower strata, will eventuate in a capitalism which is sufficiently elastic to insure their relative well-being, or whether this capitalism will first be transformed into communism.)

Such developments in the political arena, Mannheim argued, were necessarily paralleled in various forms of intellectual life:

> This process of the complete destruction of all spiritual elements, the utopian as well as the ideological, has its parallel in the most recent trends of modern life, and in their corresponding tendencies in the realm of art. Must we not regard the disappearance of humanitarianism from art, the emergence of a "matter of factness" (Sachlichkeit) in sexual life, art, and architecture, and the expression of the natural impulses in sports—must all these not be interpreted as symptomatic of the increasing regression of the ideological and utopian elements from the mentality of the strata which are coming to dominate the present situation? Must not the gradual reduction of politics to economics, towards which there is at least a discernible tendency, the conscious rejection of the past and of the notion of historical time, the conscious brushing aside of every "cultural ideal," be interpreted as a disappearance of every form of utopianism from the political arena as well?[14]

The tendencies Mannheim noted in 1929 seemed to become realities in the two decades following World War II, when the belief in diverse forms of charismatic *Wertrationalität* in the religious, economic, and political orders broke down, in part because the various ideologies and utopias proved to be failures or became routinized operational realities. Protestantism and Catholicism, fascism, capitalism, communism, and social democracy, all lost their power to inspire Western people to work hard, to live morally, or to change the world. The ideological legitimations of societies or political forces were expressed increasingly in secular *Zweckrationalität* terms, i.e., as efficiently operating social orders or representatives of interest groups.

These developments led a variety of political analysts to posit the decline of ideology, particularly as it affected the behavior of leftist or working-class movements after World War II. Thus Albert Camus, writing in the left-wing Paris daily *Combat*, in 1946, noted that socialists, by abandoning Marxism as "an absolute philosophy, limiting themselves to retaining its critical aspect . . . , will demonstrate that this era marks the end of ideologies."[15] Writing in 1949, the British sociologist (and socialist) T. H. Marshall advanced a general explanation for the rise and decline of total ideologies. He suggested that they initially emerged with the rise of new strata, such as the bourgeoisie or the working class, as they sought the rights of citizenship, that is, the right fully to participate socially and politically. As long as they were denied such rights, sizable segments of these strata endorsed revolutionary ideologies (or utopias). In turn, older strata and institutions, seeking to preserve their ancient monopolies of power and status, fostered conservative extremist doctrines. The source of the decline of such ideologies in democratic countries, from this point of view, lies in the eventual integration of these groups into society and polity.[16]

Another British scholar, Isaiah Berlin, in reviewing the development of political ideas in this century, came to similar conclusions in 1950, although from a different ideological and analytical perspective, that of a conservative political theorist. Berlin argued that the general acceptance in the postwar world of the "policy of diminishing strife and misery" through collectivist state action was resulting in an order whose "entire trend . . . is to reduce all issues to technical problems of lesser or greater complexity."

> In Western Europe this tendency has taken the . . . form of a shift of emphasis away from disagreement about political

principles (and from party struggles which sprang from genuine
differences of moral and spiritual outlook) toward
disagreements, ultimately technical, about methods.... Hence
that noticeably growing lack of interest in long-term political
issues—as opposed to current day-to-day economic or social
problems.[17]

The first extensive scholarly analysis of the "end of political
ideology" by an American was published in the spring of 1951 by a
historian, H. Stuart Hughes. Although Hughes's analysis contained
all the basic elements elaborated by subsequent commentators, his
work has been studiously ignored by critics of the thesis. Perhaps
this benevolent disregard is due to Hughes's record as a socialist
supporter of left-wing causes (e.g., Henry Wallace's presidential
campaign of 1948, SANE, TOCSIN, and other peace groups) and his
running as a third-party leftist peace candidate for United States
senator against Edward Kennedy in 1962, a record which tends to
confound attempts to give the concept ideological links. Hughes's
description, written in the first year of the 1950s, closely resembles
others which appeared later in the decade:

> The process of ideological dissolution which began thirty
> years ago with the first successes of Italian Fascism and
> which the disillusionments following the Second World
> War notably accelerated now seems to have reached its
> logical conclusion....
> Quite predictably, the Left is hardest hit. The Left,
> vociferously ideological and doctrinaire, was more vulnerable to
> this sort of slow corrosion than the Right, which has learned
> skepticism and adaptability from its defeats of the last century.
> In fact, the end of the *mystique* of the Left is the clearest sign of
> what happened....
> Socialism as a political faith has very nearly abdicated....
> Under present circumstances, a party that has chosen the
> course of participation in government can scarcely avoid the
> taint of conservatism, the negation of ideology currently
> associated with political power.
> By the same process of reclassification, the word "fascism"
> has lost most of its terrors. In conservative circles many people
> avoid the term entirely....
> Even the word "democracy" is losing its sacrosanct
> character.... Of the two major parts of the most generalized
> contemporary definition of democratic—individual freedom

and government by universal suffrage—it is only the former that
has retained its power to inspire enthusiasm and sacrifice. . . .
   What has really gone glimmering is the promise of social
equality. In the year 1950, the only sort of equality that most
cultivated Europeans can see before them is a leveling up and
down to a lower-middle-class standard of respectable
grubbiness—the kind of daily living of which George Orwell
gave so chilling a description in his *Nineteen Eighty-Four* and
of which Britain under the Labour Government has provided a
dignified foretaste. This is not the notion of equality which once
inspired death on the barricades and the consecrated lives of
revolutionaries. . . . The common man has lost his aura of
sainthood. Those who a decade ago spoke of the century of the
common man were perhaps simply in error by a hundred years:
it was the century that was ending rather than the century that
was opening before them.[18]

   In 1955, the Frankfurt Institute was again to provide a "home" for
another important expression of the thesis when Raymond Aron
published his "Fin de l'âge idéologique?" in one of their volumes.[19]
Although the leading spokesmen for "critical theory" did not agree
with their "guests," Mannheim and Aron, they were to advance their
own versions of the "end of ideology" in various works. As Martin
Jay, the historian of the Frankfurt Institute, notes: "the Frankfurt
School's version of the end-of-ideology grew out of their belief that
liberal society was being replaced by an almost totally 'administered
world' in which ideological justifications were no longer necessary."[20] Theodor Adorno, in an article published in 1951, concluded
that "in the authentic sense of false consciousness there are no more
ideologies."[21] In a collectively authored book, presented as the work
of the Institute as a whole, which appeared in 1956, they called
attention to the "weakening" of ideology from a high point reached
"around the year 1910":

   One can speak of ideology in a meaningful way only to the
   extent that something spiritual emerges from the social process
   as something independent, substantial, and with its own proper
   claims. . . . Today the characteristic of ideologies is much more
   the absence of this independence, rather than the delusion of
   their claims. . . .
   Nothing remains then of ideology but that which exists itself,
   the models of a behavior which submits to the overwhelming

power of the existing conditions.... Ideology and reality are converging in this manner, because reality, due to the lack of any other convincing ideology, becomes its own ideology.[22]

More detailed efforts to explain the decline of ideology in Western society were advanced by two erstwhile members of the Frankfurt School who remained in the United States after the main body returned to Germany after the war: Otto Kirchheimer and Herbert Marcuse. Kirchheimer in three trenchant articles contended that partisan-based ideologies waned because the ideological

> mass integration party, product of an age with harder class lines and more sharply protruding denominational structures, is transforming itself into a catch-all "people's party".... Under [the] present condition of spreading secular and mass consumer-goods orientation, with shifting and less obtrusive class lines, the former class-mass parties and denominational mass parties are both under pressure to become catch-all peoples' parties.[23]

In addition, according to Kirchheimer,

> the modern welfare state can now provide solutions to problems of many social groups. This weakens the old clashes of immediate interests and converts them into mere conflicts of priority in the time sequence of satisfactions.... This situation allows ... [party] policies to be determined by tactical requirements of the moment, relegating ideologically determined long-range goals to a remote corner.[24]

Herbert Marcuse's repeated emphases on the decline of ideology in modern society exposed him to criticism from the French Marxist sociologist Lucien Goldmann, who grouped "Aron, Marcuse, Bell, Riesman" as the sources of the "belief that Western society has been so stabilized that no serious opposition can be found within it."[25] Time and again in his writings and public lectures, Marcuse has reiterated his belief that modern industrial capitalism, through its ability to sustain abundance and entertainment, has eliminated all but the slightest possibility for mass radical protest. In 1964, he commented that

> in the capitalist world, there are still the basic classes [capitalists and workers] ... but an overriding interest in the preservation and improvement of the industrial *status quo* unites the former antagonists in the most advanced areas of comtemporary society.[26]

Marcuse's despair about the revolutionary potentiality of the working class is, of course, well known. Far less publicized is the fact that he was so pessimistic about the role of Blacks and students that he openly opposed the participation of the first in the political process and of the second in the governance of the university— because the system is able to seduce both into basically conforming to the status quo. At a symposium in 1965 at Rutgers University, Marcuse stated that Negroes have been brainwashed by American society and consequently follow middle-class norms in their political behavior:

> When asked which situation he preferred—one in which the Negroes were deprived of their civil rights, including the power to vote, or one in which they freely exercised the civil rights to choose "middle-class values," Marcuse replied: "Well, since I have already gone out on a limb, I might as well go all the way: I will prefer that they did not have the right to choose wrongly."[27]

Less than a month before the French "events" of May 1968, in an interview with *Le Monde*, Marcuse stated:

> Everywhere and at all times, the overwhelming majority of students are conservative and even reactionary. So that student power, in the event of it being democratic, would be conservative or even reactionary.[28]

By 1969, Marcuse, like many others, had learned that he was wrong. In his *Essay on Liberation*, he identified the American "ghetto population" and the student opposition as major disruptive forces. Yet, it should be noted, he still concluded that a liberating "revolution is not on the agenda" of the advanced Western industrial states; that the combination of the necessary "subjective factor" (political consciousness) and the "objective factor" ("the support and participation of the class which is at the base of production") only "coincide in large areas of the Third World."[29]

Similar ideas were advanced by the scholar who comes closer to being an exponent of Marxist analysis in American sociology than any other major figure in the field and who subsequently coauthored with Marcuse and Robert Wolff a radical tract for the late sixties, *A Critique of Pure Tolerance*. This is Barrington Moore, Jr. Writing in the fifties, Moore noted that

> as we reduce economic inequalities and privileges, we may also eliminate the sources of contrast and discontent that put drive into genuine political alternatives.... There is, I think, more

than a dialectical flourish in the assertion that liberty requires
the existence of an oppressed group in order to grow vigorously
.... Once the ideal has been achieved, or is even close to realization, the driving force of discontent disappears, and a society set-
tles down for a time to stolid acceptance of things as they are.
Something of the sort seems to have happened in the United
States.[30]

About the same time, T. B. Bottomore, who was to become the
principal senior exponent of Marxism in British sociology and the
successful candidate of the leftist forces for the presidency of the
International Sociological Association in the mid-seventies, voiced
comparable judgments with respect to the direction of change in
Western society generally. Bottomore identified the decline in
ideological conflict in the postwar world as reflecting a basic shift in
class relations. As he put it in 1955, in *Classes in Modern Society*:

> [E]ven though democratic governments still have a class
> character, this is no longer their most prominent feature, as it
> frequently was in the nineteenth century.... It should also be
> observed that in most modern democracies there is a large and
> growing area of social policy on which the main parties agree.
> The extent of this agreement on the interests of the community
> as a whole is a measure of the decline of sharp class
> antagonisms. It is a measure especially of the degree to which the
> privileged groups have surrendered their privileges and have
> abandoned the pursuit of purely selfish interests, and thus of
> the real diminution of class differences.[31]

Ten years later, in the second edition of this book, Bottomore,
reacting to the reemergence of sharp ideological controversy among
the Western intelligentsia, held up other proponents of the "end-of-
ideology" thesis to scorn for their failure to have understood that the
basic sources of radical appeal still continued under capitalism.[32]
There is not the slightest suggestion in this revised edition that
Bottomore himself had been an exponent of an extreme version of
the thesis, one which, in its social optimism, went far beyond the
analysis of such writers as Aron, Bell, Shils, and myself. He simply
dropped his 1955 contention that ideological conflict had declined
because

> property owners in the developed industrial democracies have
> ceased to be a ruling class in the sense of being able to maintain
> or improve their own situation in society or to resist the growing
> pressure for equality of condition.... The instruments of

production can no longer be used without regard for the interests of the worker; they are hedged about with restrictions imposed by democratic governments. Property no longer automatically assures to its possessor a predominant share in the political affairs of his society. Power, in the contemporary democratic societies, is dispersed among numerous social groups, employers, trade unions, and voluntary associations of many kinds, each of which brings its influence to bear upon government policy.[33]

Possibly made aware of the discrepancy between the position taken in the two editions, Bottomore, in 1967, in discussing the "end of ideology" as "a phrase which rings strangely," nevertheless went on to note that "if what is meant is that the great nineteenth-century ideologies which divided societies internally have developed cracks and appear to be crumbling, and that they no longer exercise anything like their former sway over the minds of social critics, then the characterization may be accepted as plausible."[34]

Three years later, in 1970, Bottomore, in an essay in the New Left-oriented *New York Review of Books*, once more reversed direction and severely criticized, as patently "discredited views," the "notorious doctrines proclaiming the 'end of ideology' and the achievement of 'stable democracy' in the Western industrial countries."[35] Again, there is no hint in this essay—which assumes that the exacerbation of political conflict in the late sixties constituted a self-evident refutation of the views under attack—that its author had advanced many of the arguments that he was now projecting onto the writings of others. Thus earlier, in a comparison of the Soviet Union with "the Western democracies," he suggested that the "unification of elites ... characteristic of all the Communist countries" has resulted in "the formation of a new ruling class and the consolidation of its privileges and its power over the rest of the society," while the Western countries "differ ... [in] that in them the power of one group is limited by the power of other independent groups, political parties, employers, trade unions, and a variety of other pressure groups. This is a very important difference, for the emergence of a single unified elite means the end of both freedom and equality."[36]

Bottomore included among the "notorious doctrines," linked to the "end of ideology," the concept of stable democracies, seemingly forgetting that he had once emphasized that "Universal adult suffrage has made it possible, by peaceful means, to curb the power of property owners and to change the character of government...."

Individual freedom in society can only be assured by political means, by institutions which must as a minimum exclude the single-party system and encourage dissent by the protection of minority groups."[37]

Bottomore, like other leftist critics of the "end-of-ideology school" of sociologists, in the flush of enthusiasm over the emergence of radical activism among students and sections of the intelligentsia in the late sixties, triumphantly argued in 1970 that the "source of this failing was its own unhistorical character, ... that it encouraged a propensity to regard the fleeting present as an eternal order."[38] Curiously, in view of subsequent events in the 1970s, Bottomore presented as an example of this failing my 1967 estimate that the revived movement is likely to be "one of many unsuccessful attempts ... to create a radical movement in an essentially unfertile environment," given the historical background that "in the United States, with its relatively stable social system and a fairly long tradition of political tranquillity, radical social movements of any kind have had difficulty in establishing themselves."[39] Bottomore might have better maintained his record as a prognosticator if he had held to his own pessimistic 1967 comment about student politics. He noted at the time that the possibility that the "new radicalism ... [would last longer than previous short-lived waves] depends upon whether the new radicalism can find some basis in society less ephemeral than a student movement."[40]

By 1971, in an article evaluating the by then evident decline of the student movement, Bottomore wrote that it is "difficult to foresee the development of a broad radical movement" in the United States. He saw little hope for the radicalization of the working class "in conditions of growing prosperity and declining trade unionism."[41]

Participants in and faculty supporters of the student-activist wave of the sixties could only find words of total scorn for those like David Riesman and myself who called attention to the historical pattern of recurrent rises and rapid declines of student-based movements.[42] Yet, a few years later, such generalizations were to give sustenance to radicals depressed by the evident ebbing of protest. Bettina Aptheker, a Marxist leader of the Berkeley Revolt in 1964–65, took heart in 1973 from the fact that "all social movements go in waves. You cannot sustain a level of intensity for an indeterminate length of time ...; if that analysis is right, the movement will recur."[43]

The assumption that basic structural trends in Western society had sharply reduced the factors making for intense ideological conflict was applied during the early sixties specifically to the prospects for student activism by a left-oriented scholar, Kenneth Keniston, who was to become the most significant sympathetic American student of the phenomenon during its high point in the last half of the decade. He first emphasized the "decline of Utopia" and "quiescence" among students. In commenting in the mid-seventies on the "view of the modern period as one of the 'decline of utopia' and the 'end of ideology,' " Joseph Gusfield was to emphasize the writings of Keniston, together with those of Daniel Bell and Judith Shklar, as major statements.[44] Keniston's conviction that American youth were inherently "predominantly apolitical" led him in 1963 to put "political revival" in quotation marks in the title of an article discussing "signs of increasing political activity on a number of campuses," and to devote most of the essay to analyzing the enduring structural sources of "apathy."[45] He suggested that it "almost appears that affluence and education have a negative effect on political involvement, at least in America"—a conclusion he was to reverse a few years later.

Yet the same Kenneth Keniston was to single out for scorn the writings of Daniel Bell, Seymour Martin Lipset, and Edward Shils about the end of ideology. From the assumption that this group of "liberal" theorists "predicted precisely the opposite of what has actually happened," Keniston concluded that this "fact alone should impel us to question and redefine the basic assumptions from which liberalism began."[46] One may be forgiven an expression of astonishment in reading these words, coming as they do from a research specialist on the behavior of the young who insisted, even *after* the youth revolt of the sixties began, that it could not possibly reverse the basic forces making for apoliticism and apathy among students, and directed as they are against a group of scholars who explicitly anticipated in their writings on the end of ideology the reemergence of ideological or utopian politics based on a "rebellious younger generation" (Shils), "the young intellectual" (Bell), and "the intellectuals" (Lipset).[47]

My references to the work of a number of scholars who have been identified with Marxism, or whose scholarly writings include endorsement of various forms of left-wing activism as proponents of an extreme "end-of-conflict" variant of the "end-of-ideology" thesis, are not meant to suggest that their work gives the thesis a specific leftist ideological coloration. But, given the polemical context of recent discussion, it is important to note that various political persuasions, each in its own way, lent support to the idea. These include, in addition to those discussed earlier, two prominent American sociologists, David Riesman and Talcott Parsons; Herbert Tingsten, long-time editor of Sweden's leading liberal newspaper, *Dagens Nyheter*; Gunnar Myrdal, the famous economist and Swedish socialist leader; Ralf Dahrendorf, probably the best known of contemporary German sociologists, writing in the mid-1950s while still an active socialist; Stein Rokkan, sometime president of the International Political Science Association; George Lichtheim, historian and theorist of socialism; Lewis Feuer, a current exponent of psychoanalytic approaches to social analysis; Michel Crozier and Alain Touraine, French sociologists of sharply different orientations; Mark Abrams, British pollster; Robert Lane, Yale political behaviorist, former student leader, and current socialist activist; Judith Shklar, Harvard professor, writing from the viewpoint of political theoy; and Thomas Molnar, a conservative political theorist among the many who could be cited.[48]

Although John F. Kennedy has been given credit by some as ending the political quiescence of the "silent '50s" in the United States by giving voice to a new ideological commitment to the country's egalitarian objectives, thus inspiring student political activism, Kennedy himself espoused a version of the "end-of-ideology" thesis in public discourse in statements the first drafts of which have been attributed to Arthur Schlesinger, Jr. Thus in May 1962 he proclaimed that ideological division over basic issues was over; that there was no further need for "the great sort of 'passionate movements' which have stirred this country so often in the past." A month later, in a commencement address at Yale, the young president concluded that "the central domestic problems of our time are more subtle and less simple. They do not relate to basic clashes of philosophy and ideology, but to ways and means of reaching common goals."[49]

The assumptions underlying these statements—that the basic economic problems of jobs, security, and inequality had largely been resolved—were presaged in the late fifties by two liberals who were to become the major intellectual spokesmen for the Kennedy era, Arthur Schlesinger, Jr., and John Kenneth Galbraith, both then Harvard professors. In 1957 the former wrote,

> While there are things to be done in areas of economic direction and regulation, the major problems of economic structure seem

to be solved; few liberals would seriously wish today to alter the
mix in our present mixed economy. . . . Moreover, to a great
degree, the present conservative Administration has
nominally, at least, run away with the verbal objectives of the
New Deal. . . . As Arthur Larson has suggested, we are all New
Dealers now. [50]

Five years later Schlesinger elaborated these views to a global scale,
noting that the rise of the welfare state or "mixed society" has

revealed classical capitalism and classical socialism as
nineteenth-century doctrines. . . . It is evident now, for
example, that the choice between private and public
means . . . is not a matter of religious principle. . . . It is simply
a practical question as to which means can best achieve the
desired end. . . . Indeed, I would suggest that we might well
banish the words "capitalism" and "socialism" from
intellectual discourse. [51]

His academic colleague, subsequent comember of the Kennedy
administration, fellow enthusiast for the New Politics of the 1970s,
and currently self-proclaimed socialist, Galbraith, presented similar
views, noting that

as an economic and social concern, inequality has been
declining in urgency. . . . Production has eliminated the more
acute tensions associated with inequality. And it has become
evident to conservatives and liberals alike that increasing
aggregate output is an alternative to redistribution or even to
the reduction of inequality. The oldest and most agitated of
social issues, if not resolved, is at least largely in abeyance, and
the disputants have concentrated their attention, instead, on
the goal of increasing productivity. . . .
    The ancient preoccupations of economic life—with equality,
security, and productivity—have now narrowed down to a
preoccupation with productivity and production. Production
has become the solvent of the tensions once associated with
inequality, and it has become the indispensable remedy for the
discomforts, anxieties, and privations associated with economic
insecurity. [52]

Much of the leftist criticism of the end-of-ideology theme has
focused on the writings of the so-called pluralist school of sociologists, Aron, Bell, Shils, and myself, stressing the supposed disconfor-
mation of our hypothesis, given the New Left revolt of the 1960s,
which was based largely on students, excluded minorities, and the

intelligentsia. Each of us, however, had anticipated that political protest would continue and would be supported largely by these strata. Thus, in his original article in *Encounter* in 1955, as noted earlier, Edward Shils predicted that, unless Western society undertook "great tasks" socially, "ideology," in the sense of extreme or revolutionary doctrines, would "creep in through the back door, or more particularly through a rebellious younger generation."[53] Again, in an article published in 1958, which represents his most extensive elaboration of the end-of-ideology thesis, Shils emphasized the

> tendency of intellectuals in modern Western countries, and latterly in Asian and African countries, to incline toward ideological politics ... [since] most of the traditions of modern intellectuals seem to dispose them toward an ideological outlook. It seems to be almost given by their attachment to symbols which transcend everyday life and its responsibilities.[54]

In the conclusion to his 1955 essay, "The End of the Ideological Age?," which also forms the end of his book on intellectuals, Raymond Aron explicitly denied that the decline of total ideological doctrines implies a decline of commitment to social reform and change:

> One does not cease to love God when one gives up converting the pagans or the Jews and no longer reiterates: "No salvation outside the church." Will one cease to desire a less unjust society and a less cruel lot for humanity as a whole if one refuses to subscribe to a single class, a single technique of action, and a single ideological system?[55]

A decade later, in returning to the theme in an essay whose title indicates its emphasis, "The End of Ideology and the Renaissance of Ideas," Aron reiterated that he was not anticipating an end to political outlooks or efforts to reform society but rather a decline in the appeal of total or integrated ideologies in the West. As he noted, "The breakdown of ideological syntheses does not lead to insipid pragmatism or lessen the values of intellectual controversy."[56] Aron explained his position in outlining the sources of the "anti-ideological" position of the moderate left:

> The moderate left is in fact, in the present circumstances, anti-ideological in a very precise and limited sense: in each particular situation it tries to reconcile in the best possible, or least unsatisfactory, way personal freedom, democratic

legitimacy, economic progress, and the lessening of social inequalities. It is precisely because complete reconciliation [of all
these objectives within one coherent ideology] is impossible
except as a remote rational concept that the moderate left
declares itself "anti-ideological" and stresses the diversity of
political situations and the fragility of vast syntheses. It is
because developed societies are at least partially succeeding in
achieving such a reconciliation that they cannot or will not
formulate an ideological synthesis. [57]

My own analysis in *Political Man* of the decline of ideology was
presented in the context of arguing *against* the theses of Barrington
Moore and others on the *left* who stressed the impact of these
changes in reducing class struggle. As I noted in 1960, in my book
Political Man, described by Moskvichov as the one "in which the
'twilight of ideology' thesis received its fullest and most exhaustive
analysis,"

one wonders whether these intellectuals are not mistaking the
decline of ideology in the domestic politics of Western society
with the ending of the class conflict which has sustained
domestic controversy. As the abundant evidence on the voting
patterns in the United States and other countries indicates, the
electorate as a whole does not see the end of the domestic class
struggle envisioned by so many intellectuals. . . . The predictions
of the end of class politics in the "affluent society" ignore the
relative character of any class system. [58]

In specifying the factors underlying the decline of total ideologies
in left-wing parties, I elaborated on the theme originally suggested
by T. H. Marshall, discussed earlier, that because revolutionary
mass politics in early industrial society was largely a phenomenon of
the working-class struggle for citizenship, its ideological commitments eroded when "the workers . . . achieved industrial and political citizenship, [and] the conservatives . . . accepted the welfare
state." But implicit in the assumption that "inclusion" reduces the
need for total ideologies on the part of previously excluded groups is
the recognition "that ethnic, racial, or religious groups, like American blacks or Ulster Catholics, who are still deprived in citizenship
terms, will continue to find uses for extreme tactics and occasionally
ideologies." [59]

In discussing the decline of leftist sentiment among American
intellectuals in the 1950s, I suggested, in an article first published at
the end of that decade, that it is questionable

whether a permanent change in the [adversary] relationship of
the American intellectual to his society is in process. In spite of
the powerful conservatising forces, the inherent tendency to
oppose the *status quo* will still remain.... Any *status quo*
embodies rigidities and dogmatisms which it is the inalienable
right of intellectuals to attack, whether from the standpoint of
moving back to traditional values or forward toward the achievement of the equalitarian dream.[60]

Similar assumptions about the continued concern of intellectuals,
particularly young ones, for critical ideologies were made by Daniel
Bell in his analysis in *The End of Ideology*:

The new generation of [intellectuals] ... finds itself seeking
new purposes within a framework of political society that has
rejected, intellectually speaking, the old apocalyptic and
chiliastic visions. In a search for a "cause," there is a deep,
desperate, almost pathetic anger.... In the U.S. ... there is a
restless search for a new intellectual radicalism.... The
irony ... for those who seek "causes" is that the workers,
whose grievances were once the driving energy for social
change, are more satisfied with the society than the
intellectuals. The workers have not achieved utopia, but their
expectations were less than those of the intellectuals, and the
gains correspondingly larger.

The young intellectual is unhappy because the "middle way"
is for the middle-aged, not for him; it is without passion and is
deadening. Ideology, which by its nature is an all-or-none
affair ... [is] temperamentally the thing he wants.[61]

Although the tone and ideological emphasis were quite different,
C. Wright Mills, deeply steeped in the writings of Weber and
Mannheim, reached almost identical conclusions to those of Bell
and myself. Thus, in his famous "Letter to the New Left" (published
in1960), he stated: "generally it would seem that only at certain
(earlier) stages of industrialisation, and in a political context of
autocracy, etc., do wage-workers tend to become a class-for-
themselves, etc." He described the belief of some radicals in the
revolutionary role of the working class in "advanced capitalist
societies" as running "in the face of the really impressive historical
evidence that now stands against this expectation ... a legacy from
Victorian Marxism that is now quite unrealistic."[62] And Mills also
suggested that the social group which is most likely, given its
structural situation, to be a source of continuing anti-establishment
struggle is the intellectuals:

It is with this problem of agency [of change] in mind that I have
been studying, for several years now, the cultural apparatus,
the intellectuals—as a possible, immediate, radical agency of
change . . .; it turns out now, in the spring of 1960, that it may
be a very relevant idea indeed.[63]

Similar views were expressed by John Kenneth Galbraith in 1967,
when he reiterated his views, first expressed a decade earlier, that
the modern industrial system has confounded Marx's anticipations
by its ability—a concomitant of economic affluence—to absorb class
conflict and sharply reduce conflicts about "the goals of the society
itself." Yet, like Mills, he noted the emergence of "an ill-defined
discontent, especially among students and intellectuals, with the
accepted and approved modalities of social thought."[64] Such discontent and potential for conflict with the dominant economic strata on
the part of members of the "educational and scientific estate and the
larger intellectual community" are, according to Galbraith, implicit
in the sharply varying value orientations inherent in the structural
position of the two major extragovernmental elites.

In emphasizing the role of intellectuals as a potential center for
the revival of protest in the early sixties, Bell, Mills, and I were at
variance with the assumptions of Marcuse and Bottomore. The
latter, for example, argued as late as 1964 that "at the present
time . . . it is probably the case that most intellectuals in the West
European countries and in the U.S.A. belong to the right."[65]

Daniel Bell also discussed the ideological implications of the "end
of chiliastic hopes, of millenarianism, of apocalyptic thinking"—
what he means by ideology in his use of the famous phrase. And
unlike a number of more pessimistic leftists, who espoused their
own versions of the notion, Bell saw the "end of ideology" in politics
as making realistic discussions of utopia possible for the first time:
"The end of ideology is not—should not—be the end of utopia as
well. If anything, one can begin anew the discussion of utopia only
by being aware of the trap of ideology."[66]

More recently, in his analyses of the emergence of postindustrial
society which have concerned him during the past decade, Bell has
also stressed the special propensity of intellectuals to foster antinomian ideological attitudes—attitudes which, repeatedly appearing among the culture creators, reflect their desire to reduce or
abolish restraints in order "to attain some form of ecstasy." Such
attitudes are in sharp opposition to the orientation of the workaday
world, "the economy, technology, and occupational system . . .

[which] is rooted in functional rationality and efficiency ... shaped by the principle of calculation, the rationalization of work and of time, and a linear sense of progress."[67] In various writings since the late '50s, I have also emphasized the extent to which the "adversary culture" of the intellectuals, their continued opposition to the basic values and institutions of the owners and controllers of industry and politics in capitalist and postcapitalist societies, is inherent in the nature of their work, with its emphasis on creativity, originality and "breakthroughs."[68]

Max Weber, writing soon after World War I, presciently anticipated these views, noting the desire of many intellectuals to find some form of ecstasy in a period characterized "by rationalization ... and, above all, by the 'disenchantment of the world.' " Faced with "disenchantment," with the absence of charismatic total ideologies, some will shift their value emphasis "into the transcendental realm of mystic life or into the brotherliness of direct and personal human relations." They may try "intellectually to construe new religions without a new and genuine prophecy," which can only result in "miserable monstrosities. And academic prophecy, finally, will create only fanatical sects but never a genuine community." For Weber, the most ethical reaction for the intellectual "who cannot bear the fate of the times" is to return to traditional religion. "In my eyes, such religious return stands higher than the academic prophecy, which does not realize that in the lecture-rooms of the university no other virtue holds but plain intellectual integrity."[69]

A few years later, Karl Mannheim, in the same essay in which he anticipated the decline of ideology and utopia, noted the difficulty for intellectuals of living in "congruence with the realities of ... a world, utterly without any transcendent element, either in the form of a utopia or an ideology." He foretold the rise of an emphasis on " 'genuineness' and 'frankness' in place of the old ideals."[70] And, like Weber before him, Mannheim predicted that it would be the "intellectuals ... even more than now in increasing proportions recruited from all social strata rather than merely from the more privileged ones," who, unable to accommodate to a situation without ideological conflict, will seek "to reach out beyond that tensionless situation."[71]

Returning to the theme in the late thirties, Mannheim almost seems to be describing the New Left intelligentsia of the 1960s when he notes that the intellectual critics of advanced liberal democratic society "refuse to utter even the slightest solutions for the future":

[I]t is regarded as a higher sort of wisdom to say nothing specific, to despise the use of reason in attempting to mould the future, and to require no more than blind faith. One enjoys then the double advantage of having to use reason only in criticizing one's opponents and, at the same time, of being able to mobilize without restraint and to one's own profit all the negative emotions of hatred and resentment which—according to Simmel's principle of the "negative character of collective behaviour"—can unify a large number of people more easily than any positive programme.[72]

It is interesting to note that, in commenting on the writings of Daniel Bell and myself dealing with the "end of ideology," James C. Davies suggests that the malaise that basically underlies our writings is a "sense of the inadequacy of capitalist and socialist systems . . . [to] provide adequate criteria or adequate means for developing individuals and cultures beyond the level of material abundance."[73]

One specific criticism of the concept of the "end of ideology" has been made by some radicals who, admitting a congruence of empirical judgment with their own evaluation of the erosion of ideological controversy among the major-party protagonists in the Western democracies, still argue that those who have proclaimed the "end of ideology" have failed to recognize that the concept is a conservative ideological one and that it contributes to the undermining of efforts at radical change. Thus, Stephen Rousseas and James Farganis have commented that "there can be little doubt that . . . [Bell's] arguments and that of Lipset on the decline, if not the end, of ideology as an operative force in the Western world are based largely on fact," but they go on to argue that "C. Wright Mills would agree that the end of ideology makes a fetish of empiricism and entails an ideology of its own—an ideology of political complacency for the justification of things as they are."[74] But, obviously, such an argument only repeats a component part of the analysis they are criticizing. In 1963 I attempted a comprehensive discussion of the sources and consequences of the "decline of ideology":

[N]ot only do class conflicts over issues related to division of the total economic pie, influence over various institutions, symbolic status, and opportunity, continue in the absence of *Weltanschauungen*, but . . . the decline of such total ideologies does *not* mean the end of ideology. Clearly, commitment to the politics of pragmatism, to the rules of the game of collective bargaining, to gradual change whether in the direction

favoured by the left or the right, to opposition both to an all-
powerful central state and to *laissez-faire* constitutes the component parts of an ideology. The "agreement on fundamentals,"
the political consensus of Western society, now increasingly has
come up to include a position on matters which once sharply
separated the Left from the Right. And this ideological agreement, which might best be described as "conservative socialism," has become *the* ideology of the major parties in the developed states of Europe and America. [75]

In making these contentions, I was only reiterating the argument
stated by H. Stuart Hughes in the conclusion to "The End of
Political Ideology," when he noted that "The creeds of 'progress'—
liberalism, democracy, socialism—have made their peace with what
remains of traditional conservatism. . . . Is it surprising, then, that
the new conservatism of 1950 . . . should have fused all ideologies in
an unresolved concord in which the one clear note is the name of
freedom?" [76]

In all fairness, it should be noted that a Communist critic, L. N.
Moskvichov, does recognize that the main body of writings about

> the end of ideology in industrially developed states of the West
> does not imply the demise of all ideology or the absence of any
> political or ideological differences. The phrase "end of
> ideology," according to its authors and supporters, means only
> that, first, the so-called universal ideologies no longer serve to
> guide mass political actions and this applies above all to
> Marxism-Leninism; secondly, in the advanced capitalist states,
> acute ideological and political conflicts gradually die down. [77]

It should be clear from the references to some of Aron's, Shils',
Bell's, and my own writings that, in the same works in which we
discussed the "end" or "decline" of ideology, neither we nor most of
the others who wrote on the subject ever meant the end of systems of
integrated political concepts, of utopian thinking, of class conflict,
and their correlates in political positions espoused by the representatives of different classes or other political interest groups. Rather,
what we were referring to was a judgment that the passionate
attachments of an integrated revolutionary set of doctrines to the
anti-system struggles of working-class movements—and the consequent coherent counterrevolutionary doctrines of some of their
opponents—were declining; that they were, to repeat C. Wright
Mills's term, "a legacy from Victorian Marxism." They would not
reemerge in advanced industrial or "postindustrial societies," al-

though they would continue to exist in the less-developed nations, whose social structures and processes of change resemble those of Europe during the Industrial Revolution. Ideology is not the common-sense term, meaning *any* kind of political thinking, that some of our radical critics seem to think it is. One radical sociologist, Franz Schurmann, has even argued that, from a Marxist point of view, the concept of a revolutionary ideology is meaningless. "Ideology is a tricky word. For Marx, ideology was false consciousness." And Schurmann goes on to ask (in terms reminiscent of Bell's earlier discussion of the consequences of postindustrial society for political thinking): "In this 'end of ideology,' are there the seeds of a new moral-political order?"[78]

(Parenthetically, it may be noted that the Soviet scholar L. N. Moskvichov challenges interpretations of Marx such as Schurmann's. He cites a number of passages from Marx and Engels which refer to ideology as "comprising political and legal views, philosophy and religion, by no means applying any negative connotation to the term. . . . Marx and Engels emphasized the class essence of ideology in society divided into antagonistic classes." He goes on to note that Lenin wrote of the need to "carry on propaganda for the proletarian ideology—the theory of scientific socialism.")[79]

Curiously, the strongest tribute to the concerns of the "academic sociologists" who write from the "pluralist" perspective has come from the pen of another radical sociologist, Alvin Gouldner, who in 1970 noted that a group of scholars, whom he identifies with the approach of Talcott Parsons, have "focused attention on some of the new sources and sites of social change in the modern social world":

> For example, and to be provocatively invidious about it, it was not the Marxists but Talcott Parsons and other function-alists who early spotted the importance of the emerging "youth culture," and at least lifted it out as an object for attention. It was the academic sociologists, not the Marxists, in the United States who helped many to get their first concrete picture of how Blacks and other subjugated groups live, and who contributed to such practical political developments as the Supreme Court's desegregation decision. It is the ethnography of conventional academic sociologists that has also given us the best picture of the emerging psychedelic and drug cultures, which are hardening the separation and conflict of generations.[80]

In large part the polemical controversies concerning the validity of the analyses of the end of the ideology have revolved around different meanings of the term "ideology." The critics have been able to demonstrate to their own satisfaction that ideologies continue to exist—that, with the decline in the cold war, intellectuals, the intelligentsia, and educated young people have intensified their commitment to anti-establishment outlooks. In his article on "Ideology" in the *International Encyclopedia of the Social Sciences*, Edward Shils has effectively pointed out that he and other exponents of the end-of-ideology thesis never implied that "ideals, ethical standards, general or comprehensive social views and policies, were no longer either relevant or possible in human society." And, as he stresses in his recent book,

> [I]t is obvious that no society can exist without a cognitive, moral, and expressive culture. Standards of truth, beauty, goodness are inherent in the structure of human action. The culture which is generated from cognitive, moral, and expressive needs and which is transmitted and sustained by tradition is part of the very constitution of society. Thus every society, hav- ing a culture, will have a complex set of orientations toward man, society, and the universe in which ethical and meta- physical propositions, aesthetic judgments, and scientific knowledge will be present. These will form the outlooks and suboutlooks of the society. Thus there can never be an "end" of outlooks or suboutlooks. The contention arose from the failure to distinguish these and ideology in the sense here under- stood. . . .
>
> Moreover, the exponents of the "end of ideology" did not assert or imply that the human race had reached a condition or a stage of development in and after which ideologies could no longer occur. The potentiality for ideology seems to be a permanent part of the human constitution. In conditions of crisis when hitherto prevailing elites fail and are discredited, when the central institutions and culture with which they associate themselves seem unable to find the right course of action, ideological propensities are heightened. The need for a direct contact with the sources or powers of creativity and legitimacy and for a comprehensive organization of life permeated by those powers is an intermittent and occasional need in most human beings and an overwhelming and con- tinued need in a few. The confluence of the aroused need in the former with the presence of the latter generates and intensifies ideological orientations. As long as human societies are

afflicted by crises, and as long as man has a need to be in direct contact with the sacred, ideologies will recur. The strongly ideological elements in the tradition contained in the modern Western outlook are almost a guarantee of the persistent potentiality.[81]

Much of the debate concerning the concept of the end of ideology has obviously involved ideological differences. Yet the idea in its modern format was advanced by a number of sociologists and historians as an empirical hypothesis about the consequences of social development on the character of class-related partisan controversy. For the most part, the radical critics have ignored the issue of the validity of the hypothesis; they usually have taken its falseness as *prima facie*, as self-evident—given the fact that political passions and radical protest movements continue to exist. But while some have engaged in polemics, a few others have indeed attempted to evaluate the validity of the proposition. A considerable literature, some of it quantitative in methodology, has sought to compare the intensity of ideological cleavages among different societies or to examine the changes within nations over time. Three political scientists (Rejai, Mason, and Beller, not previously involved in the controversy) examined these disparate studies and concluded that the hypothesis holds up:

> The end-of-ideology hypothesis, then, has occasioned a large body of scholarly output over the past decade. In general terms, this hypothesis seeks to establish a negative correlation between the degree of economic development and the intensity of ideological politics within a given country. The hypothesis has held up quite well in empirical investigations in a number of advanced industrial societies.[82]

More recently, another political scientist, John Clayton Thomas, systematically coded the position of fifty-four political parties in twelve industrialized nations on ten dimensions for seven five-year periods from the 1870s to the 1960s. He reports "significant patterns of convergence (i.e., declining average deviations) from the 1910s to the 1960s and from the 1930s to the 1960s."[83] Nonleftist parties, i.e., conservative, liberal, and Christian Democratic ones, "moved steadily, and sometimes dramatically, leftward between the 1890s and 1960s."[84] Similarly,

> an examination of the average amount of advocacy of change by British Commonwealth labour, Socialist/social democratic,

and Communist parties ... [revealed] consistent and sizeable
decreases in their radicalism on almost all of the issues. In many
cases the degree of deradicalization is comparable to the high
degree of depolarization the non-labour parties experienced.[85]

While Thomas' work in general provides the most comprehensive
test and apparent verification of the basic assumptions in the
end-of-ideology literature, it is important to note one major modification. He finds that the nonleftist parties have changed their policy
positions more dramatically than have the labor-oriented ones,
although most end-of-ideology writers have emphasized the shift by
leftist parties and have underplayed those by other groups. Thomas
suggests that the reason for the displaced emphases may have
resulted from the fact that the status quo in industrialized society
has shifted to the left, i.e., to the welfare-planning society. Hence,

> a party's position could change, but the change would not be
> perceived if the status quo changed in the same direction. This
> explanation could account for inattention to the massive
> depolarization of non-labour parties. Second, a party's position
> might not change, but change would nonetheless be perceived if
> the status quo changed. This would account for the exaggera-
> tion of the degree of labour party depolarization.[86]

The differences in evaluation of the thesis—between those who
have carefully sought to test it, and that of the polemical critics—led
Rejai and his colleagues to look for an explanation of how men
could reach such disparate conclusions. They found it in the fact
that most of the critics demonstrate an "apparent willingness to
disregard the empirical significance of the hypothesis in question and
to rely, instead, on semantic justification." The critics are able to
challenge it "by adopting definitions of ideology that have serious
deficiencies ... that are so vague, so general, and so broad as to
minimize their relevance for empirical investigation."[87]

It should be clear also that the revival of total ideologies among a
segment of intellectuals and students in various Western countries
does not, in and of itself, challenge the theses advanced by those
who wrote of the decline of ideology among mass-based social
movements in Western countries. As noted earlier, these writings
often *explicitly* exempted intellectuals and students from the generalization. The fact that the New Left and New Politics "post-
materialist" protest, seemingly characteristic of postindustrial
society, is based on the intellectuals and their fellow travelers among

university students and the privileged intelligentsia does not mean that it is unimportant or that it will not ultimately contribute to significant forms of social change. Elsewhere I have dealt in some detail with the emergence of forms of antinomian protest in modern society, following up on the insights and anticipations of Weber and Mannheim.[88] But such trends are only in their formative stages. John Clayton Thomas, in noting the new ideological conflicts of the late sixties, argues that, since these have not involved a "revival of the economic cleavage ..., a broadening of domestic political conflict may not be out of the question, but it seems highly improbable."[89] At the moment, the political-party systems, institutionalized to accommodate the conflicts of industrial society and ideologically moderated, as Bottomore noted, by the workings of democratic electoral systems, still remain dominant. As a quantitative study of electoral patterns in "Western party systems since 1945" by the Strathclyde political scientists, Richard Rose and Derek Urwin, indicates, there has been little change in the relative strength of the political parties, whose behavior has corresponded to Weber's anticipations:

> Whatever index of change is used—a measure of trends or of several measures of fluctuations—the picture is the same: the electoral strength of most parties in Western nations since the War has changed very little from election to election, from decade to decade, or within the lifespan of a generation.... In short, the first priority of social scientists concerned with the development of parties and party systems since 1945 is to explain the absence of change in a far from static period in political history.[90]

Efforts to find a mass base, beyond an affluent minority of the intelligentsia, on the part of New Left groups which reject the established Social Democratic, Communist, and Democratic parties, all oriented to the electoral system, have failed dramatically in areas as diverse as France, Germany, Italy, Northern Europe, and the United States. Most recently, the vast majority of American New Leftists, including some of their most prominent spokesmen, have rejoined the Democratic Party in the United States, finding sufficient ideological sustenance in the liberal and populist positions that have been identified with George McGovern.

The empirical content subsumed in the concept of the "end of ideology" has commended itself to scholars of sharply different

political persuasions. Nevertheless, some of those who have enun-
ciated it have been selectively singled out as supposedly having
denied that the sharp type of ideological controversy which emerged
in the 1960s could ever occur. This attack illustrates the extent to
which ideological evaluations of underlying motives have been
confused with validity. Professor Richard Simpson noted recently
the increase in such forms of criticism in sociology and warned:

> A central idea ... is that when we pin an ideological tag on a
> theory ... we say something about the validity of the theory.
> This notion is alarming, for it would turn sociology into sub-
> standard moral philosophy with the resonating of sentiments
> replacing reason and observation as the basis for constructing
> and judging theories. [91]

S. N. Eisenstadt

3 The Sociological Tradition: Origins, Boundaries, Patterns of Innovation, and Crises

Introduction: Traditions and Their Origins

Traditions are neither congeries of folkloristic artifacts nor bodies of fully codified and systematized knowledge and belief, although they may contain both. Whatever their composition, Edward Shils has shown that they constitute a crucial, if seemingly intangible, aspect of any continuous entity or intellectual and cultural endeavor.[1] Traditions delineate some of the most crucial and pervasive aspects of such entities or endeavors—above all, the range of their contents, their boundaries, the forms of their self-identity, and the basic types of intellectual orientations and modes of action and creativity that develop within them. The representation of their origins has been an essential element in "great" traditions and little traditions, especially in traditional societies and civilizations.[2] In many such traditions the definition of an actual or reconstructed origin, depicted in the life of the founder or in special historical or mythical events or situations, has strongly influenced the delineation of real boundaries and basic orientations and has often been paradigmatic in determining further development.

It may seem that this would not be true in the intellectual,

This paper is based on parts of a longer book on sociological theory and the crisis of sociology by the author in collaboration with M. Curelaru. I would like to thank Miss Curelaru for help in preparation of this paper and the notes; Professors T. Clark, Y. Elkana, and K. H. Silvert for detailed comments; and, above all, Professor J. Ben-David for very helpful and extensive editorial comments on an earlier draft. Because of limitations of space, the documentation in the notes has been kept to a minimum.

cognitive, and, above all, scholarly and scientific, or would-be scientific, spheres, for in these areas the boundaries and progress of an intellectual endeavor are seemingly determined by its objective contents.

To be sure, the sole primacy of purely objective-intellectual and critical-empirical analysis in actual scientific work (as distinct from its validity and validation) has been boldly questioned by Thomas Kuhn and Paul Feyerabend, and earlier, from the point of view of sociology of knowledge, in a radical way by Karl Mannheim and, more cautiously, by Robert K. Merton.[3] Yet most of these scholars analyzed either the importance of various "external" intellectual or institutional forces in the shaping of different internal controversies within a given intellectual field or, like Joseph Ben-David and Randall Collins, the institutional factors leading to the emergence of new disciplines.[4] Usually there was little inquiry into the processes that determined the boundaries of any intellectual discipline. The implicit assumption was probably that such delineation is largely determined by the objective intellectual contents of a given field, by the discovery of new fields or methods of analysis, or by a combination of the two and that only when these have been set is it possible to develop within them paradigms à la Kuhn or research programs à la Lakatos.

A closer look at the history of scholarly and scientific disciplines indicates that such a view may well be but a partial one. The distinctive boundaries and identifications of scholarly disciplines, and the intellectual orientations which develop within them, are shaped by various combinations of "objective" intellectual contents with symbolic and institutional elements similar to some of the components of other types of traditions; and one could hypothesize that, among such components, the origins of a discipline—notably, the perception by its practitioners of such origins in relation to other parts of the intellectual panorama—may be of great importance.

But the way in which the perception of the real or presumed origins of a tradition influences the development of a scholarly or scientific field differs greatly from the impact such perception has on the development of a "great" (above all, a religious) tradition. While the origins of any intellectual or scientific discipline may sometimes be fully represented by a single exemplary personality or by a series of historical events, such real or perceived origins, because of the open nature of scientific inquiry, never fully indicate further developments within a scientific discipline. They can, however, be very influential in many other ways, especially in outlining concrete research programs within a field by defining its boundaries, its intellectual identity, and its concrete research problems, as well as ways of coping with them. But the influence of the origins of any scientific field on the delineation of its boundaries and on its further development cannot be exercised, as in religious or other symbolic traditions, through some direct emanation of the image of its origins or through upholding such an image as an exemplary symbolic event. Rather, their influence is exercised through specific institutional mechanisms, and it is the study of these that should constitute the central aspect of an analysis of traditions in general and scholarly traditions in particular.

In the present paper we shall attempt to analyze some basic characteristics of the development of sociology by analyzing "open scholarly and scientific traditions," following in many ways the leads provided by Edward Shils in his pioneering studies of the development of the sociological tradition.[5] We will endeavor to explain how the origins of sociology, by shaping its initial boundaries and the self-identity of its practitioners, have influenced the patterns of theoretical innovations in the field, the patterns of their incorporation into the sociological tradition, the disputes that have developed in their name, and, above all, the evolution of self-examination as manifested in declarations about its own crisis, the last and most vociferous of which have been witnessed in the recent past.

The Origins of the Sociological Tradition and the Crystallizing of Its Distinctiveness

Sociology developed its identity and its internal boundaries, however fragile, by attaining some distinctiveness from other parts of the broader intellectual tradition of self-examination and self-inquiry that developed in Europe in the wake of the Reformation and the Enlightenment and by extending the critical approach to the basic phenomena of human and social existence. This tradition, as it developed in Europe from about the middle of the seventeenth century on, originally had its major focus in philosophy but became extended to comprise many different scholarly and intellectual areas.

Sociology developed by attaining some distinction from several components of this tradition, namely, from philosophy proper, especially the utilitarian-positivist and the romantic streams, which permeated the general public outlook in nineteenth-century Europe. Second were the traditions of social reform and reconstruction and of critical journalism and political analysis. Third were the more academic specializations of modern historiography and jurisprudence and of policy-oriented economics and statistics.

The development of the distinctiveness of sociological analysis was predicated first of all on the attainment of a certain intellectual distance from philosophical and ideological political movements and from movements for social reform. Of special importance in this development, as Edward Tiryakian has so rightly stressed, was the ambivalence of most sociologists toward commitment to political ideologies and parties in general and to liberalism and socialism in particular.[6] Perhaps even more important was the perception that the same sociological theories could be used for different political or ideological purposes. Thus, within the sociological tradition a tendency to maintain a certain distance between sociological theories and their philosophical and ideological counterparts was gradually developed. Above all, there was a general weakening of ties with philosophical and ideological optimism, as espoused by revolutionaries or evolutionary liberals, and with the pessimisms of the romantics, as applied to problems of social order in general and to the analysis of the direction of modern society in particular.[7]

The separate development of sociology was also predicated on the attainment of some degree of distance from the traditions of social reform. This was especially true in England and the United States, where there were strong traditions of social reform, and in France, where the reforming tradition of Saint-Simon, later taken up—and partly revised in reaction to Saint-Simon—by Le Play and his disciples, was influential for a time.[8] The growing distance between these traditions and sociology manifested itself not only in reduced zeal for direct action, and reduced optimism about the possible impact of such action, but also in a growing stress on the importance of a more objective and detailed—and possibly also a more critical and "demystifying"—analysis of the modern social order and of possible trends in modern society.

The most crucial shift away from the philosophical and social-reforming traditions and orientations occurred in the period between some of the forerunners of sociology, on the one hand, and its founding fathers, on the other. The early evolutionists and positivists in Europe and America, together with Marx and his followers, on the whole identified themselves with broad philosophical and ideological movements. Above all they aligned themselves with certain sets of attitudes toward the solution of the problems of modern society, even though they did not fully identify themselves with any existing political party or concrete movement.[9] However, even among the earliest of the forerunners there were some, especially among the representatives of the emerging tradition of sociopolitical analysis—men like de Tocqueville or Lorenz von Stein—who did not fully accept the viability of this attitude and did not opt for "simple" political choices—whether liberal, conservative, or revolutionary—as the single natural road for modern society.[10]

This more detached, complicated, and ambivalent attitude toward ideological and political visions became even more pronounced in the later generation, especially among the European founding fathers of the sociological tradition—Emile Durkheim and Max Weber, Georg Simmel and Ferdinand Tönnies, Alfredo Pareto, and even, to some degree, Leonard T. Hobhouse.[11] Certainly they all showed great concern with the moral problems of the social and political order and evinced a very deep commitment to the exploration of it and even to its moral strengthening; they saw in sociological inquiry a crucial instrument for bringing critical enlightenment to bear on these problems. They could also identify sociology with some very broad intellectual trends, such as rationalism or secularism, but they did so to a much lesser extent than the first generation of the forerunners of sociology, men like Auguste Comte, Herbert Spencer, Karl Marx, and their many less well-known contemporaries, among whom these problems were hotly disputed. Moreover, they on the whole refused—with the partial exception of Durkheim—to identify the sociological enterprise with any single ideological trend or political party. Even Durkheim, who attempted to make sociology the basis of a new civic morality of the Third Republic and who evinced somewhat radical political tendencies, did not equate sociology with any single ideological or political group in the Third Republic.[12]

Above all, they did not share the relatively simple social, philosophic, and/or reforming optimism or romantic pessimism of the forerunners and of many of their own lesser contemporaries. Instead, they tended to stress the ubiquity and continuity of tensions between the creative and restrictive aspects of modern life: the potential contradictions between liberty and rationality, on the one hand, and justice and solidarity, on the other.

True enough, some later outstanding sociologists—Karl Mannheim and the later Marxists, such as some members of the Frankfurt school, and, in England, Leonard T. Hobhouse and Morris Ginsberg—attempted to uphold a new optimism about the possible course of modern society and of the place of reason within it, and some of them hoped that sociology might indeed provide a basis for a new morality based on reason; others, like Hans Freyer, developed a much more profound romantic pessimism.[13] However, neither of these latter groups was fully successful in obtaining acceptance for its attitude among other sociologists or the wider intellectual public. Whatever their personal standing or outlook, they could no longer identify the sociological enterprise as such with any single philosophical, ideological, or political *Weltanschauung*. Indeed, insofar as they attempted to do so, they diverted their own and their colleagues' intellectual energies from the furtherance of sociological analysis.

The Bases of the Distinctiveness of the Sociological Tradition
The development of distance from philosophical, ideological, and political movements and from movements of social reform was, however, only a precondition for the development of sociology as a distinct intellectual discipline.

This distinctiveness was attained by an analytical and conceptual reformulation and transformation of problems which were not entirely different from those with which other intellectual traditions or academic disciplines were concerned. Indeed, sociology as it started to emerge in the nineteenth century shared many central problems with all these traditions. With the broad sociophilosophical traditions sociology shared attempts to explain the "basis" and nature of social order: How is social order possible at all? How is it related to the basic wants of individuals? What are its basic characteristics and problems? More particularly, it shared with this tradition a concern about such matters as the following: the extent to which social order or life is harmonious or conflict-ridden; the relation of individuals to social life and to the good social order; the extent to which moral and social characteristics are common to all human societies—whether they constitute something basically human or vary from place to place; the degree of givenness of the social and cultural order and the basis of such givenness in "nature" or in some divine command; and, as against such givenness, the possibility of creativity and change.

With the reformist-revolutionary tradition, sociology shared an interest not only in critically evaluating the major characteristics of modern society and the conditions of modern social life but also in investigating, evaluating, and analyzing the possibility of changing some of these conditions through various ameliorative or revolutionary programs.

The sociological tradition shared with the modern tradition of journalistic political analysis a concern with such problems as the nature of the class structure of modern society; the nature and working of different political systems (whether democracy or autocracy); the social basis of liberty and tyranny; the analysis and description of the characteristics of modern city life; and so on.

It shared with history and with ethnographic studies, and with some of the traditions of political analysis, a concern with understanding, in a scientific and critically detached way, some of the conditions and laws of development of a single society or political order, of different types of societies and political orders (or even full societies), of the institutions and customs of different people, of even, perhaps, historical development itself.

It shared with the more practical policy-oriented economic and demographic research a concern with the observation of actual patterns of contemporary social life (such as family life, patterns of consumption, and the like), with the collection of data which could shed light on these patterns, and to some extent with the development of statistical and other methods of empirical or quantitative research.

However, in attempting to analyze these problems, sociology developed approaches and a set of problems of its own, and it was around these that its distinctiveness emerged.

The distinctiveness of sociology from philosophical and ideological orientations emerged on the intellectual level, first of all, in the attempt to transform questions about the nature and bases of social order from philosophical questions into analytical problems subject to critical, potentially empirical, investigation, capable of being tested. Second, this distinctiveness emerged—in contrast to the concerns of social reformists, on the one hand, and political analysts, historians, and observers of contemporary social life, on the other—when sociologists attempted to deal with relatively concrete problems by analyzing them in relation to the general problems of social order—its nature, conditions, and variability.

On the intellectual level the distinctiveness of the sociological approach manifested itself, first, in the development of a specific sociological *Problemstellung*, which differed greatly, not only from the philosophical and ideological ones and from the concerns of social reformers, but from the ways in which political analysts, historians, ethnographers, and other observers of contemporary social life formulated their problems; second, by the development of the so-called sociological theories, namely, explanatory and analytical models of social order; third, by the development of a series of specific questions or problems relating to more concrete aspects of social life, organization, and behavior and by the attempt to connect these systematically with the broader paradigmatic problems of social order; and fourth, by the connection of all these with scholarly scientific research in general and with some generalized analytical concepts in particular.

The Specific Sociological *Problemstellung* and the Intellectual Distinctiveness of Sociology

This specific sociological *Problemstellung*, as developed very haltingly and intermittently in distinction from the philosophical, ideological, and social-reforming traditions, did not ask about the "natural" conditions or characteristics of the social order or for the single "best" type of social order. Instead, the major focus of inquiry was shifted to the analysis of the conditions and mechanisms of social order and its constituent components—of continuity and change in the social order in general and in different types of social order in particular. Thus, the basic problem of social order became gradually reformulated from how society emerged from a presocial base into how some continuous interaction among human beings is possible, given—as a sort of basic datum of human existence, a sort of evolutionary universal of mankind—the basic social interdependence of human beings, on the one hand, and their distinctiveness, on the other. True, for very long periods there persisted among sociologists a tendency to formulate the Hobbesian problem: the problem of social order in terms of a transition from a presocial individual state into some social bond;[14] but with each major steppingstone of sociological analysis the locus of this problem was shifted more and more to the institutional sphere itself, to the very construction of human society. Thus Marx stressed that alienation is rooted in the very nature of the division of labor in general and in the class division of labor in particular.[15] Similarly, Durkheim's emphasis on the inadequacy of purely contractual ties stressed that it was the process of division of labor which created the central problem of social order, while Weber's emphasis on the importance of the legitimation of material, power, or prestige interests made a basically similar point.[16]

The impact of this search for the conditions and mechanisms of social order (instead of the search for the general characteristics of society as a "natural" or purely moral fact or order) became manifest in the gradual transformation and reformulation of several central problems of social analysis. Of special importance here was the reformulation of problems of social disorder, disorganization, and social transformation—matters of interest in the philosophical speculation of all eras but in modern philosophical speculations in particular.

The existence of social disorder, the ubiquity of internal conflicts, and the demise of sociopolitical systems have long been recognized (at least since Plato and Aristotle) as constituting a basic facet of any society or polity; since Hobbes, they have been seen as the starting point for the analysis of the possibility of creating a social order.[17] But the specifically sociological concern has developed by turning the analysis of these phenomena of disorder and decline into a starting point for the understanding of the mechanisms of social order and of the conditions of its functioning and change, both in general and in various particular societies. This implies that social disorder is not prior to and hence different from social order but rather constitutes a special type of constellation of elements which in different combinations make up the core of continuity of social order itself; therefore, it implies that social disorganization may become a starting point for the analysis not only of change and transformation in the social order but of stability and continuity as well.

To be sure, the distinction between the normal and the pathological, as developed by Durkheim, or between statics and dynamics, as developed by Spencer, continued to maintain some of the old dichotomous perceptions of social order versus social disorganization; but on the whole, the major development of sociological analysis was away from such an approach.[18]

This new approach to social disorganization became, in the sociological *Problemstellung*, very closely connected with the formulation of the problems of social change. The ubiquity of change in societies has, of course, been recognized since the days of the Greeks.[19] But the important breakthrough in modern sociological thought came in the recognition that social and cultural systems may transform themselves, creating out of their own forces the impetus to, and the capability for, the creation of new types of social and cultural order, and in the further recognition that such transformative capabilities may indeed be connected with many of the phenomena of disorder.

Hence, a basic, slowly developing and crystallizing aspect of sociological thought and analysis appears in attempts to analyze the phenomena of disorder in the same terms and concepts as those of social order and to connect the analysis with an understanding of the conditions and mechanisms of social continuity, change, and transformation. In this way sociological thought became focused on the analysis of the transformative propensities of social systems and saw in these propensities not external or random events but major aspects or components of social order. This approach to disorganization and change could be found among some of the greatest figures of sociological analysis. Around it crystallized some of the more important breakthroughs. The first major breakthrough in modern sociological analysis occurred with Marx's works, and the crucial analytical concept was that of alienation as potentially given in the very construction of his environment by man and by the process of division of labor in general and by class divisions and industrialism (capitalism) in particular.[20] Of central importance here was Marx's insistence on the ubiquity of alienation and conflict in "class" society and in the possible relations among alienation, conflict, and social change. The weakness of Marx's analysis lay in his assuming that alienation and conflict in the "class" society were temporary phenomena, which would disappear in the "classless" situation;[21] these assumptions led him to concentrate on aspects of the conflict which would lead to the supposedly conflict-free society. Another breakthrough was Simmel's concept of the perenniality of conflict in social life; but Simmel's view was limited by his focus on the purely "formal" aspects of social interaction.[22]

Two further analytical contributions in this context were made by Durkheim and Weber. Both concentrated on analyzing the phenomena of disorganization as a possible central focus for a deeper understanding of social order through a systematic comparative analysis of the conditions and mechanisms of its functioning. Durkheim's analysis of social integration—in particular, his concept of "organic solidarity"—was the counterpoint of his preoccupation with anomie.[23] Weber concentrated on the confrontation between the institution-building and institution-destroying tendencies of charisma in various societal settings.[24] In common with Marx, Durkheim and Weber showed that the possibility of change and conflict is indeed one of the constitutive aspects of social order; but, unlike him, they left open the question of the ubiquity of such conflict and so devoted large parts of their analysis to the different structural conditions under which different manifestations of conflict emerge.

In close connection with this analysis of disorganization, conflict, and change, there also developed in the sociological *Problemstellung* a growing recognition of the great variety of types of social order or societies; of their internal changeability; and of the temporal (historical) dimension as at least one, if not the single, determinant of such variety and changeability. The recognition of a variety of types of social (or rather political) order goes back, of course, at least to Aristotle, as does the search for the relation between the different types and the civic attitudes and moral postures of individuals.[25] In these two respects, modern sociological analysis is very much in the Aristotelian tradition. However, in its *Problemstellung* it goes beyond this tradition. First, in its refusal to identify the social with the political order, sociological thought surpasses the Aristotelian tradition by emphasizing the greater variability of social institutions. Second, by stressing the variety of interrelations among moral commitments and transcendental orientations, on the one hand, and types of social order, on the other, sociological thought ignores assumptions about the existence of (and search for) a morally superior social order and even about necessary relations between different political regimes and different moral virtues or dispositions.[26] In this respect, as Edward Shils has stated, "Sociology has partially closed the gap left by Aristotle between the *Ethics* and the *Politics*."[27]

Similarly, modern sociology goes beyond Aristotle by attempting to incorporate, or account for, historical development as one major mechanism of the variety and changeability of types of social orders and by focusing not only on changes in social orders but also on their internal transformative capacities.

This recognition of the great variety of forms of social life and social order was, of course, very closely related to the concerns of ethnographers, historians, and jurists. But it differs from the ethnographic description of customs and institutions in its attempt to incorporate the more concrete descriptions within the framework of explanatory paradigms of sociological analysis.

In this broad sphere of comparative analysis of institutions, the first major figures of modern times were Montesquieu and some of the Scottish moralists, especially Ferguson and Millar. Later came the various ethnologists and anthropologists, such as Taylor, and, still later, the different evolutionary schools of the nineteenth century. These were followed in the twentieth century by the great upsurge of comparative studies in the social sciences in the 1940s.[28]

Because of this shift in the definition of the major problems of social order and their repercussions on the analysis of social organization and change, it became possible to apply new approaches, concepts, and problems to the analysis of different levels of social life, ranging from macrosocietal structure and process to different microorganizations and patterns of daily informal behavior. By connecting sociological inquiries with the new traditions of research which had begun to develop, beginning in the early nineteenth century in ethnography, social surveys and statistics, and political journalism, it became possible to concretize the specifically sociological *Problemstellung*.[29]

The Initial Pattern of the Institutionalization of the Distinctiveness of Sociology

The impetus generated by the development of a specifically sociological *Problemstellung* and the potential extension of it through research provided a major "natural" focus and rallying point for the continuous extension and growth of the modern intellectual tradition of critical self-appraisal. But sociology continuously competed with other intellectual traditions in the attempt to provide— according to its own *Problemstellung*—the proper approach to scholarly and critical analysis of social life in general and of modern social life in particular.

Hence, the distinctiveness of sociological analysis, as it gradually emerged in the period of the founding fathers, did not entail the complete isolation of sociology from other intellectual traditions or a fully accepted division of scientific labor between it and these other disciplines. Rather, in its formative phases, as well as in its subsequent development, sociology tended, because of the fact that it shared to some degree the same concerns, to maintain relatively close but problematic, ambivalent, and tension-ridden orientations to the other disciplines and traditions.

These ambivalent relations were rooted first of all in the fact that the distinctiveness of sociology did not entail the development of problem areas entirely different from those of other intellectual disciplines. Sociology became distinct to the degree that the problems it shared with the philosophic, ideologic, and social-reforming orientations, and with the historical, ethnographic, and sociographic approaches, were brought together and transformed according to the specifically sociological *Problemstellung*.[30]

But there was no single "royal way" in which these different components of the sociological tradition came together. The neighboring intellectual traditions were not only departure points from which a single unified, homogeneous sociology could become differentiated. In different situations and phases of the development of sociological analysis various components of sociological analysis stemming from these traditions came together in different combinations. Any combination of such components, or even any single component, when reformulated in terms of the specifically sociological *Problemstellung*, could become—as is attested by the history of sociology—the initial basis, and sometimes the continuing basis, of the institutionalization of some type of sociological analysis.

Since each of these components of sociological analysis was rooted in different intellectual and institutional traditions, they could develop to some degree independently of one another while maintaining or "reopening" connections with "parent" or "sister" disciplines and orientations. This was very often done in such a way as to minimize the relations of one component to other components of the emerging sociological tradition. Hence, whatever the exact combinations of the different components of the sociological tradition were that crystallized in any concrete situation, the tensions which developed among them tended to be closely related to the close connections between the sociological tradition and the other intellectual traditions, since each component sought to legitimate its claims to hegemony by its connections to these intellectual traditions.

The constant ambivalence of sociology's orientations to other intellectual traditions and academic disciplines was further reinforced by the crystallization of the major components, or reference orientations, of the sociologist's broad intellectual role. These role orientations developed in connection with the search for an intellectual and institutional identity and with the attempt to delineate sociology's place in that new intellectual-scientific tradition that had been emerging since the eighteenth century. These concrete problems grew out of the skepticism and self-criticism directed toward philosophical optimism in general and toward the extreme pretensions of many of the forerunners, who saw sociology standing at the apex of the humanistic sciences as a sort of secular substitute for religion or philosophy.[31]

The pursuit of scholarly analysis, together with varying types of commitment—both to a critical evaluation of society in general and modern society in particular and to possible practical applications— became the core of the intellectual identity of most sociologists. This core became not only the source of tensions—in regard to the conception and self-conception of sociology—but the focus for ongoing discussions in and around the discipline.[32]

One area of tension was very prominent in Germany in the period of the founding fathers (Weber, Tönnies, Sombart, and so on) in the late 1920s and 1930s; in the United States in the same period; for more prolonged periods of time in many of the Latin-language countries; and again—as we shall see later on—in most centers of sociological research during the 1960s and 1970s. This tension developed between a relatively strong emphasis on the critical component of the sociologist's role (with concomitant participation in ideological, reformist, political, or wider intellectual communities or publics), on the one hand, and "objective" research, or scholarly orientation (with its stronger roots in academic institutions and publics), on the other. Moreover, within the first of these two orientations, there was tension between the more prophetic conception of sociology as a sort of secular substitute for religion and a more detached, nonutopian political stance.

Another area of tension was that between the practical, applied, and professional components of sociologists' roles as against those of scholarly research or social criticism.

Within the policy orientation of sociologists tensions have developed, as Edward Shils has so succinctly pointed out, among manipulative, alienated, and consensual sociologies. "Consensual" implies the use of sociology as part of the process of transformation of the relationship of authority and subject through the enhancement of self-understanding and a sense of affinity. "Manipulative" and "consensual" are to some degree similar to the engineering and enlightenment models analyzed by Morris Janowitz.[33]

The relative importance of each of these orientations has varied greatly in different periods of the development of sociology and in different stages of its institutionalization. However, they have all been constant, if often latent, components of sociologists' self-conceptions, always there to become activated in different constellations or situations and so to provide a source of tension, controversies, and disputes.

The multiplicity of these role referents and orientations, together with the different starting points of sociological analysis, has constantly entailed participation in, or orientation to, different organizational settings and potentially different publics or clienteles.[34] It was these multiple orientations that constituted, both initially and later on, the mechanisms through which sociology became institutionalized as a distinct discipline; and it was through these mechanisms that a constant tension was maintained, not only internally, among sociologists, but also between orientations within sociology and external intellectual traditions and academic disciplines.

The Impact of the Initial Pattern of Institutionalization of Sociology on Its Development: Debates and Discontinuities in Theoretical Developments

This initial pattern of the institutionalization of sociology as a distinct discipline—a pattern characterized, as we have seen, by sociology's close relations with other intellectual traditions, by the multiple starting points and components of sociological analysis and the multiple intellectual role orientations of sociologists, by internal tensions, and by orientations to external disciplines—has shaped some of the major aspects of the development of the field.

The impact of this initial pattern can be discerned in the constant debates, in and around sociology, about the intellectual and academic identity of sociology and about what may be called meta-problems of sociological analysis.

From the beginning of its development as a special field, there have been debates centering on a clear definition of the subject matter of sociology as distinct from history, social philosophy, or ethnography, on the one hand, and from other social sciences, such as economics and political science, on the other. To illustrate only briefly: sometimes this search for a distinct subject matter led to a depiction of sociology as a sort of apex of all the social sciences; at other times the search narrowed to an analytical focus on specific elements in social life—the elements of "sociability."[35]

The problem of defining the proper subject matter of sociology was usually closely related to discussion of the proper method of sociology. The central focus of these methodological debates was whether it is at all possible—given the special nature of the data of human social experience, as well as the basic involvement of research in the fabric of social and cultural life—for the human and social sciences to develop along the same patterns as the natural sciences. Accordingly, methodological debates have tended to focus around several points.[36] Among the persisting foci were: sociology as a nomothetic versus an ideographic, a positivistic versus a humanistic, science; the appropriateness of analyses that are causal, like those of natural science, and seemingly deterministic versus those based on *Verstehen* and the imputation of meaning to people's activities; and comparative generalization versus explanations in terms of unique historical situations as the major explanatory tool in the social sciences. Closely related to these were discussions about the possibility or impossibility of "reduction" of social phenomena to individualist as against "collectivist" explanations, and discussions of the methodological and philosophical implications of the fact that the investigator in the social sciences is so closely related to the subject matter of his research.

The foci of these perennial metaphysical, philosophical, and ideological discussions have been on the possibility and limits of a value-free sociology; on the self-examination of sociology in terms of the "sociology of knowledge" approach;[37] and on the closely connected analytical examination of the major concepts in sociology.

The relative importance of these meta-analytical problems, as well as those related to the intellectual identity of sociology, has varied greatly in the different stages of sociology's development and institutionalization. Some of these problems especially those relating to the proper subject matter of sociology—have, with the continuous development of different areas of research and with the growing academic institutionalization of sociology, almost (but not quite) vanished from the spectrum of sociological controversies. Others—especially the various meta-analytical, philosophical, and methodological ones—seem to reemerge, albeit somewhat transformed, even in periods of growing consolidation of sociological analysis and research—such as the most recent period, which will be analyzed below in greater detail.[38]

Whatever their relative importance in the panorama of sociological debate, all these controversies have kept the internal tradition of sociology open, in varying degrees, toward those intellectual traditions and academic disciplines in relation to which it had attained its own distinctiveness—that is, toward philosophy, theories of scientific methods, and theory of knowledge; to some degree toward history and ethnography; and toward ideological and political movements and orientations.

A second important aspect of the development of sociological analysis—closely related both to its multiplicity of starting points and to the role orientations of sociologists and their consequences—has been, as Raymond Boudon has indicated, its relatively high degree of discontinuity, manifested above all in the extreme unevenness in the patterns of development of different types of sociological analysis and research and in sizable gaps between such developments in different periods and places.[39] These discontinuities were due above all—beyond the methodological points stressed by Boudon—to the fact that the formulations of important problems of sociological analysis could proceed from the several different departure points of sociological analysis. The choice would depend on the relative strength of the different role orientations of sociologists, and the resulting formulations would not be entirely comparable. Each of these starting points or bases of sociological analysis could become a source of new research or could lead to the reformulation of old ones. Thus, the appearance was often created of total novelty, of being different or revolutionary.[40]

To illustrate: the recent great upsurge of interest in equality, women, family, youth, and the poor and the vogue for proving social and political concern have but rarely related themselves to many earlier traditions; but related problems have long been subjected to sociological analysis—for example, Tocqueville's analyses of equality; early sociological, anthropological, and ethnological studies of sexual mores and the still earlier analyses of low-income groups and social surveys of the living conditions of the poor. Similarly, studies of modernization which developed in the 1950s out of the great interest in problems of development have been, for relatively long periods, dissociated from the traditions of comparative institutional analyses in sociology or anthropology.[41]

Some of these gaps have gradually (but only gradually) been closed; and, in the very process of closing them, the mutual discoveries of the different sociological traditions have very often made the discontinuity even more visible.[42]

Such discontinuity is perhaps not unique to sociology. It may have been more acute in other disciplines, such as philosophy or political science. But the propensity to perceive this discontinuity as problematic, or perhaps to accept it as a real problem, to be sensitive to it, to connect such perception and sensitivity to the relations to other "external" traditions and disciplines, seems to have been more acute within the sociological community and to have had a relatively stronger impact on the internal development of the discipline.

The Pattern of Incorporation of Theoretical Developments into the Sociological Tradition; Possibilities of Sectarian Debates and Declarations about the Crisis of Sociology

But however strong this sensitivity to the impact of external sources and to the discontinuities in their own discipline has been in the self-perception of sociologists or in their work, it was not, of course, continuously predominant in the discussions and controversies within the sociological community. Similarly, the various openings to other intellectual traditions could for very long periods of time subsist only as marginal to the central substantive discussions in sociology—as an almost esoteric specialization.

It was only under special intellectual and institutional conditions that these sensitivities to internal discontinuity and these "external" discussions tended to become more central in sociology and to influence the more general tenor of the pursuit of sociological analysis and research. Such sensitivity tends to develop among sociologists when, in the intellectual development of the discipline, the reformulation of the specific research problems which are central to sociological analysis at any given point in time (whether they deal with the nature of the class structure of modern societies, with the comparative analysis of institutions, or with other subjects of like importance) coincides with changes and shifts in sociological theories, in the broad explicative paradigms. Second, such sensitivity tends to be greater when it is connected with activation of different role orientations of sociologists—for example, the radical-critical or the practical ones. Third, such sensitivity is greatest when either of the former trends coincides with broader intellectual trends or social processes and movements which impinge on crucial intellectual components of sociology—for example, on the emphasis given to its critical as opposed to its scientific basis.[43]

It is therefore no surprise that this kind of sensitivity has developed above all in those historical situations in which critical junctures in the development of sociological theory have coincided with great intellectual movements, like positivism or romanticism, or with changes in the ideological perception of social reality which have raised new themes of social protest. Thus, such sensitivity to external sources developed in connection with the breakdown of the positivist-idealistic and evolutionary schools and their declining impact on internal developments in sociology and social anthropology, of which the sociological theories of Durkheim, Max Weber, Simmel, and Tönnies had been the most important illustrations.[44]

As the works of Pareto, Mosca, and other Italian writers demonstrate, a sensitivity to the scientific nature of sociology, its boundaries and relations to other intellectual disciplines, developed (even if less intensively than in Germany) in connection with the upsurge of historicism and neo-Machiavellian orientations in Italy in the late-nineteenth and early-twentieth centuries.[45] Similarly, the sensitivity which developed in the first three decades of the twentieth century, both to the "academic" standing, boundaries, and proper subject matter of sociology and to its relations to the major philosophic, political, and ideological movements of the time, could be discerned in the formulations about the nature and direction of sociology in the works of, among others, Franz Oppenheimer, Werner Sombart, and Robert Michels and, somewhat later, in Alfred Vierkandt, Hans Freyer, Alfred Weber, and Karl Mannheim.[46]

Above all, such sensitivity became evident in the 1960s in the controversies surrounding the functional-structural model. This controversy gave rise, first in the early sixties, to "countermodels," like the conflict model and the exchange model, and to the revival of the symbolic-interaction approach and the development of ethnomethodology.[47] The coincidence between these internal controversies about theory and the new types of intellectual antinomianism which characterized the student protest gave rise to pronouncements about the need for "radical" sociologies and to the contemporary outcry about the crisis of sociology.[48]

It is in such situations that external intellectual and institutional factors impinge very seriously on the various transitions, breakthroughs, and openings in sociological analysis. Above all, such impingements influence the pattern in which important theoretical changes and innovations and new research programs are incorporated into the existing framework of sociological analysis.

As a result of such impingements, central problems of sociological research are reformulated, not only in terms of the internal problematics of sociology, but also in terms of the relations of sociology to other disciplines. Internal developments in sociology are often confronted with those "external" intellectual traditions or academic disciplines which are ordinarily relegated to the periphery of sociological inquiry.[49]

Second, this tendency to combine "internal" with "external" discussions often gives rise to a shift in the central preoccupations of sociologists. In their mildest form, then, shifts result in temporary fads and fashions which move the center of sociological discourse from substantive research and theoretical analysis into marginal or external fields: social philosophy and philosophical self-examination of sociology or methodology. Instead of serving as catalysts of the major trends, these preoccupations, as it were, seize the center of sociological endeavor. Discussions of such topics as the hidden dimensions of society, the philosophical or existential possibility or impossibility of pursuing sociological research, and the existential, personal, or social bases of the pursuit—topics which in relatively normal times accompany and enliven the interpretation of social phenomena—now become the central concern of the profession, replacing, instead of aiding, substantive research and theoretical analysis.[50] This may lead to a sharp dissociation between methodological and philosophical analysis, on the one hand, and empirical research, on the other. In extreme cases the proclamation of "principled" stands on these problems is taken as the main task of the sociologist, especially when the stand so adopted contains a denial—on philosophic grounds—of the objective validity of empirical research.[51]

The full impact of these tendencies is felt when they become interwoven with another trend that in such situations tends to develop in sociological communities, namely, the transformation of sociological "schools" into metaphysical and ideological sects, each with its own combination of metaphysical, political, ideological, and analytical paradigms, all of them developing strong symbolic closure and esoteric personal or sectarian discourses.[52]

To be sure, not all "paradigms shifts" or changes in research programs in sociology or social anthropology have coincided *so closely and directly* with this type of impingement of "external forces." Among the major explicative paradigms which emerged in relative isolation from such forces was the functional model in British social anthropology and, in sociology, the structural-functional model and at least the initial development of the exchange model and the conflict and symbolic-interaction models.[53] Similarly, many research paradigms that are more "restricted"— such as those of culture and personality in its psychoanalytical and learning-theory guises, the first studies of modernization, studies of stratification in general and of status incongruence in particular, many of the more recent shifts of emphasis in the sociology of religion from the earlier functionalist model, as well as many others—have indeed developed in relative isolation from the various external forces analyzed above.[54] All these developments were, of course, greatly influenced, indirectly, by broader intellectual and social forces,[55] but not under their direct impact, as discussed above. The indirect influence of these broad forces has yet to be investigated systematically, but it is evident that their incorporation into the existing sociological tradition has not, on the whole, been initially accompanied by the various symptoms of "crisis," even though there was no dearth of the "usual" doctrinal disputes among the adherents of the different models.

Significantly enough, however, once these paradigmatic shifts were caught, as it were, in the web of external involvements, their whole mode of incorporation into the existing sociological tradition became transformed. When recent discussions of such areas as modernization, political sociology, stratification, and many others, and of theoretical paradigms in sociology, became closely connected with political and ideological discussions, they produced a growing sensitivity to the impact these external forces have on the format and direction of sociology—and, in more extreme cases, acrimonious sectarian debates.[56] It is situations like this that have given rise to recurrent declarations that sociology is in a state of crisis.[57]

These declarations usually contain several elements: a strong stress on the failure of sociology to live up to its scholarly and/or critical-intellectual premises; the impossibility of objective sociological analysis; a reopening of the problem of the identity of sociology —of its broader intellectual bases and of its relations with neighboring disciplines; an examination of the validity, limits, and possibilities of prevalent sociological concepts; concern about real and presumed methodological weaknesses of sociological research and analysis and about the tenuous relation between theory and research; and a highly critical reexamination of the approaches and major concepts of sociological analysis. Last but not least, disputes arose about the possibility of a value-free sociology.

These elements of criticism could be found in all the major declarations of crises in sociology, whether these related to the breakdown of positivism and evolutionism in the late-nineteenth and early-twentieth centuries or in the 1920s and '30s. But, as we shall see, the impact these criticisms had in the development of sociological theory was varied, and so was their impact on the pursuit of sociological work.

Such crises influenced the pursuit of sociological work in two directions. On the one hand, they could lead to abdication of the distinctiveness and autonomy of sociological analysis. This possibility became actualized when these crises produced a distinction— brilliantly analyzed by Merton in a somewhat different context— between "insiders" and "outsiders"; that is, when it was assumed that only a given racial, ethnic, or ideological group could really understand phenomena associated with that group or even with the social order in general.[58] This distinction produced a strong trend toward fragmentation and discontinuity in research—a trend which became stronger as the sense of sociological community became weakened through the bitterness of such crises or through the attempts of some of its members to escape the challenges of the crisis by retreating into philosophical meditations, dogmatic-metaphysical assertions about the nature of society and sociological inquiry, formalistic definitions of sociology, or the purely technical aspects of sociological research.

There could also be constructive outcomes of such crises. These are manifest in some of the major analytical breakthroughs in the history of sociology: in the broadening of the scope of research which was related to explicative paradigms, in the development of more continuous research programs, and in growing mutual recognition between different sociological groups and traditions.

Moreover, though many shifts in explicative paradigms and in research programs in sociology have received their impetus from the internal momentum of development of sociological analysis, the situation of combined internal and external influences, described above, has also stimulated the development of the most important sociological theories, like those of Durkheim, Weber, and Karl Mannheim, and of research programs, like those of the Frankfurt school and the more recent research programs in such areas as stratification, health, sex relations, deviance, and modernization— programs which developed in the late 1960s and early '70s in close connection with various efforts to reexamine the work of the founding fathers of sociology.[59]

It would be outside the scope of this paper to analyze the conditions—intellectual, institutional, and organizational—within the sociological community which influence whether its crises will be constructive or destructive. Instead, I should like to point out some of the background factors connected with the most recent "crisis" of sociology.

The Intellectual and Institutional Conditions of the Contemporary Debate about the Crisis of Sociology

The relations between the institutional and intellectual conditions bearing on the development of the "crisis" of sociology can be more fully discerned in contemporary controversies in and around the sociological community, for example, in the demands for a radical sociology.

The common background of the controversies that have divided the sociological community since the late '60s has been a greater awareness of external and metascientific aspects of sociological analysis in contrast to the more segregated and specialized types of discussions that were especially predominant in sociological circles in the United States and to some degree also in England, Holland, and the Scandinavian countries in the period following World War II. On the whole, those discussions were based on a rather general acceptance of the professional commitment to research and to the academic core of sociology. There was a strong, if often implicit, emphasis on the possibility of a "neutral" application of sociology and a de facto distance from broader intellectual, political, or institutional involvements or orientations outside the field.

From about the mid-1960s, as a result of the convergence of several institutional and intellectual trends which had developed within the sociological community and around it, significant changes have taken place in the whole atmosphere of such discussions. There was continuous growth during this period in most fields of sociological research—in stratification, modernization, sociology of organization, communication research, and the like—and there were attempts to codify the results, whether in the various readers published in the '50s (above all, those published by the Free Press), covering all the major areas of sociology, or in *Current Sociology*, in *Sociology Today*, or in their European (especially French, German, and Dutch) counterparts.[60] There then followed various theoretical debates centering around the structural-functional model and the development of the various countermodels mentioned above.[61] Finally, there were several attempts to bring these various areas of empirical research into closer relation to theoretical analyses.

All these internal developments attested to the gathering internal momentum and strength of sociological analysis. They raised the level of aspirations within sociology and provided a background for the constant critical examination of the different premises and achievements of different sociological theories and of sociological research—a critical examination which could easily produce intellectual dissatisfaction with the achievements of sociology.

This internal criticism of sociology was reinforced by several broader intellectual and institutional trends which impinged, not only on the professional self-perceptions of sociologists, but on the standing of sociology in the eyes of the general intellectual public.

With the growing institutionalization of sociological activities, both the sociological community and the wider public began to take seriously sociologists' claims of their ability to contribute to social change and planning and to the creation of a better society by providing direction, critical orientation, and/or technical guidance. As a result, there was a growing awareness of the complexity of the broader societal and political implications of sociological research.[62] It came to be recognized that sociologists have considerable influence on the trends of intellectual discussion and opinion formation and that sociology can contribute to critical debates about such controversial problems as poverty, race, class relations, and student rebellion. This critical awarenss of sociology and of the various ethical problems involved in research was reinforced when sociologists participated in policy-making research.

Of special importance was the allegation that sociology was developing in a technocratic direction, partly as a result of the complexity of sociological activities and partly because sociologists became involved in consultation and research for government and business.

Thus sociologists became increasingly aware that the conception of professional autonomy which had developed in the late 1940s and early 1950s—which took it for granted that sociologists stood apart from direct political involvement and which emphasized their purely "technical" and academic professional roles—was no longer generally accepted. Because of growing demands for a closer relation of their work to actual social problems and a stronger awareness of pressures from varying publics, sociologists generally became much more sensitive to the changing pattern of commitment to social problems and inquiries.[63]

These trends intensified the influence of various new publics on the sociological community and could potentially undermine the

legitimacy of the academic-professional orientations, which previously had been predominant. Above all, these trends tended to
reactivate some hitherto dormant or isolated role orientations—
especially the critical role orientation—and thus to bring them into
the center of sociologists' self-perceptions. An additional push was
thus provided for the development of a critical reexamination of
many of the premises of sociology and of the self-conception of
sociologists. [64]

This critical examination was intensified by several external
intellectual trends which had been developing slowly in the 1950s
and which gathered full momemtum in the mid-1960s. First among
these was a critical examination of the relevance of scientific
progress to the welfare of mankind. A new searching look at the
place of science was taken in the early post–World War II period.
The necessity for this was first voiced in the *Bulletin of Atomic
Scientists*; later the cry became much louder and was closely related
to the broader problems of the place of science in the contemporary
community, of the possible limits of "reason," and of the validity of
science as the basis of the major values of society. Whatever the
impact of these discussions on other sciences, it touched one of
sociology's nerve centers and questioned the standing of sociology in
the intellectual tradition. [65]

From the mid-1960s on, these discussions became closely related
to, and were intensified by, new kinds of protests against the
emerging social and economic realities of what was termed the
"postindustrial" society, on the one hand, and the events of the
international situation on the other. In extreme cases these protests
merged into a protest against the broader premises of Western
culture itself. Of crucial importance in this respect were the internal
upheavals in the United States in connection with racial questions,
problems of poverty and ghettos, and the Vietnam War. These
upheavals spread throughout the world; but they became most fully
articulated in the West (though also in Asia and Africa) with the
outburst of intellectual antinomianism that was a feature of student
protest, leftist radicalism, and both sophisticated and "crude"
Marxism.

The greater scope of the sociological community and its entry into
the more central areas of intellectual and academic life have made
sociology especially sensitive to the trends of protest and intellectual
antinomianism that, with the massive expansion of student populations, have swept over Western universities since the middle of the

1960s. This sensitivity was probably reinforced by the fact that students of sociology—and their departments—tend to exhibit social characteristics which predispose them to radicalism.[66]

The impact of these circumstances was reinforced by the unequal and uneven institutionalization of different parts of the national and, above all, the international sociological communities; and the developments within the centers of Western sociology were paralleled, and to some degree reinforced, by those in the Third World, where these problems became especially acute as a result of increased feelings of dependence on Western centers for resources and professional standards. However, Western problem-definition and research techniques, when applied to the study of Third World societies, created—after initial acceptance of these models—strong feelings of inappropriateness, imposition, and alienation.[67]

It was against the background of these intellectual trends, combined with the growing mutual influence and awareness of different parts of the sociological community and their respective publics, that many scholarly discussions were transformed into sectarian, ideological, and political disputes. A demand grew for new radical sociologies, and acrimonious debates developed between adherents of different sociological paradigms. The result was a feeling of dissatisfaction and crisis in sociology, and some sociologists found themselves oscillating between their perception of sociology as a scientific or scholarly endeavor and sociology as a substitute for religion or philosophy—which could lead to the abdication of sociology's autonomy and distinctiveness.

In these outcries and discussions about the crisis of sociology, all the elements that we have mentioned as characterizing crisis situations were manifest, but the convergence, in the contemporary setting, of three trends has given rise to a rather paradoxical constellation of the different elements of "crisis." These three trends were (1) the stronger internal momentum of sociological analysis and research, (2) the greater density of the sociological community, with resulting intensity of contacts between its different parts, and (3) the politicization of many of the debates about the state of the sociological community. This constellation has stimulated, as we have seen, a more serious examination than ever before of various aspects of sociological analysis, theory, and research areas and methodology, and this examination may open up many new avenues of development and growth.

On the other hand, this intense preoccupation with external, meta-analytical problems and, above all, the combination of this preoccupation with political involvements of sociologists and with growing dependence of sociologists on their academic positions and clientele have created a much more "nihilistic" atmosphere, a potentially total denial of the validity, not only of selected aspects of sociological work, but of the entire enterprise. Many of the contemporary critics of sociology have based their criticisms not on criteria derived from other intellectual disciplines—from philosophy or history, for example—but rather on purely ideological and political grounds.[68]

Thus the contemporary crisis in sociology has presented the sociological community with a much more difficult but also potentially more fruitful challenge than earlier declarations of crises.

The Institutionalization of Sociology and the Sensitivity of Sociologists to External Influences

The preceding analysis brings us to one of the major points of dispute among sociologists about the nature of the sociological enterprise and its institutionalization. The crux of the dispute is whether these special features of the institutional aspects of sociological work—especially the various orientations and sensitivities to external sources, to multiple publics, which produce a sense of discontinuity within itself—will, as Merton seems to intimate, disappear with the growing institutionalization and "maturity" of sociology, or whether, as Bendix states, they will remain with us, if not forever, then at least for a very long period of time. Merton's approach may seem to be supported by the fact that the various conditions conducive to discontinuities in the development of sociological analysis and to intensification of the connection between such discontinuities and the openness to "external" intellectual factors have indeed developed most visibly in relation to the relatively low level of institutionalization of sociology in the nineteenth and twentieth centuries and to the relatively long period of its differentiation from other disciplines.[69]

Moreover, as Merton has shown, some of the disputes about sociology that have been taking place are not dissimilar from those which characterized the earlier phases of development of the natural sciences.

And yet our analysis indicates—as indeed Merton's own later analysis of some aspects of the "crisis of sociology" indicated[70]— that these various discontinuities and their derivatives did not characterize simply the initial stages of development of sociology; they erupted again, in somewhat different form but with undiminished intensity, during the recent period of greater institutionalization of sociology—a period marked by increasing continuities in many fields of research, by closer relations between research programs and both middle-range and more general theories, and by growing momentum and vigor in the development of different paradigmatic models and research programs.

Yet this "internal" push or momentum was only one source of the recent wave of innovations or reformulations of problems of sociological research and analysis. Significant to an even greater degree than before was the impact exerted by various external intellectual and ideological trends and by the intense activation of different role orientations of sociologists—especially the activation of the critical as against the contemplative scholarly component in these roles.

Thus it may well be that, though the specific focus of the internal discontinuities, and of the sensitivities of sociological work to external factors, changes according to the level of institutionalization of sociological activities, yet in some way or other the sensitivities themselves—and possibly also the discontinuities—are given in the very nature of the sociological enterprise and may become intensified in periods when sociology is becoming more dense and institutionalized.

Indeed, it may well be that here we witness one example of the possibility that different scientific and scholarly traditions may develop not only different degrees, but also different patterns, of institutionalization. It may well be, too, that an important condition of these different patterns may reside in some of the basic aspects of these traditions, pointed out in the beginning of this paper—for example, the original delineation of their boundaries and their self-perceptions. Thus it can perhaps be hypothesized that as long as the specific conditions of the sociological tradition, analyzed above, continue, they will indeed make sociology sensitive to these external influences and will continuously confront the sociological community with the necessity of coping with them in a constructive way.

The possibility of constructive development of sociological analysis has been predicated first of all on maintaining the internal momentum of analytical and research programs. To do this in the face of external pressures depended on the ability to contain these external forces within the analytical and conceptual frameworks of the sociological *Problemstellung* and within programs of empirical research. Meeting these challenges constructively would ensure the continuity of the scholarly-scientific tradition of sociology as well as its contribution to the critical evaluation of changing social reality.

Morris Janowitz

4

The Journalistic Profession and the Mass Media

Journalists do not ordinarily create culture. They disseminate the contents of culture, with varying degrees of conscientiousness and competence, to large publics. The journalists who have achieved the first rank of cultural creativity—comparable to that of eminent scientists, writers, scholars, and artists—are few indeed. Prestigious newspapers have produced an occasional commentator, like Walter Lippmann, who can be described as an effective conservator and/or strategic innovator of culture. However, such people often have entered journalism after making contributions in other sectors of intellectual life.

Thus, the role of the journalist in the cultural process is not to be assessed in terms of contributions by eminent personalities. This role involves the day-to-day tasks of a distinct professional group. To create culture—to contribute to its continuity and modification—is to produce and implant a perception of reality. In our contemporary society, with its rapid and extensive obsolescence of intellectual, scientific, and humanistic endeavors, elements of culture persist because there are institutions which serve to reinforce and reinterpret past and present accomplishments. The machinery of education and communication agencies gives culture its vitality and societal consequence. Journalists participate in this cultural process by selecting and rejecting content and thereby determining what will come to the attention of the various audiences and publics in a "mass" society. A "mass society" is an industrialized society which aspires to include all of its members as active political participants and to integrate them into its central institutions.[1]

It is possible to think of the contents of the mass media as consisting of public affairs (news and commentary); humanistic and artistic subjects; and entertainment. Of course, these distinctions involve an arbitrary element, and each type of material serves to enhance or detract from the impact of the others.[2] In this paper I shall deal only with the first of these contents, namely, the strategy and rhetoric of the journalist in handling public affairs. That this is an important reflection of the condition of culture in contemporary society is a view neatly formulated by Walter Lippmann: " ... on the whole, the quality of the news about modern society is an index of its social organization."[3]

Competing Models: Gatekeeper or Advocate

Since the end of World War I, journalists have come more and more to consider themselves as professionals and to search for an appropriate professional model. The initial efforts were to fashion journalism into a field similar to medicine, where the journalist would develop his technical expertise and also create a sense of professional responsibility. This model and its aspirations can best be called the "gatekeeper" model of the journalistic profession. In particular, this image of the journalist sought to apply the canons of the scientific method in order to increase his objectivity and enhance his effective performance. This model was reinforced in part by the increased prestige of the academic social researcher, and it involved the assumption that, through the application of intellectually based techniques, objective and valid results could be obtained.

The gatekeeper orientation emphasized the aspirations of searching for objectivity and the sharp separation between reporting fact and disseminating opinion and commentary. Coverage of the real world required the journalist to select what was important from the mass of detailed information; therefore, the notion of the journalist as gatekeeper rested on his ability to detect, emphasize, and disseminate what was important—important as news, opinion, and human interest. From this perspective, the performance of the journalist as cultural agent did not derive from the specific tasks he performed but from the logic under which he operated and the mode of discourse which he created.[4] Under the gatekeeper concept of professionalism, the journalist encountered institutional pressures and personal limitations in his search for objectivity and in separating fact from opinion. But to the extent that he thought of himself as a professional or hoped to make journalism into a profession, he had little doubt about standards of performance, although there was much debate about their clarity and how to apply them.

Of course, there were powerful barriers to the implementation of such a professional conception. Journalists were subject to internal and external pressures in their day-to-day work. In particular, they did not have sufficient time or resources to pursue their investigation. However, individual journalists have increasingly developed areas of extensive expertise and competence. In the period immediately after World War I, the printed media were dominant. The format of "yellow journalism"—which had little to do with gate-keeping—was deeply entrenched but was on the wane. We are not asserting that a body of documentation exists which would testify to overall improvement in the standards of performance, although a case could be made that such a trend occurred. We are, rather, asserting that professional norms, as goals to be achieved, became more and more explicit and that they rested on the search for objectivity and the separation of news from editorial content. There can be no doubt that the emergence of this professional orientation reflected the impact of the technical achievements of other professional groups, particularly in medicine and law. It represented the belief that the scientific method was productive in various sections of society and that it had broad substantive and cultural relevance for the journalist.[5]

In the middle of the 1960s, this gatekeeper model of journalistic professionalism was called into question by certain working journalists. They recommended replacing the scientific method by a conception of the journalist as critic and interpreter. During the sociopolitical tensions of the mid-1960s "objectivity" was being criticized in various intellectual quarters. A number of outspoken academic social scientists became doubtful of their ability to be objective and claimed that the search for objective reality led to a retreat from personal and political responsibility. Some working journalists also proclaimed that objectivity in reporting was impossible or at least doubtful and that the task of the journalist was to represent the viewpoints and interests of competing groups, especially those of excluded and underprivileged groups. This new orientation became especially pronounced among television news personnel. One sociological investigator sympathetic to this viewpoint drew the conclusion from her field research into the practice of journalists that objectivity was a "strategic ritual" by news personnel to defend themselves from the "risks of their trade" and from "critical onslaught."[6]

In the view of the new journalists, there is a series of conflicting interests, each of which creates its own contribution to the definition of reality. Therefore, the role of the journalist is to insure that all perspectives are adequately represented in the media, for the resolution of social conflict depends on effective representation of alternative definitions of reality. The journalist must "participate" in the advocacy process. He must be an advocate for those who are denied powerful spokesmen, and he must point out the consequences of the contemporary power imbalance. The search for objective reality gives way to a struggle to participate in the sociopolitical process in terms of knowledge and information.

The issues of confidentiality are crucial in distinguishing between the gatekeeper and the advocate-journalist. Before the outbreak of World War II, the frequency with which these issues pressed into the daily routine of the working journalist was limited, although they were of real importance. Before 1941, the national-security aspect of public affairs was circumscribed, and only a few journalists were working on such topics and the associated issues of confidentiality. However, progressively, matters of national security and associated record-keeping have expanded the day-to-day problems of confidentiality. In the contemporary scene, the advocate-journalist has developed outspoken opinions on confidentiality. It is not that he has a consistent set of principles or a body of procedures; rather, the issues of confidentiality are very salient to him and supply a means of exposing his professional ideology. But the importance of confidentiality also derives from the self-conceptions of the advocate-journalist. The advocate-journalist believes that his tasks involve collecting information and revealing the contents whenever it is, in his view, in the public interest or in the interest of submerged or repressed social groups.

As a result, three central themes guide the advocacy notions of confidentiality. First, the journalist believes in the absolute confidentiality of his sources in certain circumstances. Young journalists are increasingly prone to go to jail rather than expose those sources which need to be protected and which require protection if additional information is to be collected. But the issue is broader than sources, for the advocate-journalist thinks of himself as representing the interest of his clients—that is, those who supply him with information, especially the submerged groups about whom he writes. Therefore, he is prepared to keep information supplied to him confidential when he believes that doing so is in the interest of his clients.

Second, the advocate's professional role now has come to outstrip, under most conditions, his citizen role. In the past, the conventional journalist sought to balance his professional role with his citizen role. Thus, if information about criminal behavior came to his attention, the reporter would consider cooperation with governmental officials and balance this obligation with his interest as a journalist. The advocate-journalist has come to believe that, if he obtains information bearing on a criminal prosecution, he is not required to assist the legal process. In 1972, Professor Blasi of the Law School of the University of Michigan completed an ad hoc questionnaire survey of approximately 1,000 journalists' views on confidentiality. The result was by no means a representative sample, but the findings indicate that a minority have accepted the essentials of the advocate point of view. Almost 20 percent of the journalists declared that they would not supply the "prosecution" with information they had collected in confidence that could be used to establish the innocence of a defendant facing an erroneous indictment on a serious criminal charge.[7]

Third, the mechanisms of confidentiality are not symmetrical, especially with respect to government sources. The advocate-journalists believe that personal records of income taxes, social security, and criminal behavior should be kept confidential to insure the right to individual privacy. However, since they believe that government, in conducting its business, either withholds or manipulates information, journalists have a widely ranging obligation to expose the information which government agencies label as confidential.

Advocate-journalists came to think of themselves as conforming to a conception of the legal profession, with their concern to speak on behalf of their "client" groups by means of the mass media. However, it is abundantly clear that the legal model of professionalism cannot be effectively applied to journalism. The journalistic mode of work does not allow for the basic safeguards presumed to operate in the legal profession: cross-examination of witnesses, the role of the judge, and the appeals procedure, for example. The movement toward the advocacy format, in fact, represented a partial break with the idea of professionalism and was in part a political act. Some critics have described it as the "Europeaniza-tion" of the American press.[8] The advocacy format does raise the possibility and reality of a more explicitly partisan press. However, during the past decade the American press cannot be seen as having been Europeanized, since it has not moved toward more and more explicit linkages with organized political parties and factions. The advocacy format in the American scene has been a much more individualistic expression, with only a diffuse ideology and a strong anti-"authority" overtone.

The differences and common ground in these two professional perspectives are not clarified by the label each group has applied to the other. The advocate-journalist speaks of the distinction between "neutral" and "participant." The gatekeeper speaks of the distinc-tion between "responsible" journalism and "sensational" journal-ism. There is obviously a gap between professional perspectives and goals and day-to-day performance in any profession. This is partic-ularly the case in journalism, where immediate pressures mean that journalists must turn out a required product regardless of their self-conception. Moreover, the very notion of advocacy journalism as it evolves has its elements of ambiguity. Skeptical observers of the journalistic profession can therefore hold that there is a tendency to overemphasize the new trend. But to recognize that aspirations no doubt outrun actual practices is hardly to deny the extent and impact of the emerging norms. Moreover, the ideology and accom-panying discontents of journalists, as well as their actual perfor-mance, need to be understood.

In this paper, therefore, I shall explore various aspects of the role of the journalist with a view to highlighting the conditions which reinforce each of the two competing role conceptions, namely, that of gatekeeper and that of advocate. The central trend influencing journalists, as well as those in a variety of other occupations, has been the effort to achieve professionalization. The competition between the two conceptions has taken place within this general framework. However, it will be necessary to examine the factors which condition and limit professionalism in journalism. These include not only its particular knowledge base, which engenders a wide range of discretion, but also the relations between journalism and academic intellectuals, as well as the particular issues of professional client relations in journalism.

The Professional Organization of Journalists

Compared with medicine and law, journalism is a much smaller profession, even with the inclusion of practitioners in the electronic media. In the 1960 census, approximately 160,000 persons were classified as editors, reporters, authors, publicity writers, and public-relations specialists—a categorization much broader and more inclusive than "journalists." John Johnstone estimates that, in 1971, the total full-time personnel in the English-language news media in the United States who were engaged in news and editorial work was 69,500.[9] Of this number, a "relatively small cadre of news and public affairs personnel—some 7,000 at most," staffs the primary information services in the United States.

The profession is indeed loosely structured, with a variety of patterns of educational background, different routes to entrance, extensive job mobility, and diverse professional association of limited impact and consequence. For those who occupy the elite positions, there is a more structured career pattern. Each year a large number of undergraduate college students major in journalism or take some journalism courses. Between 1964 and 1971, 27,886 persons received bachelor's degrees in journalism from United States colleges and universities. These educational programs stress the technical aspects of writing and production and provide a smattering of liberal education. With some exceptions, they fail to attract the most outstanding students. A considerable percentage of these journalism majors never enter journalism, or they practice journalism for only a short time. They man the bulk of the minor and routine journalism jobs, and only a limited number of the top journalists come from this background.

The alternative career route is through attendance at a prestigious liberal-arts school or a superior state university.[10] Students who go this route avoid undergraduate journalism courses and are likely to be involved in collegiate journalism or campus politics instead. They enter journalism as junior staff members on reputable newspapers. Before World War II, such persons tended to major in English, humanities, and history; in recent years, the trend has been toward studying the social sciences. Because there are no formal criteria for recruitment, the decision to enter journalism can be a late one. Moreover, it is a profession with limited opportunities for continuing education, although such opportunities have been growing.

Journalists tend to come from middle-class backgrounds, a sizable number from the "solid" upper-middle class. A family background which stresses verbal and literary skills seems important. Until recently, journalism did not attract working-class sons and daughters or members of minority groups. The journalistic profession has been heavily white Anglo-Saxon Protestant, but there has been a gradual increase in minority-group members. Jews have been somewhat overrepresented, especially in the more prestigious outlets, but their overrepresentation in journalism is hardly so pronounced as in medicine or law.

Most journalists belong to some professional association. Often the association is a local or regional one, and there are alternative associations, but no single one or two dominate. Journalism has been gradually organized into white-collar unions. The professional norms are also maintained—to the extent that they are—by informal and face-to-face contacts. The personal relations of the corps of Washington correspondents described by Leo Rosten represent the epitome of such informal contacts. Likewise, in varying degrees, journalists join their own social cliques and frequent particular social clubs, bars, and restaurants where shop and professional issues are discussed.

Is it possible to make an estimate of the proportion of working journalists who adhere to the gatekeeper versus the advocacy norm? What are the factors which condition the orientation of journalists toward the gatekeeper or the advocacy persuasion? From John Johnstone's 1971 interview survey of a sample of over 1,300 journalists, some measures of the relative concentration can be drawn. First, responses to particular questions establish the broad parameters. The broadest and most diffuse measure of even a milder orientation toward the advocate outlook could be found in the answer to the question of whether the journalist thought there were too few crusaders in the media; 34.9 percent of the sample did. On the other hand, the narrowest and sharpest measure of the advocacy model came in willingness to endorse the activities of the underground press without qualification. Only 11 percent held this viewpoint—the strong partisans of advocacy journalism.

By means of a scale of items, Johnstone distinguishes the "neutral" from the "participant" journalists, and the results confirm the responses on the single items. Of his sample, 8.5 percent were predominantly participants in outlook, and 21.4 percent were moderately participant. In addition, 35.4 percent held balanced views, 25.1 percent were moderately neutral, and 9.7 percent were predominantly neutral. These findings underline the conclusion that the bulk of the profession holds "moderate" views and that only a small minority are polarized at each end of the continuum.

The drift toward the advocacy persuasion does not essentially represent socioeconomic background or minority-group protest but, rather, a personal, intellectual, and, in turn, political trend. It appears to be more a result of "socialization"—that is, of age, education, and career experience—and undoubtedly involves elements of social personality. Johnstone's survey findings confirm direct observations and reporting. In his conclusion, he states that "participant views of journalistic responsibility would appear to emerge out of one's experience in higher education, while neutral values are a product of apprentice type experiences, of career lines in which one learns to be a journalist in the context of practical skills, and concrete routines rather than abstract principles and theories." His data emphasize the importance of youth and of residence in large metropolitan centers in conditioning advocacy orientations. Journalism is a comparatively young profession; his survey points out that one-third of the journalists in the early 1970s were between twenty-five and thirty-four years old and that the majority were in "their twenties and thirties." Within this age distribution, it is the younger cohorts who are the strongest carriers of the "new" professional norms of advocacy.

Johnstone presents some data on the social and educational background factors which produce journalists in the advocacy mold. One must rely on direct observations and impressions as well. I have observed that, since the middle of the 1960s, some of the most outspoken carriers of the advocacy orientation have been the younger journalists educated at prestigious liberal-arts schools and state universities. They have been exposed to student movements and, more important, to academic writings and to professors deeply critical of contemporary society. They tend to find their desired life-style in the major metropolitan centers. On the other hand, the gatekeeper personnel tend to be older and more often educated in journalism. It would not be unfair to speak of two subcultures in journalism, highly age-graded. This is particularly the case since the gatekeeper personnel appear to be more involved in professional associations, while the subculture of the advocates is linked to intensive primary groups, that is, to face-to-face and informal networks and controls. For the advocates, some of these networks are linked to college associations, work on underground newspapers, or associations resulting from participation in efforts to manage local journalism reviews.

Surveys of journalists' political opinions show that they are skewed to the left of center. While there is hardly a one-to-one linkage between political orientation and professional norms, the advocates appear to be concentrated more to the left side of the political spectrum than the gatekeepers. Those who have written on the culture of journalism have repeatedly pointed to the reformist impulse which has motivated men and women to enter the field. This reformist impulse is accompanied, not by an urge to exercise power, but by a desire to bring about change through moral criticism. The contemporary thrust of advocacy journalism is clearly a manifestation of such motivation, which has a long tradition in the ideology of American journalists.

The Historical Background of Advocacy Journalism

The rise of the advocate-journalist will not be understood if it is considered as being the direct result of the agitation and unrest of the 1960s, especially on the campuses. It is an oversimplification to conclude that activist students moved off campus and into public life, including positions in the mass media, taking with them the notion of advocacy journalism. The intellectual basis of the advocate in journalism has had a long tradition. In the United States, the mass-circulation newspaper developed—in contrast to the European press—as a nonparty press. It was and remains a commercial enterprise; and its social and political roles were grafted on as a result of the efforts of the muckraker novelists and journalists. The reformist tradition was an expression of ethical and religious impulses grounded in a philosophy of pragmatism. The crusading editor and reporter, the individual in defiance of organized interests and corrupting forces, searched for the facts and presented them dramatically. The muckraker represented, moreover, the belief that the newspaper had the potential—through the power of the press and public opinion—to overcome the weaknesses of political institutions. In this there is a direct line of continuity between the muckraker and the advocate.

By the early 1920s, when Walter Lippmann wrote *Public Opinion*, he was fully aware of the distinction between the gatekeeper and the advocate in journalism and of the ambiguities involved in professionalizing the press and in balancing these roles. He did not use these terms. However, it is striking that he anticipated that the advocate role in the press was gaining and would gain in prominence and importance. Lippmann defined the essential public and cultural dimensions of the gatekeeper when he stated that "the function of news is to signalize an event."[11] He was hardly naive or simplistic, since he recognized the difference between news and "the truth." But this distinction did not, in his view, relieve the journalist of his professional responsibilities to dig for the objective facts. On the contrary, he was concerned that the press was beginning to be "regarded as an organ of direct democracy, charged on a much wider scale, and from day to day, with the function often attributed to the intitiative, referendum and recall."[12] In short, he anticipated the advocate definition of the journalist and rejected its political implications.

It was almost twenty-five years later that the Commission on the Freedom of the Press issued its report, which sought to explicate and extend the debate about the role of the journalist. Originated and supervised by Robert M. Hutchins, and sponsored financially by Time, Incorporated, the commission was composed of thirteen distinguished men—eleven academics, plus Beardsley Ruml, formerly a professor and then a banker, and Archibald MacLeish. Not a single member was a working journalist or manager in the mass media. Clearly, the intellectual and cultural perspectives of the academic, as epitomized by Robert M. Hutchins, who later became an occasional newspaper columnist, constituted the essential ingredient.

The commission—the Hutchins Commission, as it came to be called—prepared a range of research studies which are a lasting contribution to the scholarly literature on the mass media. But its main impact was in its "General Report," dated 10 December 1946, which rejected government intervention and stressed the need for self-regulation.[13] This theme came to dominate discussion about the mass media in schools of journalism and professional associations. Considered in retrospect, the commission appears to have been committed to a gatekeeper conception of journalism—like many such critical intellectual endeavors—but it had the unanticipated effect of justifying the advocate role.

The commission criticized extensively the absence of appropriate standards of press performance and the ineffectiveness of the mass media in solving the problems of a democratic society. Its formulation deemphasized the "factual" and the "intelligence" aspects of public affairs and stressed the interpretative role of the press. Whether it intended to or not, it moved in the direction of strengthening and justifying an expansion of the advocate role, which was its long-term consequence.

The report reflected a broad historical perspective and a profound philosophical and legal concern with individual freedom of expression. Its recommendations, however subtle and penetrating, were general and had very limited specific results. These recommendations can be contrasted with the less overarching outlook of the comparable British Royal Commission; its report, issued in June 1949, led, as described below, to the establishment of the British Press Council.

Clearly, the Hutchins Commission's exploration of basic issues remains viable. But it did not lead to collective efforts involving journalists, mass-media managers, and representatives of the public in "institution-building." The exclusive academic composition of the commission, plus the failure to establish a body of journalists, publishers, and representatives of the "public" after the commission had issued its report, weakened its effectiveness. The commission's effort reflects a continuation of the academic outlook of benign contempt for the professional journalist—enriched by the particular intellectual moralizing of Robert M. Hutchins.

If the Commission on the Freedom of the Press gave unanticipated legitimacy to the advocacy position, the findings and recommendations of the Kerner Commission, established to investigate the causes (and prevention in the future) of the tragic race riots of the 1960s, gave explicit support to the trend. In contrast to the penetrating intellectual quality of the reports and recommendations of the Commission on the Freedom of the Press, the quality of the writing and analysis of the Kerner Commission left no enduring scholarly residue.[14] Nevertheless, this commission had an immediate and direct impact. The Kerner Commission criticized the media for failing to give adequate coverage to the plight of minorities and for their ineffective editorial support for necessary social and political change.[15] The recommendations of the Kerner Commission included the employment of additional minority-group members in the mass media, in order to guarantee that the minority point of view would be adequately represented. These recommendations epitomized the advocacy orientation and were analogous to the argument used to support the claims at that time for black direction of black-studies programs on university campuses. The critics of this aspect of advocacy journalism hold that reporting on the state of minority groups can be done through an effective gatekeeper outlook concerned with objectivity; to hold that only minority-group members can perform that function is to distort reality and to politicize excessively recruitment into the profession.

The Kerner Commission and subsequent efforts of the federal

government at equal employment resulted in the increased employment and visibility of blacks and other minority-group members in
journalism. Such steps, and the social and political tensions of the
1960s, served to heighten the institutionalization of the advocacy
function in the mass media.

Barriers to Professionalism

The pervasive differences between the gatekeepers and the advocates reflect the persistent barriers to professionalization in journalism. Sociologists emphasize that professionalization involves a
series of institutional steps or stages. An occupational group
becomes a profession when (1) it practices on a full-time basis; (2)
it participates in the establishment of an educational facility in
order to establish advanced educational qualifications; (3) it orga-
nizes a professional association; (4) it has representatives who seek
to gain recognition in order to control their working conditions; and
(5) it issues a formal code of ethics.[16]

The journalistic profession has these arrangements, but, nevertheless, the scope of its professionalization has been limited. This is
a result of the absence of the more essential prerequisites of
professional development, namely, the development of a knowledge
base and a set of accepted procedures of legal control of working
conditions. There has also been little formalization of ethical and
other professional procedures, because, in order to prevent government interference with the press, journalists, in contrast to other
professions, have refrained from seeking legal protection of their
professional arrangements.

Effective professionalization is a function of a knowledge base.
And a knowledge base can be grounded in scientific research, as in
the case of medicine, or in a mode of reasoning, a grammar, or a
logic, as in the case of the legal profession. Obviously, a professional
is not a scientist, since professional practice involves the combination
of knowledge with a variety of other skills and expertise. Journalists
require effective writing and speaking skills. The need for these skills
does not necessarily stand as a barrier to professional standards in
journalism. There is a wide element of discretion in the practice of
journalism which reflects the limited knowledge element—either
about the subjects being reported or about the effects of the mass
media on society. This pattern of discretion permeates the work of the
journalist and gives it a distinctive ethos.

In the absence of effective professional procedures, the journalist is subject to influence by the sociopolitical process as he seeks to report it. Obviously, any professional group is deeply conditioned by the setting in which it works, and the journalist especially responds to the special character of his work setting. Harold D. Lasswell's classic article on this issue, "The Person: Subject and Object of Propaganda," has been all but forgotten.[17] Yet its content remains a touchstone for assessing the professional role of the journalist and his response to the institutions of contemporary society. The special ethos of the journalist, and thereby his cultural role, reflects the fact that he works and lives in a world of symbols and that his interactions with the institutions of society are mediated by the special environment in which he works. This means that journalists are particularly subject to the impact of the intellectual and cultural trends of society. They react to them, incorporate them, and modify them with greater speed and intensity than other professional groups and segments of society.

Thus, the professional and cultural definitions of the journalist—and especially the elaboration of the advocacy outlook—reflect the contacts which journalists have with intellectuals. In contemporary society, intellectuals tend overwhelmingly to be university-based. The interaction between journalists and humanists and social scientists is hardly based on mutual respect, nor is it productive of stable standards of performance. Perhaps it would be more appropriate to speak of the ambivalence which limits mutual respect and weakens professional standards.

In the academic disciplines of the humanities, there is little by way of a community of interest which would include journalists as men of letters. This is partly because the humanistic disciplines in the university setting have become "historical" and "critical" rather than centers of creative culture. More often than not, the writings of the humanities faculties of American universities present the dominant theme of the corrupting influences of the mass media on contemporary culture and the media's inability to educate the mass public effectively.[18] But these intellectual critics are at the same time fascinated and obsessively attracted by the mass media. One cannot but be impressed by the extent to which prestige in the university is influenced by the ability to present oneself in the mass media. However, this involvement is easily rationalized for many humanists by the belief that, while the inherent impact of the mass media is to degrade culture, their particular contributions in the mass media work in different, if unspecified, ways. The professional journalist is aware of the profound ambivalence in these attitudes of university professors. As a result, journalists derive little cultural reinforcement from the academic humanist.

The link between the social scientists and the media professionals is less distrustful but still contains important elements of cultural discontinuity. Professional media personnel see the academic social scientist as a source of legitimate news, while the social scientist is more prepared to cooperate and interact with the journalist, since he takes the mass media as given in contemporary society.

Journalists are selective in choosing what they will use from the findings of social science and in determining which pronouncements of social scientists are newsworthy. A considerable amount of what social science generates is no more than a new type of human-interest story and is criticized as such by the media. The findings of public-opinion polls and surveys have achieved a measure of journalistic acceptance. Moreover, since the social sciences—especially economics—have entered the mainstream of public debate, their findings have become more and more newsworthy.

Tension and mistrust develop between the journalist and the social scientist when research into the impact of the mass media is discussed. Most journalists look at market research on the mass media with considerable skepticism. They see it as an effort to focus on purely commercial considerations at the expense of professional responsibilities. They tend to believe that market research contributes to lowering standards and to inhibiting creativity. More than most professional groups, journalists resist academic investigations of their enterprise, especially of the impact of the mass media. They believe that their own standpoint on these issues is superior to that of the academic specialist.

Of course, journalists have been deeply interested in the effect of their work on contemporary society. It would be understandable if they overemphasized the impact of the mass media on society; this would be no more than an expected self-exaggeration. In general, the professional believes in the crucial importance and pervasive influence of the mass media. This influence potential is what leads the majority—those of the gatekeeper orientation—to be concerned vaguely with professional ethics and the adherents of advocacy journalism to pursue their efforts energetically, since they believe that they have an all-powerful instrument.

At the same time, a minority of journalists, either through realism or cynicism, emphasize the powerful limitations on the communication process. In fact, journalists are often uncertain of the effect and effectiveness of their efforts. If one is seeking for a measure of the fragmentation of the profession, it would be not only in its diversified and unstable career lines, weak professional association, and weak self-control, but also in journalists' limited agreement in assessing the consequences of their efforts in the mass media.

On the other hand, it must be asserted that academic research into the impact of the mass media has not been a commanding topic of intellectual achievement, although some of the most seminal thinkers in social science have been interested in the study of the mass media. Nor has this research field produced a consistent and cumulative body of documentation, findings, and analytic interpretation.[19] The study of the impact of the mass media arose in response to the dramatic and pervasive propaganda and political-warfare campaigns of World War I.[20] No doubt there were elements of oversimplification and an overemphasis on the influence of the mass media in these pioneer studies, but they were of enduring value because they demonstrated that collective, and especially political, decision-making was dependent on the management of the mass media. The findings of this first period of research, which extended until World War II, were at least compatible with the observations and experience of many professional journalists.

In the period which began during World War II and intensified in the 1950s, a new direction developed in the study of the mass media. The findings created a gap between the more outspoken and visible academic research worker and the professionals in the media. The new direction, stimulated by the social psychology and survey research of Paul F. Lazarsfeld and his associate, Bernard Berelson, deemphasized the impact of the mass media.[21]

The Lazarsfeld-Berelson methodology studied, through direct interviews, the responses of persons to particular messages or campaigns. This approach deemphasized the consequences of the mass media, since it could not encompass the media's capacity to define the sociopolitical setting and the alternative paths for change, nor could such a methodology estimate adequately the cumulative effects of the mass media through time. The Lazarsfeld-Berelson strategy had the merit of calling into question overgeneralized conclusions of the earlier period. However, because of its limited time frame, its results could hardly be the basis for assessing the cumulative sociopolitical and cultural impact of the mass media in an advanced industrial society; nor did it supply a basis for relating university research to the journalistic profession.

Of course, within social-science circles, there were persistent critics of this mode of mass-media research. Thus it was not surprising that a third phase came into being, of research that was more realistic and more attuned to the strategic impact of the mass media. For example, the impact of television, and particularly of televised violence, was a topic in which careful experimental studies and more cumulative results from surveys identified the discernible negative influence, as was summarized by the Surgeon General's survey of available literature.[22] Research on the political effects of the media produced a "second look," which highlighted the importance of the mass media both in "defining the situation" and in influencing marginally involved voters.[23] These researches returned to earlier academic conceptions of the impact of the mass media.

Thus, as research into mass communication has matured, it has not served as an effective link between the academy and professional journalists, nor have its findings motivated journalists to make concrete efforts to improve their standards of performance. Some journalists remain powerfully resistant to research efforts because these are seen as attempts at manipulation rather than as undertakings designed for mutual enlightenment and self-clarification. Therefore, although social science can provide a potential basis for journalistic professionalism, the results of social research are in effect too limited substantively.

Institution-Building for Journalism

The very limited impact of media research on the journalistic profession has been paralleled by a failure by university intellectuals to contribute to a central concern, namely, to the development of an independent audit of press performance. In effect, each programmatic statement or policy proposal of the past thirty years which has addressed itself to improving journalism has concluded that an independent audit of press performance is essential. But there has been no meaningful movement in this direction in the United States. In 1946, the final report of the Commission on the Freedom of the Press, *A Free and Responsible Press*, stated that "we recommend the establishment of a new and independent agency to appraise and report annually upon the performance."[24] In the same vein, John Wale, the British journalist, ended his study of the British press by observing that the evaluation of press content remains a neglected topic and that academic research should probe the "accuracy, fullness and fairness" of what journalists write and broadcast in haste.[25]

Of course, a great variety of reasons can be cited to account for the failure of an independent press audit to develop, but, given the vast academic effort in "media research" and the extensive resources of private foundations, there is no effective explanation. Obviously, one can point to vested interests and institutional inertia. The financial owners, the operational managers, and the working press have each demonstrated resistance to implementing independent audits. Second, there must be professional justifications for auditing the press, and these seem to be weak or absent. In the United States, norms about freedom of expression have had the consequence of eliminating any role for the government, even a facilitating one, in auditing press performance. The realities of the federal government's press relations, especially the sharp criticism of the media by Richard Nixon and Spiro Agnew, plus the extensive apparatus of media information and contrived leaks, have reinforced the journalist's opposition to any setting of standards by government agencies. Given the central importance of the protection of press sources and the reluctance of the courts to protect such sources, journalists also view the judicial branch with considerable skepticism as an agency for setting standards.

Even those who accept the idea of an independent audit do not support it energetically. In fact, the increased salience of the distinction between the gatekeeping journalist and the advocate-journalist serves to generate counterpressures. On the abstract level, the gatekeeping journalist's outlook is compatible with an independent audit of press performance. But the day-to-day pressures on the journalist—including the most creative and professional journalist—are such as to lead him to doubt its effectiveness. There is also doubt about the mechanism of implementation, a doubt that runs as follows: men and women who really know journalism are not likely to take up such tasks; therefore, the likelihood is that academics without realistic knowledge of the press will become involved and will produce sterile and mechanical results.

On the other hand, the advocate-journalist is indifferent or openly hostile to such enterprises. Because he lacks a commitment to objectivity, the audit for him recedes as a device of professional consequence. The advocate-journalist paradoxically sees the competitive process as the basis of self-regulation and is interested in increasing the scope and intensity of divergent points of view in any given media outlet. In addition, in recent years, the advocate-journalist has launched various journalism reviews—local magazines designed to compete with and to counterbalance the existing news institutions rather than to work for the establishment of independent press audits.

Third, there can be no doubt that the methodology of the press audit presents very difficult problems and requires considerable resources. Basically, a distinction can be made between the case-study approach, which focuses on a series of specific items, and a broader analytic approach, which is concerned with overall standards of performance. Given the development and aspirations of the social sciences in the United States, it is understandable that there would be extensive efforts to apply quantitative and systematic content analysis to the evaluation of mass-media performance. The objective is not to focus on specific items but to chart patterns and trends. The results of such efforts have unfortunately been disappointing. While the logic of content analysis should be particularly suitable for this task, it has not fulfilled its promise or been effectively organized as a research procedure.[26] In recent years, there has been some increase in interest in the quality and imaginativeness of content-analysis studies, but systematic content analysis of press performance has not produced a solid array of results that could command both academic and journalistic attention.

In particular, the formulation of categories which not only describe media content but also incorporate evaluative criteria and can be reliably applied has proved to be the major source of difficulty. The Commission on the Freedom of the Press itself tried to launch a series of studies on the application of quantitative content analysis and announced the forthcoming publication of a volume, to be prepared by Millon D. Stewart, in which "standards are proposed as an essential tool for gauging the freedom and accountability of the press in actual operation." Statistical analysis was made of the media coverage of the first United Nations conference by considering about "seventy daily newspapers, forty general magazines, the four major radio networks, the five leading newsreels, and several hundred group publications."[27] This effort, which represented one of the most comprehensive content-analysis studies, produced mountains of data. However, the sheer weight of the material contributed to the demise of the effort and even to the absence of a published monograph. Research journals such as *Public Opinion Quarterly* and *Journalism Quarterly* contain important but at best fragmentary content-analysis studies, with insufficient emphasis on evaluating media performance.

Instead, the major effort at mass-media evaluation has been in the form of case studies and is epitomized by the penetrating writing of A. J. Liebling.[28] The amount of such critical reporting and writing has been limited, although in the 1960s it became institutionalized in publications such as the *Nieman Reports* and the various efforts at creating journalism reviews. As with systematic content analysis, it is difficult to point to a discernible impact, but no doubt this type of evaluation by critical case studies serves to maintain the present levels of performance and has in turn contributed to the strengthening of the professional outlook of the advocate-journalists.

In essence, the movement toward an independent audit of the mass media has been weaker in the United States than in Great Britain. In Great Britain, the effort resulted in the emergence of a press council. Characteristically, the British thrust has been less in the direction of the analytic categories and formal standards of performance that reflect United States social science; instead, the work has been of the case-study variety. The efforts have been on a national basis and in response to parliamentary concern. The direction has been toward formulating a "common law" arising from the examination of an ongoing series of complaints about specific media events and practices, from the invasion of the royal household to the allegation of "ghoulish" reporting of the Aberfan coal-mine disaster to specific charges of bribery and corruption.

The British Press Council has, in effect, sought to develop a series of decisions about cases that are designed to serve in a manner analogous to legal ones. The underlying assumption of this council conforms essentially to the gatekeeper persuasion. The history of the British Press Council, as recorded by H. Phillip Levy, reveals an interesting example of cultural institution-building.[29] When the British Press Council was first organized in July 1953 in response to the recommendations of a royal commission, it consisted only of representatives from the journalist groups and from the owners' association. Its initial support was limited and its efforts sporadic at best.

The initial Royal Commission on the Press was followed by a second government inquiry, the Shawcross Report. As a result, the Press Council was reorganized in July 1963. It became a larger, more elaborate organization, with more explicit functions. More important, it was organized on a tripartite basis—the journalistic profession, the owners, and representatives of the public. In response to the new format, the council was invigorated. The number of complaints greatly increased, rising from 283 for 1963-64 to 436 for 1965-66.[30] One measure of the relevance of the council's work was that, while about 20 percent of the complaints were dismissed as frivolous, of the remaining, 50 percent were upheld. There is no statutory basis for the Press Council, and it does not have legal or administrative sanctions. It proceeds on the basis of publicity. Its decisions are printed in its annual reports, which seem to develop a body of custom. An offending newspaper is asked to publish the council's final decision, and only in an isolated case or two has the newspaper involved refused. Clearly, the acceptance and procedures of the Press Council reflect British cultural patterns. It is difficult to assess its impact, but it does exist. Its very existence makes a cultural contribution to some limited degree, because there is at least a national institution of redress.

The existence of the British Press Council has stimulated the very gradual development of counterparts in the United States. Local press councils received some stimulus because of the financial support offered by the Mellett Fund for a Free and Responsible Press in 1967 for organizing such councils in six local communities. A national news council was organized in 1972, and its program has been slow in developing. Publishers and editors-in-chief appear prepared to offer more verbal support of these efforts than might be implied by published editorials.[31] Moreover, there is some empirical evidence that the local press councils have a positive, if limited, effect.[32]

However, journalists in the United States have been more concerned with their professional autonomy than with mechanisms for auditing their performance. The extent to which they believe that they have made progress in this respect is striking. Journalists are subject to a constant stream of external pressures. Public-information officers and public-relations agents seek to have organizations and clients mentioned in the mass media. Professional journalists take such activities for granted and without resentment make use of the provided material as they see fit. They are, of course, more deeply concerned with pressure and criticism from the top level of the executive branch of government and with court decisions seeking to force them to reveal their sources. While these court decisions raise fundamental professional issues, the journalistic corps have responded with vigor and enthusiasm to the attacks from the White House and Watergate-associated sources, since these are news and the basis for new journalistic reputations.

The issue of professional autonomy focuses more and more on the internal procedures of the media agencies. The journalist wants to select his own stories, to treat them as he feels appropriate, and to avoid being rewritten and edited by members of his organization. The sheer size of a mass-media organization creates a division of labor and a set of supervising officers who impinge on autonomy, so defined. Nevertheless, Johnstone's survey indicates that United States journalists, as of the early 1970s, tend to be relatively satisfied with the amount of freedom they have in "deciding which aspects of a news story should be emphasized."[33] They are more constrained by their organization in selecting the stories on which they work, but even in this regard they overwhelmingly believe that they have effective freedom. The differences between the gatekeepers and the advocate-journalists are real and noteworthy. The advocate-journalists are less satisfied with their professional freedom and autonomy, but they are hardly fundamentally dissatisfied. No doubt to some extent they feel that they are able to operate as advocates.

Institution-building in journalism involves, as well, the complex issues of professional-client relations. Of course, the journalist has clients and has professional relationships with his clients. The audience of a medium are the initial clients of the journalist, and he has the obligation to perform services which are "good" for the client and on his behalf, regardless of the client's preferences and beliefs. But his client linkage is weak because of the ease with which the audience can shift its loyalties. Moreover, in a democratic society the media are open, and unintended audiences figure as clients.

But the issue is more complex. The journalist does not perform a specific service for a particular individual (this is the difference between the journalist and the public-relations "counselor"). He seeks to assist the members of his audience to relate themselves symbolically to the institutions of collective problem-solving. The journalist thereby performs a task designed to create the conditions under which the individual citizen, and administrative and political leaders, can take action. There is an analogy with the schoolteacher, in that the journalist too is concerned with mind sets and thought processes in the first instance; and here lies the core element of professional-client relations in journalism.

The adherents of the gatekeeper outlook would hold different conceptions of their client relationships than those oriented toward the advocate role. In the gatekeeper conception, the emphasis is placed on the client's ability to make judgments of his own self-interest. The task of the journalist is to process information and commentary in order to place information in a proper cultural perspective and to assist the client in understanding his relationship to the sociopolitical process. In short, it is to enhance his underlying rationality. This requires the journalist to present the client with information which may be unpleasant and which he has a powerful tendency to resist. It is hardly a purely "rationalist" interpretation, since it recognizes the irrational and emotional elements in social relations. The professional-client relationship assumes that the audience members have the potential to respond and that this potential needs to be maximized. It is based on a notion of a self-correcting system of social and political control.

In contrast, the advocate's conception of professional journalism highlights the barriers to sociopolitical change in contemporary society and in the limitations that particular segments of the society face in achieving their legitimate self-interests. For these groups to achieve their legitimate objects, the active intervention of the mass media, as well as other key institutions, like the educational and judicial systems, is required. Professional relations with clients have special reference to subject groups covered by the mass media, especially to those groups suffering inequalities and injustices. Therefore, it is the professional responsibility of the advocate-journalist to speak on behalf of these groups. Thus, the advocate-journalist would like to relate to his clients in the role of the lawyer but in the setting of the mass media. But this is to confuse the legal process with that of mass communications and to overlook the elaborate system of internal controls which the legal system has created.

Conclusion

The cultural tasks of journalism and its strategic influence are related to its ability to contribute to effective collective problem-solving both by the information and comment it disseminates and by the form and style of public rhetoric it generates. In an advanced industrial society, this essentially means that the journalist has the professional responsibility to assist individuals in overcoming their personal experiences and prejudices. This is precisely what is involved in the cultural role of the journalist, whether he is a famed specialist or a workaday reporter.

It is not condescending to reiterate our initial statement that journalists do not occupy a central position in creating culture, although the mass media have the power to attenuate cultural themes. Journalists can reinforce those elements of culture required to maintain the essential elements of political consent in a democratic society. Political consent does not imply the suppression of genuine differences of opinion or interest but the clarification and extension of areas of agreement which permit democratic political institutions to function without resorting to mass manipulation.

Although the professionalization of journalism has been slow, there have been relevant advances. At the present, the basic issue in the professionalization of journalism rests in assessing and juxtaposing the functions and consequences of the two competing models. The gatekeeper can be considered as the ideal of the enlightenment of the mass public; the advocate, as the ideal of the lawyer and almost that of the politician.

There are difficulties in the gatekeeper model, but there is an inherent clarity of purpose and goal. The professional task at issue is to retain and develop the essential concern with the inherent search for objectivity that is linked to the scientific method. The gatekeeper is a form of "public servant." In explicating this idea, the case of the higher civil servant, more in the ideal type of the British system than in the American reality, can be of relevance. The gatekeeper journalist, like the civil servant, must reach conclusions within a short time and must operate in a political context yet remain objective. The higher civil servant is supposed to be aware of the limitations of his capacities in day-to-day routines and of his greater power in a crisis—a set of circumstances which bears on the work of the journalist.

The gatekeeper journalist is aware of the economic realities which provide the resources for his endeavors and which can serve to thwart or distort the impulse toward objective journalism. But as Herbert Gans has pointed out, there are organizational factors in the contemporary mass media which continue to reinforce the professional norm of objectivity.[34] In particular, the journalist in the main works for organizations with heterogeneous audiences. To build and to retain mass audiences, journalists soon discover a powerful incentive to produce output that is viewed by such heterogeneous audiences as relatively objective. These audiences respond with sharp criticism to content that distorts that part of the environment with which they are directly familiar, and persistent distortion runs the risk of the loss of specific audience segments.

On the other hand, there is no professional model to fit the advocacy conception of journalism. As has been reiterated, the journalist is not the equivalent of a lawyer because of the absence of an analogy to legal procedures. Nor is he in effect a European type of party journalist, because he is committed to a libertarian ethic and because he opposes excessive confidentiality. These aspects of the self-imposed tasks of the advocate-journalist imply that it is essential for him to have a basis for his professional independence. This requirement perforce, and even unintentionally, leads him back toward the gatekeeper ideal.

The resolution of the dichotomy between the gatekeeper and advocate perspectives rests not in a mechanical synthesis but, rather, in a clear differentiation. The core task of the journalist— given both the ambiguity of the advocacy model and the centrality of information for a democratic society—rests in the gatekeeper role. The advocate role as a distinct and a secondary role, if it is to persist with effectiveness and responsibility, will require an element of professionalization to insure its independence and to define its limits and potentialities.

Harry G. Johnson

 Economics and the Radical
Challenge: The Hard Social
Science and the Soft Social Reality

The Myth of "The Hard Social Science"

To understand the nature and the limitations of the problem in
intellectual analysis to which this essay is devoted, it is essential to
appreciate that the concept of economics as "the hardest" or "the
only hard" social science is a very recent (post-World War II)
development and that it is also almost solely an American conception. For this there are fairly obvious reasons, stemming both from
the intellectual evolution and academic professionalization of the
subject and from American social and political history since the
beginning of World War II.

Economics had its intellectual origins, like the other "social
sciences," in philosophy rather than in natural science; as an
academic discipline it was not effectively formally separated from
philosophy until the late nineteenth century and pre-World War I
period, and until well into modern times it retained some connection
with philosophy by being paired with political science in the subject
description "political economy." Already before World War I the
leading economists had begun to build, and to emphasize the need
for building, a scientific quantitative base for the subject through
statistics and economic history—particularly the latter, since the
techniques of economic statistical analysis available were as yet
rudimentary in the extreme.[1] This program of gradual science-
building was, however, forestalled by the economic and political
disturbance ensuing on World War I, and particularly by the
problem of mass unemployment, which plagued Britain throughout

the interwar period and, after 1929, the whole capitalist world, most notably the United States. In consequence, especially in Britain but also in the United States in the 1930s, economics was to many of its leading practitioners not a science but a branch of applied philosophy concerned with politics and concerned in particular with a definition of the debating ground and rules of debate between political radicals and political conservatives. Economics was the main area of political controversy at the time, just as, at other times, politics has focused on choice of foreign allies or morality of government administration.

This remained the case in the period immediately after World War II; indeed, the war and the enforced suspension of normal market-competitive economic life, together with wartime full employment and the alternative politicoeconomic explanations that could be given for it, provided fresh material for and interest in the philosophical and ideological aspects of the subject. This interest was expressed in a variety of now largely forgotten and unrecorded or poorly recorded ways: at the popular level, treatment of Keynes himself as a sinister intellectual figure and of "Keynesianism" as a subversive radical movement; at the professional level, suspicion of the competence of Keynesian economists and doubts about their collegial reliability; at the academic level, great interest and rather naive faith in the possibilities of national economic planning (notably in the early stages of the Marshall Plan for European economic reconstruction), allied with emphasis on student understanding of the whole long list of reasons why a competitive system may produce socially nonoptimal allocative results; and, at the scientific level, considerable interest in the construction of mathematical models of Marx's analytical system and the solution of "the transformation problem" (the problem of rendering consistent a system of "values" determined by labor cost of production with a system of prices determined by competitive equalization of rates of return on capital).[2]

This period of political-philosophical preoccupation was short lived in the United States. It is important to note that its short life was largely related to particular political developments in the United States, developments which were not characteristic of other countries in the Anglo-Saxon tradition of economics, and that to an important extent its transience reflected deliberate or unconscious repression of an aspect of the traditional concerns of the subject that remained dormant under sedation but ready to bestir itself once the sedation was removed. In the other countries in the Anglo-Saxon tradition, most notably the United Kingdom, the radical interest and the political orientation remained alive and self-consciously and self-confidently vocal. In this they were actually strengthened, and had their way facilitated, by a sort of conspiracy of silence on the part of the American profession with respect to radical politics and social-policy issues, which on the one hand permitted economic radicalism elsewhere to fuse prestigiously with political anti-Americanism, and on the other hand relieved radicalism of the necessity it had been under, up until the immediate post–World War II period, of demonstrating maintained competence in the common scientific ground of accepted theory, concepts, and factual knowledge. In the United States, by contrast, the genuine radicals were forced to retreat into the smaller liberal-arts colleges, where their effective influence was confined to a local oral tradition, soon forgotten by the students they graduated, and their radicalism was confined to the social small talk of a scientific professional specialist and to endorsing public-policy positions respectably expressible within the framework of Democratic Party politics. 184415

The transition from social philosophy to social science, in the American profession's view of itself and of its social role and responsibilities, occurred very rapidly, in response to a combined social push and social pull and to the internal logic of scientific and professional development itself. The social push came from the agonies of the McCarthy period, the period of witch-hunting on behalf of cultural purity and loyalty that has twice followed involvement of an immigration-based new nation in a totalitarian-democratic foreign war, for reasons that need not be entered on here. The relevant point is that to raise the question is to win the argument, in the sense that, despite the largely successful defense of academic freedom at the time, the longer-run effect was the inculcation of habits of self-censorship which directed economists toward research and toward theorizing about how the American economic system worked and could be made to work better and away from dangerous thoughts about the justice of the system and the possibility of revolutionizing it. Those who did not conform found themselves sorted out into marginal or ultramarginal positions in the profession, unless—as may be said (rather unfairly) of John Kenneth Galbraith—they had the wisdom and the literary skill to tramp on corns while pretending to break toes. Somehow, reasons were found to explain why the respect due to such distinguished avowed Marxists as Paul Sweezy did not extend to appointment at a major university and why older and undislodgeably tenured "radical" scholars found themselves without professional hearing or promising students.

The social pull came from the needs of the American government for professional services involving either direct commitment to government goals or transactions and confrontations with foreign governments and opposite numbers in foreign countries of a kind that subordinated domestic dissent to loyalty, in foreign affairs, to national interest. American foreign policy involved a large and at times mushrooming growth of demand for professional economic skills throughout most of the period, beginning with the war itself and its demand for general economic skills in wartime economic management and for particular applications, as represented by the Office of Strategic Services. The demand then continued, in the postwar period, with the professional-staffing needs of the Marshall Plan for European economic reconstruction; and, when the Marshall Plan proved successful, the same techniques—of capital transfers combined with economic planning—were used to promote the economic development of poor countries. Along with these general demands for professional economic services there were substantial demands, financed by the government and by foundations, for economic research into the Japanese economy, into Russian and East European economic planning, into the economy of mainland China, and into the economic problems of Latin America. On the domestic side of American policy, the war had given a great impetus to the development of Leontief's input-output analysis, which thereafter suggested itself as an obvious technique for research into a great variety of problems on both the state and national levels. In addition, the military interest in economic analysis as a technical logic of achieving efficiency in "the allocation of scarce means to given ends," very broadly defined, produced continued support for scientific economic research through the RAND Corporation and its less-publicized counterpart, the Office of Naval Research. Later, with the post-Sputnik (1957) surge of interest in science and scientific research as a general panacea for the domestic and international problems of American society, economics, much more than the other social sciences, enjoyed a free ride on the bandwagon.

It is worth noting, again, that the position of economics as a "hard" science in the United States is unparalleled, in comparison to its position in other countries, both "Western" and "communist." In the "West" its ideological aspects are popularly recognized; in the "communist" sector, they are economics' *raison d'être*. This unique character can, in turn, be associated with more fundamental characteristics of American society, though the subject can be mentioned only cursorily here. Most societies are stable enough, sufficiently static, and enough used to poverty to make sharing what there is a major political issue, one way or another. By contrast, American society—to some extent in common with recent-settlement countries—emphasizes production and efficiency. This includes maximizing output per person, which raises acute problems when human lives have to be deliberately sacrificed in military ventures. Hence economics, which in its production aspect emphasizes minimizing inputs, becomes a "science," whereas, when the problem is sharing what is available fairly among the claimants, it remains philosophy. Therefore, economics in the United States, in the particular guise of the social science concerned with the substitution of capital and technology for labor, acquires a *cachet* of "hardness" denied to it in societies in which the central conflicts appear to be between man and man rather than between man and nature. In contrast to the natural sciences, however, economics has had no serious difficulty either in accommodating to the more recent phase of disillusionment with science and scientific method as a panacea for society's problems or in maintaining its reputation as an instrument for efficient solution of such problems.

Apart from, or as a supplement to, the influence of political developments in the United States and its international relations, developments in the economics profession itself were in various ways promoting the view of economics as a "hard science" among the economists themselves. In the early post-World War II period, much of this can be associated with the activities and intellectual ethos of the Cowles Commission, then located at the University of Chicago. Three scientific contributions in particular are worth noting. One was the development of linear programming—originally in connection with the military problems of routing merchant shipping and supplying Air Force bases—as a technique for actually computing numerically the solutions to economic maximization and minimization problems previously "solved" by economic theorists only in qualitative or algebraic terms. This development made economic theory practically and operationally useful and made economics an "applied science" comparable to the applied natural sciences. Another was the recognition and solution of "the identification problem" (the problem of knowing whether one was really measuring a demand relationship or a supply relationship, on the basis of *ex post* data which embodied the interaction of demand and supply factors); this paved the way for the application of econometrics to whole systems of interdependent relationships, in place of single relationships of doubtful interpretative meaning. The third was T. C. Koopmans' powerful methodological attack on the inductive fact-gathering methods of studying business cycles employed by the National Bureau for Economic Research, which up to then had had a virtual monopoly of empirical research in economics. Koopmans attacked these methods on the grounds that they were "measurement without theory." This cleared the way for a fusion of economic theory with empirical research under the rubric of "hypothesis-testing" in place of "measurement" (the two terms suggest the shift from social philosophy to social science), and it led to a flowering of econometrics. [3]

Apart from these specific contributions to the development of economics as a "hard" science, the Cowles Commission was a major center for the expression and diffusion of the aspirations of economists of the younger generation to be regarded as "scientists" enjoying parity of esteem with their natural-science colleagues. These aspirations themselves reflected both the prestige of natural science in the United States—resulting from its successful application in the conduct of World War II, especially the production of the atomic bomb—and the exposure of the younger economists to natural-science techniques and standards in the course of learning the mathematics requisite to the pursuit of general-equilibrium theory. A few sample manifestations may be mentioned: an influential article in *Econometrica* discussing the application of the first law of thermodynamics to economics and speculating on the applicability of the second law of thermodynamics; a boast by Paul Samuelson to the effect that mathematical economists had at last begun to produce theorems that real mathematicians found interesting; and a transient tendency to christen various pieces of analytical connectedness as "effects"—in obvious imitation of the terminology of physics, such as the Pigou effect, the Tobin effect, the Keynes effect, the Patinkin effect, or the real-balance effect, the wealth effect, the interest effect, and so on—of which only the "Pigou effect," or "real-balance effect," now survives. [4]

A more pervasive influence has been the development of economics as an academic discipline providing training up to and beyond the Ph.D. level for large numbers of young people destined for a variety of lucrative and socially important professional careers, especially in the period of rapid expansion of university training from the latter 1950s up until the end of the 1960s. Already in the immediate postwar period, when large numbers of GI Bill-supported veterans were undergoing graduate training, it had become clear that the least-risk way for the graduate student to surmount the hurdle of the Ph.D. qualification and establish his professional reputation was to develop and apply some new mathematical or statistical technology. At the same time, testing and certifying competence of this kind was a more manageable task for the academic teachers than certifying Ph.D's by the traditional university standard of demonstrated knowledge of an extensive literature and originality of some ill-defined kind in devising and solving an intellectual problem, particularly in view of the large numbers of students to be processed and the large number of institutions and departments, often of rather pedestrian caliber, involved in processing them. Thus the use of scientific method became in an important sense a substitute for the existence and self-conscious understanding of the science itself.[5] This characteristic in turn produced both crucial strengths and crucial weaknesses in the radical challenge, and in the responses to it, as these manifested themselves in economics. It strengthened the radical challenge, since few among the orthodox majority understood the questions and the scientific weakness and basically unscientific and emotional foundations of the radical challenge; but it weakened it, too, through the pervasive acceptance and tolerance of ostensibly scientific disagreement, expressed in the language of civilized scientific debate and conforming to its rules. For the professional response, there was weakness in the tendency to assume that the radical protesters were scientifically rational and maturely sincere in their protests and so deserving of a civilized hearing and a scientific response, including accommodation to demands and criticisms that appeared reasonable. Against this, there was strength in the possession not only of a methodology of debating ideologically charged issues, developed in the aftermath of "the Keynesian revolution" and emphasizing arbitration by testing against empirically established facts, but also of an extensive body of empirical knowledge, the amassing and refinement of which had required bringing into the purview of economic theory—and making scientific sense of them—various

social facts, influences, and arrangements that radicals as general
social critics have tended to treat, extremely superficially, simply as
evil social phenomena that can and must be changed or destroyed
but whose existence radicals *qua* economists are obliged by their
professional training to recognize.

The Radical Challenge and the Professional Response

For purposes of describing and analyzing the radical challenge and
the response of the economics profession to it, it is helpful to
distinguish three major areas of professional activity and responsibility: academic teaching and course content at the undergraduate
and graduate levels; scientific research and writing; and professional activity in and through the professional association. Various
strengths and weaknesses with respect to the second area—scientific
content—have already been mentioned; parallel points with respect
to the first and third will be made in due course, in this section.

First, however, it is necessary to recall briefly the salient points of
developments in American society leading up to and through the
appearance of the radical challenge, since these in an important
sense prepared the profession at least partially for the rise of
radicalism. In particular, there was, in the transition from the
Kennedy to the Johnson administration, a shift of governmental
orientation from external to internal policy problems, expressed in
the declaration of the War on Poverty and resulting in the devotion
of considerable professional attention (incidentally, generally well
paid) to the problems of poverty and, more generally, income
distribution. From the scientific point of view, this novel[6] subject of
research and theory prompted the deployment of a great deal of
scientific, highly technical new analysis of the economics of human
capital, education, labor-force participation, and so on, for the
understanding of a social-policy problem; it also revealed the
existence of a surprising measure of agreement among economists
of ostensibly sharply opposed political beliefs and of disagreement
between economists and noneconomists on both causes and cures.[7]
From the point of view of policy understanding, it was largely
through the increasingly careful application of methods of economic
measurement that the problem of poverty was recognized as very
largely overlapping the problem of pervasive discrimination against
American blacks (and other nonwhite groups; more accurately, the
quantitatively most important aspects of poverty lay in the area of
intersection between the two discriminand groups of blacks and

women). The central point, however, was that the concern about poverty in the mid-1960s was the occasion of a dress rehearsal of the latest developments in economic theory and the tested empirical knowledge relating to inequalities of income and wealth. This in turn meant that, when the radicals came on the scene, those of them who intended to be serious and to be taken seriously confronted an established body of scientific knowledge and scientific research techniques requiring considerable intellectual effort to master—and which they had to master.

On the side of academic teaching of the subject, economics had, in confrontation with the general demand for "relevance" in social-science teaching, the advantage of providing a professional training leading to a fairly clearly defined set of career opportunities; in consequence, its students were predominantly pragmatic, career-minded, and socially and philosophically incurious, in contrast, say, to sociology, which, with its promise of teaching them to understand society, tended to attract socially dissatisfied individuals and then turned them out into a world which offered few careers to those possessing their presumed expert knowledge of how society works. On the other hand, the structure of course offerings in economics, especially at the undergraduate level, was weak and vulnerable to radical criticism and student dissatisfaction in various significant respects. The undergraduate course retained strong humanistic elements in its concern with the history of Western civilization and its great problems; yet concern with these issues had been pretty well stamped out at the graduate level of instruction, in favor of mathematical theory and statistical techniques, with the result that new teachers were not well qualified to teach what they were supposed to teach and so tended to teach it badly, superficially, and unsympathetically. They naturally tended to concentrate on the kind of mathematical manipulations they had learned with so much effort in graduate school and to neglect, as far as they could, the humanistic side. The student seeking for enlightenment and philosophical understanding tended to get, instead, diagrams, mathematics, and elaborate literary-logical exercises, which, if they had practical reference, referred to problems that in terms of his own experience were not real to the undergraduate. Further, thanks to the increasingly mathematical orientation of economic theory, it was (and is) frequently unclear to the teacher himself what contribution, if any, mathematical knowledge makes to economic understanding. It is therefore not surprising, either, that radical criticism focused on mathematics and statistics as symbols of the "irrelevance" of conventional economics and that the teachers frequently had great difficulty in providing for this concentration a rationale that was convincing even to themselves. (The difficulty may be understandable if we recall a once widely quoted definition of economics, that "Economics is what economists do.")

This weakness of economics in the face of radical criticism is, of course, a standard problem of academic or formal instructional organization. In the absence, and indeed deliberate suppression, of any clear market test of course structure and content, these tend to be determined by the interaction between the preliminary requirements of the next stage of the academic structure and the intellectual and research interests of those who, having passed the next or higher stage successfully, are fed back as instructors into the lower echelons of instruction. Two other standard problems of instructional organization have also contributed to the weakness of economics, in common with other disciplines.

One is the natural tendency of the academically most successful to preempt the most interesting levels and subjects of teaching for themselves, leaving the less attractive and more elementary teaching to their younger and less successful colleagues. This tendency has reached the point, in economics, where not merely the more eminent scholars concentrate on graduate work, leaving to young men the elementary teaching that, in an important sense, demands the most maturity, perspective, wisdom, and inspiration, but the senior professors in the graduate schools shun the teaching of the "required" or "core" courses of the first or even the second graduate year in order to concentrate on work in small seminars and graduate research groups on narrowly defined topics of direct personal interest. This has important implications for successful radical challenge. First, the elementary teaching falls to untenured instructors, assistant professors, and associate professors, and, especially, to graduate teaching assistants, who have personal-anxiety reasons for fearing and resenting the system of apprenticeship and the enforcement of scientific standards. To put it in terms of the crudest economic determinism, such persons, having got so far into the system of academic privilege, have strong motives of self-interest for demanding an equal sharing of the remaining rents of differentiated monopoly. Moreover, it seems obvious that if the most eminent senior men find it beneath their dignity to teach—and often even to know—the contents of the basic courses, these

required courses are an inequitable and unnecessary barrier, standing between youth and the just rewards of youthful ability.

The other standard problem of the academic instructional setting
is the ambiguous role of the college student as simultaneously
intellectual child and physical, mental, and social adult, as simultaneously student and colleague, or, in economic terms, as simultaneously work in progress and finished product. This ambiguous
role makes the task of the radical student a delightfully subtle game
of role-alternation and motivation-concealment; and, correspondingly, the task of the academic confronted by the radical student
becomes excruciatingly difficult, since the teacher's orientation is
necessarily toward treating the student as a rational and dis-
passionate adult colleague whose ideas deserve respectful consideration and reasoned discussion, even though this particular rational
adult colleague may be a clever, hostile adversary, and the clever
young fellow academic may be an irrational spoiled child. This
problem has understandably been most acute in the old, prestigious,
elitist universities and the long-established small colleges, where
consciousness of shared privilege promotes exceptional staff respon-
siveness to student demands and the strength of historical social
position and established academic prestige encourages considerable
flabbiness in contemplating the implications for future generations
of yielding to the demands of the current generation of students. It
is for this reason that the first shock wave of radical student protest
concentrated on the most established and reputable centers of
academic learning; that the radicals won a surprising degree of
success there, on the basis of which radicalism spread through the
lower levels of the university and college system; and that the eastern
private universities have probably incurred the most serious and
lasting damage, through the replacement of structured course work
by permissive electives and through the acceptance of "Marxist" or
"radical" courses and their teachers on an academic par with
"conventional" or "orthodox" economics courses.

Turning to the academic content of economics courses and the
choice of research topics and approaches to them, we find that the
corollary of the changes on the teaching side, just discussed, has been
a trend toward "Marxist" research in a broad sense. As regards pure
theory, the initial post–World War II interest in the mathematics of
Marxian models was never completely submerged; and for those
interested in studying the matter, it quickly appears that (as is true
in other areas of economics and social science generally) Marx was

not that good a mathematician. The social intuition and emotional response were the main message of the claim to science; and if one wants to explore and elaborate the message, modern economic science is a better tool than the classical economic science available to Marx, and it will be used unless a really brilliant and original Marxist mind appears on the scene—which seems very doubtful, in terms of the commonly accepted view of the nature of original scientific discovery. On the applied side, there has been considerable effort to rework the economics of inequality, education, and human capital from a "radical" point of view, but it has scored no brilliant successes. A certain amount of empirical work has been done on the measurement of Marxist concepts, notably "the rate of surplus value" in underdeveloped countries, but the resulting contribution to understanding is by no means obvious. Most recently, the "radicals" have been tending to shift, for scientifically understandable reasons, into the study of economic history and the associated set of "great questions" posed by Marx about the origins and nature of capitalism. In this field, however, the essentially literary, philosophical, and semantic techniques of Marxist scholarship confront the more revolutionary aims and vastly more scientific techniques of cliometrics, with its emphasis on the painstaking assembly and theoretical and econometric evaluation of microeconomic data.

One strongly suspects, in fact, that academic economics will rapidly digest and largely excrete the radical challenge, not so much through understanding of, confrontation with, and scientific triumph over the challenge as through the power of established academic institutions and scientific communities to ingest, extract nourishment from, and extrude all sorts of rough intellectual fodder. One can, in fact, already observe the processes at work. The "radical" courses at the undergraduate level command little attention at the level of admission to graduate work, as compared with a quantitative background (not necessarily in economics). The graduate-level courses and the later workshops and seminars oriented toward radicalism remain for the most part optional, and the students, particularly in this period of inflation, unemployment, and falling college enrollments, must be fully aware that, wherever the jam is, the real butter is on the bread of the quantitative subjects. The "radical" assistant professors appointed a few years back to teach radical courses in the leading universities are somehow failing to win tenure and are descending the ladder of academic prestige into the second-string state universities and colleges, where they will gradually be submerged among the coarse and unimaginative careerist professional pedants and project researchers. The trend of radical student interest toward economic history and the history of economic thought—a trend which, incidentally, repeats in some respects the radicals' scurry for cover in the McCarthy period—will in effect steer them toward teaching in liberal-arts colleges and to professing courses which are safely historical and cultural, not to be confused with real present-day life, in the teaching of which a certain amount of radicalism is condoned and even expected as spice to an otherwise dull display of enervating erudition.

One final aspect of the radical challenge and the response to it remains to be discussed here. This, the aspect which has excited the most discussion and concern in the other social sciences, is the impact the radical movement had on the proceedings of the American Economic Association.

In contrast to the riotous proceedings that have characterized the annual meetings (specifically the business meetings) of some other professional associations, an attempt to disrupt the annual A.E.A. meetings was made on only one occasion and then unsuccessfully. This was at the 1969 New York meetings, when about twenty-five members of "a group of radical economists" attempted to take over the microphone and the platform from the president in order to read a denunciatory statement, failed to gain the microphone,[8] read their statement while the meeting discussed the agenda, were then allowed the floor, read their statement over the microphone, and departed (see the official account in the Appendix). On the other hand, the annual business meeting became, and has continued to be, a very lengthy and argumentative affair, concerned most recently with equal rights for women, although the proceedings have been punctiliously parliamentary and polite. Moreover, the program sessions have come regularly to include sessions on "radical" subjects, organized and participated in by "radical economists." Behind this comparatively peaceful and civilized experience of "the radical challenge" lie, on the one hand, the fact and historical experience of a profession that has, in the memory of living and still active senior members, been through the wringer of attempted politicization before, and, on the other hand, an interesting case for study of the influence of institutional forms and practices in restraining or fostering certain kinds of political behavior.

As regards the experience and consequent behavior principles of the profession, there is first the general fact that the senior members of the profession include *both* a significant number of German-language refugee scholars—academically, the disbanded remnants of the once-famous "Austrian School" of marginalism and capital theory—who are predominantly liberals in the European intellectual tradition rather than the American New Deal Democrat mold; *and* a high proportion of Jews either of European refugee origin or of American origin but raised while anti-Semitism was still a strong social force in America. Both groups are insistent on respect for individual rights but are equally fastidious about, and resistant to, claims to rights that implicitly seek special rights for one or reduce the rights of others.[9] Second, and more specifically, a number of still-active economists passed through the witch-hunting for leftists in the McCarthy period and, before that, but especially afterward, the academic discrimination against, and virtual ostracism of, right-wing economists by the majority belonging to the dominant New Deal Keynesian school; they have had, as a result, to think out and live by a workable philosophy of democratic government and procedure.[10] Finally, many economists have had experience with governmental processes in many different contexts at many different levels as part of their professional activity—including, not negligibly, the experience with local politics that is accumulated osmotically by most educated people who have a family to raise and taxes to pay in the type of city in which most universities and colleges are located; hence they are tolerant of, but not seriously moved by, emotive youthful caricatures of political and social processes and structures.[11]

As regards the institutional characteristics of the American Economic Association, there are three points to be noticed. The first is that the president-elect, the vice-presidents, and the executive committee are elected by postal ballot from a selection of candidates produced by a nominating committee, itself chosen to represent different geographical, occupational, and other differential aspects of the profession's work by the president;[12] however, space is left on the ballot for write-in votes. One of the nominating committee's responsibilities is to use the record of past write-ins as a guide in selecting suitable candidates for nomination. The vice-presidents serve for one year, but the executive-committee members serve for a period of years, so that only a minority of them is elected in any given year. Only one person is nominated as president-elect; this reflects an unfortunate historical experience in which an eminent foreign candidate was defeated in favor of a native candidate better known to the membership. The nomination is for president-elect, who becomes president automatically the following year because of a decision in the late 1950s that the duties of preparing and superintending the annual program, delivering a presidential address, and representing the profession on increasingly frequent ceremonial occasions had become too onerous for one man to perform in a single year.[13] The result of this patrician-democratic system of self-government by the Association is that the Association is impervious to revolutionary change of management but is adaptable gradually, and with a long lag, to changes in majority professional opinion and interests. The most that could be accomplished by a radical minority would be the forced passage of politically motivated resolutions, but even these (refer again to the Appendix) are restricted in scope and language by the Association's constitution.

Second, the possibility of successfully carrying through a politically radical (or for that matter reactionary) resolution is reduced virtually to negligibility as the serendipitous result of a change in programing introduced for a quite unrelated reason. Up until the late 1960s, the business meeting was scheduled as the final event on the last day of the annual meetings. But the inconvenient timing of the meetings (December 27–30), in conjunction with the ready availability of early escape by air from the small number of large cities to which the members attending the meetings limited the venue, had the effect of reducing attendance to the point where it became embarrassingly necessary to impress an executive-committee member to move the vote of thanks to the program and local-arrangements committees. More seriously, as a result of what was then a standard and academically reputable but is essentially an economically irrational policy for handling the funds of academic societies, namely, the establishment of an investment committee that invests for growth of capital value rather than dividends and therefore shows little accounting income, thereby inducing the treasurer to insist on current expenses being covered by current subscription income so as to avoid "dipping into capital," the Association had become wealthy to the figure of over $500 per member, and there was a very real fear that a voting coalition requiring no more than twenty or so members attending the business meeting—or, worse, a score of noneconomist one-year subscribers to the Association's journal—could and perhaps would vote the closing-down of the Association in order to realize the handsome capital gain from liquidation of the assets. To guard against this possibility, and also the aforementioned embarrassment of meetings of members with no purely civilian members present, the business meeting was rescheduled to follow immediately after the presidential address, delivered on the preceding evening, in the hope of catching a quorum of civilians too physically feeble or too bereft of alternative opportunities for amusement to make it to the nearest exit between the end of the presidential address and the beginning of the business meeting, and with the expectation that the meeting would nevertheless take no more than the previous customary twenty to thirty minutes.

The result has been the proverbial mixture of good news and bad. The bad news has been that the business meeting, instead of ending limply at 9:30 or so, in good time for a nightcap or two at a publisher's party, has typically gone on until 11:00, midnight, or even 1:00 A.M. and beyond, with the executive and the conservative establishment frozen in their places in alertness against the familiar left-wing tactic of boring the conservatives down in numbers to a voting minority against a small, determined group of radicals. The good news has been that the conservative or pragmatic majority has voted down—partly with the unwelcome assistance of the rapid attrition of the Association's earlier paper wealth by inflation and falling stock-market values—the more irresponsible and expensive radical demands, for example for Association sponsorship of a new journal to provide an academically reputable publication outlet for radical criticisms of government policy, or Association financing of a round-the-clock reporting service on actual and scheduled committee hearings in Washington. They have also continued to insist on properly academic wording of resolutions. At the same time, the semicaptive presence of several hundreds of members, many of whom personally live and work in rather homogeneous and narrow university or college environments, undoubtedly serves to make the general membership more aware of the existence, nature, and substance of radical dissent than they otherwise would be.[14]

Finally, it is relevant to note that the American Economic Association, unlike the American associations of some other social sciences and unlike economic associations in some other countries (for example, the Royal Economic Society in Britain), serves its members more in the fashion of an umbrella than in the fashion of a raincoat. The annual meetings are organized as a cooperative enterprise in alliance with other associations in fields closely related to economics, according to a pattern that changes from year to year, though on a regular cycle. Any sufficiently numerous group of reasonably reputable economists may form its own association and mount a program of its own at the meetings, with the support of the Association and often with official recognition in the form of one or more joint sessions. In the past, such associations have been formed by Catholic economists, black economists, economists interested in comparative economic systems (more accurately, communist economics), economists interested in "the grants economy," and, more recently, radical economists, women economists, and economists interested in United States-Mexican and United States-Canadian economic relations. Less formally, the Association's own program always provides sessions for subjects that interest enough economists to generate the necessary number of paper-writers and discussants or to provide a sufficiently distinguished discussion panel.[15] In fact, therefore, the Association exercises little control, positive or negative, over what economists do and the academic credit they get for doing it, apart from its presidential and vice-presidential posts and its honorary memberships and two honorary medals, all of which (except possibly its Clark Medal, for the best economist under forty years of age) are awarded too late in professional life to excite much ambition. Its main function is to represent its members, and that not in the elevated sense of Burke's *Letter to the Electors of Bristol*. Its prime responsibility is to accommodate flexibly to its members' activities and interests. In consequence, it affords an exceedingly measly trophy for successful political strategy.

Concluding Remarks

The title of this paper contrasts the "hard social science" with "the soft social reality." The contents attempt to describe and explain the response of the economists to the radical challenge. The profession was in fact "soft," inasmuch as the radicals, and a larger number of others who were swayed by them, obviously neither understood nor respected the scientific academic pursuit in which the profession was ostensibly engaged, while most of their opponents equally failed to understand the true nature, and the fragility, of the claims to scientific status that economists have generally assumed to possess legitimacy. Nevertheless, the profession and the discipline survived the radical challenge reasonably intact, partly by virtue of the collective conservative strength of traditional academic organizations, partly by virtue of the institutional characteristics (including accidental ones) of its professional association. In contemplating the experience, one is forcibly led back to the thinking of Popper and Polanyi on the nature of scientific procedure and of the republic of science. It is not the brilliance and comprehensive understanding of the individual scientist but rather the collective result of the democratic interaction of many often pedestrian and blinkered minds, agreed on scientific rules for evaluating theoretical propositions against empirical evidence, that turns social philosophy into social science. In this sense, economics can justly claim to be the "hardest," or even the only "hard," social science. But it is a humbling thought that economics in the period under review has been as unscientific as other "softer" social sciences in its willingness to confuse the scope and limits of social-scientific inquiry with the questions currently regarded as permissible in the interests of American society and that in this willingness it has provided seemingly high-powered ammunition to radicals who ought to study rather than reject the rules of scientific inquiry—study, that is, whether radicalism is really, as it claims to be, an ethical philosophy and not, as some classic writers have suggested, merely an appealing life-style for a particular personality type.

APPENDIX

Proceedings of the American Economic Association (*Annual Business Meeting, December 29, 1969, New York Hilton Hotel, New York, New York*)
The Eighty-second Annual Business Meeting of the American Economic Association was called to order by President W. J. Fellner in the Trianon Ballroom of the New York Hilton Hotel, New York, New York, at 9:30 P.M. on December 29, 1969. At this point, a group of approximately twenty-five members of "a group of radical economists" filed into the meeting room. Their spokesman, Arthur MacEwan, demanded, on behalf of the group, that he be permitted to present a statement to the meeting. President Fellner informed Mr. MacEwan that he could present his statement when the meeting considered unfinished or new business. Even though ruled out of

This Appendix is an extract from the *American Economic Review,* May 1970, pp. 487–89.

order by Martin Shubik, who announced that he had been asked to give advice as parliamentarian, and in the midst of confusion brought about by attempts of other members of the radical group to join him on the platform, Mr. MacEwan began immediately to read his statement. Meanwhile, President Fellner, using the microphone, proceeded to a consideration of the items as they appeared on the agenda prepared for the meeting. Despite the confusion occasioned by the fact that Mr. MacEwan was still reading his statement and was being interrupted by members of the audience, it was VOTED: (1) to approve the minutes of the Association's Business Meeting of December 29, 1968; (2) to ratify the minutes of the Executive Committee meetings held on December 27, 1968, and March 7–8, 1969; and (3) to accept the reports of the Secretary and the Treasurer, which had been circulated in written form to the members. (These reports are published below.)

At this point, President Fellner recognized Mr. MacEwan, who presented over the microphone the statement of the radical economist group, printed as Exhibit I to these minutes.

Following the reading of the statement, the group left the meeting. In the discussion that followed, the President recognized Gordon Tullock, who made the statement printed as Exhibit II to these minutes.

The President recognized Gerhard Tintner, who moved that a vote of censure of the United States Department of State for refusing to grant a visa to the Marxian economist Mandel, who had been invited to make a series of lectures in the United States. The motion was seconded. Martin Shubik moved that the original motion should be amended to read, "It is the sense of this meeting that no member of the economics profession, regardless of his views, should be prevented from accepting an invitation to visit the United States to present lectures or to accept a teaching assignment." The motion was seconded. The question was raised as to whether the motion as amended was in violation of Article III, Section 3, of the charter of the A.E.A. that "the Association as such will take no partisan attitude, nor will it commit its members on practical economic questions." Following a discussion, it was voted 112 for and 7 against to adopt the motion as amended.

Exhibit I
We have come to denounce the American Economic Association,

and to denounce the dominant economics for which the A.E.A. provides the organizational support.

Economists in the United States work as a group and work contrary to the interests of the masses of people. The affluence and the power of the economists derive from their support of the elite, the elite which controls the institutional structure and the sources of power that perpetrate and reproduce the oppression of millions—the economists are the sycophants of inequality, alienation, destruction of environment, imperialism, racism, and the subjugation of women.

Economists are the priests and prophets of an unjust society. They preach the gospel of rational efficiency, justifying the reduction of man and nature to marketable commodities; they treat human beings as capital and tell us the poor are poor because they lack "productive skills"; all they tell us about the war in Vietnam is how to fight it more efficiently; they apply mathematical models that "prove" that foreign investment helps the development of poor countries; they tell us that racism is the result of "personal preference"; they tell us that private property and wage differentials present a system of personal material incentives "necessary" for "growth."

But the economists do not merely praise the system; they also supply the tools—indeed, they are the tools—instrumental to the elite's attainment of its unjust ends. They show how to manipulate people so that the system's hinges are smoothly oiled. Economists are minimizers of just discontent: in the face of police riots in cities, it is the economists who develop "people appeasement" programs to prevent rebellion; when a reactionary government controls a poor country, economists are sent to "rationalize" and "stabilize" its economy; when students rebel on campuses, it is the industrial relations economists and game theorists, the rational arm of the police, who provide the program for repression.

The American Economic Association must be denounced as the organization through which these economists operate. But further, the A.E.A. plays directly destructive roles in our society. It serves to insure the perpetuation of professionalism, elitism, and petty irrelevance. It serves to inhibit the development of new ideas, ideas which are reflective of social reality.

Our conflict with the A.E.A. is not simply an intellectual debate. The A.E.A. cannot lessen our condemnation by their willingness to partake in debate, or by their willingness to provide a room to radical economists at this meeting. Our conflict is a basic conflict of interests. The economists have chosen to serve the *status quo*. We have chosen to fight it.

Exhibit II

May I begin by saying how happy I am that certain people are now leaving the meeting.

As those of you who know me are aware, the particular political and economic point of view which I happen to hold is a minority one, both in this society and in the larger society within which we live. I have become accustomed to being in the minority in majority voting. Nevertheless, I am here this evening to speak in favor of democracy within the American Economic Association—a system in which I almost always lose: Democracy may not be the best possible form of government either for a nation or for a voluntary association such as the A.E.A. You may recall that Winston Churchill once said democracy was the worst of all possible forms of government, except, of course, for those others that had been tried from time to time. Nevertheless, it is at the moment the best form of government which we have available. It is particularly suitable for voluntary societies such as this one, since minorities are free to leave and set up new societies if they find this one objectionable. It may be so that, over time, we will discover better ways of running such associations, but we have not done so at the moment.

Under the circumstances, it is necessary that we attempt to conduct our business in a reasonably orderly way. In democracy, everyone has a right to speak, but if they all speak at once, no one can be heard. Rules as to who speaks first are essential and cannot be objected to, provided they do not deprive anyone of the right to speak eventually. The disturbance which has just terminated did not arise because the disturbers were denied the right to speak, but simply because they were told they could not speak at exactly the time they chose without any consideration for other persons' rights. They refused to obtain the floor by parliamentary methods apparently because they felt they had a superior right. This superior right, I presume, derives from the fortunate fact that they knew the truth and were here to proclaim it, whereas those who might otherwise wish to talk were in error. The rules which provide for the presenting of different points of view in an orderly manner would, thus, be unnecessary. The fact that the disrupters left immediately after reading their statement in order to prevent themselves from being contaminated by anything that anyone else might say is a further illustration of this attitude.

Clearly, the position taken by these people is profoundly undemocratic. They know the truth and propose to act on it, and they have no feeling that any particular procedure or routine has any value in itself. Any orderly process of making decisions will impose delay. It is certainly true that it would be better to reach the right decision instantaneously. Unfortunately, we have no instantaneous method of "aggregating preferences." Until one is invented, we will have to follow processes which can make errors and which take time.

As I said before, it is by no means obvious that democracy is the ultimate or ideal form of government. We may discover something better in the future. For the moment, however, we are stuck with democracy simply because it is better than any known alternative. It seems to me, therefore, very important that we not only conform to rules of democratic behavior ourselves, but enforce these rules on others. There is a certain irony in my pressing this point of view because, as I noted at the beginning of my remarks, I have almost always been in the minority in the past and it seems likely that I am doomed to be in the minority in the future. Nevertheless, until I can suggest some better method, I feel that I must accept the majority decisions and, as a matter of fact, the majority appears to be quite tolerant of various points of view, even the points of view of members of extremely small minorities like myself.

Reinhard Bendix

 Province and Metropolis: The Case of Eighteenth-Century Germany

Edward Shils has suggested the distinction between province and metropolis as one focus for the analysis of intellectual groups. The present essay makes use of this distinction for an interpretation of middle-class culture in eighteenth-century Germany. The first part deals with the provincialism of German society, its reflection in the class structure, and the paradox that within this localized society there was a burgeoning interest in literature. The second part outlines the impact of French metropolitan culture on German court society and the social and literary formulations of an emerging middle-class identity in response to that impact. The essay concludes with a survey of German reactions to the French Revolution.

Province and Intellectual Mobilization
In seventeenth- and eighteenth-century Europe, England and France were powerful and relatively unified societies. By contrast, "Germany" existed only as an institutional anachronism. Based on the Treaty of Westphalia (1648), the Holy Roman Empire of the German nation consisted of sovereign territories belonging to 8 Electors (*Kurfürsten*, of which the Austrian, Prussian, Bavarian, and Saxon Electors were the most important), 27 lay princes (*weltliche Fürsten*), 95 Imperial Knights (*Reichsritter*), 42 Imperial Bishops (*Reichsbischöfe*), and 50 free Imperial towns (*freie Reichsstädte*).[1] All the small sovereign territories depended on the Empire for their survival, and so did an additional 4,000 hometown communities (*Kleinstädte mit Selbstverwaltung*)—small towns

119

which for diverse historical reasons possessed certain rights of self-government.[2] A basic definition of the hometowns is that there was almost no penetration into their internal affairs from the outside; each unit found protection for its peculiar institutions by adding its own specifications to the existing complexity of jurisdictions. Much the same can be said of the other petty principalities and jurisdictions.

An estimated 20 to 25 percent of the people lived in diminutive hometowns, and the provincialism of eighteenth-century middle-class culture is best understood with reference to the conditions of local home rule. There was little economic differentiation in these hometowns and relatively little economic or administrative intrusion from the outside. The *Bürgerschaft* was content with a moderate level of living and used its powers of exclusion to maintain the status quo. On that basis it was possible to avoid the cleavage between a patriciate and an artisan class that was pronounced in the few towns of larger size and greater outside involvement. The self-conscious localism of these hometown residents is not adequately conveyed by the term "petty bourgeois," with its implication of frustrated ambition and of a slightly pathetic imitation of a bourgeois way of life. As Walker has suggested, this strongly conservative small-town *Bürgertum* is important in its own right, a point that is missed by the commonplace that "Germany lacked a strong liberal bourgeoisie" like that of England or France.[3] Hometown localism is not unique to Germany, of course, but only there did it enjoy strong institutional support through the political fragmentation of the Empire.

Until the 1850s, between 65 and 70 percent of the population lived in the countryside. Here, local rule was typically more autocratic, and less insulated from external involvements, than in the hometowns. Even so, local government in the countryside was quite as insistent on its autonomy as the hometowns and used its jurisdiction for similar defensive purposes. To a degree, such rural localism persisted even in the larger states, despite their more effective administration. Naturally, localism was more pronounced in the smaller territorial enclaves—those of the Imperial Knights, the Bishoprics, and the numerous petty principalities. When conservatives of the period extolled the virtues of tradition, they had in mind the hometowns and small territorial domains as neighborhood communities. They idealized the narrow horizon of provincial living and freely applied their model to all the territorial enclaves threatened by absolutist regimes and enlightened thought. In the process,

they disregarded the fierce, if often tacit, coercion typical of familial
and neighborhood interdependence.[4] The point is that, in the towns
as in the countryside, personal coercion of the autocratic or oligar-
chic variety characterized the lives of most people in eighteenth-
century Germany.

Thus, since the Treaty of Westphalia of 1648, a European balance
of power had preserved a power vacuum in the center of Europe in
which a great multiplicity of jurisdictions survived. The institutions
of the Holy Roman Empire did not accomplish any positive political
purpose, but they were resilient enough to preserve this political
particularism until the Napoleonic invasions destroyed its balance.
Paradoxically, this politically fragmented structure possessed certain recognizable social strata. People usually distinguished between
nobility, *Bürgertum*, and peasantry, attributing each individual to
one of these estates by a combination of birth and status. The
subcultures of social and political experience tended to cut across
these distinctions. Nobles and peasants lived in the same rural
world. On the other hand, a hometownsman and, say, a banker in
Hamburg lived in quite different worlds. Not only were urban
residents more diverse, but certain categories like civil servants, free
professionals, and others stood outside the old system of estates.
Walker has suggested a threefold distinction between countrymen,
hometownsmen, and movers and doers to cope with the increasing
number of people who "did not fit." These categories are meant to
encompass different ranks of society, like nobles and peasants in the
countryside or merchants, master craftsmen, journeymen, and
others in the towns. The third category is the smallest and most
heterogeneous. It includes all the residents of the larger towns:
government officials, teachers, clergymen, merchants, manufacturers, artisans, workers in industry, and, finally, intellectuals and
free professionals. If an aristocrat became an officer or administra-
tor, or an occasional hometownsman left his community to ply a
trade in a larger town, he joined this more mobile social world.[5] The
persons and occupations in Walker's third category are obviously
very diverse, but in contrast with the people in the countryside and
the hometowns they have the element of mobility in common. It is
misleading, however, to call them "doers" as well. Certainly, some
of them were. Bankers, wholesale traders and manufacturers,
landless laborers, free-lance journalists, and civil servants were
among them. Yet, many officials, teachers and clergymen, merchants and laborers, even free professionals and writers, were

movers without being doers. They might be mobile, but they fitted well into the parochial world of eighteenth-century Germany. Last but not least, it is important to mention married women. The vast majority of them were quite conservative in outlook; yet, in the middle ranks of society, many of them had time on their hands, and they became an audience for the printed word.

This is the paradox of eighteenth-century German society. Its great political fragmentation and intense parochialism coincided with a rapid cultural mobilization which made the elite and increasing segments of the "middle ranks" of society aware of fashions, ideas, and important events abroad, especially in France, the leading country of eighteenth-century Europe. The following discussion provides evidence for this cultural mobilization. Its consequences are analyzed in the second part of this essay.

Political fragmentation combined with mercantilist policies to produce a mushrooming bureaucracy, which increased the potential audience for newspapers, journals, and books. In the eighteenth century, absolutist rulers took it for granted that they must promote the economy as well as strengthen their military and political power. In the smaller territories the same impulses prevailed, even though the military and political aspects of absolutism turned into travesties. In spirit if not in detail, economic priorities followed the precedents set by French mercantilism. They comprised promotion of trade and industry, a substantial involvement of government in the conduct of economic enterprises, and a detailed regulation of social and economic life. A burgeoning officialdom was the inevitable accompaniment of absolutist rule, and in eighteenth-century Germany every state, down to the smallest Imperial Knight, required a corps of officials! Moreover, many of these "states" were composed of scattered, rather than consolidated, territories. Even though under the same sovereign, the separate territories each possessed its own administration and judiciary, requiring additional numbers of officials. In this connection, Biedermann estimates that there were some 2,000 separate territories.[6] The ranks of the "bureaucracy" were swelled further by the general practice of treating all teachers—and, in Protestant territories, all clergymen— as employees of the state. In Germany, bureaucratization is an enduring legacy of eighteenth-century absolutism, not a by-product of advanced capitalism and complex organization.

Ever since the eighteenth century, officials, teachers, and clergymen have represented an important segment of the German *Bürger-*

tum. No appropriate English equivalent is available for this term, and the French "bourgeoisie" is a literal, but inappropriate, translation.[7] It is a symptom of these linguistic and conceptual difficulties that after another half-century of economic development and at the high point of German liberalism in the revolution of 1848, 58 percent of the delegates to the Paulskirche consisted of civil servants, teachers, and clergymen, while another 24 percent consisted of lawyers, writers, and other free professionals. By contrast, only 9 percent of the delegates were merchants, manufacturers, artisans, and landed proprietors of nonnoble origin.[8] These figures suggest that, by contrast with England and to a lesser extent with France, the most active segment of the German middle class consisted to a disproportionate extent of state employees. Obviously, in Germany as elsewhere, free professionals and entrepreneurial types from many walks of life played an important role as well; from the beginning of the eighteenth century the German *Bürgertum* included employees of the state as a distinct group; and under the influence of this group and the free professionals, education became so important a feature of the *Bürgertum* as a whole that special phrases (*Bildungsbürgertum* or *gehobenes Bürgertum*) are used to distinguish this class of people from the persons who lack education. For this reason I use the phrase "educated commoners" in the discussion below.

Perhaps the rapid increase of intellectuals in the late eighteenth century was as important a phenomenon as bureaucratization. There is no simple causal relation between this "intellectual mobilization," to which I now turn, and the proliferation of officials induced by political particularism. Certainly, literacy was not confined to officials, teachers, and clergymen. Indeed, all too many of these state employees were at a low cultural level, lording it over those below them while cringing in deference to those above. Yet in terms of status and education this stratum stood clearly above the common people. Contemporary descriptions of officials idling away their time or attending to business on a hit-or-miss basis also mention that they read newspapers. Government officials and ministers of the church may have been slovenly and narrowly provincial in their outlook, but to some extent they depended on the printed word; and in relatively well-governed states like Prussia, military discipline and reformist zeal saw to it that the servants of state and church did their duty.[9]

This mixed picture of the officials is more generally characteristic of a kind of crazy-quilt relation between absolutism and intellectual awakening. To a degree, absolutist rule, with its large aspiration of controlling all available resources, depended upon officials with a modicum of education. Autocratic rulers promoted education in the interest of improving production and tax collection, though they might adumbrate such efforts with conventional religious appeals. At any rate, their intent was profoundly conservative, and they insisted on censorship in the interest of orthodoxy and loyalty. Yet the effects of this absolutist position were double-edged. The same education which helped make officials better instruments of the royal will also increased the possibility of a reaction against absolutism. Absolutist sponsorship of education, the Protestant concern with the salvation of souls, and the free thought encouraged by the Enlightenment helped to spread an interest in literature and philosophy, with potentially subversive results.

The foundation years of "German" universities reflect these diverse influences and suggest the intense concern of absolutist rulers with an education that would be useful for administration. Sixteen universities were medieval foundations (before 1500); nine were founded in the sixteenth century, the period of the Reformation. Twenty-four universities were founded in the seventeenth and eighteenth centuries, and four more in the early nineteenth century, so that the total number under absolutist auspices came to twenty-eight. Until the early eighteenth century, academic practice often remained antiquated, especially in the older institutions. Only the universities of Halle (founded 1694), Göttingen (1736), and Königsberg (dating back to 1544) were notable centers of innovation. Even in these advanced universities the Prussian and Hannoverian governments exercised strict control over academic affairs. Universities were organized to prepare young men for their official duties in government, church, and school, especially after 1740, when university study became increasingly a condition of public employment. Scientific or general education was irrelevant to the training of competent "royal servants." In effect, German universities were schools of public officials and clergymen, since three-quarters of the students attended the faculties of law and theology.[10]

In this way, higher education would serve strictly delimited purposes. Official Protestantism considered *every* authority sacrosanct; and, for much of the eighteenth century, the German Enlightenment remained preoccupied with theological problems and did not challenge symbols of authority on a broader front, as in

France. The record of censorship indicates how absolutist rule sought to combine its interest in the status quo with the intellectual mobilization needed for more effective government. In this respect much depended on the outlook of the ruler and the degree to which he wanted publishing controlled. Under Frederick the Great, Prussia was the state with the most enlightened attitude toward freedom of the press—at any rate by the standards of the day. But Frederick also disparaged German literature publicly, and his successors went back to a much more restrictive policy toward the press. In any case, Prussia was *not* the center of German cultural life.

In fact, Germany lacked a cultural center like London or Paris. The consequences of this fact are vividly described in a review article by Goethe:

> Nowhere in Germany is there a center of social life and education [*gesellschaftlicher Lebensbildung*], where writers can congregate and develop, each in his own field, but in a unified fashion. Born dispersed, educated very differently, mostly left to themselves and to impressions from very different situations; swept away by the preference for this or that example of native or foreign literature; impelled to all kinds of dabbling attempts in order to test their powers without guidance; only through gradual reflection convinced of what one should undertake; instructed by practice in what one can accomplish; led astray time and again by a large public without taste, which devours the bad and the good with just the same delight; then again encouraged through acquaintance with the educated multitude scattered through all parts of the *Reich*; strengthened by contemporaries engaged in collaborative endeavors; thus the German writer finally finds himself in the age of manhood, in which worry about his livelihood and a family compels him to look around. Often he is forced, with the saddest feeling, to obtain his living through works he himself does not respect, in order to be allowed to create what his mature mind would wish solely to be occupied with. What respected German writer will not recognize himself in this picture and confess, with humble sadness, how often he has sighed for an opportunity to subordinate the peculiarities of his creative genius to a national culture, which unfortunately did not exist? For the cultivation of the higher classes through foreign fashions and a foreign literature prevented a German from developing as a German early on, however much advantage such cultivation has brought us as well.[11]

In our context, Goethe's description is best read as an account of the peculiar stamp which these conditions put upon cultural life. In a fragmented country like Germany, the petty circumstances of daily life were not relieved by larger public preoccupations, such as those of Paris or London. Nonetheless, cultural life flourished, especially in the south and west. In the Electorate of Saxony, Leipzig was the center of book fairs, and allowance was made for this economic asset by rather lenient censorship. Even so, newspapers were not permitted to discuss religious questions. Early in the century, the rulers of both Saxony and Saxony-Weimar had issued decrees prohibiting "untruthful newspaper writings," declaring that they wanted "no reasoners for subjects."[12] Württemberg witnessed both an intensification of intellectual life and the most arbitrary suppression of individual writers. Later in the century, Saxony-Weimar became suddenly the most famous center of high culture—under the aegis of Goethe and his patron, Grand Duke Carl August. As will be shown below, it was in the absence of a national center and a national public that German literary aspirations came to focus on humanity as a whole.

Political particularism and the mixed record of censorship suggest that absolutism could intervene in, but could not control, the cultural life of the country. With so many sovereign territories in which the same language was spoken, it was relatively easy to escape censorship by moving the place of publication, when necessary, to a neighboring state. Active men could not fail to make invidious comparisons between German disunity and the successful polities of England and France; and this sense of backwardness, together with efforts to compensate for it, aided the "intellectual mobilization" of the educated public. At this point I want to consider the evidence for this mobilization in the latter part of the eighteenth century; for, backward and disunited as the country was, both economically and politically, beginning in the 1770s it witnessed a springtide of cultural interest and achievement.

The number of book publications provides a rough index for the growth of the reading public during the eighteenth century. The following compilation is based on the listing of printed works in the Leipzig book fair. As a whole, these listings are reasonable approximations, even though they include some double counting, and some works were announced and not published or were published but not listed. The bulk of the books was published in Latin, German, and French; and we need only note that in the course of the century Latin declined, while German and French increased many times. It seems clear from table 1 that after the middle of the eighteenth century the country witnessed an upsurge in the arts and sciences.

TABLE 1: Number of Books in Leipzig Book-Fair Catalogues, by Year and Field

FIELD	TOTAL NUMBER OF BOOKS LISTED BY YEAR					
	1700	1720	1740	1760	1780	1800
Theology*	430	374	436	269	389	241
Law	85	86	172	52	149	143
Medicine	63	79	101	70	191	198
History†	157	209	221	277	469	631
Philosophy‡	197	198	334	392	968	1,590
Poetry§	46	33	62	138	476	1,209
Total	978	979	1,326	1,198**	2,642	4,012

SOURCE: Gustav Schwetschke, ed., *Codex Nundinarius Germaniae Literatae Bisecularis, Mess-Jahrbücher des Deutschen Buchhandels* (Halle: G. Schwetschkes Verlagsbuchhandlung, 1850, 1877), pp. 78, 198, 218, 238, 273, 313.

*Theology includes both Protestant and Catholic writings, but the former predominate throughout.

†Based on the more detailed breakdown in 1801 and subsequent years, one can assume that "history" includes biography, classics, politics, geography, and travel.

‡On similar assumptions, "philosophy" includes education, philology, natural science, economics, "cameralistics," technology, mathematics, military science, and business.

§"Poetry" also includes music, novels, plays, and art books.

**Probably, the numbers for 1760 would have been higher if book publishing had not been affected by the Seven Years' War (1756-63).

The data in table 1 indicate only the general trend in book publications, not their absolute magnitude. For example, the listings for the Leipzig fair show 2,642 publications for 1780, but a contemporary bookseller estimated a total of some 5,000 German books and pamphlets, not counting foreign-language books or occasional publications. Another estimate for 1783 suggests that some 2,000 separate publications were issued in editions totaling 2 million volumes. Similar estimates were given for the number of writers living in Germany, a figure that is supposed to have doubled, from 3,000 to 6,000, between 1773 and 1787. Estimates of the number of writers in specific areas or individual towns are probably more reliable, but all such estimates are rather rough. In any case, there is little doubt about the general trend. Obviously, this profusion of reading matter was a mixed lot, with novels, plays, travelogues, biographies, religious tracts, and historical and scientific literature at one end, and encyclopedias, almanacs, cookbooks, household manuals, calendars, and a profusion of lurid, if not pornographic, booklets at the other.

Often books were serialized in the various journals which also proliferated in the last decades of the century, and here the figures seem to be quite reliable. According to the most comprehensive study available, 2,191 new journals were published between 1766 and 1790; that is, there were 248 new ones in 1766-69, 718 in the 1770s, and 1,225 in the 1780s. The total for this period was three times larger than the corresponding total for 1741-65. Thirty-four percent of the new journals in the period 1766-90 were devoted to light reading or fiction (*Unterhaltungsliteratur*). In other subjects, new journals for the whole twenty-five-year period were distributed as follows:

History	10.0 percent
Literature	10.0
Theology	7.3
Pedagogy	5.0
Medicine	5.5
Science	4.9
Economics (Cameralistics)	4.0
Popular science	8.5

The remaining 10.8 percent were distributed among military science, music, and philosophy. Thus, the sudden increase in the publication of journals coincided with a striking degree of specialization at this early time. Nor was this development confined to particular areas, since there were fifty-six different towns, many of them quite small, in which at least three new journals were published between 1766 and 1790.

In the minds of contemporaries there was no doubt that this whole intellectual mobilization represented a major change. "Our literature begins in the 1740s," one journal declared in 1784. The philosopher Fichte stated in 1805 that a new trade in books had developed in the second half of the eighteenth century. At the same time, there were mounting expressions of surprise and concern at this proliferation of "scribblers." People began to worry about the dangers of reading as a fad and of glutting the literary marketplace with shoddy products. But whatever the evaluation, there is no doubt that all parts of Germany underwent a major intellectual mobilization in the last decades of the eighteenth century.[13]

In sum, eighteenth-century Germany was a society steeped in its provincial particularism. Concern with local affairs predominated in the hometowns and the countryside. The people involved took pride in their local affairs. At a high artistic level, one can appreciate this sense of positive well-being and community in Goethe's *Hermann und Dorothea* (1797), a poetic celebration of the parochial spirit, which regarded refugees from the French Revolution with sympathy and detachment in the happy thought that one was not oneself involved in these world affairs.[14] No doubt, even in this quiescent population there was, here and there, a rebellious spirit. Most of these spirits were to be found, not among the residents of the hometowns or the countryside, but among the people who did not "fit" into the old estate order and railed at the confining world in which they had to live. In 1799, Hölderlin wrote a famous outburst which castigated what Goethe had held up to admiration:

> It is a harsh statement, and yet I say it, because it is the truth: I cannot think of a people more torn apart than the Germans. You see artisans, but not men, thinkers but not men, masters and servants, youths and established people, but not men. Is it not like a battlefield where hands and arms and legs lie about dismembered, while the spilt lifeblood melts into the sand?[15]

Clearly, among the seven million hometownsmen of "Germany" the vast majority would have approved of Goethe's attitude rather than Hölderlin's—if they had known of it. But for all the difference in their attitudes, Goethe *and* Hölderlin were part of the intellectual agitation which sought to cultivate and mobilize a docile, parochial population toward a concern with larger issues. The paradox is the evidence of so much intellectual mobilization in the midst of so provincial a society.

Reference Societies and Reference Groups

The provincialism of German society was a fact of European politics. France's hegemony rested in part on the balkanization of central Europe, and her preeminence ceased only with the final defeat of Napoleon in 1815. Throughout the eighteenth century, French cultural influence dominated the society of the German courts. Imports of French luxury goods contributed largely to the

fact that between 1700 and 1790 the German territories had a
negative trade balance with France of some 18 million marks
annually.[16] In view of this great cultural influence and the proximity
of the two countries, it was inevitable that the French Revolution
also had many repercussions. But there was no revolution in
Germany. The hierarchic view of society associated with the *ancien
régime* proved strong enough to resist the revolutionary impulses
emanating from France. In modified form, the political fragmentation continued into the nineteenth century. Spokesmen for the
church, scholars, jurists, and officials provided intellectual sanction
for the authority of rulers in even the smallest sovereign territory.
The German *Bürgertum*—the educated commoners of German
society—resisted the impulses of the Revolution in a manner that
contributed to the flowering of German classical literature. Thus, in
considering the impact of French culture and the French Revolution, we will be concerned directly with certain major characteristics
of German society itself.

Under Louis XIV (1643-1715), France had become the most
powerful nation in the world. The French monarch overwhelmed his
enemies at home and abroad not only in the military field but by the
exemplary magnificence of his buildings and by the works of art and
the elaborate ceremonial which distinguished his court. The ruling
circles of German society responded with alacrity to the latest
fashion at Versailles—but in territories frequently extending over
only a few square miles. The resources of these territories were small
and their power negligible. In actuality the German courts could
produce but a sorry imitation of their model; yet, in their little
worlds, many German rulers expressed their aspirations by buildings and festivals, by liveried servants and ceremonial displays,
which made up in outward splendor what they lacked in political
substance. Such magnificence was seen as the proper attribute of a
ruler who represented God on earth. If the maintenance of such a
court meant the cruel exploitation of the people, then this was
considered part of the divine order.

The German courts received encouragement from France. French
emissaries frequented the residences of German rulers, and these in
turn, or their representatives, were received at Versailles. The
culture of the French court was encouraged by the 30,000 French
Huguenots who had fled to Germany after 1685. Dependent upon
the powerful among their German hosts, these refugees promoted
French fashions through the luxury trades in which they were en-

gaged. Frenchmen replaced Germans as private tutors at courts and in aristocratic households. Young aristocrats made a special tour of the French capital a part of their education. Even after the Seven Years' War, many sons of German ruling houses volunteered for service in the French army! At the German courts, imitation of French fashion, use of French as the language of high society, demonstrations of homage to the French monarch—these seemed a small price to pay for an unofficial but unchallengeable verification of sovereign status. With psychological hindsight one can see in this German Gallomania an overcompensation for a weak position and perhaps the ambivalence of love and hate.

A few details may be mentioned because they suggest the kind of thing contemporaries were likely to hear and gossip about. In some court circles, French conversation became so customary that native German came to be seen as a vulgar, provincial dialect, and persons of low social rank were referred to as those who could not speak French. The children were taught French first, and sometimes outsiders wondered whether such people still knew German. Even early German classics, like some plays by Lessing, had to be translated into French in order to be performed (in the Electorate of Brunswick). Naturally, the veneer often cracked; then German was spoken, interlarded with French phrases.

The French model was not, moreover, confined to language, fashion, and culture. At Versailles, young German aristocrats could observe the seamier side of court life. Sexual license seemed an attribute of such life, and, the higher the rank, the greater the license. The French hardly invented the practice, but Versailles seemed to give it the stamp of cultural approval. Sometimes a single instance can illuminate a general condition, as in the exclamation of a resident in the capital of a small German principality when he witnessed the wedding procession of the reigning sovereign: "Now our prince lacks nothing but a beautiful mistress!" He had seen the father and grandfather with their mistresses and simply thought this an attribute of princely dignity.[17] In addition to illicit, if eminently public, love affairs, court society was preoccupied by a seemingly endless round of activities. There were the lavish and long-drawn-out banquets with a multitude of guests, and in the evenings one gathered again to watch a French comedy or an Italian opera. For persons of standing, entry to these entertainments was free of charge. Hunting and large parties organized for the hunt were a frequent preoccupation. There were longer journeys to the fairs of

Leipzig or Frankfort, as well, and to the many famous spas—each visit involving a large entourage and much display. Many special festivals were arranged to celebrate the birthday of the prince or his mistress, or the special days of the princely family, or the presence of a visiting dignitary. For that matter, festivities were often arranged on the spur of the moment. Many of these events received baroque elaborations through various allegorical devices. All of these activities were stimulated further by much visiting back and forth between courts. In 1721, some 400 foreign aristocrats passed some time at the Saxon court in Dresden in an eight-month period. Many of these cavaliers were foreign-born aristocrats like Casanova, who set the tone by their prodigal manner. They would spread the word concerning the customs and splendor they had witnessed elsewhere and thus encourage further competition among petty rulers, who were already vying with one another in their amorous conquests and baroque displays and frivolities.

All this activity required elaborate preparations, which could bring commotion to a whole area for weeks or even months. It was taken for granted that the ruler was free to call on the people of "his" realm and their possessions to serve the needs of his court. All of this was most conspicuous at the small courts, because of the discrepancy between their pretense and the world outside; but even at the Prussian court the French fashion prevailed. I have mentioned that Frederick II expressed contempt for the German language and its literature. He designed his Academy of Science on the French model, with Maupertius as its first president; he invited Voltaire, who found that everyone spoke French. Frederick would pay Frenchmen more than Germans; he hired an obscure French librarian at twice the salary he was willing to pay Winckelmann, the famous German classicist. At the Potsdam court, French fashion and culture were combined with puritanical ordinances, which the king applied to himself first of all and imposed upon his entourage as well. Little of that Prussian spirit was to be found elsewhere in German court society.[18]

As a result of emulating Versailles, the German courts and courtiers were divided by an unbridgeable gulf from the people at large. In Saxony the aristocracy demanded that its sons be entirely segregated from the sons of bourgeois families because a common education would unfit them for their social role. Religious ceremonies like christenings or weddings were to be conducted in aristocratic homes rather than in the church because it would be demeaning to christen aristocratic babies with the same water as ordinary children. Men of standing preempted high offices, while the actual work was done by bourgeois menials. Any social contact with persons of lower status was regarded as a special favor or even demeaning, but the bastard children of a ruler's mistress or, for that matter, cavalier adventurers with aristocratic pretensions were readily accepted as equals. In such a setting, affairs of court and state were in the hands of rulers and their confidants, while commentaries on such affairs by persons outside that circle were a social presumption that was rejected out of hand. A public was absent in the specific sense that no one outside the ruling circle had the right to an opinion.[19]

Defenders of the status quo supported this hierarchic view of society. As employees of the state, clergymen, teachers, and officials were hardly in a position to dissent from an interpretation which legitimized their own role in society. But the same view was shared by the people at large, especially by those in the middle strata of society—entrepreneurs of various kinds and members of the professions, like lawyers, doctors, and writers—who in France stood in the forefront of intellectual and political mobilization. As a contemporary observer put it: "Every nation has its [own] great impetus: in Germany it is obedience, in England freedom, in Holland commerce, in France the honor of the king. It would take very great transformations, in order to alter the whole direction of a way of thought."[20] Obedience toward established authority was a stronger force in Germany than "the honor of the king" was in France. The character of this obedience requires our attention, because it helps to explain the German reaction to the French Revolution.

There is considerable evidence on this point. In the seventeenth century, the English Civil War and the execution of Charles I in 1649 were the single most important events next to the reign of Louis XIV and France's European hegemony. German writings on these events were unanimous: they condemned the execution of a crowned head in the strongest terms, excoriated the Cromwellian regime, and then welcomed the restoration of Charles II to the English throne.[21] This acceptance of every legitimate ruler's sovereign authority remained the prevailing opinion in the eighteenth century, even after journals and newspapers began to appear in greater numbers, beginning in the 1720s. To see such acceptance in proper perspective, it is necessary to refer back to the German Reformation. Luther had rejected the monastic ideal of medieval Catholicism and demanded that every Christian believer prove himself in this world, but he considered man both intellectually incapable of achieving knowledge and morally incapable of achieving virtue. In his view, man can be reborn by faith alone, each in the calling in which God has placed him. This doctrine proved highly suitable for aristocratic rule and mercantilist practices. Everyone is called to do his best in his appointed role, having due regard for the traditional modes of work and profit. Competition and striving after wealth are dangers to the soul, but with faith as his guide the Christian believer will have a modest living. At the same time, the ruler and his officials have responsibility for the country's welfare, which is of no concern to the ordinary citizen. The horizon of artisans and merchants is confined to their calling and their religion. It is the task of rulers and aristocrats at court to know diplomacy, the practices of court life, and the affairs of the world. In this religious construction of the social world, intellectual interests belong to high society, not to the narrow life of commoners.

We have at least an indirect clue to this widespread attitude in the so-called moral weeklies, a type of eighteenth-century publication modeled after such English journals as the *Tatler* and the *Spectator*.[22] The content of these weeklies provides the best available evidence of the prepolitical or prepublic reactions of strata educated and leisurely enough to read but excluded from all political participation and hence from the formation of public opinion. These reactions reflect the efforts of educated commoners to develop self-assurance in facing up to a court society that was socially and politically exclusive and culturally more French than German. Fortunately, something can be said about the readers of these moral weeklies, even in the absence of statistical information. It is a projective type of evidence: the journals themselves characterized the social world to which their homilies were addressed. There is little reference to occupations or estates but considerable attention to a middle level of education and interest. The weeklies were written so as to be understandable to everyone of ordinary intelligence—"neither too bad or pedestrian [*niedrig*] for the scholar, nor too lofty and incomprehensible for the unlearned," as the Hamburg *Patriot* put it. They addressed themselves to those "for whom study is not even an ancillary activity." They wanted to be useful and attractive to all estates, but in practice they counted officials, clergymen, professionals, merchants, and, above all, women among their readers. The households depicted in them have servants; the sons travel and go to universities, while the daughters learn French. There is leisure for reading and conversation. Men of proven virtue may have aristocrats for friends but not artisans, peasants, or servants. [23]

Moreover, courtiers (though not landed gentry) are rare in the imaginative scenarios of these writings. Only a few aristocrats figure in the two or three subscription lists which have survived. The great majority of subscribers are state employees, so that one may speak of a *Beamtenbürgertum* (literally, "officials as townspeople"), which in itself shows how remote this eighteenth-century social world is from the more familiar connotations of the word "bourgeoisie." [24]

The moral weeklies of the eighteenth century made an effort to instill a sense of purpose and self-assurance among these "middling" strata of society. Their message of virtue certainly included the demand that everyone promote the common welfare, especially in large towns like Hamburg, which had a civic tradition of their own. Still, this message was addressed primarily to questions of fashion, child-rearing, and proper conduct in everyday life. The cultivation of virtue by itself was considered a way of promoting the common good. The object of these discussions was to suggest in what ways the common man—*by staying within his proper sphere*—contributes to the welfare of the whole. To be concerned with politics is not his task; and ridicule is heaped on those who presume to judge affairs of state, which require a higher level of knowledge than is compatible with the circumstances of private persons. In accordance with these views, the moral weeklies had nothing to say about the rights of man but a good bit to say about his duties. When rights are mentioned at all, they refer to the ways in which a man can maintain his happiness and his peace of mind by being sociable, living up to his contractual obligations, and obeying the authorities; for if he fails in these respects, he will be punished and his peace will be disturbed.

There is no mention of the injustice and arbitrary tyrannies that were rampant in the eighteenth century—not even in moral weeklies published in towns that prided themselves on their freedom. Here is an example from the *Alte Deutsche*, published in Hamburg. Just one issue of this weekly deals with the freedom of the city, which is praised for a condition that is unusual in Germany. But the essay emphasizes the duties which freedom requires. Disorderly conduct is condemned, as is any willful opposition to authority. One contributes to freedom in this way:

> I do not meddle in public affairs. I do not have the proper calling for that. But still I possess love and honesty for the general welfare. As I see it, freedom is therefore nothing else than the opportunity and the effort to promote the general good according to one's own fitness [*nach seinem Masse*]. As I see it, he is not worthy of freedom who grumbles when he is called upon to contribute his due share to the support of the general good. . . . To be bound by laws is not slavery; to resist the laws is not freedom but wickedness.[25]

Just as the common man has his duties, so, indeed, do those in authority. The moral weeklies never question or challenge kings or princes. They express only the wish that rulers should be fatherly, surrounded by honest advisers, and act for the welfare of their subjects. With varying intensity, the moral weeklies appealed to the unpolitical self-assurance of educated commoners. They were not animated by servility or anxious submission. They conveyed the sense that commoners have their proper and important position in the social order. This self-definition in relation to the higher ranks of society and to those below provides the most general background for the "German reaction" to the French Revolution.

The moral weeklies gave *no* direct attention to the affairs of the courts. Other papers might report the rampant gossip about the luxuries, intrigues, and scandals that were occurring in over two hundred sovereign households; but for the moral weeklies, the world of the court is a dangerous and disquieting sphere which the honest man is well advised to avoid. Careers at court are a matter of luck. To achieve power and wealth in that setting is hazardous to one's conscience and one's life. Courtly splendor is a false veneer, service at court empty of purpose, and the rational and capable man can do far more useful things elsewhere. But if the weeklies denounced fawning and deceiving courtiers and, with them, the whole courtly way of life, the political implications of that description were never mentioned. This critique posed no challenge to the institution of the court or to the legitimacy of sovereign authority; it voiced, rather, a moral and cultural judgment. The discussions of court society provided a foil against which the ethical outlook of the educated commoner, with its emphasis on virtue, general welfare, diligence, family happiness, sociability, and contentment, could be displayed to good advantage.

By such contrasts the moral weeklies defined the meaning of politics! Seventeenth-century writings on the courtly arts, like those of Baltasar Gracián, had advised the man of fashion and good breeding how to conduct himself in order to achieve his personal ends. In practice this amounted to advice on the personal manipulation of others and an iron-willed control over one's own emotions— all under the outward guise of personal grace and an elaborate etiquette. It was this type of conduct that the writers in the moral weeklies called "political":

> I understand here by the term political man someone who loses sight of faithfulness and honesty in order to realize his unjust intentions; who perjures himself, lies, and knows how to dissemble, not in order to achieve something good in secret, but in order to do an evil deed that much more securely. Such politics is attributed to courtiers who are told that they must not have a conscience, that they must not hesitate to violate the holiest alliance or covenant [Bündnis], and that they must be adroit enough always to invent a pretext. But one meets with such politics also very frequently in ordinary life and in all kinds of commerce. It is undeniable that this politics is an invention of hell and the most shameful vice, in that it destroys entirely the good faith [Treu und Glauben] which is the soul of society. Nevertheless, this vice has found its admirers, defenders, and even preachers, who have made out of it an art and science and laid down its rules and laws. And in this way the art of being unfaithful appears under the name of politics.[26]

Writers in the moral weeklies did not want to be concerned with such politics. Rather, they wished for the man at court to be honest so that the virtues of the educated commoner could flourish there. One should add that these writings do *not* attribute such virtues to some ancient and pure German tradition, nor do they attribute the vices of court life to the evil influence of French culture. In the spirit of the Enlightenment, virtue is accessible to every reasonable man, and vice is the result of unreason and a lack of faith.[27] Hindsight may suggest that this definition of politics had very dangerous implications for the future of German society; but as it appears in the moral weeklies of the time, the definition was a means of rejecting court society and raising the self-assurance of the *Bürgertum*.

This approach did not imply a demand for equality. Men are equal only before God. Religion and reason call every man to the practice of virtue, and each must practice virtue in the station to which God has called him. Indeed, inequality comes from God, and we must try (though we sometimes fail) to understand that differences of temperament, occupation, and status are for the best. To change the social structure would be a highly reprehensible undertaking. A man who is not content with his station in life would be discontented with every other as well.

This conservative acceptance of social hierarchy coexisted with a critical approach to the aristocracy. The moral weeklies denounced the frivolity and wantonness of courtiers. They were equally vehement in denouncing aristocratic haughtiness, based on heraldry and long lineage. Pride of blood and status cannot bear comparison with such virtues of commoners as effort, work, unselfishness, good faith, and reason. Much moral indignation is expressed toward the disdain with which aristocrats often treat worthy commoners. What had these gentry to be proud of, with their hard drinking, loose living, coarse manners, their debts and lack of culture, and their obsession with horses, dogs, and the hunt? At the same time, these negative images were balanced by sympathetic portraits of honest and cultured members of the landed gentry with whom the pseudonymous authors of the weeklies liked to associate. All these critical writings passed the scrutiny of censors easily because they did not challenge the established order, and many rulers of the time would have welcomed a reform of aristocratic culture. The ideal of the moral weeklies may be summed up by saying that virtue based on religion and reason is the desired attribute of both the educated commoner and the honest aristocrat. Differences of status become inconsequential where thought and action are inspired by the same convictions.

In the course of the eighteenth century, there was an increase in the number of German commoners who could entertain social aspirations. Free professionals, artisans, merchants, manufacturers, and the "civil-service intelligentsia" acquired an education and were exposed to a considerable intellectual mobilization. Yet these educated commoners were confronted with the French culture of an aristocratic society from which they were excluded and which made up by cultural distance and personal arrogance what it lacked in political stature. Commoners were not only denied political participation and the right to be concerned with public affairs; they themselves doubted their own capacity to form relevant opinions. They might enjoy a level of comfort or even a degree of affluence, but they were under the tutelage of an absolutist state and its officials. In thousands of hometowns, commoners were primarily concerned to keep this official world from intruding into their community affairs, though one can speculate that here and there some of them developed aspirations reaching beyond their provincial confines. Probably such aspirations increased in proportion to political and economic intrusions from the outside. In the larger communities such encapsulation was in any event not feasible. Moreover, the *Beamtenbürgertum*—that middling stratum of teachers, officials, and clergymen—stood in still closer proximity to the world of affairs; and the closer such educated commoners were to the court society from which they were so pointedly excluded, the more likely they were to search for some sense of value in their own sphere. This was the audience in which the moral weeklies sought to instill a sense of self-assurance.

The homilies concerned with virtue and a reasoned ordering of civic life tell us something about how these commoners felt: they wanted to have a sense of their own worth in society. A projection of this concern is a major theme of classical German literature. Goethe portrayed the demeaning exclusion of the young Werther (1774) from an aristocratic gathering as a searing personal experience—and his novel was a great popular success. In his *Wilhelm Meister* (1795–96) he drew a telling contrast between the nobleman and the citizen (or commoner):

> Personal cultivation is only possible for the nobleman ... a certain dignified grace in common things, a sort of easy delicacy in serious and important ones, becomes him well, for he lets it be seen that he is everywhere in equilibrium. He is a public person, and the more cultivated his movements, the more sonorous his voice, the more restrained and measured his whole being, the more perfect he is.... He may be cold, but with a clear head; playing a part, but clean.... Everything else which he has in him and about him—capacity, talents, riches—all seem to be only extra gifts.
>
> Now imagine a citizen only thinking of making some claim to these advantages; he must absolutely fail and he must be all the more unfortunate the more Nature may have given him of impulse and capacity to that mode of being....
>
> If the nobleman by his personal carriage offers all that can be asked of him, the citizen by his personality offers nothing and can offer nothing. The former has a right to seem, the latter only to exist, and what he wishes to seem becomes ridiculous and in bad taste. The former is to ask and make, the

latter is to effect and procure—he is to cultivate individual
capabilities so as to become useful, and it is already pre-
supposed that there is no harmony in his manner of existence
nor can there be, because he is obliged to make himself useful
in one direction and must, therefore, neglect everything else.[28]

Goethe himself had little hope for major changes in the condition he
diagnosed. Eventually Meister finds the personal fulfillment he
seeks in the company of aristocrats and under their educative
influence. Most writers of the classical period shared Goethe's
pessimistic estimate of Germany's educated commoners.

These writers were close to the scene to which the moral weeklies
had addressed themselves. In one novel or play after another, the
world of the courts, with its masterful men, some good and many
evil, is contrasted with the world of commoners, with its ideals of
feeling and piety, of diligence and rectitude. The courts may be a
place of vice, but they are also the locus of power; the virtue of the
commoner is without the power to achieve its ends. Until the middle
of the century, novels and plays tended to meet this conflict by
idealizing equanimity and contentedness. Man should not quarrel
with God but should accept the fate which befalls him as part of a
divine dispensation. This approach precludes all subjective claims
on life, any idea that by his personal intervention a man can change
his fate. Indeed, the dramatic heroes of this literature are almost
always aristocrats—even when their actions idealize the typical
virtues of the educated commoner. The world of commoners was
inevitably narrow, and the greatness of classical German literature
consists in part in the effort to break out of this identification of
passivity as the virtue of the *Bürger*. In *Emilia Galotti* (1772), virtue
is preserved when a father kills his own daughter rather than allow
her to be violated by the evil designs of the prince; passivity is
overcome, but at the price of turning action against the virtuous
commoner himself. Many subsequent plays show the great difficulties besetting the virtuous man of action, and Schiller's *Wilhelm
Tell* (1804) is one of the few plays in which a commoner's right to
individual assertion is finally vindicated. Among educated commoners in Germany, reconciliation with one's fate had become a
way of life, and the inward struggle over the problem of self-
assertion provided the classic writers with one of their major
themes.[29]

With this outlook on life, how did German commoners respond to
the signal event of the French Revolution? How did they react—

these men who felt humble and insecure toward their betters in a country where princely rule was often paltry—when they witnessed events that presaged the ultimate abolition of despotic abuses and the coming of a new equality in human affairs? There can be no single or simple answer to these questions, but I believe that Schiller's work may be taken as representative in the symbolic sense of that word. Certainly Schiller confronted these questions directly. In a letter of 1793, addressed to Duke Friedrich Christian von Augustenberg, he justified his own preoccupation with aesthetic problems—but only after giving full weight to the political preoccupations of the day. He allowed that the events of the last decade seemed to require the unremitting attention of philosophers, poets, and every thoughtful citizen. He cited Solon's condemnation of citizens who did not take a stand in the face of rebellion. If ever there had been a case in which this principle applied, it was the present time,

> in which the great destiny of mankind is called into question,
> and in which it appears that one cannot remain neutral without
> becoming guilty of the most unpardonable indifference toward
> the most holy concerns of man. A spirited, courageous nation,
> which has been considered exemplary for a long time, has
> begun to take violent leave of its established social order and
> return to the state of nature in which reason is the sole and
> absolute lawgiver. An affair which ordinarily only opportunism
> and the right of the stronger would have decided has been
> brought before the judgment seat of *pure reason* and at least
> makes some pretense of being decided in accordance with
> *principles*. Every thinking person may consider himself ... an
> associate judge in this court of reason, although as man and
> world citizen he is also a party to the case and involved in its
> success.[30]

Yet, after stating the promise of the revolution in strong terms, Schiller denied even more strongly that this promise would be fulfilled. One would indeed be justified in bidding the muses goodbye *if* lawmaking had become rational, *if* man was being treated as an end rather than a means, *if* the law had been made supreme and true freedom the foundation of the state. But none of these assumptions applied. The attempt of the French people "to institute the holy rights of man and achieve political freedom has revealed only that the people are incapable and unworthy." Elsewhere he says that "a moment so prodigal of opportunity finds a generation unprepared to receive it." The "moral opportunity is lacking" because the lower classes desire only animal satisfactions, while the cultivated classes offer a repugnant spectacle of lethargy and moral depravity.[31]

One must reform the character of the people without recourse to the state, since under present conditions one cannot rely on the people to reform the state.[32] In reaching this conclusion Schiller declared that he was addressing the political issues of his day, not evading them. One need not accept this evaluation of his own role, but Schiller's assessment of the German public was probably realistic. The people to whom the moral weeklies appealed were not prepared to undertake the political reconstruction of their country. They stood across a gulf from their aristocratic rulers, both psychologically and culturally. In Schiller's view, the poet's task was to bridge that gulf:

> Ours is no longer the Homeric world, in which all members
> of society were at approximately the same stage in their feelings
> and opinions and hence could recognize themselves readily in
> the same description and meet one another in the same
> emotions. Today, a large gulf is visible between the elite and
> the mass of the nation, due in part to the fact that moral
> ennoblement and the enlightenment of ideas form a coherent
> whole, but nothing is gained by mere fragments [of this pro-
> cess]. In addition ... the members of the nation have become
> extremely unlike one another in their feelings and expres-
> sions.... In our times, a poet of the people has to make a
> choice between the easiest and the most difficult [course].
> Either he accommodates himself exclusively to the com-
> prehension of the large crowd and foregoes the applause
> of the educated class. Or he pursues both purposes in combina-
> tion and by the greatness of his art vanquishes the enormous
> distance existing between the two.[33]

Thus, Schiller explicitly defines his artistic task as educational. And his dramatic work certainly reveals that he used his superb poetic gifts to present his audience with an understanding of the realities and the problematics of personal power.[34]

Clearly, this was not the only German response to the French Revolution. But before considering the more directly political responses to that event, a question of interpretation must be posed. Along with many other writers of the day, Schiller emphasized the central significance of character formation in pointed contrast to

that "all-pursuing demon of criticizing the state," as he put it in the
prepublication announcement of his journal, *Die Horen* (1794).[35]
He believed that under the banner of truth and beauty a higher
interest in purely human concerns beyond the narrow tensions of the
day could help to unite a politically divided world. For Schiller and
his friends this was an affirmation, however much we may consider
it a misguided illusion. It was an appeal to high-minded Germans of
the day whose homeland was in disarray while the banner of
humanity was being raised in Paris. Men of good will and liberal
sentiment thought there was little prospect of revolution in a
fragmented country, and soon enough they were doubtful about the
wisdom of revolutions. With politics defined as court intrigue, they
had little taste for politics and no access to it in any case. Yet as
spirited men they could hardly be expected to forego high aspirations for themselves and their country. Under these circumstances,
the appeal to *Bildung* appeared as a worthwhile alternative in its
own right and, in the long run, of political significance as well. In
their eyes this was not an evasion but a constructive step ahead, a
way of defining a specifically German contribution to an enlightened age, made still more compelling by the superb talent of the
writers involved. With such a contribution as a seemingly viable
alternative, many spirited men would not opt for a political struggle
that appeared hopeless.[36]

Schiller did not see the flaw in this approach, despite his concern
with the political and educational implications of art. Education is a
long-run process, and its success is always proximate if not equivocal. To aim at the unification of classes in a hierarchic society, to
achieve a greater unity of moral and intellectual culture: these are
worthy goals in a fragmented country. But this high-minded message was simply asking too much of ordinary people. Schiller
himself had an inkling of this when he wrote:

> Kaum hat das kalte Fieber der Gallomanie uns verlassen,
> Bricht in der Gräkomanie gar noch ein hitziges aus.
>
> Hardly has the cold fever of Gallomania departed
> Than a hotter fever, Grecomania, erupts.[37]

Yet Schiller contributed to the trend he lampooned by idealizing
classical Greece as a frame of reference for the dramatic artist and
the political and aesthetic analyst. Similarly, Wilhelm von Humboldt declared that no people could rival the ancient Greeks in

combining "so much simplicity and nature with so much culture,"
and Humboldt was to play a major role in reforming Prussian
university education. This whole approach was given public sanction
when F. A. Wolf was called to the University of Halle in 1783. A
classical philologist, Wolf justified ancient Greece as the principal
subject of general education by pointing out that no other people
could serve so well as a model. Significantly, this idealization of
Greece singled out the most glaring defect of all other cultures: their
tendency to subordinate high culture to the most urgent needs of
daily existence. Wolf considered it proper to use German in writing on
"political, economic, medical, military, mathematical and other
useful subjects. But in everything which goes beyond these voracious
demands of civilization" only classical Greek can reveal the "many-
sidedness and depth of culture."[38] We have encountered this
antipolitical and antiutilitarian attitude before as a boost to the
self-assurance of educated commoners. In the hands of common
men (in the pejorative sense of the word), *Bildung* could become a
means of social and national self-assertion. It is an ironic reflection
that perhaps the fault lay in the very talents of writers like Schiller:
psychologically and artistically their aspirations were simply too
high for ordinary people to cope with.

German Reactions to the French Revolution

In concluding this essay, I want to consider the more political
reactions to the French Revolution. The question is how Germany's
educated commoners responded when they had come to terms with
this event, not in the elevated context of *Bildung*, but in the more
mundane one of public affairs. One of Goethe's Venetian epigrams
is an apt introduction to this topic, highlighting as it does the
Gallomania at the courts and the lack of self-assurance and political
experience on the part of educated commoners:

> Lange haben die Grossen der Franzen Sprache gesprochen,
>   Halb nur geachtet den Mann, dem sie vom Munde nicht floss.

> Nun lallt alles Volk entzückt die Sprache der Franken.
>   Zürnet, Mächtige, nicht! Was ihr verlangtet, geschieht!

> Long have the Great spoken the Frenchies' language,
>   Little regarding those who did not master the tongue.

> Now, delightedly, all people babble the language of France.
>   Mighty ones, do not rage! What you demanded, occurs![39]

The ruling groups of German society had taken the French monarchy as their model and had exploited the people (though Goethe does not say so) to support the luxuries of a French type of court life. Now, suddenly, the French Revolution had replaced the old model with a new one. With subtle irony Goethe suggests that the "mighty ones" could not now object if people still followed the French model that had been set before them. Indeed, every impulse emanating from the successive phases of the Revolution now provided Germany with models that encouraged the articulation of grievances for which, previously, no outlet had existed.

The responses so elicited covered a wide range of opinions, from conservative rejections of the Revolution, root and branch, at one end, to democratic and socialist proposals for a republican constitution and an equalization of property, at the other. Both extremes were in an awkward position. A complete rejection of revolutionary ideas implied more than simple support of the status quo in Germany. It meant, more specifically, an endorsement of political particularism and social hierarchy at a time when the foremost European power was advancing the cause of nationalism and equality. Accordingly, a good many conservatives accepted the necessity of reforms, albeit holding fast to the principles of a hierarchic social order and monarchic rule.[40] At the other end, a complete acceptance of revolutionary ideas now brought German radicals into the same dependence on French precedent and support that had been the bane of the German courts under the *ancien régime*. Certainly, radical democrats developed their ideas in Germany quite independently of French revolutionary propaganda; but their credibility was impaired by their intellectual affinity with French affairs, and they lost ground, in any event, when the revolutionary impetus declined in France.[41]

Within this gamut of opinions I shall focus attention on the liberal center, because the Revolution and its Napoleonic aftermath made change inevitable and undercut both the unyielding defenders of the status quo and the radical democrats, whose time had not yet arrived. I said earlier that critical reactions to the abuses of absolutist rulers surfaced in Germany wherever censorship allowed it. The main difficulty was the absence of a "public" to which critics of government could appeal. As matters stood, writers had to address their wishes and complaints to the court and its entourage, since ordinary folk accepted the official view that they were not qualified to pass judgment. Hence, critical comments were couched in a language of humble submission; they hinted that the well-meaning fatherly ruler was ill-served by his subordinates, or they wrote of good or bad models of rulership in far-off places—with obvious applications closer to home.[42] This atmosphere was changed by the Revolution, which presented the world with a cornucopia of political experience. The Revolution made it clear that reform through collaboration with the enlightened aspects of absolutist regimes was *not* the only way of effecting change. But, beyond this, doubt and confusion prevailed.

To the "liberal center" of Germany, revolution presented an insoluble dilemma. Its ideological thrust was aimed at many of the targets which had aroused personal indignation and veiled protest for almost two generations. Among these targets, the most important were, perhaps, aristocratic privilege, the exclusiveness and immoralities of high society, and specific abuses, like hunting rights or the infamous impressing of men for military service in foreign countries. Even conservatives like the publicist Schlözer and the historian Johannes von Müller deplored these and other aspects of the status quo and hence welcomed a revolution which promised to do away with them. Schlözer was a highly respected and staunchly monarchist publicist who had strongly opposed the American Revolution. Yet this man wished the blood of the revolution on the despots who had made the French Revolution necessary. Cancerous lesions could not be healed with rose water, he maintained. For his part, Müller was a skeptical critic of the Enlightenment and greatly feared radical change. Yet he thought it was a good idea that kings and magistrates should learn that they also were human. In his view, censorship would do no good, because news of the Revolution would spread anyway and carry its own message.[43] One must remember that even conservatives had been well prepared for a favorable reaction to the French Revolution. The policies of the enlightened despots—especially Frederick II and Joseph II—had been inspired by ideas similar to those of the Revolution, and French society and culture had held an unrivaled prestige throughout the century. Where relatively conservative men greeted the Revolution so warmly, more liberal spirits responded much more eagerly.

Yet this ready acceptance of an emancipatory ideal was matched by a very widespread rejection of the Revolution itself. Valjavec has documented that many German enthusiasts for the Revolution turned against it when Louis XVI was executed in 1793 and the Terror followed. Then, with the fall of Robespierre in 1794, when

France herself experienced a retrenchment under the Directory, the German sympathizers of the Revolution could maintain their liberal attitudes without abandoning their traditional acceptance of authority. Moreover, as skepticism toward the Revolution turned into outright condemnation, German liberals turned for inspiration to the English experience with constitutional government and to the doctrines of the English classical economists.[44]

As a model for German aspirations, France had become tarnished. The artificiality of French culture at the German courts had become transparent. France had now become the citadel of liberty; but intellectual mobilization had antedated the revolution by decades, and there was no need to continue Germany's political tutelage. To be sure, nothing could be done about the country's political fragmentation. Still, considerable progress had been made in reforming the abuses of absolutism. A system of laws had been established. Enlightened rulers had become concerned to protect the little people against the privileged, to promote elementary and higher education, to clear swamps and develop the economy. Governments had become relatively free of corruption, and the better rulers checked on the execution of their commands by trained officials. Oppressive orthodoxy had been alleviated in the interest of toleration. There was no call for revolution in the face of such promise, even if it was as yet only half-fulfilled. On the contrary, there was a sense, indeed an exaggerated one, that the German territories were finding their way of realizing the goals of the Enlightenment.[45]

Thus, by the end of the eighteenth century, educated commoners had acquired a sense of their own identity not only in the cultural realm but in affairs of state. In 1791 the publicist Schlözer declared that, of all peoples, the Germans were the most prepared for the "quiet reconquest of the lost rights of man":

> To be sure, the revolution will be slow, but it is occurring. Enlightenment is rising from below, as in France; but it is also meeting with enlightenment up above: nowhere are there more cultivated sovereigns than in Germany.... From all appearances it will be more the work of professional writers [Schriftstellerei] than of cabinets; this [revolution] is occurring slowly, without mischief, without anarchy. Princes will remain princes, and all Germans will become free men.[46]

That same year, the Prussian finance minister, Struensee, had seemed to despair of reforming the thousand and one anachronisms of absolutist rule, but by 1799 he declared that "the beneficial revolution which ... Frenchmen have conducted violently from below, we Prussians will conduct gradually from above."[47] Later, Goethe articulated the same idea in a manner that aptly characterizes this outlook on reform under the auspices of enlightened absolutism:

> It is true, I could not be a friend of the French Revolution, for its horrors touched me too directly and revolted me daily and hourly, whereas its beneficial consequences could not yet be envisaged at that time. Nor could I be indifferent when in Germany one sought to introduce in an *artificial manner* similar scenes, which in France were the consequence of a great necessity.
>
> But neither was I a friend of an arbitrary autocracy. I was also completely convinced that a great revolution is never the fault of the people, but rather of the government. Revolutions are quite impossible whenever governments are perpetually just and alert so that through timely improvements they meet [the revolution] half way and do not resist until the necessary [reforms] are forced upon them from below.[48]

In Goethe's view, necessary change must, to be successful, be an outgrowth of a nation's own circumstances, not the cheap imitation of another country. He resented being labeled a defender of the status quo. He was no friend of what was antiquated, bad, and unjust under existing conditions. He only wanted the good to be recognized where it existed. For the rest, he was convinced that even good institutions require constant attention and reform. In fact, this had been the constant concern of the Grand Duke Carl August, whom he had served for half a century.[49]

Goethe's reflections of 1824–25 are an appropriate conclusion to a discussion of intellectual mobilization in a provincial setting in which "men of spirit" responded to the metropolitan challenges of the day. To be sure, Goethe was a unique figure. A man of extraordinary gifts and Germany's most illustrious poet, he had been at the same time the highest-paid official in the service of Grand Duke Carl August of Saxony-Weimar-Eisenach. Not surprisingly, his outlook tended to the conservative side of the political spectrum. Nevertheless, his combination of official duties and intellectual concerns, his respect for the aristocracy, combined with the humanistic ideals of the educated commoner, were typical of the rising intelligentsia of the period. Goethe's work and personality idealized a citizenship of the world (*Weltbürgertum*), which was a favorite slogan of the period. Perhaps unwittingly, Goethe helped to make "cultural capital" out of the antipolitical and antiutilitarian orientation which I have described.

Clifford Geertz

7

Centers, Kings, and Charisma:
Reflections on the Symbolics
of Power

Introduction

Like so many of the key ideas in Weber's sociology—verstehen, legitimacy, inner-worldly asceticism, rationalization—the concept of charisma suffers from an uncertainty of referent: does it denote a cultural phenomenon or a psychological one? At once "a certain quality" which marks an individual as standing in a privileged relationship to the sources of being and a hypnotic power "certain personalities" have to engage passions and dominate minds, it is not clear whether charisma is the status, the excitement, or some ambiguous fusion of the two. The attempt to write a sociology of culture and a social psychology in a single set of sentences is what gives Weber's work its orchestral complexity and harmonic depth. But it is also what gives it, especially to ears less attuned to polyphony, its chronic elusiveness.

In Weber, a classic instance of his own category, the complexity was managed and the elusiveness offset by his extraordinary ability to hold together warring ideas. In more recent and less heroic times, however, the tendency has been to ease the weight of his thought by collapsing it into one of its dimensions, most commonly the psychological, and nowhere has this been more true than in connection with charisma.[1] Everyone from John Lindsay to Mick Jagger has been called charismatic, mainly on the grounds that he has contrived to interest a certain number of people in the glitter of his personality; and the main interpretation of the rather more genuine upsurge of charismatic leadership in the New States has

150

been that it is a product of psychopathology encouraged by social disorder.[2] In the general psychologism of the age, so well remarked by Phillip Rieff, the study of personal authority narrows to an investigation of self-presentment and collective neurosis; the numinous aspect fades from view.[3]

A few scholars, among them prominently Edward Shils, have, however, sought to avoid this reduction of difficult richness to neo-Freudian cliché by facing up to the fact that there are multiple themes in Weber's concept of charisma, that almost all of them are more stated than developed, and that the preservation of the force of the concept depends upon developing them and uncovering thereby the exact dynamics of their interplay. Between the blur produced by trying to say too much at once and the banality produced by dismissing mysteries there remains the possibility of articulating just what it is that causes some men to see transcendency in others, and what it is they see.

In Shils's case, the lost dimensions of charisma have been restored by stressing the connection between the symbolic value individuals possess and their relation to the active centers of the social order.[4] Such centers, which have "nothing to do with geometry and little with geography," are essentially concentrated loci of serious acts; they consist in the point or points in a society where its leading ideas come together with its leading institutions to create an arena in which the events that most vitally affect its members' lives take place. It is involvement, even oppositional involvement, with such arenas and with the momentous events that occur in them that confers charisma. It is a sign, not of popular appeal or inventive craziness, but of being near the heart of things.

There are a number of implications of such a glowing-center view of the matter. Charismatic figures can arise in any realm of life that is sufficiently focused to seem vital—in science or art as readily as in religion or politics. Charisma does not appear only in extravagant forms and fleeting moments but is an abiding, if combustible, aspect of social life that occasionally bursts into open flame. There is no more a single charismatic emotion than there is a single moral, aesthetic, or scientific one; though passions, often enough distorted ones, are undeniably involved, they can be radically different from case to case. But my concern here is not to pursue these issues, as important as they are to a general theory of social authority. It is to probe into another matter Shils's approach causes to appear in a novel light: the inherent sacredness of sovereign power.

The mere fact that rulers and gods share certain properties has, of course, been recognized for some time. "The will of a king is very numinous," a seventeenth-century political divine wrote; "it has a kind of vast universality in it"—and he was not the first to say so. Nor has it gone unstudied: Ernst Kantorowicz' extraordinary *The King's Two Bodies*—that magisterial discussion of, as he put it, "medieval political theology"—traced the vicissitudes of royal charisma in the West over two hundred years and a half-dozen countries, and more recently there has been a small explosion of books sensitive to what now tends to be called, a bit vaguely, the symbolic aspects of power.[5] But the contact between this essentially historical and ethnographic work and the analytical concerns of modern sociology has been weak at best, a situation the art historian Panofsky once analogized, in a different context, to that of two neighbors who share the right to shoot over the same district, but one of them owns the gun and the other all the ammunition.

Though still very much in process, and cast sometimes on too apodictic a level, Shils's reformulations promise to be of enormous value in overcoming this unuseful estrangement because they encourage us to look for the vast universality of the will of kings (or of presidents, generals, führers, and party secretaries) in the same place as we look for that of gods: in the rites and images through which it is exerted. More exactly, if charisma is a sign of involvement with the animating centers of society, and if such centers are cultural phenomena and thus historically constructed, investigations into the symbolics of power and into its nature are very similar endeavors. The easy distinction between the trappings of rule and its substance becomes less sharp, even less real; what counts is the manner in which, a bit like mass and energy, they are transformed into each other.

At the political center of any complexly organized society (to narrow our focus now to that) there is both a governing elite and a set of symbolic forms expressing the fact that it is in truth governing. No matter how democratically the members of the elite are chosen (usually not very) or how deeply divided among themselves they may be (usually much more than outsiders imagine), they justify their existence and order their actions in terms of a collection of stories, ceremonies, insignia, formalities, and appurtenances that they have either inherited or, in more revolutionary situations, invented. It is these—crowns and coronations, limousines and conferences—that mark the center as center and give what goes on there its aura of being not merely important but in some odd fashion connected with the way the world is built. The gravity of high politics and the solemnity of high worship spring from liker impulses than might first appear.

This is, of course, more readily apparent (though, as I shall eventually argue, not any more true) in traditional monarchies than in political regimes where the ingenerate tendency of men to anthropomorphize power is better disguised. The intense focus on the figure of the king and the frank construction of a cult, at times a whole religion, around him make the symbolic character of domination too palpable for even Hobbesians and Utilitarians to ignore. The very thing that the elaborate mystique of court ceremonial is supposed to conceal—that majesty is made, not born—is demonstrated by it. "A woman is not a duchess a hundred yards from a carriage," and chiefs are changed to rajahs by the aesthetic of their rule.

This comes out as clearly as anywhere else in the ceremonial forms by which kings take symbolic possession of their realm. In particular, royal progresses (of which, where it exists, coronation is but the first) locate the society's center and affirm its connection with transcendent things by stamping a territory with ritual signs of dominance. When kings journey around the countryside, making appearances, attending fetes, conferring honors, exchanging gifts, or defying rivals, they mark it, like some wolf or tiger spreading his scent through his territory, as almost physically part of them. This can be done, as we shall see, within frameworks of expression and belief as various as sixteenth-century English Protestantism, fourteenth-century Javanese Hinduism, and nineteenth-century Moroccan Islam; but however it is done, it is done, and the royal occupation gets portrayed as being a good deal more than merely hedged with divinity.

Elizabeth's England: Virtue and Allegory

On 14 January 1559, the day before her coronation, Elizabeth Tudor —"a daughter, whose birth disappointed her father's hopes for succession, and thus, indirectly, caused her mother's early demise; an illegitimized Princess whose claim to the throne was, nevertheless, almost as valid as those of her half-brother and half-sister; a focus of disaffection during Mary's reign; and a survivor of constant agitation by Imperial and Spanish emissaries to have her eliminated"—rode in a great progress (there were a thousand horses, and she sat, awash in jewels and gold cloth, in an open litter) through the historical districts of the City of London. As she moved, a vast didactic pageant unfolded, stage by stage, before her, settling her into the moral landscape of the resilient capital that five years earlier had done as much, or tried to, for Philip of Spain.[6]

Starting at the Tower (where she aptly compared her seeing the day to God's delivery of Daniel from the lions), she proceeded to Fenchurch Street, where a small child offered her, for the town's sake, two gifts—blessing tongues to praise her and true hearts to serve her. At Gracechurch Street she encountered a *tableau vivant* called "The Uniting of the Houses of Lancaster and York." It took the form of an arch spanning the street, covered with red and white roses and divided into three levels. On the lowest, two children, representing Henry VII, enclosed in a rose of red roses, and his wife Elizabeth, enclosed in one of white, sat holding hands. On the middle level there were two more children, representing Henry VIII and Ann Boleyn, the bank of red roses rising from the Lancaster side and the bank of white ones from the York converging upon them. And at the top, amid mingled red and white, perched a single child, representing the honored (and legitimate) Elizabeth herself. At Cornhill, there was another arch with a child on it representing the new queen, but this one was seated on a throne held up by four townsmen dressed to represent the four virtues—Pure Religion, Love of Subjects, Wisdom, and Justice. They, in turn, trod their contrary vices—Superstition and Ignorance, Rebellion and Insolence, Folly and Vainglory, Adulation and Bribery (also impersonated by costumed citizens)—roughly under foot. And lest the iconography be too oblique, the child addressed an admonitory verse to the sovereign she mirrored, spelling out its message:

> While that religion true, shall ignorance suppresse
> And with her weightie foote, break superstitions heade
> While love of subjectes, shall rebellion distresse
> And with zeale to the prince, insolencie down treade
>
> While justice, can flattering tonges and briberie deface
> While follie and vaine glory to wisedome yelde their handes
> So long shall government, not swarve from her right race
> But wrong decayeth still, and rightwisenes up standes.[7]

Thus instructed, the queen moved on to Sopers-Lane, where there were no less than eight children, arranged in three levels. These, as tablets hung above their heads announced, represented the eight

beatitudes of Saint Matthew, which a poem recited there described
as grained into the character of the queen by the hurts and perils
she had surmounted en route to the throne ("Thou has been viii
times blest, O quene of worthy fame / by meekness of thy spirite,
when care did thee besette").[8] From there she passed on to
Cheapside, confronting at the Standard painted likenesses of all the
kings and queens arranged in chronological order down to herself;
receiving at the Upper End two thousand marks in gold from the
City dignitaries ("Perswade you selues," she replied in thanks,
"that for the safetie and quietness of you all, I will not spare, if
nede be to spend my blood");[9] and arriving, in the Little Conduit, at
the most curious image of all—two artificial mountains, one
"cragged, barren and stony," representing "a decayed commonweal"; one "fair, fresh, green, and beautiful," representing "a
flourishing commonweal." On the barren mountain there was a
dead tree, an ill-dressed man slumped disconsolately beneath it; on
the green one a flowering tree, a well-appointed man standing
happily beside it. From the branches of each hung tablets listing the
moral causes of the two states of political health: in the one, want of
the fear of God, flattering of princes, unmercifulness in rulers,
unthankfulness in subjects; in the other, a wise prince, learned
rulers, obedient subjects, fear of God. Between the hills was a small
cave, out of which a man representing Father Time, complete with
scythe, emerged, accompanied by his daughter, Truth, to present to
the queen an English Bible ("O worthy Queene . . . words do flye,
but writing doth remain"), which Elizabeth took, kissed, and,
raising it first above her head, pressed dramatically to her breast.[10]

After a Latin oration by a schoolboy in Saint Paul's churchyard,
the queen proceeded to Fleet Street, where she found, of all people,
Deborah, "the judge and restorer of the house of Israel," enthroned
upon a tower shaded by a palm tree and surrounded by six persons,
two each representing the nobility, the clergy, and the commonalty.
The legend inscribed on a tablet before them read, "Deborah with
her estates consulting for the good gouerment of Israel." All this,
its designer writes, was to encourage the queen not to fear, "though
she were a woman; for women by the spirite and power of Almyghtye
God have ruled both honorably and pollitiquely, and that a great
tyme, as did Deborah."[11] At Saint Dunstan's Church, another child,
this one from Christ's Hospital, made another oration. Finally, at
Temple Bar, two giants—Gogmagog, the Albion, and Corineus, the
Briton—bore a tablet on which were written verses summarizing all
the pageants that had been displayed, and the progress ended.

This progress. In 1565 she goes to Coventry; in 1566 to Oxford; in 1572 she makes a long journey through the provinces, stopping for "masques and pageants" at a whole host of noble houses. She also enters Warwyck in that year, and the next she is in Sandwich, greeted with gilt dragons and lions, a cup of gold, and a Greek Testament. In 1574 it is Bristol's turn (there is a mock battle in which a small fort called "Feeble Policy" is captured by a large one called "Perfect Beauty"). In 1575 she visits the earl of Kenilworth's castle near Coventry, where there are Triton on a mermaid, Arion on a dolphin, the Lady of the Lake, and a nymph called Zabeta who turns lovers into trees; and later she enters Worcester. In 1578 the red and white roses and Deborah reappear in Norwich, accompanied by Chastity and Philosophy putting Cupid to rout. And they go on, "these endless peregrinations, which were so often the despair of her ministers"—in 1591 to Sussex and Hampshire, in 1592 to Sudeley, and, once again, Oxford.[12] In 1602, the year before she dies, there is the last one, at Harefield Place. Time emerges, as he had that first day in Cheapside, but with clipped wings and a stopped hourglass.[13] The royal progress, Strong remarks of Elizabeth—"the most legendary and successful of all [its] exponents"— was "the means by which the cult of the imperial virgin was systematically promoted."[14] The charisma that the center had (rather deliberately, as a matter of fact) fashioned for her out of the popular symbolisms of virtue, faith, and authority she carried, with a surer sense of statecraft than those pragmatical ministers who objected, to the countryside, making London as much the capital of Britain's political imagination as it was of its government.

That imagination was allegorical, Protestant, didactic, and pictorial; it lived on moral abstractions cast into emblems. Elizabeth was Chastity, Wisdom, Peace, Perfect Beauty, and Pure Religion as well as queen (at an estate in Hertford she was even Safety at Sea); and being queen she was these things. Her whole public life—or, more exactly, the part of her life the public saw—was transformed into a kind of philosophical masque in which everything stood for some vast idea and nothing took place unburdened with parable. Even her meeting with Anjou, possibly the man she came closest to marrying, was turned into a morality: he entered her presence seated on a rock, which was drawn toward her by Love and Destiny pulling golden chains.[15] Whether you want to call this romanticism or neo-Platonism matters little; what matters is that Elizabeth ruled a realm in which beliefs were visible, and she but the most conspicuous.

The center of the center, Elizabeth not only accepted its transformation of her into a moral idea, she actively cooperated in it. It was out of this—her willingness to stand proxy, not for God, but for the virtues he ordained, and especially for the Protestant version of them—that her charisma grew. It was allegory that lent her magic, and allegory repeated that sustained it. "How striking and meaningful it must have been to the spectators," Bergeron writes of that gift of an English Bible from the daughter of Time, "to see Truth in visible union with their new sovereign. . . . Morally Truth has chosen between good—the flourishing hill, the future, Elizabeth—and evil—the sterile mount, the past, false religion and a false queen. Such is the path to salvation."[16]

Hayam Wuruk's Java: Splendor and Hierarchy

There are other ways of connecting the character of a sovereign to that of his realm, however, than enveloping him in pictured homilies; as moral imaginations differ, so do political, and not every progress is that of a Pilgrim. In the Indic cultures of classical Indonesia the world was a less improvable place, and royal pageantry was hierarchical and mystical in spirit, not pious and didactic.[17] Gods, kings, lords, and commoners formed an unbroken chain of religious status stretching from Siva-Buddha—"Ruler over rulers of the world . . . Spirit of the spiritual . . . Unconceivable of the unconceivable"—down to the ordinary peasant, barely able to look toward the light, the higher levels standing to the lower as greater realities to lesser.[18] If Elizabeth's England was a swirl of idealized passions, Hayam Wuruk's Java was a continuum of spiritualized pride. "The peasants honor the chiefs," a fourteenth-century clerical text reads, "the chiefs honor the lords, the lords honor the ministers, the ministers honor the king, the kings honor the priests, the priests honor the gods, the gods honor the sacred powers, the sacred powers honor the Supreme Nothingness."[19]

Yet even in this unpopulist a setting, the royal progress was a major institution, as can be seen from Indic Java's greatest political text, the fourteenth-century narrative poem *Negarakertagama*, which is not only centered around a royal progress but is in fact part of it.[20] The basic principle of Indonesian statecraft—that the court should be a copy of the cosmos and the realm a copy of the court, with the king, liminally suspended between gods and men, the mediating image in both directions—is laid out in almost diagrammatic form. At the center and apex, the king; around him and at his feet, the palace; around the palace, the capital, "reliable, submissive";

around the capital, the realm, "helpless, bowed, stooping, humble"; around the realm, "getting ready to show obedience," the outside world—all disposed in compass-point order, a configuration of nested circles that depicts not just the structure of society but, a political mandala, that of the universe as a whole:

> The royal capital in Majapahit is Sun and Moon,
> peerless;
> The numerous manors with their encircling groves
> are halos around the sun and moon;
> The numerous other towns of the realm ... are stars
> and planets;
> And the numerous other islands of the archipelago
> are ring-kingdoms, dependent states
> drawn toward the royal Presence.[21]

It is this structure, the deep geometry of the cosmos, which the poem celebrates and into which, half as rite and half as policy, it fits the royal progress.

It opens with a glorification of the king. He is at once Siva in material form—"The Daymaker's Equal," upon whose birth volcanoes erupted and the earth shook—and a triumphant overlord who has vanquished all the darkness there is in the world ("Exterminated are the enemies ... Rewarded, the good ... Reformed, the bad").[22] Next, his palace is described: North, the reception areas; East, the religious shrines; South, the family chambers; West, the servants quarters; in the center, "the Interior of the Interior," his personal pavilion. Then, with the palace as center, the complex around it: East, the Sivaite clergy; South, the Buddhist clergy; West, the royal kinsmen; North, the public square. Then, with the complex as center, the capital in general: North, the chief ministers; East, the junior king; South, the Sivaite and Buddhist bishops; West, though not in fact mentioned, probably the ranking commoners.[23] Then, with the capital as center, the regions of the realm, ninety-eight of them, stretching from Malaya and Borneo on the North and East to Timor and New Guinea on the South and West; and, finally, the outermost ring, Siam, Cambodia, Campa, Annam—"Other countries protected by the Illustrious Prince."[24] Virtually the whole of the known world (later parts of China and India are mentioned as well) is represented as turned toward Java, all of Java as turned toward Majapahit, and all of Majapahit as turned toward Hayam Wuruk—"Sun and Moon, shining over the earth-circle."[25]

In cold fact, hardly more than the eastern part of Java was so oriented, and most of that in an attitude not properly described as either helpless or humble.[26] It was to this region, where the kingdom, however invertebrate, at least was more than a poetic conceit, that the royal progresses were directed: west to Pajang, near present-day Surakarta, in 1353; north to Lasem on the Java Sea in 1354; south to Lodaya and the Indian Ocean in 1357; east to Lumajang, nearly to Bali, in 1359.[27]

Only the last of these, which was probably the greatest, is described in detail, however—more than four hundred lines being devoted to it. The king left the capital at the beginning of the dry season, visiting no less than 210 localities scattered over about 10,000–15,000 square miles in about two and a half months, returning just before the west monsoon brought the rains. There were about 400 ox-drawn, solid-wheel carts; there were, more for effect than anything else, elephants, horses, donkeys, and even camels (imported from India); there were swarms of people on foot, some carrying burdens, some displaying regalia, some no doubt dancing and singing—the whole lurching along like some archaic traffic jam a mile or two an hour over the narrow and rutted roads lined with crowds of astonished peasants. The core section of the procession, which seems to have come in the middle, was led by the cart of the chief minister, the famous Gajah Mada. Behind him came the four ranking princesses of the realm—the sister, mother's sister's daughter, mother's sister, and mother of the king—together with their consorts. And behind them, seated on a palanquin and surrounded by dozens of wives, bodyguards, and servants, came the king, "ornamented with gold and jewels, shining." Since each of the princesses represented one of the compass points (marked on her cart by traditional symbols and on her person by her title, which associated her with the quarter of the country in the appropriate direction from the capital), and the king represented the center in which they all were summed, the very order of the march conveyed the structure of the cosmos—mirrored in the organization of the court—to the countryside.[28] All that was left to complete this bringing of Heaven's symmetry to earth's confusion was for the countryside, struck with the example, to shape itself, in turn, to the same design.

The stops this lumbering caravan made—at forest hermitages, sacred ponds, mountain sanctuaries, priestly settlements, ancestral shrines, state temples, along the strand (where the king, "waving to the sea," composed some verses to placate the demons in it)—but reinforce the image of a metaphysical road show.[29] Everywhere Hayam Wuruk went, he was showered with luxuries—textiles, spices, animals, flowers, drums, fire-drills, virgins—most of which, the last excepted, he redistributed again, if only because he could not carry them all. There were ceremonies everywhere, crowded with offerings: in Buddhist domains Buddhist, in Sivaite ones Sivaite, in many places both. Anchorites, scholars, priests, abbots, shamans, sages, entered into his Presence, seeking contact with sacred energies; and in virtually every town, sometimes at mere encampments, he held public audiences, also largely ceremonial, for local authorities, merchants, and leading commoners. When there were places he could not reach—Bali, Madura, Blambangan—their chieftains journeyed to meet him, bearing gifts, "trying to outvie each other" in the forms of deference. The whole was a vast ritual seeking to order the social world by confronting it with magnificence reaching down from above and a king so exactly imitative of the gods that he appeared as one to those beneath him.

In short, instead of Christian moralism, Indic aestheticism. In sixteenth-century England, the political center of society was the point at which the tension between the passions that power excited and the ideals it was supposed to serve was screwed to its highest pitch; and the symbolism of the progress was, consequently, admonitory and covenantal: the subjects warned, and the queen promised. In fourteenth-century Java, the center was the point at which such tension disappeared in a blaze of cosmic symmetry; and the symbolism was, consequently, exemplary and mimetic: the king displayed, and the subjects copied. Like the Elizabethan, the Majapahit progress set forth the regnant themes of political thought —the court mirrors the world the world should imitate; society flourishes to the degree that it assimilates this fact; and it is the office of the king, wielder of the mirror, to assure that it does. It is analogy, not allegory, that lends the magic here:

> The whole of Java is to be as the capital of the King's
> realm;
> The thousands of peasant huts are to be as the courtiers'
> manors surrounding the palace;
> The other islands are to be as the cultivated lands,
> happy, quiet;
> The forests and mountains are to be as the parks, all
> set foot on by Him, at peace
> in His mind.[30]

Hasan's Morocco: Movement and Energy

It is not necessary, of course, that power be dressed up in virtue or set round with cosmology to be perceived as more than force in the service of interest: its numinousness can be symbolized directly. In traditional Morocco, "the Morocco that was," as Walter Harris called it, personal power, the ability to make things happen the way one wants them to happen—to prevail—was itself the surest sign of grace.[31] In a world of wills dominating wills, and that of Allah dominating them all, strength did not have to be represented as other than what it was in order to suffuse it with transcendent meaning. Like God, kings desired and demanded, judged and decreed, harmed and rewarded. *C'est son métier*: one did not need an excuse to rule.

One, of course, did need the capacity, and that was not so easily come by in a vast and shifting field of literally hundreds of political entrepreneurs, each concerned to build a smaller or larger configuration of personal support about himself. Morocco did not have either the hierarchism of medieval Hinduism or the salvationism of Reformation Christianity to canonize its sovereign; it had only an acute sense of the power of God and the belief that his power appeared in the world in the exploits of forceful men, the most considerable of whom were kings. Political life is a clash of personalities everywhere, and in even the most focused of states lesser figures resist the center; but in Morocco such struggle was looked upon not as something in conflict with the order of things, disruptive of form or subversive of virtue, but as its purest expression. Society was agonistic—a tournament of wills; so then was kingship and the symbolism exalting it. Progresses here were not always easy to tell from raids.

Politically, eighteenth- and nineteenth-century Morocco consisted of a warrior monarchy centered in the Atlantic Plain, a cloud of at least sporadically submissive "tribes" settled in the fertile regions within its immediate reach, and a thinner cloud of only very occasionally submissive ones scattered through the mountains, steppes, and oases that rim the country.[32] Religiously, it consisted of a sharifian dynasty (that is, one claiming descent from Muhammad), a number of Koranic scholars, jurists, teachers, and scribes (*ulema*), and a host of holy men, living and dead, possessed of miraculous powers, the famous marabouts.[33] In theory, Islamic theory, the political and religious realms were one, the king was caliph and head of both, and the state was thus a theocracy; but it was not a theory that anyone, even the king, could regard as more than a lost ideal in the face of a situation where charismatic adventurers were constantly arising on all sides. If Moroccan society has any chief guiding principle, it is probably that one genuinely possesses only what one has the ability to defend, whether it be land, water, women, trade partners, or personal authority: whatever magic a king had he had strenuously to protect.

The magic was perceived in terms of another famous North African idea: *baraka*.[34] Baraka has been analogized to a number of things in an attempt to clarify it—mana, charisma, "spiritual electricity"—because it is a gift of power more than natural which men, having received it, can use in as natural and pragmatical a way, for as self-interested and mundane purposes, as they wish. But what most defines baraka, and sets it off somewhat from these similar concepts, is that it is radically individualistic, a property of persons in the way strength, courage, energy, or ferocity are and, like them, arbitrarily distributed. Indeed, it is in one sense a summary term for these qualities, the active virtues that, again, enable some men to prevail over others. To so prevail, whether at court or in a mountain camp, was to demonstrate that one had baraka, that God had gifted one with the capacity to dominate, a talent it could quite literally be death to hide. It was not a condition, like chastity, or a trait, like pride, that shines by itself but a movement, like will, that exists in its impact. Like everything the king did, progresses were designed to make that impact felt, most particularly by those who might imagine their own to be comparable.

Rather than occasional or periodic—and therefore a schedule of set pieces—the Moroccan progress was very nearly continuous. "The king's throne is his saddle," one saying went, "the sky his canopy." "The royal tents are never stored," went another. The great late-seventeenth-to-early-eighteenth-century consolidator of the dynasty, the man who made its baraka real, Mulay Ismail, seems to have spent most of his reign "under canvas" (during the first half of it, a chronicler notes, he did not pass a single uninterrupted year in his palace); and even Mulay Hasan (d. 1894), the last of the old-regime kings of Morocco, normally spent six months of the year on the move, demonstrating sovereignty to skeptics.[35] The kings did not even keep a single capital but instead shifted the court restlessly among the so-called Imperial Cities—Fez, Marrakech, Meknes, and Rabat—in none of which they were really at home. Motion was the rule, not the exception; and though a king could not, like God, quite be everywhere at once, he could try, at least, to give the impression that he was: "No one could be sure that the Sultan would not arrive at the head of his troops on the morrow. During such times the most adamant peoples were ready to negotiate with [his] officials and reach terms which suited the sovereign."[36] Like its rivals, the center wandered: "Roam and you will confound adversaries," another Moroccan proverb runs, "sit and they will confound you."

The court-in-motion was referred to either as a *mehalla*, literally, "way station," "camp," "stopover," or as a *harka*, literally, "movement," "stirring," "action," depending upon whether one wanted to emphasize the governmental or military aspects of it. Normally the king would remain camped in an area for anywhere from several days to several months and would then move, by gradual stages, to another, where he would remain for a similar period, receiving local chieftains and other notables, holding feasts, sending out punitive expeditions when need be, and generally making his presence known. This last was hardly difficult, for a royal camp was an impressive sight, a great sea of tents, soldiers, slaves, animals, prisoners, armaments, and camp followers. Harris estimated that there were nearly 40,000 people in Mulay Hasan's encampment (a "strange mixture of boundless confusion and perfect order that succeeded each other in ... quick succession") in the Tafilalt in 1893, and fifty or sixty tents within the royal compound alone. Even as late as 1898, when all this was more or less drawing to a close, Weisgerber speaks of "thousands of men and beasts" in Mulay Abdul Aziz's encampment in the Chaouia, which he also describes, less romantically, as a vast lake of infected mud.[37]

The mobility of the king was thus a central element in his power; the realm was unified—to the very partial degree that it was unified and was a realm—by a restless searching-out of contact, most of it agonistic, with literally hundreds of lesser centers of power within it. The struggle with local big men was not necessarily violent or even usually so (Schaar quotes the popular maxim that the king employed ninety-nine ruses, of which firearms were but the hundredth), but it was unending, especially for an ambitious king, one who wished to make a state—one scuffle, one intrigue, one negotiation succeeded by another.[38] It was an exhausting occupation, one only the tireless could pursue. What chastity was to Elizabeth, and magnificence to Hayam Wuruk, energy was to Mulay Ismail or Mulay Hasan: as long as he could keep moving, chastening an opponent here, advancing an ally there, the king could make believable his claim to a sovereignty conferred by God. But only that long. The traditional shout of the crowds to the passing king, *Allāh ybarak f-ᶜamer Sīdī*— "God give you baraka forever, my Master"—was more equivocal than it sounds: "forever" ended when mastery did.

There is no more poignant example of the degree to which this fact dominated the consciousness of Morocco's rulers, and no bitterer witness to its truth, than the terrible last progress of Mulay Hasan. Frustrated by the failure of his administrative, military, and economic reforms to bear fruit, threatened on all sides by intruding European powers, and worn out by twenty years of holding the country together by the main force of his personality, he decided, in 1893, to lead a massive expedition to the shrine of his dynasty's founder in the Tafilalt, a desert-edge oasis 300 miles south of Fez. A long, arduous, dangerous, expensive journey, undertaken in the face of what seems to have been nearly universal advice to the contrary, it was quite possibly the greatest mahalla ever made in Morocco—a dramatic, desperate, and, as it turned out, disastrous effort at self-renewal.

The expedition, of 30,000 men drawn from the loyal tribes of the Atlantic Plain, mounted mostly on mules, left Fez in April, crossed the middle and high Atlases in the summer and early autumn, and arrived in the Tafilalt in November.[39] Since only one European, a French doctor, was permitted to go along, and he was an indifferent observer (there do not seem to be any native accounts), we do not know much about the trip except that it was grueling. Aside from the simply physical obstacles (the highest passes reached nearly 8,000 feet, and the road was hardly more than a trail scratched across the rocks), the burden of baggage, tents, and armaments (even cannons were dragged along), and the logistical problems involved in feeding so many people and animals, the whole area was dotted with contentious Berber tribes, who had to be prevented, half with threats and half with bribes, occasionally with force, from "eating the caravan." But though there were some difficult moments and the expedition was seriously delayed, nothing particularly untoward seems to have happened. The sheikhs came, accompanied by dozens of tribesmen; royal hospitality was extended; and, amid flamboyant riding and shooting displays, gifts were exchanged, tea drunk, bulls sacrificed, taxes gathered, and loyalty promised. It was only after the shrine had been reached and the prayers accomplished that the trouble began.

It is likely that the king, his timetable disrupted by the slowness of the Atlas passage and his army fevered and malnourished, would have preferred to remain in the oasis through the winter, but a combination of factors caused him to stay less than a month. The Berber tribes were still a worry, particularly as the southern ones were even more belligerent; there was a fear of assassination by French agents directed from southern Algeria; and there were reports of severe fighting between Moroccans and Spaniards at the other, Mediterranean, end of the country. But perhaps the most important factor in the decision to try to make it back to the plains at so unsuitable a time was Mulay Hasan's own failing powers. Harris, who saw him at Tafilalt, found him terribly aged from only two years earlier (he was apparently in his mid-forties)—tired, sallow, prematurely gray; and the same sense of lost momentum that propelled him south apparently turned him north again when his journey to his origins failed to restore it.

In any case, the expedition, now but about 10,000 strong, left in December for Marrakech, three weeks' march over the High Atlas to the east, through a region even more forbidding, geographically and politically, than that through which it had already passed. In addition, it was winter now, and the whole affair soon turned into a retreat from Moscow:

> By the time his army had reached the foothills the winter snows had begun; as they climbed higher into the main massif more and more of the camels, mules and horses, weak with starvation, stumbled into deep snowdrifts and died. Little but their carcasses stood between the remnants of the *harka* and starvation, and the surviving beasts staggered on and upwards laden with what little meat could be salvaged from the corpses of their companions. The army was attended by clouds of ravens, kites and vultures. Hundreds of men died daily, they were left unburied in the snow, stripped of whatever rags they had still possessed.[40]

By the time Marrakech was reached, more than a third of the already reduced army had been lost; and the himself rather mobile Harris (he was the London *Times* correspondent), who was on hand for the arrival, found the king no longer merely aging but dying:

> What was noticeable at Tafilet was doubly apparent now. The Sultan had become an old man. Travel-stained and weary, he

rode his great white horse with its mockery of green-and-gold trapping, while over a head that was the picture of suffering waved the imperial umbrella of crimson velvet. Following him straggled into the city a horde of half-starved men and animals, trying to be happy that at last their terrible journey was at an end, but too ill and too hungry to succeed.[41]

The king remained in Marrakech until spring, attempting to regather his powers; but then, renewed anxiety about the deteriorating situation in the North, and the need for his presence there, set him in motion again. He had got as far as Tadla, about a hundred miles from Marrakech, when he collapsed and died. The death was, however, concealed by his ministers. They were concerned that, with the king gone, the caravan would dissolve and the tribes fall upon it and that conspirators supporting other candidates would contrive to prevent the accession of Mulay Hasan's chosen successor, his twelve-year-old son, Mulay Abdul Aziz. So he was represented as being merely indisposed and resting privately, his corpse was laid in a curtained palanquin, and the expedition was launched into a forced march, brutal in the summer heat, toward Rabat. Food was brought to the king's tent and then taken away again as though consumed. The few knowledgeable ministers hurried in and out of his presence as though conducting business. A few local sheikhs, cautioned that he was sleeping, were even permitted to look in upon him. By the time that the progress neared Rabat, two days later, the king's corpse had so begun to stink that his death announced itself; but by then the dangerous tribes had been left behind, and Abdul Aziz, his backers informed of events by a runner, had been proclaimed king in the city. In two more days the company, largely reduced to the old king's ministers and personal bodyguard—the others having drifted away or straggled behind—limped into Rabat, engulfed in the stench of royal death:

> It must have been a gruesome procession from the description his son Mulai Abdul Aziz gave me [Walter Harris wrote]: the hurried arrival of the swaying palanquin bearing its terrible burden, five days dead in the great heat of summer; the escort, who had bound scarves over their faces—but even this precaution could not keep them from constant sickness—and even the mules that bore the palanquin seemed affected by the horrible atmosphere, and tried from time to time to break loose.[42]

And so, its motion spent, the progress that had begun more than a year before ended, and with it two decades of rushing about from one corner of the country to another, defending the idea of religious monarchy. Indeed, this was more or less the end of the whole pattern; for the next two kings—one of whom reigned for fourteen years, the other for four—attempted only a few rather desultory harkas in a rapidly disintegrating situation, and the French, who took over after them, made palace prisoners of the two kings who followed. Immobilized, Moroccan kings were as dead as Hasan, their baraka impotent and theoretical. It was neither as embodiments of redemptive virtue nor as reflections of cosmic order but as explosions of divine energy that Moroccan kings recommended themselves to their subjects, and even the smallest explosion needs room in which to happen.

Conclusion

Now, the easy reaction to all this talk of monarchs, their trappings, and their peregrinations is that it has to do with a closed past, a time, in Huizinga's famous phrase, when the world was half-a-thousand years younger and everything was clearer. All the golden grasshoppers and bees are gone; monarchy, in the true sense of the word, was ritually destroyed on one scaffold in Whitehall in 1649 and on another in the Place de la Révolution in 1793; the few fragments left in the Third World are just that—fragments, relic kings whose likelihood of having successors diminishes by the hour.[43] England has a second Elizabeth, who may be as chaste—more so, probably—than the first, and who gets properly lauded on public occasions, but the resemblance rather ends there; Morocco has a second Hasan, but he is more a French colonel than an Arab prince; and the last of the great line of Javanese Indic kings, Hamengku Buwono IX, his royal office legally abolished, is the self-effacing, rather ineffectual, vaguely socialist vice-president of the Indonesian Republic, around whom not even the smallest planets revolve.

Yet, though all this is true enough, it is superficial. The relevance of historical fact for sociological analysis does not rest on the proposition that there is nothing in the present but the past, which is not true, or on easy analogies between extinct institutions and the way we live now. It rests on the perception that though both the structure and the expressions of social life change, the inner necessities that animate it do not. Thrones may be out of fashion, and pageantry too; but political authority still requires a cultural frame in which to define itself and advance its claims, and so does opposition to it. A world wholly demystified is a world wholly depoliticized; and though Weber promised us both of these—specialists without spirit in a bureaucratic iron cage—the course of events since, with its Sukarnos, Churchills, Nkrumahs, Hitlers, Maos, Roosevelts, Stalins, Nassers, and De Gaulles, suggests that what died in 1793 (to the degree that it did) was a certain view of the affinity between the sort of power that moves men and the sort that moves mountains, not the sense that there is one.

The "political theology" (to revert to Kantorowicz's term) of the twentieth century has not been written, though there have been glancing efforts here and there. But it exists—or, more exactly, various forms of it exist—and until it is understood at least as well as that of the Tudors, the Majapahits, or the Alawites, a great deal of the public life of our times is going to remain obscure. The extraordinary has not gone out of modern politics, however much the banal may have entered; power not only still intoxicates, it still exalts.

It is for this reason that, no matter how peripheral, ephemeral, or free-floating the charismatic figure we may be concerned with—the wildest prophet, the most deviant revolutionary—we must begin with the center and with the symbols and conceptions that prevail there if we are to understand him and what he means. It is no accident that Stuarts get Cromwells and Medicis Savonarolas—or, for that matter, that Hindenburgs get Hitlers. Every serious charismatic threat that ever arose in Alawite Morocco took the form of some local power-figure's laying claim to enormous baraka by engaging in actions—*siba*, literally, "insolence"—designed to expose the weakness of the king by showing him up as unable to stop them; and Java has been continuously beset by local mystics emerging from meditative trances to present themselves to the world as its "Exemplary Ruler" (*Ratu Adil*), corrective images of a lost order and an obscured form.[44] This is the paradox of charisma: that though it is rooted in the sense of being near to the heart of things, of being caught up in the realm of the serious, a sentiment that is felt most characteristically and continuously by those who in fact dominate social affairs, who ride in the progresses and grant the audiences, its most flamboyant expressions tend to appear among people at some distance from the center, indeed often enough at a rather enormous distance, who want very much to be closer. Heresy is as much of a child of orthodoxy in politics as it is in religion.

And both heresy and orthodoxy, however adept the secret police, are universal, as we learn when workers explode in East Germany, Tolstoyan romantics reappear in Russia, or, strangest of all, soldier-populists surface in Portugal. The enfoldment of political life in general conceptions of how reality is put together did not disappear with dynastic continuity and divine right. Who gets What, When, Where, and How is as culturally distinctive a view of what politics is, and in its own way as transcendental, as the defense of "wisedom and rightwiseness," the celebration of "The Daymaker's Equal," or the capricious flow of *baraka*. Nor is it any less capable of yielding spectacle, center-praising or center-challenging:

> I accompany the Humphrey press to one of Hubert's stops, a school for handicapped children, for the deaf and the retarded. He shakes hands with every single Sister. Every one. And every child he can reach. Schedule allows for twenty minutes. Thirteen used for shaking hands. The talk goes on for twenty minutes, *on* for twenty-five, *on* for thirty. The hands of the poor priest who is trying to translate into sign language are wearing out ... thirty-five minutes—another man takes over as translator ..." And some of the greatest men in history had handicaps"—he tries to think of one, his eyes flash, cheeks acquire that familiar beaming, knowing look.—"Thomas Edison. We *all* have handicaps ..." "What's the most important word in the English language?" "Service!" "And the other most important word is 'love!' " "And what are the last four letters in the word American? I CAN. Look at them. Spell it. I can. You *can*. You're great. You're wonderful. God bless you." The tears are in the corners of his eyes, the tears that cause him such grief on television. His head chucks up and down happily as he wades back through the crowd of distracted, uncertain, uncomprehending kids.

> In Madison Square Garden, then, on July 14, a celebration of moral purity is held. "Together with McGovern at the Garden," it is called. Its purpose is to raise funds. Mike Nichols and Elaine May come back together just for the event; so do Peter, Paul, and Mary; and Simon and Garfunkel. The contrast between such a rally and a Wallace rally—or, say, a gathering of Bob Hope and Billy Graham for Richard Nixon—explodes the circuits of the mind. Comparative liturgies! June 14 is Flag Day. But there are no flags on stage. No flags surround the Garden. The evening celebrates the resurrection of the youth culture. The liturgy of a new class is performed. Peter, Paul, and Mary, Dionne Warwick, Simon and Garfunkel in every song celebrate

the mobile, lonely, vulnerable, middle-class life. Dionne
Warwick warbles in blue-flowered, cottony, innocent, white
gown: "Imagine!—No heaven—no hell—no countries—no
religions! When the world will live as one." Simon and Gar-
funkel offer "Jesus loves you, Mrs. Robinson!" and the most
revealing line: "I'd rather be a hammer than a nail." No
Lawrence Welk. No Johnny Cash. No Benny Goodman. The
music is singlemindedly sectarian. At 11:05, the entire cast
gathers on stage, flashing peace signs. Then a great chant goes
up: WE WANT MCGOVERN!" "It's a wonderful night of coming
together," McGovern says. He tells them how he "loves this
country enough to hold it to a higher standard, away from the
killing, death, and destruction now going on in Southeast
Asia." "I love this land and cherish its future. I want to set
about making this country a great, decent, and good
land ... to be a bridge from war to peace ... a bridge across
the generation gap ... a bridge across the gaps in justice in
this country ... As the prophet wrote: 'Therefore, choose
life ... be on the side of blessing, not cursing' ... on the side
of hope, health, life. And peace for ourselves and peoples all
around the globe."

At Racine, the rally is on again, this time in Memorial Hall,
well after working hours and publicized through radio spots.
The crowd assembles early; some are turned away at the door.
1200 sit inside, 330 in the balcony, standing room for 250.
Excitement crackles. The loudspeakers are tuned just right,
then turned up louder. "I've laid around and played around this
ole town too long." Billy Grammer is singing, his blue eyes
flashing. And: "Horseshoe diamond ring." Mr. Karl Prussian,
twelve years a counterspy, is introduced by George Magnum, in
the latter's high nasal best: "If you've been followin' the Conservative movement in the U.S., you'll know the man ah'm
about to intr'duce to you." "George Wallace," Karl Prussian
says, "is a man of God." "God bless you!" George Magnum
says. We're in Protestant territory now and the symbols are
colliding, and sparks are shooting. It's meetin' time, and everyone's at ease. George Wallace, Jr., his hair as long as John
Lennon's, swings out gently. He flourishes his dark electric
guitar, tenderly, with restraint. No wild vulgar rock, no Mick
Jagger here, but son of a man misunderstood, a young, patient,
and determined Alabaman. "Gentle on my mind ..." is his
first number, and his second is: "I shot a man in Reno just to
watch him die." Then the Governor, half-reluctant, half-
jubilant, explodes across the stage. Pandemonium. He likes the

crowd. His eyes begin to shine. Nervousness falls away and his movements become fluid, confident. Each gesture draws a response. "I tell you we're gonna give St. Vitus dance to the leadership of the Democratic party." "Ah'm sick of permissiveness in this society. Ah'm tired of false liberals!" "Ah'm sick'n' tired of giving up 50 percent of my income to the United States, to waste half of it overseas on nations that spit on us and half of it on welfare." "An' now they tell us Vietnam was a mistake. A mistake that cost the average citizen 50,000 lives, 300,000 wounded, 120 billion dollars down the drain. Ah don' call that a mistake. It's a tragedy." Like David Halberstam, he puts the blame upon the best and brightest—"them." *This* is how *they* run our lives.[45]

So the progresses continue. If the material were from Germany or France, India or Tanzania (to say nothing of Russia or China), the idiom would be different, as would the ideological assumptions upon which it rested. But there would be an idiom, and it would reflect the fact that the charisma of the dominant figures of society and that of those who hurl themselves against that dominance stem from a common source: the inherent sacredness of central authority. Sovereignty may rest now in states or even in the populations of states, as Humphrey, McGovern, and Wallace alike assume; but the "vast universality" that inheres in it remains, whatever has become of the will of kings. Neither nationalism nor populism has changed that. It is not, after all, standing outside the social order in some excited state of self-regard that makes a political leader numinous but a deep, intimate involvement—affirming or abhorring, defensive or destructive—in the master fictions by which that order lives.

Saul Bellow

8

Writers and Literature
in American Society

Preface

What was it, in the thirties, that drew an adolescent in Chicago to the writing of books? How did a young American of the depression period decide that he was, of all things, a literary artist? I use the pretentious term literary artist simply to emphasize the contrast between such an ambition and the external facts. A colossal industrial and business center, knocked flat by unemployment, its factories and even its schools closing, decided to hold a World's Fair on the shore of Lake Michigan, with towers, high rides, exhibits, Chinese rickshaws, a midget village in which there was a midget wedding every day, and other lively attractions, including whores and con men and fan dancers. There was a bit of gaiety, there was quite a lot of amoebic dysentery. Prosperity did not come back. Several millions of dollars were invested in vain by businessmen and politicians. If they could be quixotic, there was no reason why college students shouldn't be impractical too. And what was the most impractical of choices in somber, heavy, growling, low-brow Chicago? Why, it was to be the representative of beauty, the interpreter of the human heart, the hero of ingenuity, playfulness, personal freedom, generosity, and love. I cannot even now say that this was a bad sort of crackpot to be.

The difference between that time and this is that in the thirties crackpots were not subsidized by their families. They had to go it alone for several years. Or at least until the New Deal (thanks largely

to Harry Hopkins) recognized that a great government could *buy* the
solution of any problem and opened WPA projects in many parts of
the country. I think it possible that Hopkins and Roosevelt, seeing
how much trouble unhappy intellectuals had made in Russia,
Germany, and Italy between 1905 and 1935, thought it a bargain to
pay people twenty-three dollars a week for painting post-office
murals and editing guidebooks. This plan succeeded admirably. If I
am not mistaken, America continued to follow the Hopkins hint in
postwar Europe and perhaps in Vietnam.

I know, for instance, that John Cheever has been conducting
creative-writing courses at Sing Sing. Writers and criminals have
often found that they have much in common. And correctional
officials seem to understand, thanks to the psychology courses they
take in the universities, that it is excellent therapy to write books and
that it may soften the hearts of criminals to record their experiences.
Politicians, too, when they fall from power or retire, become writers
or university professors. Thus Hubert Humphrey and Dean Rusk
became lecturers, Eugene McCarthy became a poet, and an altogether different sort of politician, Spiro Agnew, a novelist. Inter-
viewed not long ago in the New York *Times*, Mr. Agnew said that,
having suffered greatly, he felt the need to do something creative to
recover his spirits and was setting to work writing a novel because he
was not yet strong enough to do serious mental work.

But I started out to recall what it was like to set oneself up to be a
writer in the Midwest during the thirties. For I thought of myself as
a midwesterner and not a Jew. I am often described as a Jewish
writer; in much the same way one might be called a Samoan
astronomer or an Eskimo cellist or a Zulu Gainsborough expert. I
sense, at times, that in the eyes of the public, or of that portion of
the public that is still identified with the Protestant majority, there is
some oddity about it. I am a Jew, and I have written some books. I
have tried to fit my soul into the Jewish-writer category, but it does
not feel comfortably accommodated there. I wonder, now and then,
whether Philip Roth and Bernard Malamud and I have not become
the Hart, Schaffner, and Marx of our trade. We have made it in the
field of culture as Bernard Baruch made it on a park bench, as Polly
Adler made it in prostitution, as Two Gun Cohen, the personal
bodyguard of Sun Yat-Sen, made it in China. My joke is not broad
enough to cover the contempt I feel for the opportunists, wise guys,
and career types who impose such labels and trade upon them. In a

century so disastrous to Jews, one hesitates to criticize those who believe that they are making the world safer by publicizing Jewish achievements. I myself doubt that this publicity is effective.

I did not go to the public library to read the Talmud but the novels and poems of Sherwood Anderson, Theodore Dreiser, Edgar Lee Masters, and Vachel Lindsay. These were people who had resisted the material weight of American society and who proved—what was not immediately obvious—that the life lived in great manufacturing, shipping, and banking centers, with their slaughter stink, their great slums, prisons, hospitals, and schools, was also a human life. It appeared to me that this one thing, so intimately known that not only nerves, senses, mind, but also my very bones wanted to put it into words, might contain elements that not even Dreiser, whom I admired most, had yet reached. I felt that I was born to be a performing and interpretive creature, that I was meant to take part in a peculiar, exalted game. For there are good grounds to consider this, together with other forms of civilized behavior and ceremony, a game. At its noblest this game is played, under discipline, before God himself—so Plato said, and others as well. The game can be an offering, a celebration, an act of praise, an acknowledgment also of one's weaknesses and limitations. I couldn't have put it in this manner then. All that appeared then was a blind, obstinate impulse expressing itself in bursts of foolishness. I loved great things. I thought I had a right to think of that exalted game. I was also extremely proud, ornery, and stupid.

I was, in 1937, a very young married man who had quickly lost his first job and who lived with his in-laws. His affectionate, loyal, and pretty wife insisted that he must be given a chance to write something. Having anyone pay attention to my writing wasn't a real possibility. I am as often bemused as amused at the attention my books have since received. Neglect would have been frightful, but attention has its disadvantages. The career of a critic, when I am feeling mean about it, I sometimes compare to that of a deaf man who tunes pianos. In a more benevolent mood I agree with my late father that people must be encouraged to make as honest a living as they can. For this reason I don't object to becoming a topic. When I visited Japan, I saw that there were prayer-and-fortune-telling papers sold for a penny at each temple. The buyers rolled up these long strips of paper and tied them by threads to bushes and low trees. From the twigs there dangled hundreds of tightly furled papers. I sometimes compare myself to one of these temple trees.

So I sat at a bridge table in a back bedroom of the apartment, writing something, while all rational, serious, dutiful people were at their jobs or trying to find jobs. My table faced three cement steps that rose from the cellar into the brick gloom of a passageway. Only my mother-in-law was at home. A widow, then in her seventies, she wore a heavy white braid down her back. She had been a modern woman and a socialist and suffragette in the old country. She was attractive in a fragile, steely way. You felt Sophie's strength of will in all things. She kept a neat house. The very plants, the ashtrays, the pedestals, the doilies, the chairs, revealed her mastery. Each object had its military place. Her apartment could easily have been transferred to West Point.

Lunch occurred at half past twelve. The cooking was good. We ate together in the kitchen. The meal was followed by an interval of stone. My mother-in-law took a nap. I went into the street. Ravenswood was utterly empty. I walked about with something like a large stone in my belly. I often turned into Lawrence Avenue and stood on the bridge looking into the drainage canal. If I had been a dog I would have howled. Even a soft howl would have helped. But I was not here to howl. I was here to interpret the world (its American version) as brilliantly as possible. Still I would have been far happier selling newspapers at Union Station or practicing my shots in a poolroom. But I had a discipline to learn at the bridge table in the bedroom.

No wonder a writer of great talent and fine intelligence like John Cheever volunteers to help the convicts with their stories. He knows how it feels to be locked in. Maybe he thinks the prisoners, being already locked in, may as well learn the discipline. It is the most intolerable of privations for people whose social instincts are so highly developed that they want to write novels to be confined in rooms. Nuns fret not, perhaps, but writers do. Bernanos, the French religious novelist, said that his soul could not bear to be cut off from its kind, and that was why he did his work in cafés. Cafés indeed! I would have kissed the floor of a café. There were no cafés in Chicago. There were greasy-spoon cafeterias, one-arm joints, taverns. I never yet heard of a writer who brought his manuscripts into a tavern. I have always taken an interest in the fact that Schiller liked to smell apples when he was writing, that someone else kept his feet in a tub of water. The only person whose arrangements seemed to me worth imitating was the mystic and guru Gurdjieff. Gurdjieff, when he had work to do, set forth from headquarters in Fontainebleau with his disciples in several limousines. They carried hampers with caviar, cold fowl, champagne, cheese, and fruit. At a signal from the master the cars would stop. They would picnic in a meadow, and then, with all his followers around him, Gurdjieff did his writing. This, if it can be arranged, seems to me worth doing.

I am glad to say that I can't remember what I was writing in Ravenswood. It must have been terrible. The writing itself, however, was of no importance. The important thing was that American society and S. Bellow came face to face. I had to learn that by cutting myself off from American life in order to perform an alien task, I risked cutting myself off from everything that could nourish me. But this was the case only if you granted the monopoly of nutrients to this business-industrial, vital, brutal, proletarian, and middle-class city that was itself involved in a tremendous struggle. It was not even aggressively hostile, saying, "Lead my kind of life or die." Not at all. It simply had no interest in your sort of game.

Quite often, in the Hudson belonging to J. J., my brother-in-law, my mother-in-law and I drove to the cemetery. There we tended her husband's grave. Her trembling but somehow powerful spotty hand pulled weeds. I made trips with a Mason jar to the faucet and made water splotches about the nasturtiums and sweet williams. Death, I thought, Chicago-style, might not be such a bad racket after all. At least you didn't have to drive down Harlem Avenue in rush hour back to the house with its West Point arrangements, with its pages of bad manuscript on the bridge table and the silent dinner of soup and stew and strudel. After which you and your wife, washing dishes, enjoyed the first agreeable hours of the day.

J. J., my brother-in-law, born Jascha in the old country, practiced law in the Loop. He was a Republican, member of the American Legion, a golfer, a bowler; he drove his conservative car conservatively, took the *Saturday Evening Post;* he wore a Herbert Hoover starched collar, trousers short in the ankle, and a hard straw hat in summer. He spoke in a pure Hoosier twang, not like a Booth Tarkington gentleman but like a real Tippecanoe-country dirt farmer. All this Americanism was imposed on an exquisitely oriental face, dark, with curved nose and Turkish cheekbones. Naturally a warmhearted man, he frowned upon me. He thought I was doing something foreign.

There was an observable parallel between us. As I was making a writer of myself, this exotic man was transforming his dark oriental traits and becoming an American from Indiana. He spoke of Aaron

Slick from Punkin' Crick, of Elmer Dub: "Ah kin read writin', but ah can't read readin'." He had served in the Army—my wife wore his 1917 overcoat (too small for me)—and he told old, really old, La Salle Street Republican sex jokes about Woodrow Wilson and Edith Bolling. It was common in that generation and the next to tailor one's appearance and style to what were, after all, journalistic, publicity creations and products of caricature. The queer hunger of immigrants and their immediate descendants for true Americanism has yet to be described. It may be made to sound like fun, but I find it hard to think of anyone who underwent the process with joy. Those incompetents who lacked mimetic talent and were pure buffoons were better off. I remember a cousin, Arkady, from the old country who declared that his new name was now, and henceforth, Lake Erie. A most poetic name, he thought. In my own generation there were those immigrants who copied even the unhappiness of the Protestant majority, embracing its miseries, battling against Mom; reluctant, after work, to board the suburban train, drinking downtown, drinking on the club car, being handed down drunk to the wife and her waiting station wagon like good Americans. These people martyred themselves in the enactment of roles that proved them genuine—just as madly wretched in marriage as Abe Lincoln and Mary Todd. Cousin Arkady, a clown who sold dehydrated applesauce on the road, giving dry-applesauce demonstrations to housewives in small-town department stores, was spared the worst of it. He simply became "Archie" and made no further effort to prove himself a real American.

The point of this brief account, as I see it, is to evoke that mixture of imagination and stupidity with which people met the American Experience, that murky, heavy, burdensome, chaotic thing. I see that my own error, shared with many others, was to seek sanctuary in what corners of culture one could find in this country, there to enjoy my high thoughts and to perfect myself in the symbolic discipline of an art. I can't help feeling that I overdid it. One didn't need as much sanctuary as all that.

If I had to name the one force in America that opposes the symbolic discipline of poetry today as much as brutal philistinisms did before World War II, I would say the Great Noise. The enemy is noise. By noise I mean not simply the noise of technology, the noise of money or advertising and promotion, the noise of the media, the noise of miseducation, but the terrible excitement and distraction generated by the crises of modern life. Mind, I don't say that philistinism is gone. It is not. It has found many disguises, some highly artistic and peculiarly insidious. But the noise of life is the great threat. Contributing to it are real and unreal issues, ideologies, rationalizations, errors, delusions, nonsituations that look real, nonquestions demanding consideration, opinions, analyses in the press, on the air, expertise, inside dope, factional disagreement, official rhetoric, information—in short, the sounds of the public sphere, the din of politics, the turbulence and agitation that set in about 1914 and have now reached an intolerable volume. Nadezhda Mandelstam, writing of poets in the Soviet Union, says of the Russian noise: "Nowhere else, I believe, were people so much deafened as they were here by the din of life—one after another poets fell silent because they could no longer hear their own voices." She adds: "The noise drowned out thought and, in the case of millions, conscience as well."

William Wordsworth nearly two hundred years ago expressed his concern over the effects of modern turbulence on poetry. He was right, too. But, in the language of my youth, "He didn't know the half of it."

Some Questions and Answers

Q: How do you, a novelist from Chicago, fit yourself into American Life? Is there a literary world to which you belong?

A: When I entered the Restaurant Voltaire in Paris with the novelist Louis Guilloux some years ago, the waiter addressed him as "maître." I didn't know whether to envy him or to smile. No one had ever treated me so reverentially. And as a student I had sat in Chicago reading of *salons* and *cénacles*, of evenings at Magny's with Flaubert and Turgeniev and Sainte-Beuve—reading and sighing. What glorious times! But Guilloux himself, a Breton and a former left-winger, seemed uncomfortable with his title. It may be that, even in Paris, literary culture is now preserved by smarmy headwaiters. I am not altogether sure of that. What is certain is that we have nothing like it in America—no *maîtres* except in dining rooms, no literary world, no literary public. Many of us read, many love literature, but the traditions and institutions of literary culture are lacking. I do not say that this is bad; I only state it as a fact that ours is not a society which creates such things. Any modern country that has not inherited them simply does not have them.

American writers are not neglected. They mingle occasionally

with the great; they may even be asked to the White House, but
no one there will talk literature to them. Mr. Nixon disliked
writers and refused flatly to have them in, but Mr. Ford has
invited them, together with actors, musicians, television news-
casters, and politicians. On these great evenings the East Room
fills with celebrities who become ecstatic at the sight of other
celebrities. Secretary Kissinger and Danny Kaye fall into each
other's arms. Cary Grant is surrounded by senators' wives, who
find him wonderfully preserved, as handsome in the flesh as on
film, and they can hardly bear the excitement of personal contact
with greatness. People speak of their diets, of travel and holidays,
of vitamins and the problems of aging. Questions of language or
style, the structure of novels, trends in painting, are not discussed. The writer finds this a wonderful Pop occasion. Senator
Fulbright seems almost to recognize his name and says, "You
write essays, don't you? I think I can remember one of them."
But the senator, as everyone knows, was once a Rhodes Scholar.

It is actually pleasant on such an evening for a writer to pass,
half-disembodied and unmolested by small talk, from room to
room, looking and listening. He knows that active public men
can't combine government with literature, art, and philosophy.
Theirs is a world of high-tension wires, not of primroses on the
river's brim. Ten years ago Mayor Daley in a little City Hall
ceremony gave me a five-hundred-dollar check on behalf of the
Midland Authors Society. "Mr. Mayor, have you read *Herzog*?"
asked one of the reporters, standing by. "I've looked into it,"
said Daley, yielding no ground. Art is not the mayor's dish. But
then, why should it be? I much prefer his neglect to the sort of
interest Stalin took in poetry, phoning Pasternak to chat with
him about Mandelstam and, shortly afterwards, sending Mandelstam to die.

Q: Are you saying that a modern industrial society dismisses art?
A: Not at all. Art is one of those good things toward which it feels
friendly. It is quite receptive. But what Ruskin said about the
English public in 1871 applies perfectly to us: "No reading is
possible for a people with its mind in this state. No sentence of
any great writer is intelligible to them." Ruskin blamed avarice:
" ... so incapable of thought has it [the public] become in its
insanity of avarice. Happily, our disease is, as yet, little worse
than this incapacity of thought; it is not corruption of the inner
nature; we ring true still, when anything strikes home to us ...

though the idea that everything should 'pay' has infected our every purpose so deeply . . ."[1]

Q: You don't see avarice as the problem, do you?

A: No. "A people with its mind in this state" is where I lay the stress. We are in a peculiarly revolutionary state, a critical state that never ends. Yesterday I came upon a description of a medical technique for bringing patients to themselves. They are exposed for some minutes to high-frequency sounds until they are calm enough to think and to feel out their symptoms. To possess your soul in peace for a few moments you need the help of medical technology. It is easy to observe in bars, at dinner tables, everywhere, that from flophouse to White House Americans are preoccupied by the same questions. Our own American life is our passion, our social and national life against a world background, an immense spectacle presented daily by the papers and the television networks—our cities, our crime, our housing, our automobiles, our sports, our weather, our technology, our politics, our problems of sex and race and diplomacy and international relations. These realities are real enough. But what of the formulas, the jargon, the principles of selection the media prefer? TV creates the exciting fictions, the heightened and dramatized shadow events accepted by the great public and believed by almost everyone to be real. Is reading possible for a people with its mind in this state?

Q: Still, a book of good quality can find a hundred thousand readers. But you say that there is no literary public.

A: An influential book appears to create its own public. When *Herzog* was published, I became aware that there were some fifty thousand people in the United States who wanted to read my novel. They had evidently been waiting for something like it. Other writers have certainly had the same experience. But such a public is a temporary one. There is no literary culture that permanently contains all of these readers. Remarkably steady and intelligent people emerge from the heaving wastes of the American educational system. They survive by strength, luck, and cunning.

Q: What do they do while waiting for the next important event?

A: Exactly. What can they read, month in, month out? In what journals do they keep up with what matters in contemporary literature?

Q: What about the universities? Haven't they done anything to train judgment and develop taste?

A: To most professors of English a novel is an object of the highest cultural importance. Its ideas, its symbolic structure, its position in the history of Romanticism or Realism or Modernism, its higher relevance, require devout study. But what has this sort of cultural study to do with novelists and readers? What they want is the living moment; they want men and women alive, and a circumambient world. The teaching of literature has been a disaster. Between the student and the book he reads lies a gloomy preparatory region, a perfect swamp. He must cross this cultural swamp before he is allowed to open his *Moby-Dick* and read, "Call me Ishmael." He is made to feel ignorant before masterpieces; unworthy, he is frightened and repelled. And if the method succeeds, it produces B.A.s who can tell you why the *Pequod* leaves port on Christmas morning. What else can they tell you? No feeling for the book has been communicated, only a lot of pseudo-learned interpretation. What has been substituted for the novel itself is what can be said about the novel by the "educated." Some professors find educated discourse of this kind more interesting by far than novels. They take the attitude toward fiction that one of the Church Fathers took toward the Bible. Origen of Alexandria asked whether we were really to imagine that God walked in a garden while Adam and Eve hid under a bush. Scripture could not be taken literally. It must yield higher meanings.

Q: Are you equating Church Fathers with professors of literature?

A: Not exactly. The Fathers had sublime conceptions of God and Man. If professors of humanities were moved by the sublimity of the poets and philosophers they teach, they would be the most powerful men in the university and the most fervent. But they are at the lower end of the hierarchy, at the bottom of the pile.

Q: Then why are there so many writers at the universities?

A: A good question. Writers have no independent ground to stand on. They belong to institutions. They work for newsmagazines and publishing houses, for cultural foundations, advertising agencies, television networks. And they teach. There are only a few literary journals left, and those are now academic quarterlies. The big national magazines don't want to publish fiction. Their editors want to discuss only the most significant national and international questions and concentrate on "relevant" cultural matters. By "relevant" they mean political. The "real" questions facing us are questions of business and politics—energy, war, sex, race, cities, education, technology, ecology, the fate of the automobile industry, the Middle East crisis, the dominoes of Southeast Asia, the moves of the Russian Politburo. These are, of course, matters of the highest importance. More accurately, there are questions of life and death at the heart of such important public matters. But these life-and-death questions are not discussed. What we hear and read is crisis chatter. And it is the business of the cultural intelligentsia (professors, commentators, editors) to produce such chatter. Our intelligentsia, completely politicized and analytical in temper, does not take much interest in literature. The members of this elite *had* literature in their student days and are now well beyond it. At Harvard or Columbia they read, studied, and absorbed the classics, especially the modernist classics. These prepared them for the important, the essential, the incomparable tasks they were destined to perform as functionaries in the media, the managers of scores of new enterprises. Sometimes I sense that they feel they have replaced writers. The cultural business they do is tinged by literature, or rather the memory of literature. I said before that our common life had become our most passionate concern. Can an individual, the subject of a novel, compete in interest with corporate destinies, with the rise of a new class, a cultural intelligentsia?

Q: Do you suggest that when we become so extremely politicized we lose interest in the individual?

A: Exactly. And that a liberal society so intensely political can't remain liberal for very long. I take it for granted that an attack on the novel is also an attack on liberal principles. I view "activist" art theories in the same way. The power of a true work of art is such that it induces a temporary suspension of activities. It leads to contemplative states, to wonderful and, to my mind, sacred states of the soul.

Q: And what you call "crisis chatter" creates a contrary situation?

A: I should like to add that the truth is not loved because it is *better* for us. We hunger and thirst for it. And the appetite for truthful books is greater than ever, sharpened by privation.

Q: To return for a moment to the subject of a literary world . . .

A: No tea at Gertrude Stein's, no Closerie de Lilas, no Bloomsbury evenings, no charming and wicked encounters between George Moore and W. B. Yeats. Reading of such things is very pleasant indeed. I can't say that I miss them, because I never knew anything like them. I miss certain dead friends. Writers. That

Molière put on the plays of Corneille, that Louis XIV himself may have appeared, disguised, in one of Molière's farces—such facts are lovely to read in books. I'd hardly expect Mayor Daley to take part in any farce of mine. He performs in his own farces only. I have, however, visited writers' clubs in Communist countries and can't say that I'm sorry we have no such institutions here. When I was in Addis Abbaba I went to the emperor's zoo. As Selassie was the Lion of Judah, he was perhaps bound to keep a large collection of lions. These poor animals lay in the filth of dim green cages too small for pacing, mere coops. The leonine brown of their eyes had turned blank and yellow, their heads were on their paws, and they were sighing. Bad as things are here, they are not so bad as in the emperor's zoo or in writers' centers behind the Iron Curtain.

Q: Not so bad is not the same as good. What of the disadvantages of your condition?

A: There are moments of sorrow, I admit. George Sand wrote to Flaubert, in a collection of letters I looked into the other day, that she hoped he would bring his copy of her latest book on his next visit. "Put in it all the criticisms which occur to you," she said. "That will be very good for me. People ought to do that for each other, as Balzac and I used to do. That doesn't make one person alter the other; quite the contrary, for in general one gets more determined in one's *moi*, one completes it, explains it better, entirely develops it, and that is why friendship is good, even in literature, where the first condition of any worth is to be one's self." How nice it would be to hear this from a writer. But no such letters arrive. Friendships and a common purpose belong to a nineteenth-century French dream world. The physicist Heisenberg in a recent article in *Encounter* speaks of the kindly and even brotherly collaboration among scientists of the generation of Einstein and Bohr. Their letters to one another were quoted in seminars and discussed by the entire scientific community. Heisenberg believes that in the musical world something of the same spirit appeared in the eighteenth century. Haydn's relations with Mozart were of this generous, affectionate kind. But when large creative opportunities are lacking, there is no generosity visible. Heisenberg says nothing about the malice and hostility of less lucky times. Writers today seldom wish other writers well. Critics use strength gathered from the past to pummel the present. Edmund Wilson wouldn't read his contemporaries at all. He stopped with Eliot and Hemingway. The rest he dismissed. This lack of good will, to put it at its mildest, was much admired. That fact speaks for itself. Curious about Canadians, Indians, Haitians, Russians, studying Marxism and the Dead Sea scrolls, he was the Protestant majority's big literary figure. I have sometimes thought that he was challenged by Marxism or Modernism in the same way that I have seen the descendants of Orthodox Jews challenged by oysters. Historical progress demands that our revulsions be overcome. A man like Wilson might have done much to strengthen literary culture, but he dismissed all that, he would have nothing to do with it. For temperamental reasons. Or Protestant-majority reasons. Or perhaps the Heisenberg principle applies: men are generous when there are creative opportunities, but when such opportunities dwindle, they are ... something else. But it would have made little difference. At this moment in human evolution, so miraculous, atrocious, glorious, and hellish, the firmly established literary cultures of France and England, Italy and Germany, can originate nothing. They look to us, to the "disadvantaged" Americans, and to the Russians. From America have come a number of great irrepressible solitaries like Poe or Melville or Whitman—alcoholics, obscure government employees. In busy America there was no Weimar, there were no cultivated princes. There were only these obstinate geniuses writing. Why? For whom? There is the real *acte gratuit* for you. Unthanked, these writers augmented life marvelously. They did not emerge from a literary culture, nor did they create any such thing. Irrepressible individuals of a similar type have lately begun to show themselves in Russia. There Stalinism utterly destroyed a thriving literary culture and replaced it with a horrible bureaucracy. But in spite of this, and in spite of forced labor and murder, the feeling for what is true and just has not been put out. I don't see, in short, why we should continue to dream of what we have never had. To have it would not help us. Perhaps if we were to purge ourselves of nostalgia and stopped longing for a literary world, we would see a fresh opportunity to extend the imagination and resume imaginative contact with nature and society.

Q: Other people, scholars and scientists, know a great deal about nature and society. More than you know.

A: True. And I suppose I sound like a fool; but I nevertheless object that their knowledge is defective—something is lacking. That something is poetry. Huizinga, the Dutch historian, in his recently published book on America says that the learned Americans he met in the twenties could speak fluently and stimulatingly; but he adds,

> More than once I could not recognize in what he wrote the living man who had held my interest. Frequently repeated experience makes me hold the view that my personal reaction to American scholarly prose must still rest upon the qualities of the prose itself. I read it with the greatest difficulty; I have no sense of contact with it and cannot keep my attention fixed on it. It is for me as if I had to do with a deviant system of expression in which the concepts are not equivalent to mine, or are arranged differently. [2]

The system has become more deviant during the past fifty years. I want information, and I know that certain highly trained and intelligent people have it—economists, sociologists, lawyers, historians, natural scientists. But I read them with the greatest difficulty, exasperated, tormented, despairing. And I say to myself, "These writers are part of the educated public, your readers. You make your best efforts for them, these unpoetic or anti-poetic people. You've forgotten Ortega's philistine professional, the educated Mass-Man ... et cetera." But none of this matters. Philistine intellectuals don't make you stop writing. Writing is your *acte gratuit*. Besides, those you address are *there*. If you exist, then they exist. You can be more certain of their existence than of your own.

Q: But whether or not a literary culture exists ...

A: Excuse me for interrupting, but it occurs to me that Tolstoi would probably have approved of this and seen new opportunities in it. He had no use for literary culture and detested professionalism in the arts.

Q: But should writers make their peace with the academic ivory tower?

A: In his essay "Bethink Yourselves," Tolstoi advises each man to begin at the point at which he finds himself. Better such towers than the cellar alternatives some writers choose. Besides, the university is no more an ivory tower than *Time* magazine, with its strangely artificial approach to the world, its remote-making managerial arrangements. A writer is offered more money, bigger pensions, richer security plans, by Luce enterprises than by any university. The ivory tower is one of those platitudes that haunt the uneasy minds of writers. Since we have none of the advantages of a literary world, we may as well free ourselves from its banalities. Spiritual independence requires that we bethink ourselves. The university is as good a place for such thinking as any other. But while we think hard about the next step, we should avoid becoming academics. Teachers, yes. Some are even moved to become scholars. The great danger for writers in the university is the academic danger.

Q: Can you conveniently give a brief definition of "academic"?

A: I limit myself arbitrarily to a professorial type to be found in the humanities. Owen Barfield refers in one of his books to "the everlasting professional device for substituting a plethora of *talk*" about what matters for—what actually matters.[3] He is sick of it, he says. Many of us are sick of it.

A World Too Much with Us

Wordsworth in 1807 warned that the world was too much with us, that getting and spending we laid waste our powers, that we were giving our hearts away, and that we saw less and less in the external world, in nature, that the heart could respond to.

In our modern jargon we call this "alienation." That was the word by which Marx described the condition of the common man under capitalism, alienated in his work. But for Marx, as Harold Rosenberg has pointed out,

> it is the factory worker, the businessman, the professional who is alienated in his work through being hurled into the fetish-world of the market. The artist is the only figure in this society who is able not to be alienated, because he works directly with the materials of his own experience and transforms them. Marx therefore conceives the artist as the model man of the future. But when critics influenced by Marxist terminology talk of alienation they mean something directly contrary to Marx's philosophical and revolutionary conception. They mean not the tragic separation of the human individual from himself, but the failure of certain sensitive spirits (themselves) to participate emotionally and intellectually in the fictions and conventions of mass culture. And this removal from popular hallucination and inertia they conceive as a form of pathos. Nothing could be more vulgar in the literal meaning of the word than whining about separation from the mass. That being oneself and not others should be deplored as a condition of misery is the most unambiguous sign of the triumph in the indi-

vidual of the ideology of mass culture over spiritual independence. It is a renunciation of everything that has been gained
during the past centuries through the liberation of mankind
from the authoritarian community.[4]

Thus Rosenberg. And why do I associate him with Wordsworth?
Simply because we have now a class of people who cannot bear that
the world should not be more with them. Incidentally, the amusing
title of Mr. Rosenberg's essay is "The Herd of Independent Minds."

I have two more quotations to offer. The first is from a recent
statement by Soviet President Nikolai Podgorny. He warns Russian
writers that any deviation from the principles of Socialist Realism is
inadmissible, and he says, "At a time when ideological struggle
between socialism and capitalism is becoming sharper, our art is
called upon to constantly raise its ideological arsenal, its irrecon-
cilability to manifestations of alien views, to combine the assertion
of the Soviet way of life with the deflation of apolitical consumer
psychology."

Since Mr. Podgorny speaks of "our art," I shall claim the same
privilege. In the West *our* art is far from apolitical, if you allow me
to give the word politics my own definition. When I say "political," I
mean that the world is very much with us. The world is more
populous, more penetrating, more problematical, more menacing
than it was in 1807. We can no longer think of it in contrast to
Nature as Wordsworth did. This is an all made, rather than a
naturally created, world—a world of artifacts, products of the mind.
This world lives so much in us and upon us, so greatly affects our
thoughts and our souls, that I can't help thinking of it as having
a political character. "Either too much is happening too quickly, or
it is simply much more visible and audible than it was in earlier
centuries. Society has become more alive," writes Edward Shils.
"The populace [Professor Shils is speaking of the West] has become
more demanding of services, benefits, attention and a share of
authority. This adds to the visibility and audibility ... The exhilara-
tion, titillation and agitation have become a continuing feature of
our societies."[5] I am inclined to go beyond this. We are in a state of
radical distraction; we are often in a frenzy. When Baudelaire spoke
of a *frénésie journalière,* he was, like Wordsworth and his all-too-
present world, describing the condition in its earlier states. The
frenzy has accelerated unbearably in our time. We have been, as it
were, appropriated mind and soul by our history. We are often
cautioned not to exaggerate, not to see our own as the worst or most

trying of historical periods. Every generation has assailed itself in
this way and cried out against its pains and burdens. But things have
happened in the twentieth century for which words like war,
revolution, even holocaust, are plainly inadequate. Without exaggeration we can speak of the history of this century of ours as an
unbroken series of crises. Not everyone, of course, responds to crisis
with the same intensity, and some of us are more convulsed by
events than others. Some take it with existentialist anguish and feel
obliged, they say, to suffer through it as nakedly and acutely as
possible. Others are more tough-minded or better armored or simply
disinclined to give up their lives to an interpretation of history—or to
surrender their imaginations, since historical interpretations of this
sort deprive the imagination of its ability to make independent
judgments. But I don't see how we can be blind to the political
character of our so-called consumer societies. Each of us stands in
the middle of things, exposed to the great public noise. This is not
the materialism against which Wordsworth warned us. It goes much
much deeper. All minds are preoccupied with terror, crime, the
instability of cities, the future of nations, crumbling empires,
foundering currencies, the poisoning of nature, the ultimate
weapons. To recite the list is itself unsettling. The late John
Berryman once told me that T. S. Eliot could no longer read the
daily paper. "It was too *exciting,*" he said. A poet is of course more
likely to be unbearably excited, in his tender-mindedness, than a
Kansas manufacturer or a Harvard economist. In any case, it is
business and economics that most people are thinking about. Their
minds are turned toward social problems. They are not thinking
much of the time about painting or narrative poetry or Platonism or
tragedy. They are far too extensively politicized for that. I am not
sure that I want to deplore this and complain, Victorian style, of the
gross insensitivity, even of intellectuals, to art. I simply note, as one
who has lived among serious people and knows something about
American intellectuals, that they can't be said to take literature very
seriously. It's simply not important to them. It is not a power in life.
Power lies in science, technology, government, business, in institutions, politics, the mass media, the life of nations. It is not in novels
and poems. Few people, very few, will be considering, as Henry
James did, that art gives meaning to existence or will be wondering
whether they can afford to neglect the faith of Joseph Conrad. He
believed that to understand a human event, to see the color of
experience, to grasp it morally, to feel its subtleties we must have

novels—the temperament of a reader must immerse itself in that of a writer. Not even novelists and poets now share this faith. Men like Osip Mandelstam, who believed that there were in Russia only two real powers, the power of Stalin and the power of the truth manifesting itself in poetry, are very rare indeed. The artist must evidently find in his own spirit the strength to resist the principal alienating power of our time, and this alienating power comes, not from the factory or "the fetish world of the market," but from politics. Marx's "mode! man of the future" apparently appeared prematurely in Russia.

The man whom I wish to contrast with Podgorny is Goethe. His view of the writer's social duty is very different. He said in 1830, "I have never bothered to ask in what way I was useful to society as a whole. I contented myself with what I recognized as good or true. That has certainly been useful in a wide circle, but that was not the aim."

Nations and societies torn by conflict, enduring famine, beset by deadly enemies, fighting to survive, may not feel kindly toward Olympian, contemplative Goethe. Russia during its civil war, and again when Hitler invaded it, was such a nation. That, however, was thirty-five years ago. But we are all familiar with the tycoon who weeps about his poor childhood and justifies his vices and villainies by telling us how underprivileged he was. Israel is at this moment a country in great peril, but it refrains from ordering writers to enter the struggle. It does not deprive them of the right to make the Goethean choice. The creators and rulers of prison states, dictators and oligarchs, terrorists and their intellectual strategists, the cruelest, most deformed part of our species, force politics upon us and then tell us what "our art" is called upon to do.

In the privileged democracies we find people who force politics upon themselves. I think, for instance, of a Jean-Paul Sartre, who expresses his commitment to justice by demanding "action," i.e., terror and murder. He tells us in his introduction to Franz Fanon's *The Damned* that the Third World finds manhood by its burning ever-present hatred and its desire to kill us. Us? By us he means guilty and hateful Europe, and "that super-European monstrosity, North America." Sartre explains,

> The native cures himself of colonial neurosis by thrusting out the settler through force of arms. When his rage boils over, he rediscovers his lost innocence, and he comes to know himself in

that he creates himself.... Once begun, it is a war that gives no quarter. You may fear or be feared, that is to say, to abandon yourself to the dissociations of a sham existence or conquer your birthright of unity. When the peasant takes a gun in his hands, the old myths grow dim and the prohibitions are one by one forgotten. The rebel's weapon is the proof of his manhood. For in the first days of the revolt you must kill: to shoot down a European is to kill two birds with one stone, to destroy an oppressor and the man he oppresses at the same time. There remain a dead man and a free man; the survivor, for the first time, feels a national soil under his foot.

Sartre reminds us not altogether unjustly of our "ideology of lies," our "striptease of humanism," and of "the fat pale narcissism of Europe." All that is fair enough. But can we take him seriously when he insists that the oppressed must redeem themselves by violence? I have already suggested that the imagination is being given up by writers. Embracing causes, they have contracted all kinds of political, sexual, ideological diseases; their teeth chatter and their brains are filled with feverish fantasies of purgation and liberation by murder.

Suppose that Sartre had written a novel about the damned. He is not a good novelist, but the art itself would have obliged him to deal with real, or approximately real, human beings, not the zombies of a pamphleteer. Suppose the white imperialist killed in a revolt had been a real person. Would Sartre then have been able to show the slave who had butchered his master redeemed by violence? Would it be certain that he was at last a free man? I strongly suspect that the banality of this would have sickened the author of *La Nausée.* War certainly filled Tolstoi with fury, but everything in *War and Peace* is humanly tested in full detail, page by page. The novel is for Tolstoi a method of dealing justly. He subjects his own beliefs and passions to the imaginative test and accepts the verdict of an artistic method. His novel shows human beings rooted in reality, and it shows that their need for truth is a vital need, like the need to breathe. Swift's Platonist horses in *Gulliver's Travels* spoke of a falsehood as the thing that is not. By truth I mean simply what is. "Truth, Clearness, and Beauty naturally are public matters," writes Wyndham Lewis. "Truth or Beauty are as much public concerns as the water supply." The imagination I take to be indispensable to truth, so defined. *It* is the prior necessity, not the desire or the duty to perform a liberating action. Sartre declares that in the eighteenth century a work of the mind was "doubly an act, since it produced ideas which were to lead to social upheavals and since it exposed its author to danger. And this act, whatever the book we may be considering, was always defined in the same way: it was a *liberator*. And doubtless in the seventeenth century, too, literature had a liberating function."[6]

It is not inconceivable that a man might find freedom and identity by killing his oppressor. But as a Chicagoan, I am rather skeptical about this. Murderers are not improved by murdering. Unchecked, they murder more and become more brutish. Perhaps fertilizers and modern methods of agriculture would benefit the peasantry of a famished world more than the melodrama of rebirth through bloodshed. It may do more for manhood to feed one's hungry children than to make corpses.

It is true that the writer no longer holds the important position he held in the eighteenth and nineteenth centuries. He has lost out. He is not at the center of things. The bullying idea that he has a social responsibility, that he must cause upheavals, and that in the service of justice he must thrust himself into danger is the result of a certain sense of diminished importance and of a boyish nostalgia for eighteenth-century roles. A work of art has many other ways to attain social meaning. The writer whose imagination is passionately moved by political questions and who follows his deepest convictions will write political novels worth reading. But the ideological package, complete with historical interpretations, has no value. I have the greatest admiration for the courage of writers who, having had politics thrust upon them by the ruling brutes of their respective countries, honorably stood their ground. I have great sympathy for them as well. They had no choice but to write as oppositionists. From their side, looking at us in the West, they must be struck by our innocence, our apparent ignorance of the main facts, our self-indulgent playing about with ideological toys, our reckless rocking of the boat. They must often wonder as well at the dull, refractory minds, the sleepiness of many of us. For one part of mankind is in prison; another is starving to death; and those of us who are free and fed are not awake. What will it take to rouse us?

I said earlier that we live in a state of distraction, even of frenzy, and I called this unavoidable immersion in the life of society political. I said also that intellectuals in America do not really take literature seriously but are professionally preoccupied with various scientific, technological, or social questions. They are told at their universities that art is very important and are quite willing to believe it, they are prepared to accept and even to respect those who are described (quite often by themselves alone) as artists. But that is as far as it goes.

Experts know certain things well. What sort of knowledge have writers got? By expert standards they are entirely ignorant. But expertise itself produces ignorance. How scientific can the world picture of an expert be? The deeper his specialization, the more he is obliged to save the appearances. To express his faith in scientific method he supplies what is lacking from a stock of collective fictions about Nature or the history of Nature. As for the rest of us, the so-called educated public, the appropriate collective representations have been pointed out to us, and we have stocked our heads with pictures from introductory physics, astronomy, and biology courses. We do not, of course, see what is there but rather what we have been directed or trained to see. No individual penetration of the phenomena can occur in this way. Two centuries ago the early Romantic poets assumed that their minds were free, that they could know the good, that they could independently interpret and judge the entire creation; but those who still believe that the imagination has such powers to penetrate and to know keep their belief to themselves. As we now understand knowledge, does imagination *know* anything? At the moment the educated world does not think so. But things have become dreary and humankind tired of itself because the collective fictions of alleged knowledge are used up. We now bore ourselves by what we think we know. Either life has already given up its deepest secrets to our rational penetration and become tedious, or we have developed a tedious sort of rationality by ruling that certain kinds of knowledge are illegitimate. I am inclined to argue that the tedious rationality of our educated heads is a great breeder of boredom and of other miseries. Scientists of the rank of Einstein had no more to do with this tedious sort of rationality than a Matisse or a Stravinsky. But it was not Einstein who taught the college courses and wrote the textbooks. He did not beget the head-culture I refer to. This head-culture inordinately respects the collective powers of mind and the technical developments that have produced the most visible achievements of this civilization; it takes little stock in the imagination or in individual talent. It greatly esteems action. It seems to believe that artists should be harnessed to the social system as intellectual workers.

The Western world does not compel the writer to be an intellectual worker or functionary. But, feeling no power in the imagination and needing to attach himself to power, under innumerable social pressures and politicized by crisis, the writer begins to think he too must be an activist and exert influence. He must do something, make himself available, be heard in just causes. We are, however, in a position to review the achievements of writers in politics. These are not especially breathtaking. The Tolstois, the Zolas—yes, those were great. But what of the Célines, the Ezra Pounds, the Louis Aragons, the hundreds who supported Stalinism: And what, after all, can be said for the view that it is the writer's duty to cause social upheavals? How many of these upheavals have not brought to birth a police state? And if one yearns to live dangerously, is it not as dangerous to persist in the truth as to rush to the barricades? But then it is always more agreeable to play the role of a writer than to be a writer. A writer's life is solitary, often bitter. How pleasant it is to come out of one's room, to fly about the world, make speeches, and cut a swath.

For a very long time the world found the wonderful in tales and poems, in paintings and in musical performances. Now the wonderful is found in miraculous technology, in modern surgery, in jet propulsion, in computers, in television, and in lunar expeditions. I am not sure that what the public admires most in these achievements is the miraculous. It admires the power of instruments and procedures, not the thought that underlies them. It is certain, however, that literature cannot compete with wonderful technology. Writers, trying to keep the attention of the public, have turned to methods of shock, to obscenity and supersensationalism, adding their clamor to the great noise now threatening the sanity of civilized nations.

But isn't there a branch of the wonderful into which wonderful technology cannot lead us? If there is, how shall we know it? Why, we shall recognize it at once by its power to liberate us from the tyranny of noise and distraction. Since 1914, in all spheres of life, crisis has ruled over us, survival anxiety has become permanent with us, and public unrest has been set into our souls. To be free from this would indeed be wonderful. It would mean nothing less than the restoration or recreation of culture. Indispensable to such a restoration is the recovery of significant space by the individual, the reestablishment of a region about every person through which events must make their approach, a space in which they can be received on decent terms, intelligently, comprehensively, and contemplatively.

At a time when we are wildly distracted and asking ourselves what will happen when the end will come, how long we can bear it, why we should bear it, these notions of culture and significant space may seem hopelessly naive. But for art and literature there is no choice. If there is no significant space, there is no judgment, no freedom, and we determine nothing for ourselves individually. The destruction of significant space, the destruction of the individual—for that is what it amounts to—leaves us helplessly in the public sphere. Then to say that the world is too much with us is meaningless, for there is no longer any us. The world is everything. But it is apparently in the nature of the creature to resist the world's triumph. It is from this resistance that we infer truth to be one of his vital needs. And he has many ways of knowing the truth. If not all of these ways can be certified by our present methods, so much the worse for those present methods of certification.

The German philosopher Joseph Pieper speaks in one of his essays ("Leisure, the Basis of Culture") of a purely receptive attitude of mind in which we become aware of immaterial reality. "Is there," asks Pieper, "such a thing as intellectual contemplation ... ? ... in antiquity the answer given was always yes; in modern philosophy, for the most part, the answer is no."

According to Kant, Pieper continues, knowledge is exclusively discursive, the opposite of receptive and contemplative. To Kant knowledge was an activity. Any other claim to know was not genuine because it involved no work. In Pieper's own words, "The Greeks— Aristotle no less than Plato—as well as the great medieval thinkers, held that not only physical, sensuous perception but equally man's spiritual and intellectual knowledge included an element of pure receptive contemplation or, as Heraclitus says, of listening to the 'essence of things.' " Am I proposing, then, that we should take refuge from crisis and noise in a contemplative life? Such a thing is unthinkable. I am saying, rather, that there is a mode of knowledge different from the ruling mode and that this other mode is continually operative: the imagination assumes that things will deliver something of their essence to the mind that has prepared itself and that knows how to listen. I am saying also that full immersion in the great noise will kill us. Perpetual crisis will tear our souls from us. Indeed, this tearing sensation is experienced daily by many people. What can art and poetry do with this great threat to Life? Has the crisis grown too vast? Is it now unmanageable? Only the imagination, by its acts, can answer such questions.

Just now writers are asking themselves how they can be interesting and why they should be taken seriously. Interest follows power, and they do not appear to command the sort of power that is now valued by most of mankind—the power of states or institutions, the power of money or resources, the power of politics, of science and technology, the power that once belonged to religion, the power of ideas, et cetera. What can make a writer truly interesting is an inadmissible resource, something we all hesitate to mention though we all know it intimately—the soul. I don't know what else can possibly obtain and hold the attention of the modern reader, who has already become peculiarly difficult to reach. Granted that his tolerance level is low. Bad and boring novels have made him impatient. But he tends to resist all literary influences, especially if he is, or considers himself to be, an intellectual.

Coming from me, this may sound a bit odd, for I am thought in America to be something of a highbrow. But it should be noted that the character of the public has changed, that it has become more intellectual, that writers themselves have more intellectual interests and have become as concerned to analyze, to investigate problems, or to consider ideological questions as to tell stories. The attitude of intellectuals toward literature has become a "serious" one (the quotation marks are heavy). They see in novels, poems, or plays a creative contribution, often unconsciously made, to the study of society or psychology or religion. The plots of Dickens are psychoanalytically investigated, *Moby-Dick* supplies Marxists with material for the study of the factory system. Books are strongly shaken to see what usable things will fall out of them to strengthen a theory or support some system of ideas. The poet becomes a sort of truffle hound who brings marvelous delicacies from the forest. The writer himself begins to accept this truffle-hound role, acknowledging the superior value, the greater dignity, of ideas and explanations over fancy, play, verve—over imagination. The intellectual makes discourse—a plethora of talk. The novelist and even the painter and musician now imitate him and before long become themselves intellectual workers, discourse makers, serious persons, and even functionaries. Obsessive or even monomaniacal professionals do not make wonderful readers. The world is very much with them, and their hearts are difficult to reach. One might even call it a political feat to reach their hearts, to penetrate their preoccupied minds and interest them in a story.

The general view now seems to be that the writer's true province is the unconscious. It is from the unconscious that he brings in his truffles. No one can doubt the existence of the unconscious. It is there, all right. The question is what it contains. Is it only the seat of animal nature, of instinct, the libidinal forces, or does it also contain elements of higher life? Does the human need for truth, for instance, also have roots in the unconscious? Why, since the unconscious is by definition what we do not know, should we not expect to find in it traces of the soul as well as of aggression? In any case, the unconscious is today the sole source of impulse and freedom that one branch of science has reserved for art.

What I am saying is that the accounts of human existence given by the modern intelligence are very shallow by comparison with those that the imagination is capable of giving, and that we should by no means agree to limit imagination by committing ourselves to the formulas of modern intelligence but should continue as individuals to make free individual judgments.

Wordsworth warned that we laid waste our powers by getting and spending. It is more serious than that now. Worse than getting and spending, modern distraction, worldwide irrationality, and madness threaten existence itself. We may not make it. Under the circumstances, I have no advice to offer other writers. I can only say, speaking for myself, that the Heraclitean listening to the essence of things becomes more and more important.

**Priscilla P. Clark
and Terry Nichols Clark**

9 Patrons, Publishers, and Prizes: The Writer's Estate in France

Creative writers have long given France a special reputation. The notion that Paris is somehow more congenial to writers than other cities has been perpetuated over several centuries in a multitude of novels, memoirs, biographies, and correspondence. But if French writers might understandably agree with Molière that "hors de Paris il n'y a point de salut," what explains the similar attraction for foreigners, from Horace Walpole, Heine, and Turgenev through Joyce, Borges, Richard Wright, and Beckett? Just what is distinctive about the writer's estate in France?[1] There have been remarkably few serious attempts at answers. An answer must surely begin with the importance of Paris as the preeminent center—to use Edward Shils's term—of French society. From this geographic and demographic concentration, much else follows. The proximity of writers to social and political elites, to leading actors in the mass media, to critics, publishers, and booksellers, offers possibilities not present in most other countries but still does not say what is distinctive about writers.

Consider the most simple (and commonly offered) explanation: the writer in France is more "respected" than elsewhere.[2] This alleged respect might plausibly follow from the concentration of writers in Paris, along with other elites. To test this interpretation, we replicated in France a study of occupational prestige already

It is a pleasure to acknowledge the assistance accorded P. Clark by the National Endowment for the Humanities and by the Research Board of the University of Illinois at Chicago Circle. Thanks are also due Lucie Yassa for research assistance.

197

widely used in other countries. While some results distinguished the
French population, the ranking of "author" did not figure among
them; indeed, that ranking was virtually identical in France and the
United States—a country often thought of as particularly inhos-
pitable to the literary spirit.[3]

Is, then, the French public more cultured than others, with avid
readers who assure writers of royalties, which in turn assure them a
privileged position?[4] The available evidence is mixed, but there is
certainly not unqualified support for this second interpretation.[5]

Might then French writers be more generously supported than
their fellows in other countries? Do prizes, sinecures, and *bourses* of
every sort fill their coffers and raise their self-esteem?[6] The practice
of sending French men of letters (among others) on lecture tours
abroad—on "missions"—as envoys of the ministry of education or
the ministry of foreign affairs continues the tradition of cultural politics dating from the Renaissance. Perhaps the writers so deployed
become highly visible and thus perpetuate this image abroad?
Depending on the definition of "culture" and "writer," this third
interpretation is variously supported. The admittedly sporadic and
uneven evidence does not by any means suggest that French support
for writers is dramatically superior to American support.[7] It is true
that the data we present are recent, and the situation in earlier years
may well have been different.

Since these various interpretations, which initially appeared
plausible enough, were seen, on closer inspection, to have only
negligible support, we looked elsewhere for the distinctive elements
of the writer's estate in France. What we found was four basic
patterns of support: traditional support, especially traditional patronage; the market; institutionalized patronage; and professional
association. Each of these developed in a specific historical context,
although no one source ever fully supported all writers at any given
time. And while no one of these sources of support is unique to
France, the distinctive combination of all four has created a
structure of support that is characteristically French.

Traditional support includes, first, *traditional patronage*, which
involves donations from a patron to a writer. Patrons may be distant
figures, friends, parents, or even a spouse, so that traditional
patronage shades into *self-support*, wherein the writer supports
himself from activities other than writing. Before the nineteenth

century, French writers more often than not came from comfortable or even affluent circumstances and reasonably elevated social origins. For this reason, many, from La Rochefoucauld to Montesquieu and Voltaire, from Chateaubriand to Flaubert and Proust, never expected significant material return from their literary labors.[8]

The *market* could and sometimes did provide dramatic support for writers, but the logic of commerce came into equally dramatic conflict with writers' traditional elitist outlook, a view reinforced by centuries of patronage. The logic of the market—which rewards the entrepreneur who optimally adapts a product to the demands of consumers—was accepted by some French writers and vociferously resisted by others. In France as elsewhere the market has continued to grow. In France, however, more than in many countries, the working of the market is complemented by the other basic supports.

The third type of support is *institutionalized patronage*, support given not by an individual, as in traditional patronage, but by or through an official body of some sort. While the French government dispenses patronage through a number of sources, clearly the leading institution, certainly the one with the longest tradition and the greatest resonance in the world of letters, is the Académie française. By investing the forty Immortals with responsibility over the French language, by providing regular stipends to members and irregular funds to others, by dispensing prizes for works dealing with a broad spectrum of subjects, and by rewarding virtuous deeds as well as literary excellence, the Académie française itself occupies, and has created for literature, a special place in French culture. However, the Académie française, like the market, has been resisted by writers jealous of their independence.

Professional association is the fourth type of support. For writers, the ideology of art for art's sake and the development of associations like the Société des Gens de Lettres and especially the Académie Goncourt illustrate tendencies toward professionalization—but only tendencies; for if these organizations provide stipends and prizes, and if, more generally, they articulate the concerns of many writers, their efforts still fall considerably short of ideal-typical professionalization.[9]

Each of these sources of support both complements and tempers the effect of the others. The presence of all four gives the writer more autonomy in France than in countries where fewer options exist, and it is the interaction of all four that characterizes—and, in characterizing, distinguishes—the writer's estate in France.

Traditional Support

Traditional support consists either of *self-support* or the socially more complex *traditional patronage*. So widespread are the ideologies of romanticism, on the one hand, and of art for art's sake, on the other, and so tenacious is the image of the writer as a marginal man that the virtual absence of such conceptions prior to the early nineteenth century appears somehow incongruous. That patrons and the writers whom they patronized generally shared a cultural style—a congruence which seems so anomalous to postromantics— was less a function of authoritarian censorship (although such censorship did exist) than of broadly similar social outlooks.

Neither immutable nor a necessity, such harmony between patron and patronized is nevertheless not on the whole surprising, particularly in light of the relatively high social origins of writers. The four leading writers of the seventeenth century—Corneille, Racine, Molière, and Boileau—participated in the social and especially the cultural life of the court; and while such participation was much diminished for the four leading writers of the eighteenth century— Montesquieu, Voltaire, Rousseau, and Diderot (due in part to the displacement of cultural life from the court to the Parisian salons)— still, five of the eight (excepting Racine, Molière, and Rousseau) had independent means at the outset of their careers. If all (except Montesquieu) enjoyed traditional patronage at some point in their careers, patronage was never their sole source of support.[10] The irregularity of disbursement and the variability of subventions (characteristics of traditional patronage which many later writers would not have countenanced) were less noxious when patronage provided only ancillary revenues.

Patronage involved much more than money; for through patronage and the social relations it implied, writers participated in a system of traditional authority in which, as Max Weber has pointed out, the spontaneous desire of the patron was the very foundation of legitimate authority. Aristocratic writers like the duc de la Rochefoucauld or the baron de Montesquieu were born into upper-class and court society. Writers lower in status, like Corneille, Racine, Voltaire, and Rousseau, found in patronage not only a certain subsistence but also, and perhaps most importantly, an entry into the social circles of the patron.[11]

Writers frequented the court and Parisian salons in company with other elites—military leaders, landowners, judicial officials. In keeping with the ideal of the *honnête homme*, firmly set against specialization of any sort, many writers were content to write, but not assiduously enough for writing to become anything like an occupation. Writing was one means of participating in an elite social milieu; and, since he wrote for his audience as well as about them, the man of letters did not experience the constraints imposed by an unknown public. Nor, for this same reason, was there anything like the overt conflict with the public that embittered so many writers in the nineteenth century and envenomed so much of their writing.

Acceptance of patronage signaled integration into an elite and acceptance of the style of life associated with that elite. Certain writers who could have assured themselves a minimal, even a comfortable, living on their own (whether through self-support or the market) nevertheless readily accepted royal and other largesse both to signal their membership in the elite milieu and to keep up with its standard of living.

If writers thus gained entry into upper-class circles, or *le monde*, what benefits accrued to the literary patron? Legitimation of social status and authority have long been basic functions of patronage of the arts. The almost legendary Maecenas (*mécène* in French refers specifically to a patron of the arts, and *le mécénat* is the usual term for "patronage") dispensed patronage for the Emperor Augustus, who sought to legitimate and stabilize his rule. Virgil's *Aeneid* provided the Roman Empire and the emperor with a history and a tradition to justify the present—and to justify as well the patronage received.

Legitimation of authority was also a primary concern of Louis XIV, the monarch whose name is virtually synonymous with patron of the arts. His childhood had been marked by turbulent civil strife and contested monarchical authority. By making the grandeur of Versailles integral to the authority of the regime, by keeping courtiers involved in a continual round of activity, the king attracted potentially disruptive malcontents and disarmed them in advance. Occupied by the cultural activities of Versailles or engaged in military service abroad, they had little time and less inclination to foment rebellion in the provinces or otherwise to challenge monarchical authority, especially in view of the direct subsidies from the king, which attached many aristocrats to the monarchy in much the same way as patronage attached the writer.[12] In this context writers performed a significant political role alongside the architects, builders, painters, and decorators, the composers and performers of ballets and operas. With patronage from Louis, they all helped, as he would have said, to "couronner sa gloire."

Patronage placed the recipient in the patron's debt and identified the patron with the work of art. In this respect the writer was at a distinct disadvantage, for, unlike painters and sculptors (but like musical composers and scientists), writers create reasonably public goods in the technical sense of the term.[13] A painting can be sold to a single individual, and the painter supported thereby; a novel, once printed, becomes more or less widely available, so that potential patrons, while possibly attracted by fulsome dedications, have less exclusive claim to a work of literature than to a painting or sculpture. Literary works are, then, perfectly suited to mass distribution and the market.

Patronage obviously altered the social and hence the political meaning of a writer's work. Engagement in activities acceptable to the king left the writer less time for other activities. At the same time, the writer in receipt of patronage obligated himself to the king—and, in principle, more than an artist who created a more private good. This obligation could be made good by deference, in person as well as in writing.[14] Since patronage is most efficaciously reciprocated with works of literature that can be consumed in the public ritual of stage performance, traditional patrons have preferred plays and operas—performed, hence consumed, in public—over novels and poetry, which are consumed in private.

The identification of patronage of the arts as an elite activity, its prestige further heightened by the prestige of Louis XIV, inspired royalty great and small, in Russia, Prussia, Poland, and elsewhere, to dispense patronage, particularly to things French.[15] The identification of French culture and the French language with civilization itself gave the French writer a privileged position even abroad. Voltaire was patronized by Frederick the Great, Diderot by Catherine the Great. Supporting a live, speaking (French of course) *Kulturträger* captured for a peripheral court some of the rays emanating from the Sun King.

Insofar as one of its goals was to affect the cultural content of the work of art and, through that, the orientation of its consumers, the very logic of traditional patronage demanded that the patron maintain the writer in debt. The patron's munificence must not in any way become taken for granted or be accepted as "earned." To avoid routinization, patronage had to flow "spontaneously" or at least irregularly. It is true that Louis XIV in 1663 had Colbert draw up a list of illustrious writers, artists, scholars, and scientists as candidates for royal largesse. To recompense activities which enhanced the realm, Louis provided an initial 77,500 livres, to be allocated annually, in sums ranging from 600 to 3,000 livres, to 98 individuals. This total rose to 110,000 livres in 1669, but it dropped to 49,000 livres in 1676, a year of heavy military engagement. Corneille not so subtly complained of the long lean years in wishing to the king: "Puissent tous vos ans être de quinze mois / Comme vos commis font les nôtres."[16] Moreover, the list was revised annually, and those no longer in favor were unceremoniously deleted (like the aging Corneille in 1674). Others had their stipends increased (Racine's initial 600 livres in 1663 grew to 2,000 by 1680).

Molière offers an instance of the vagaries of patronage all the more significant for his supposedly ideal relationship with his patron. Unlike Corneille, Molière had no independent means and was thus particularly fortunate to receive 3,000 livres for himself and his company from Louis XIV after a single performance in 1660. The next year he received 1,500 livres for himself and the same for his company. In 1663, 1,000 livres came to him from Colbert's list, as well as 2,000 more for a single performance of *L'Impromptu de Versailles*. Then in 1665 the troupe was awarded an annual pension of 6,000 livres and was declared La Troupe du Roi, in which capacity it was granted various monopolies (*privilèges*) for all performances in the Palais Royal theater. In 1669 Louis personally authorized the performance of *Le Tartuffe*, which five years earlier had been interdicted under pressure from the church. Finally, the personal nature of the patronage relationship was evident when Louis stood as godfather to Molière's son, with the king's sister-in-law acting as godmother.

Although Molière can be said to have enjoyed traditional patronage to the full, he certainly did not enjoy it to the end. In 1672, when Molière was still as productive as ever, the king accorded the composer Lully a monopoly on all musical performances, a move which deprived Molière of a staple of his repertory, the *comédie-ballet*, and drastically reduced his income. Such a precipitous fall from grace was not out of the ordinary; when Racine and Boileau pleased the king, he appointed them royal historiographers (1678) and summarily dismissed the previous incumbent.[17]

Because patronage was so personal, not only were the amounts and circumstances irregular, but the forms it took also varied with the whims and the resources of the patron. Outright gifts, pensions, and subsidies were only part of the picture. A writer might benefit from free room and board, as did La Fontaine at Mme de la Sablière's, Corneille with the duc de Guise for a time after 1662, and Voltaire at the court of Frederick the Great. One might receive offices (*charges*) which carried considerable revenue and sometimes carried ennoblement as well. Racine was given nominal ecclesiastical posts (*bénéfices*) as well as the office of Gentilhomme ordinaire de la chambre du roi.[18] A writer might also have his works printed free at the royal press or be guaranteed a sale of a minimum number of copies. Some positions were outright sinecures, but by no means all: La Bruyère served as tutor to the grandson of the Prince de Condé (although after his pupil came of age, La Bruyère remained a member of the household, with quite vaguely defined duties).

Upon their appointment as royal historiographers, Racine and Boileau were ordered forthwith to collect information and document the history of the reign, which they did to the extent of following the king about on his all too frequent military campaigns. Racine's case in particular illustrates the diversion of a talented writer into nonliterary activities uncompelled by economic reasons. Participation in court life and its ethos implied subordination of activities which conflicted with that ethos. For Racine, no doubt, saw the appointment as historiographer as a means to "crown his (own) glory" along with the glory of the king. In any event, he did not write another play for twelve years and then did so only at the behest of Mme de Maintenon, the king's morganatic spouse.

The difficulties inherent in traditional patronage are evident. A relationship satisfactory to both parties depended on a delicate equilibrium of goods exchanged and services rendered. The comment made by Corneille after Richelieu's death might well sum up the situation of many another writer: "Il m'a fait trop de bien pour en dire du mal, / Il m'a fait trop de mal pour en dire du bien."[19]

Not all patrons were affluent aristocrats, but those aristocrats who were patrons set the style for others to imitate. For this reason the Revolution was disastrous for traditional patronage. When the émigré aristocrats returned to France, they were sadder no doubt, wiser perhaps, poorer assuredly. The Restoration government (1815–30) partially compensated many for confiscated property but normally did not restore the property itself; the result was that few émigrés were in a position, or of a humor, to squander their now relatively scarce resources on the arts. Moreover, if those inclined to patronize by tradition no longer had the means to do so, only occasionally did the newly rich develop the habit. What Gabriel Tarde called the laws of imitation could not operate if there was nothing to be imitated.

But if the nineteenth century ended the *ancien régime*, it also saw the extension of the literary market, which in France, as in most other Western countries, was transformed from a minor to the major source of support for writers. In the United States, and to a lesser degree in England, the absence of a strong legacy of traditional patronage has lent the market greater legitimacy than in France,[20] where, with the model of traditional patronage as an ideal—increasingly glorified as it became ever more distant—the market and all it stood for were resisted. Eventually these criticisms of the market, which evolved from a sense of deprivation through patronage lost, prompted the development of various mechanisms which substantially mitigated the workings of the market. Even though traditional patronage in France had become largely immaterial by the nineteenth century, its ideological legacy carried down to the present.

The Market
Success in the market demanded very different talents from those needed for success under a system of traditional patronage; and just as not all writers had been the compleat courtier required by traditional patronage, so, too, many writers in the nineteenth century, especially those imbued with the ideals of romanticism, refused to follow market demands. Still, few could ignore the stupendous potential offered by the market. The smell of success was uncommonly sweet, and a few writers became uncommonly wealthy; but, precisely because the lure was so great, many tried, and many, inevitably, failed—by market criteria.

Nineteenth-century writers were not the first to realize income from the sale (and, in the case of playwrights, the production) of their works; however, prior to its nineteenth-century expansion to meet the demands of a larger public, writers could not, and in any event did not, find in the market a steady or sure source of support. Those writers often cited as proof that a living could be made from the market in the eighteenth century turn out, upon closer inspection, to prove the aleatory nature of the market rather than its viability. This being so, it is not surprising that the writers listed in Table 1 (see Appendix) supplemented their market income considerably. Rousseau took to copying music so as to have an occupation with a steady income; Voltaire was an astute speculator: "J'ai vu tant de gens de lettres pauvres et méprisés que j'ai conclu dès longtemps que je ne devais pas en augmenter le nombre."[21] Lesage and Prévost by and large did earn their livings through writing, and both were poor and constantly in debt. Prévost forged checks and bitterly complained of the "littérature alimentaire," especially journalism, to which necessity reduced him. Yet even he was not entirely without patronage at various times in his very checkered career.[22] Diderot was not poor, but this was in spite of, rather than because of, the market. From 1730 to 1750 Diderot received a total of about 10,000 livres from his father; in the 1760s, his eventual inheritance comprised about 30 per cent of his income. The remainder came primarily from the *Encyclopédie*, both from its sales and from his salary as editor—a basically administrative task. Still dissatisfied, and worried about a dowry for his daughter, Diderot accepted the patronage of Catherine the Great.[23]

If Diderot was a market success, what was the situation for others? The few "professional" writers were likely as not Grub Street hacks whose literary activities shaded into police spying, pornography peddling, and similar unsavory pursuits. They had considerably more in common with Rameau's nephew—made famous by Diderot—than with the high priests of the Enlightenment.[24]

Why was it so difficult to depend on the market in these years? Apart from the small size of the reading public, two factors compounded difficulties for the French writer. First was the ideology of amateurism. Leading writers in the eighteenth century continued to depend heavily on traditional sources of income—patronage and self-support—and their social milieux complemented their economic bases, since both encouraged the sentiment that literature was a "noble" activity (in contrast to painting, for example, which was too artisanal, too close to manual labor).[25] If writing was thought to celebrate in some measure one's own status, one's patron, and one's milieu, it was as inconceivable for a writer actively to seek profit by his labor as for an aristocrat to seek material reward for fencing or hunting.

Such at least were the norms. In fact writers might not be in the least disinterested. Corneille was noted (though reproved) for his commercial attitude ("Corneille est excellent, mais il vend ses ouvrages"), while Boileau took to task those of his fellow writers who violated the code of amateurism and *honnêteté* by making "d'un art divin un métier mercenaire."[26] Haggling was for publishers and other lesser creatures, in theory if not in practice.

Publishers were understandably not loath to exploit this aristocratic amateurism, and their success in this was virtually assured by the legal-commercial arrangements which regulated publishing during the *ancien régime*—arrangements which were extremely disadvantageous to the authors. To publish his work, a writer had to contract with a publisher, and that publisher had to belong to the book guild. Once his manuscript was in the hands of a publisher, the author had no further connection with it. He might receive a fee from the publisher; he also might receive only free copies of the work (Descartes received 200 copies as his sole payment for *Discours de la méthode*). The publisher applied for a *privilège du roi*, which guaranteed him a sales monopoly on the book for one, two, ten, or even fifty years. The publisher alone negotiated censorship permits, set the price, and fought against pirated editions, and he alone could renew the *privilège*.[27]

Here as elsewhere the Revolution wrought changes. The book guild was abolished in 1790, and when the Convention proclaimed the *droits de l'homme* for all citizens, it decreed that authors should have *droits d'auteur*. Henceforth, upon the expiration of a contract with a publisher, the rights to the manuscript reverted to the author, who might then sign a new contract as and with whom he saw fit.[28]

This enhanced legal status put writers in a position to benefit from the growth of the market. The educational changes initiated by the Revolution, the Napoleonic reorganization, and the Third Republic reforms of the schools increased literacy; from under 30 per cent of the French population in the Restoration, it grew to 60 per cent in 1870 and to 95 per cent by 1895. The total French population also expanded: from 27 million at the end of the eighteenth century to 39 million in 1911 and to 50 million in 1970. Technological developments were important, too: the faster and more efficient rotary press, new inks and papers, various networks of lending libraries (*cabinets de lecture*), and the growth of mass journalism. It was this last development—mass journalism—that radically changed the world of literature, especially the novel. In 1828 Emile de Girardin introduced advertising in his newspaper and dropped the sales price. This strategy was soon imitated, with the result that sales of Parisian newspapers rose from 54,000 in 1824 to 70,000 in 1836 and to 200,000 in 1846. By 1870 *Le Petit Journal* alone printed 1,000,000 copies.[29]

The especial beneficiary of these developments was the novelist. The novel was a "new" genre, eminently adaptable to the tastes of a literate and enthusiastic, if not particularly educated, public. Newspapers presented an ideal vehicle of diffusion, and the serial novel was created (again by Girardin) to take advantage of this new market. Advertising kept costs low, while novels attracted the readers whom the advertisers wanted to reach. A short novel by Alexandre Dumas brought *Le Siècle* 100,000 subscribers in three weeks. In 1844, when *Le Constitutionnel* ran Eugène Sue's *Le Juif errant*, circulation rose from 3,000 to 40,000 (aided by a drop in price). [30]

It did not take long for successful writers to realize incomes hitherto undreamed of. By 1831 the still débutant Balzac had a contract of 500 francs per month with the *Revue de Paris* for short stories as yet unwritten; by 1835 he had contracted with a consortium of publishers for a 50,000-franc advance plus 1,500 francs a month or one-half the profits, again for works unwritten. Alexandre Dumas's success was even more prodigious: in a single year he signed one contract with *La Presse* for 64,000 francs and another with *Le Siécle* for 150,000 francs. Eugène Sue was guaranteed 100,000 francs a year for fifteen years in return for his exclusive collaboration during that period with *Le Constitutionnel*. The notoriety of *L'Assommoir* (1877) boosted Zola's royalties to 1,500 francs a month in the year following its publication. [31]

These were more than comfortable incomes. The novelist might become a celebrity and very rich indeed. Some did, many did not; Gérard de Nerval estimated that he earned no more than 1,800 francs a year from all his literary endeavors; Champfleury put his earnings, from criticism as well as short stories, at 3,000 francs a year. Not only were Baudelaire's *Fleurs du mal* (1857) prosecuted for obscenity, but total sales amounted to no more than 250 francs. The prosecution of *Madame Bovary*, on the contrary, stimulated sales; but this did not benefit Flaubert, who had sold the rights to the publisher for five years in return for a paltry 800 francs. [32]

How did writers react to these developments? A handful embraced the challenge of the market. Echoing the ideology of *laisser-faire*, which flourished briefly for a few years in mid-nineteenth-century France, Zola was nothing if not forthright: "Comme il est ... sain d'être seul et libre avec sa poitrine nue au grand soleil! ... la force est tout, dans la bataille des lettres. Malheur aux faibles! Ceux qui tombent ont tort de tomber, et c'est tant pis si on les écrase." [33] For every Zola and Balzac who found the market invigorating, there were many more writers who did not and who remained exceedingly critical. Stendhal went further than most in dedicating his works to "The Happy Few" and predicting (quite correctly) that he would find his public in 1880 or 1930.

The market was resisted for a variety of reasons, among them disdain for commercial undertakings on the part of these mostly bourgeois writers, who styled themselves the new aristocracy, the *aristocratie de l'esprit*. That the market could be resisted, however, was due to the alternatives available. As under the *ancien régime*, families and friends were not infrequently called upon to subsidize writers. Gérard de Nerval squandered a legacy of 30,000 francs and died, a suicide, in poverty (the Société des Gens de Lettres paid for his funeral and burial). Flaubert achieved independence through his inheritance, carefully managed, as Baudelaire's was not. Balzac began his career in a garret, the rent for which was paid by his father, and he ended it in debt to his mother (45,000 francs), to his wife for at least double the 130,000 francs acknowledged, and to various and sundry others. Balzac spent extravagantly and treated with aristocratic disdain all but the most pressing of his creditors (and these he would often avoid by maintaining a secret apartment). Others needed funds to subsidize their publications. Hugo's brother financed the *Odes* (1822), and Hugo himself heavily subsidized the staging of *Hernani* (1830).[34] Proust lived his entire life on his inheritance and paid the publishing costs of the first volumes of *A la recherche du temps perdu*. Self-support clearly enabled some writers to ignore the market.

Traditional patronage in the strict sense, may have withered but it persisted or at least altered other institutions in myriad ways. Publishers adopted certain of the trappings of traditional patronage. Commercial considerations came first, but publishers still often enjoyed injecting a personal, patronal note into their dealings with authors. Dr. Véron, a physician who was also the editor of the *Revue de Paris* and later *Le Constitutionnel*, in the early 1830s took a weekly "course in comparative literature." On his round of personal calls to a dozen or so of "his" leading writers, Véron would consult on manuscripts, offer encouragement, remind them of deadlines, and the like. Buloz, editor and publisher of the important *Revue des Deux Mondes*, made substantial loans to George Sand. Flaubert's publisher, Charpentier, may not have been overly generous; but as Flaubert's personal fortune declined, Charpentier's wife joined with several others in arranging a state subsidy for him.[35]

Many French publishers and journal editors have made special efforts to conduct themselves with at least some disdain for the forces of the market. More than in the United States (or at least at a later date than in the United States) French publishers have firmly adhered to distinctive aesthetic, literary, and ideological outlooks, and even today writers tend to publish one book after the other with "their" publisher (sometimes by contract) rather than shop around. The literary associations of the *Nouvelle Revue Française* were distinctive (and distinguished) enough for Proust to persist (after an initial rejection by Gide) until the *NRF* agreed to publish *A la recherche*. Mame was a leading publisher of Catholic works, and the Editions de Minuit has been a major patron of avant-garde literature, while Laffont is known for its American-style best-sellers.[36]

No detailed material documents the degree to which publishers have or have not seriously respected profit maximization. Scattered evidence suggests that they have not done so by any means, even in the United States.[37] If the forces of the market are mitigated from within, they are also attenuated by other institutions important for literature and the writer's estate in France.

Institutionalized Patronage
The end of the *ancien régime* marked the end of absolute personal power. The king no longer ruled by divine right, and political leaders were increasingly called upon to justify their acts. These postrevolutionary regimes faced the difficulty discussed most pointedly by Max Weber—the problem of routinizing charisma so as to maintain a leadership at once cohesive and legitimate. Two related responses in most of Europe were nationalism and bureaucratization; these combined to produce those elite commissions and committees of one kind and another that are found in many countries but are used with particular effectiveness in France.

In the arts and sciences French nationalism became bureaucratized in the five academies which were founded under Louis XIV and combined in 1795 to form the Institut de France. For writers the most important of these academies is also the one which is most visible to Frenchmen, namely, the Académie française, founded by Richelieu in 1635. Originally an extension of the monarch, latterly of the government (which even today must approve membership),[38] it bestowed something of the national charisma on the forty members, "les Immortels" (from the seal of the Académie, "A l'Immortalité"). From its inception, the Académie has had a core of men of letters, which for a long time was only a core; the

Académie française has always carefully included members from many elites. Among the 500 members from 1635 until 1906 were to be found 3 members of ruling families, 20 dukes, 48 cardinals, archbishops, or bishops (at one point in the eighteenth century 18 of the 40 were members of the clergy), 48 members of the Académies des Sciences (pre- and post-revolutionary), 15 prime ministers, 49 ministers, and 6 marshals.[39]

Members are named for life, meet weekly, and receive a standard annual fee which amounted to 1,500 francs through the nineteenth century and is today 4,500 francs (or about $900). They work in committees and as a whole, determining usage of the French language; in few countries does language have such central meaning for cultural, political, and even economic matters: "La principale fonction de l'Académie sera de travailler ... à donner des règles certaines à notre langue et à la rendre pure et capable de traiter les arts et les sciences" (Statute 24, *Règlements de 1635*). The increasing use of English and the resultant "franglais" in the mid-twentieth century have led the Académie to publish periodic *mises en garde* to censure incorrect expressions and "pour opposer une barrière à la prolifération des mots fabriqués contre le génie de la langue."[40]

However, neither its linguistic duties nor the direct monetary rewards account for "la fièvre verte" (from the green uniform worn by Academicians) or for the repeated candidacies of Balzac or Zola. Each of these writers might earn more in a single month than the annual stipend of an Academician, but they submitted their names two and twenty-four times, respectively.

The Académie française has performed many functions of signal importance for literature. By selecting distinguished writers for membership, it elevated the status of literature as a whole (as Richelieu intended that it should). The fact that it is an association with a general elite membership rather than a specialized literary body made it explicit that the Académie française serves as the guardian of good taste in general, not of aestheticism. Members elected and works honored were and are intended to represent the best of French culture in the broadest sense. Because the Académie draws its members from many elites and is consequently not a uniquely literary body, its influence is broadly cultural. For members—for writers in particular—the Académie française continues a tradition, represents the glory of literature in the broadest sense, and incarnates *l'esprit français*. Few writers, however critical of the Académie française, are immune to its mystique.[41]

This elitism goes far to explain the role of the literary prizes awarded by the Académie française. While the prizes offer no substitute for commercial success, they may offer compensation, of another nature, for lack of such success; for these prizes betoken the valuation of an elite and, by implication, rejection of the votes of the many. The Académie française was a visible, and prestigious, source of support for literature, if not for every man of letters.

Institutionalization eliminated many of the disadvantages of traditional patronage, but it created, at the same time, in the process, an official literature of sorts. The novel long remained an upstart genre, excluded from the Académie. The Bohemian artist, too, was anathema, and the naturalists were never accepted.[42]

"Immortality" was limited to forty men. Others might submit their works in Académie française prize competitions.[43] During the *ancien régime* there was usually a single annual prize (which became 1,500 francs after 1795), awarded in alternate years for poetry and eloquence (the latter consisting of an essay on an announced subject). This original prize was funded personally by some Academicians, then through the official budget. During the nineteenth century, numerous individuals established prizes on divers subjects to be awarded by the Académie. By 1850 the Académie française annually disbursed 20,000 to 25,000 francs in five prizes;[44] by 1895 these had grown to approximately 50,000 francs for 33 prizes. By 1974, 143 literary prizes totaled about $55,000.

Furthermore, at a time when traditional values were increasingly questioned, when new literary aesthetics, like realism and naturalism, were destroying the eternal verities of the classical tradition, such legacies to the Académie française reaffirmed the traditions— reaffirmed the inseparability of the Good, the True, and the Beautiful and their identification with the glory of France—in one of the few institutions to survive the Revolution almost intact. The late nineteenth century saw a great resurgence of perfervid nationalism, in which the Académie française played its part, defending French values along with the language which gave them expression.[45]

The Académie française, then, was the pinnacle of state-provided patronage, but it was only that. Throughout various ministries, libraries, and other governmental institutions one could find writers who had been fortunate enough to find a government sponsor. Under relatively authoritarian leaders, the path to patronage was

clear: the writer had to appeal to the head of state himself, a path
not without pitfalls. Much of Napoleon III's patronage to writers
from his personal funds was never acknowledged, and it proved
something of an embarrassment when he and the Empire were
discredited in 1870. Such was the case for Leconte de Lisle, who
received a secret subsidy of 3,400 francs from Napoleon III as well
as 2,000 francs from his native Ile Bourbon (la Réunion).[46] Many
desperate but politically unknowledgeable writers wrote to all sorts
of officials, pleading poverty and worthiness. Most were rejected,
including Baudelaire, who once applied to the ministry of public
instruction for funds to undertake a "voyage purement artistique."
The more successful had recourse to more complex approaches. The
labyrinthine negotiations leading to Flaubert's securing a sinecure
illustrate both the highly personal nature of the matter and the
complexities involved. The Princesse Mathilde (cousin of the de-
posed Napoleon III, still active in salon society) and Mme Charpentier (wife of Flaubert's publisher) initiated the effort; the Russian
novelist Turgenev saw senators, ministers, and Gambetta, the
premier; Taine and Maupassant became involved; and eventually
Flaubert himself visited the president of the Republic. Flaubert had
steadfastly refused appointment to a post at the Mazarine Library
(for which he would have received 6,000 francs) because any sort of
job was distasteful; but he eventually accepted an entirely honorific
post, also at the Mazarine, which provided 3,000 francs.[47]

Flaubert's negotiations may have been more complex than most,
for he was quite demanding; and indeed, until he was absolutely
hounded by creditors, he was a most reluctant recipient of patronage. Others, less retiring, actively sought posts in one part of the
bureaucracy or another; libraries in particular were congenial to
men of letters. At the end of the *ancien régime* Chamfort was royal
librarian, a post viewed as honorific even then. After 1840 Sainte-
Beuve received 4,000 francs as head of the Mazarine Library;
Musset received 3,000 francs from his appointment as librarian of
the ministry of the interior in 1837; the poet Leconte de Lisle was
appointed sublibrarian at the Comédie française in 1878; and
J. M. Heredia became librarian at the Arsenal Library in 1901.[48]

Institutionalized patronage of writers in nineteenth-century
France was symbolically important for the writer's estate and
significant for a few writers. But patronage was no longer the usual

means of support, as it had been under the *ancien régime*. On the contrary, it had become an unusual and very accessory source of income, gratefully accepted but not expected.

Prizes and Professional Association

The precipitous decline of traditional patronage and the nearly simultaneous extension of the market constituted two prime sources of alienation for French writers. What remained of traditional patronage, in its institutionalized form, exacerbated discontent by favoring some literature and some writers over others. The Académie française had always been associated with established national traditions; in the nineteenth century its literary conservatism became more evident by contrast with the many striking and new views of literature, from literary liberalism (Hugo's definition of romanticism) to the aestheticism of *l'art pour l'art*. The inclination of the Académie, evident in its elections to membership and its awarding of prizes, to single out writers who incarnated established virtues could only create dissatisfaction among writers who conceived it to be their mission to question precisely those verities.

Increasingly in the early nineteenth century, writers celebrated not the nation but the artist, who was typically portrayed in lonely battle against a hostile world. The "marketing" of his work necessarily brought the writer into close contact with this world, in activities associated with *le bourgeois*, loathed creature that he was—with publishers, journalists, and all the intermediaries upon which commercial success depends. The cult of the misunderstood genius, of the romantic artist as Prometheus against the archenemy, *le bourgeois*, was a basic element of an ideology shared by many writers. The yearning to *épater le bourgeois*, the linguistic hermeticism and outrageous bohemian behavior (vide Gautier's notorious pink vest, Gérard de Nerval's insouciant deambulation through Paris with a lobster on a leash), were more than sartorial and behavioral eccentricities; they were attempts to define the artist and art: the singularity, distinctiveness, and unicity of literary creativity. There was more to art than this, but art was also this. The success of these early-nineteenth-century artists in defining a new world outlook may be judged by the extent to which these same themes remain a significant current, or undercurrent, in many parts of the artistic world today.

But if man does not live by bread alone, neither does he subsist on ideology and oddities. Literary affinities needed translation into more substantial terms. Unlike scientists and scholars, who increasingly found support in academies and universities, writers could not bypass the market. They could, however, seek to influence it, and many writers turned to literary criticism in order to do just that. Writers became critics in order to address an audience who, deemed woefully deficient in understanding, might, it was hoped, be influenced or "educated" to the writer's point of view.[49]

When writers turned to criticism (in part, of course, to supplement their incomes), they hoped to reach a broad audience to sell their work and, beyond that, their conceptions of literature. The large-circulation journals offered the perfect medium, and they published most "writers' criticism." Failing acceptance in an established journal, writers occasionally established journals of their own. Victor Hugo and his brother founded *Le Conservateur littéraire* (1819), Balzac started the *Revue de Paris* (1833), Gautier became editor of *L'Artiste* (1856), each in an attempt to publicize a point of view inadequately aired elsewhere or not at all.

Still, no single individual, however energetic, could affect the market very dramatically. Organization was one response to a situation increasingly judged as untenable. The Société des Gens de Lettres was founded in 1838 to further the interests of writers in a number of ways. Beyond its official goal of reinforcing "la fraternité littéraire," the Société engaged in more mundane matters; it sought redress for defamation of individual authors in the press, lobbied for changes in copyright laws, instituted pensions for older members and scholarships for their children, nominated candidates for the Légion d'Honneur, raised subscriptions for statues of authors, and so forth. Some literary prizes were also established, much like those of the Académie française, though they were fewer in number and lesser in prestige.[50]

In general, however, the Société sought neither to affect the basic forces of the market nor to rival the Académie française. Its primary activities were directed more toward alleviating the distress of unsuccessful writers and helping to obtain recognition for writers in general and in particular. After 1848 it received an annual subsidy from the ministry of public instruction and the ministry of the interior. Additional funds came from occasional collections published by the Société, which included a piece from each member, the proceeds of which went to the pension fund (each member being entitled to a pension). Money was also raised by gifts and fund-raising activities, such as lotteries, tombolas, and public readings.

In contrast to the Académie française (in many periods) and most journals, the Société des Gens de Lettres did not seek to advance any distinctive aesthetic; four published works was the sole entrance requirement. Nor did it seek to elevate aesthetics above morality; on the contrary, during the Franco-Prussian War of 1870, the Société donated two cannons for the army. Moreover, members could be expelled for unseemly conduct (as were Jules Vallès and another writer, both in exile for their activity in the Paris Commune). It was a protective, not a professional, association. And by its circumspect action, it did succeed, since it was at least partially responsible for the revision of the copyright laws.[51]

Where the Société des Gens de Lettres aspired to be more than simply a protective association (its monthly dinners were designed to strengthen "la fraternité littéraire"), the Goncourt brothers were more ambitious. Edmond and Jules de Goncourt were prominent naturalist writers whose considerable inherited income enabled them to pursue their artistic goals without regard to either sales or state subventions. Their commitment to literature—conceived of as "professional" writing unhampered by the exigencies of journalism —was such that they bequeathed the whole of their estate to found an academy whose ten members would receive an annual income of 6,000 francs and would partake in a monthly dinner. The members' primary obligation was to award an annual prize of 5,000 francs to an imaginative work in prose, preferably a novel.

Created in deliberate opposition to the Académie française, the Académie Goncourt was to be, or so the gossip ran, "une académie vengeresse et consolatrice."[52] The ideal, then as now, was one of literary professionalism untainted by any extraneous considerations. Edmond de Goncourt's will stipulated that "pour avoir l'honneur de faire partie de la Société, il sera nécessaire d'être homme de lettres, rien qu'homme de lettres, on n'y recevra ni grands seigneurs, ni hommes politiques."[53] Indeed, so negative an example was the Académie française that Académie Goncourt regulations forbade any of its members to belong to the rival organization.

In France, where so much is done under direct government auspices, the need for an "independent" organization to justify itself is far greater than in Britain or the United States. Those of leftist political persuasion might logically contrast the Académie Goncourt with the government, high society, and the Académie française. But a political conservative, Léon Daudet, drew a different distinction between the two academies. Clearly, for him (as for other partisans), the Académie Goncourt awarded its prizes on strictly literary grounds: "car il y a un excellent, un médiocre et un mauvais en littérature, et le critère n'y est pas subjectif ... dans l'attribution de notre prix." By contrast, "A l'Académie française il y a le respect humain, qui fait qu'une oeuvre un peu vive, dans la forme ou le fond, n'a pas de chance d'être couronnée." But, unlike many, Daudet attributed the conservative nature of the Académie française not to its official status but to its penetration by *le monde*—the aristocratic and upper-bourgeois circles which maintained a distinctive style, particularly through their salons, into the 1930s (when Daudet recorded these observations). This *monde*, in Daudet's view, perpetuated a *politesse*, as vapid as it was refined, which stifled creativity: "L'Institut dépersonnalise ... le monde aussi ... le monde ne fait que des salonards, esclaves de conventions changeantes, mais molles et négatives."[54]

The Académie Goncourt made two signal contributions to the French literary scene. First, it sought for the first time to create and support an institution fiercely devoted to the promotion of literature alone. A few wealthy individuals had permitted themselves this luxury in earlier years, and *cénacles* had provided informal forums for literary debates; the Académie Goncourt was unique as an institution with a not inconsiderable financial base. Compared to the Société des Gens de Lettres, the Académie Goncourt was elitist and narrow in scope; it neither lobbied for medals or laws nor dispensed much charity.

The second distinct contribution of the Académie Goncourt was the impact its prize came to have on the market. Apparently, when the Académie Goncourt was founded (1902), the various prizes awarded by the Académie française did not receive much publicity, nor did they seriously affect sales. It took only a few years after the first Prix Goncourt was awarded in 1903 for publishers and writers to become aware of the increase in sales to be expected by a book which won the prize. About 1915, sales of the Prix Goncourt winner were estimated at 8,000 to 10,000 copies, a few thousand over the average; by the mid-1960s, when printings of novels averaged 3,000 to 5,000 copies, a Prix Goncourt book could expect to sell 200,000 to 400,000 copies. Since fewer than one half of 1 per cent of French literary productions sell over 100,000 copies, and only 10 per cent sell over 10,000 copies, the Prix Goncourt, by all accounts, provides a substantial increment. Halo effects are relatively limited; a number of authors have remarked that their subsequent books generally fall back to 10,000–15,000 copies (which is still above average). In the late 1950s only a handful of best-selling serious writers—Aragon, Montherlant, Simone de Beauvoir—could hope for sales over 70,000 without a prize.[55]

As the sales potential of the prize was recognized, publishers understandably did all they could to obtain recognition for their books. In the long run, they can promote an author from their own "stable" for the jury. In the short run, preparing for each competition, they can seek to publicize favorable information about one or more of their authors likely to be considered, and they make the official gesture of sending a copy of these authors' books to each member of the Académie Goncourt.

Other prizes followed the Goncourt example. The Académie française itself, in 1915, created the Grand Prix du roman. The most influential of subsequent additions include the Fémina (1904), Renaudot (1926), Interallié (1930), and Médicis (1958). Although there are currently some 800 literary prizes in France, these, with the Goncourt and Académie française novel prize, are the major prizes, which significantly influence sales.[56] All are announced near the end of the calendar year, so that the preparations, rumors, and publicity surrounding them dominate the publishing world through October and November. Newspapers like Le Monde and Le Figaro often speculate—and on the front page—about the merits of candidates, as well as give front-page space to the actual announcements. Detailed reviews on the literary pages follow. Advertising then flows into newspapers and journals, and red cover bands are rushed to bookstores to identify the prizewinners—for example, "Prix Goncourt, 1967"—which soon fill the display windows. Such publicity, together with the by now established tradition of the Goncourt, attracts many persons who may read only one or two novels a year to make "le Goncourt" one of them.[57]

Such success has understandably generated malcontents. While Proust and Malraux won the Goncourt, in the long term the losers have been more distinguished than the winners—Giraudoux, Colette, Apollinaire, Julien Benda, Montherlant, Céline, to go no further than 1932. Publishers have received much of the blame, critics (including renegade members of the Académie Goncourt itself) commonly alleging that prizes rotate among leading publishing houses. Furthermore, all winners to date have been novels. Not only do essays, poetry, and drama suffer; so do nonfictional works (there are, of course, other prizes for all of these, but none has the impact of the novel prizes). More seriously, it is held that the Goncourt jury, cognizant of the influence it wields, avoids crowning works which would not maintain the expected sales or would sour its reputation with the general public. When the sometimes difficult-to-read *nouveaux romans* of the 1950s failed to receive a Goncourt, the Prix Médicis was created (in 1958) specifically to emphasize more avant-garde works.[58] But one observer suggests, more generally, that "whenever a book which does not, above all, tell a good conventional story carries off a prize, the public is confused, sales do not reach their customary level, and the jury is quick to correct its aim the following year."[59]

The associations of writers, their prizes, and related activities have brought distinctive additions to the French world of letters. Although created largely as associations of peers to judge one another's work and provide modest rewards and recognition, these "professional" associations now occupy a major position in the French literary system.[60] Most purchasers of "le Goncourt" know nothing of the author or jury members, but the general aura of the prize is no less real or effective. This prize, like the prize system as a whole, depends for its effects on a respect for elite (professional) opinion and judgment. Expert judgments by juries of peers and respect for and acceptance of expert judgments—these elements of professionalism are clearly present in the French literary prize system; and however limited these professional tendencies, they serve to distinguish the French literary system and, in large measure, the writer in France.

Conclusion

To return to the question with which this inquiry began—What is distinctive about the writer's estate in France?—we see that the answer does not depend on exceptional prestige accorded by the general public, or on extraordinary sales of books, or again on especially generous subsidies. Rather, it is in the particular combination of sources of support that the French literary system is exceptional.

Traditional patronage, of course, has long since disappeared as a source of material support, but the memories of glories past that linger on keep traditional patronage very much alive as a standard of comparison and thus as a source of criticism for current alternatives.

The market clearly provides the greatest material support for writers. In France as in other Western countries the market supports more sorts of writing than ever before, even though few writers are fully supported by the market. Especially given the relatively limited public for serious, difficult, or avant-garde writers, the market has engendered criticism. The perceived deprivation relative to the past emphasizes the symbolic importance of institutionalized patronage, on the one hand, and professional association, on the other.

Institutionalized patronage, most unambiguously in the Académie française, continues traditional patronage by associating writers with other national elites. The specific authority of the Académie française is symbolic of a more general cultural authority which devolves upon the guardians of *l'esprit français*. The writer, with other members of the Académie française, shares the burden of adapting to continually changing circumstances the values of French society manifest in French language and literature.

Such official support is complemented by the system of literary prizes awarded by juries of leading writers and critics. The Goncourt, Renaudot, Fémina, Interallié, and Médicis juries each year single out one work through a process which sets off considerable debate and generates much publicity. While only a few works and writers actively participate, the general excitement provides a sense of national celebration for the world of letters as a whole. And for the authors whose works are crowned, the celerity of the market response is impressive (if not especially durable).

These four supports combine to create a distinctive situation for the writer in France. That this situation has been particularly attractive to writers is due to the importance, symbolic as well as material, of forces outside the market, of sources of support which mitigate market mechanisms and represent the suffrage of elites— of general social elites, governmental elites, scholarly and cultural elites, and, finally, a quasi-professional literary elite. It is these elite associations which do so much to define the writer's estate in France and to make it distinctive.

APPENDIX

In order to go beyond the generalizations commonly based on little more than anecdotes and impressions, we have endeavored to estimate the importance of patronage for writers in France in the past and for France and the United States at present.

Table 1 indicates the relative incidence of patronage for four leading writers from the seventeenth through the nineteenth centuries. (The writers were chosen according to general literary opinion and the space allotted each in the standard general reference, the *Larousse Trois Volumes* [Paris, 1965].) The assessment represents a distillation of scattered biographical information and

TABLE 1: Estimated Sources of Income of the Four Leading French Writers of the Seventeenth, Eighteenth, and Nineteenth Centuries

	PATRONAGE	INDEPENDENT MEANS	MARKET	OTHER JOBS*
Seventeenth Century:				
Corneille	2	2	2	1
Racine	2	0	1	0
Molière	2	0	1	1
Boileau	2	2	1	0
	8	4	5 †	2
Eighteenth Century:				
Voltaire	1	2	0	0
Rousseau	2	0	1	2
Diderot	2	2	1	2
Montesquieu	0	2	0	0
	5	6	2	4
Nineteenth Century:				
Hugo‡	1	0	2	0
Balzac	0	1	2	0
Zola§	0	0	2	2
Flaubert	0	2	1	0
	1	3	7	2

0 = insignificant (less than 10% of total income).
1 = medium (approximately 10–30%).
2 = high (over 30%; includes both direct and indirect income).

Rankings are based on general literary opinion as well as space allotted in the *Larousse Trois Volumes* (Paris, 1965).

*Unrelated to patronage (Historiographer and other such posts not included).
†Due to three playwrights among the four who derived more income from performances of their works than from sales of printed editions.
‡Hugo's pensions were received exclusively in the early part of his career; investments of royalties gave him an independent income, but the source was ultimately the market. He was, however, a member of the Académie française and as such received a yearly stipend of 1,500 francs.
§Zola's journalism was significant only in the early part of his career.

clearly constitutes only the most general of indications of the changes in income distribution over time. Still, whatever the insufficiencies, the trend clearly marks the increasing importance of the market and the concomitant decline in patronage as sources of support for writers.

Table 2 estimates direct support currently available to writers in France and the United States. Once again, whatever the measurement error, the basic orientations of the two literary systems are evident: governmental monies and literary prizes are more prominent in France, while private monies and fellowships play the greater role in the United States.

Literary Prizes

Lists of prizes awarded in France and the United States are available, although they are not strictly comparable. The *Guide des Prix littéraires* claims to include all literary prizes awarded in France, while the *Grants and Awards Available to American Writers*, primarily intended as a guide for writers seeking support, lists only awards over $500. The mean award for the 622 prizes awarded outside the Académie française and the Centre National des Lettres was approximately $100; the range was from somewhat over $2,000 to 0, and there are numerous prizes of $0.60, $1.00, $5.00, and so on. The prizes created in 1975 by the Centre National des Lettres are clearly substantial; there is one prize of 20,000F ($4,700) and there are six of 10,000F ($2,300) each. [1]

The total amounts for prizes obviously represent rough approximations for both countries, but we may note that, with four times the population of France and a per capita GNP that is one and one-half times greater, [2] the United States awards about four times as much money in literary prizes. The $635,000 figure in Table 2 was generated by estimation procedures. [3] When only numbers and sums actually specified in the source were used, the result was $478,000.

Private Support—Fellowships

Similar procedures were applied for United States fellowships and grants to individual writers. [4] Results from the *Grants and Awards Available to American Writers* ranged from a definite amount of $566,000 to an estimate of $1,000,000. The minimum figure included only those awards whose amounts and numbers were specified (or verified through other sources, as for the Guggenheim

TABLE 2: Summary of Support Currently Available to Writers in France
and the United States

FRANCE		UNITED STATES	
Literary prizes:		*Literary prizes:*	
143 prizes awarded by the		804 prizes (est.)	$635,000
Académie française, 1974	$65,000		
	(279,600 F)		
7 prizes created by the			
Centre National des			
Lettres, 1975	19,000		
	(80,000 F)		
622 prizes awarded from			
other sources	81,000		
	(350,000 F)		
Total prizes	$165,000	Total prizes	$635,000
	(709,600 F)		
Private fellowships:		*Private fellowships:*	
No major private sources of		Grants for drama, poetry,	
support were located,		novels, humanities, and	
apart from literary prizes		literature (est.)	$1,000,000
Government fellowships:		*Government fellowships:*	
20 fellowships to younger		78 fellowships, National	
writers, $6,000 each		Endowment for the Arts	
(24,000F), created in 1975	$111,600	($5,000 each)	$390,000
	(480,000 F)		
Short-term fellowships			
(6 months maximum)			
for younger writers	49,000		
	(210,000 F)		
8 fellowships for established			
writers, $14,000 each			
(60,000F)	111,600		
	(480,000 F)		
Total government support	$272,000	Total government support	$390,000
	(1,170,500 F)		
Total support	$437,000	Total support	$2,025,000
	(1,880,100 F)		

Sources: (1) Académie française, personal communication from the Secretary;
(2) Centre National des Lettres, personal communication from the Secretary-
General; (3) *Grants and Awards Available to American Writers,* 7th ed. (New York:
PEN Center, 1975); (4) The John Simon Guggenheim Memorial Foundation,
Annual Report for 1968, 1969, 1973, and 1974 (5) *Guide des Prix littéraires,* 5th
ed. (Paris: Cercle de la Librairie, 1965); and (6) National Endowment for the Arts,
Annual Report for 1974 and 1975.

fellowships) for categories of drama, poetry, novels, humanities, and literature.[5] If other categories of grants are included (journalism, culture, and civilization) and estimated, the figure should be raised to $1,000,000. The major private source of fellowships for writers is the Guggenheim Foundation, whose awards for creative writing have varied in recent years, from 14 in 1968 to 24 in 1973 and 26 in 1974. Here, as elsewhere, we have not computed support to institutions. Some private support in the form of grants-in-aid or loans is also available from organizations like the PEN Center in the United States and the Société des Gens de Lettres in France.

Government Support
Although a few relatively brief lecture tours for writers were sponsored by the United States Information Service and the United States Information Agency in earlier years, and while the Fulbright-Hays fellowships may have benefited writers (although not specifically for writing), the primary source of government support for writers in the United States is the National Endowment for the Arts. Founded in 1965 with a total budget for all the arts of $2.5 million, the appropriation increased dramatically, to almost $75 million, in 1975.

The NEA literature section maintains a fellowship program, but the bulk of its support to literature is in grants to institutions (aid to independent presses, sponsorship of poetry programs in schools and colleges, and others). The figures given represent rounded means of a biennial appropriation for 1973–75 of $775,000 for 155 fellowships.

Support to writers in France is channeled by the Centre National des Lettres, created in 1973 to replace the Caisse des Lettres (founded in 1930). It is part of the secretariat (formerly ministry) of cultural affairs. As with NEA, the support of the CNL goes beyond money given to individual writers to include grants-in-aid (a function of PEN in the United States), pensions to older writers, subsidy of various publications, journals, colloquia, regional literary centers, and social security contributions for writers who draw at least half their income from royalties. The CNL also subsidizes publication of works of "le patrimoine français": critical editions and the correspondence and complete works of important French authors of the past. (In the United States this is a function of the National Endowment for the Humanities.)

Notes to the Appendix

1. Another prize of 35,000F was not included, since it is reserved for the purchase of 1,000 copies of the work chosen. Some of the money comes to the writer indirectly, as royalties.

2. GNP per capita in 1968-70: France—$2,130; United States—$3,980. GNP per capita in 1972-74: France—$3,620; United States—$5,590. (Figures from *World Bank Atlas* [1974], pp. 12-20.)

3. To calculate the amounts, the following procedures were employed. Prizes in foreign currencies were excluded, as were gifts in kind (wine, jewelry, etc.). Prizes noted as biennial or triennial were counted as annual, and the monies awarded were divided accordingly. For American prizes, unspecified numbers of prizes were computed at 5 when "some," "few," or the plural, "prizes," were used; at 3 when "one or more" were indicated; and at 10 when "several" or "numerous" awards were noted.

4. Besides the estimates for numbers indicated above, amounts listed as "royalty payments" were calculated at $1,000, and unspecified "major grants" at $7,000. More precision does not seem possible without checking each source.

5. These figures are only estimates. Another source, both more inclusive, because it lists awards under $500, and more exclusive, because it restricts those awards to fiction and poetry, yielded only $726,000 for prizes and fellowships; see James Thomas, *Money and Where It's Hiding: Grants, Awards, and Prizes for Writers* (Bowling Green, Ohio: Bowling Green State University, 1974).

Jack Goody

10 Literacy, Criticism, and the Growth of Knowledge

Much of our thinking about the development of human thought from its first beginnings, and about differences between traditional and modern cultures today, is set in a binary framework. We still speak in terms of "primitive" and "advanced," almost as if human minds themselves differed in their structure like machines of earlier and later design. The emergence of science, whether seen as occurring at the time of the Renaissance in Europe, in ancient Greece, or, earlier still, in Babylonia, is held to follow a prescientific period, in which magical thought predominated. Philosophers describe this process as the emergence of rationality from irrationality (Wilson 1970), or of logico-empirical from mythopoeic thinking (Cassirer 1953), or of logical from prelogical procedures (Lévy-Bruhl 1910). More recently, others have attempted to get over the difficulties raised by a purely negative definition of the situation (e.g., rational-irrational) by means of more positively phrased dichotomies, the wild and domesticated (or cold and hot) thinking of Lévi-Strauss (1962), and the open and closed situations of Robin Horton (1967, applying Popper).

I do not find that any such simple design provides an adequate framework for the examination of human interaction and development. Yet neither is it possible to accept the opposing tendency,

This paper was first read to the Van Leer Foundation, Jerusalem, in March 1974. I am grateful to many people for stimulation on the subject of this paper, especially D. Gjertsen, R. Horton, E. Mendelsohn, E. Shils, and I. P. Watt. And I am indebted to my hosts and listeners on this and other occasions.

adopted by many social scientists heavily committed to cultural relativism, which leads them to treat all societies as if their intellectual processes were essentially the same. Similar yes, the same no. And once one allows this case, the specification of difference is not in itself enough; one needs also to point to mechanisms, to causal factors.

Toward this end I want to pursue further an argument that has been outlined elsewhere[1] and to illustrate the thesis by reference to developments in the growth of human knowledge and in the growth of man's capacity to store and augment that knowledge. For some, at least, of the differences in intellectual processes that are indicated in a very general way by means of terms like "open" and "closed" can be related not so much to differences in "mind" but to differences in systems of communication.

In using the words "thought" and "mind," I am referring to what might more technically be described as the content and processes of cognition. I take it as axiomatic that these two aspects are very closely intertwined, so that a change in one is likely to effect a change in the other. In other words, we are dealing with what Cole and Scribner, following Luria, describe as "functional cognitive systems" (1974:194). I am interested here in certain general dimensions of such systems that are related to what historians of culture perceive as "the growth of knowledge." While this has to do with "content," it also presupposes certain processes which are related, I argue, to the modes of communication by which man interacts with man and, more especially, transmits his culture, his learned behavior, from generation to generation.

Culture, after all, is a series of communicative acts, and differences in the mode of communication are often as important as differences in the mode of production, for they involve developments in the storing, analysis, and creation of human knowledge. My specific proposition is that writing, and more especially alphabetic literacy, made possible the kind of scrutiny of discourse (by giving oral communication a semipermanent form) which made possible the increase in scope of critical activity (and hence of rationality, skepticism, and logic—to resurrect memories of those questionable dichotomies). And at the same time as it increased the potentialities of criticism (because writing laid out discourse before one's eyes in a different kind of way), it also increased the potentiality for cumulative knowledge, especially of an abstract kind, because it changed the nature of communication (beyond that of face-to-face contact) as well as the system for the storage of information (thus making a wider range of "thought" available to the reading public). No longer did the problem of memory storage dominate man's intellectual life; the human mind was freed to study static "text" (rather than be limited by participation in the dynamic "utterance") —a process that enabled man to stand back from his creation and examine it in a more abstract, generalized, and "rational" way.[2] By making it possible to scan the communications of mankind over a much wider time span, literacy encouraged, at the very same time, criticism and commentary on the one hand and the orthodoxy of the book on the other.

To argue this way is not to subscribe to a "great-divide" theory; it is an attempt to get away from the nondevelopmental perspective of much thinking about human thought and, at the same time, to link the discussion to the history of scientific endeavor in its broadest context—an undertaking that involves modifying certain categories of most historical and philosophical approaches to the subject.

Let me start at the beginning. It might be argued that there is all the difference in the world between the scientific attitude toward the control of nature that is adopted by the modern world and the mystical attitude seen as characteristic of preliterate societies. But is this a difference as radical as it appears? Robin Horton, who has given us the most intelligent account of African traditional thought and its relationship to Western science, denies that this is so. He attempts to treat African traditional religious beliefs as "theoretical models akin to those of the sciences" and argues that if we recognize the aim of theory to be the demonstration of a limited number of *kinds* of entity or process underlying the diversity of experience (1967:51), then recent analyses of African cosmologies make it clear that "the gods of a given culture do form a scheme which interprets the vast diversity of everyday experience in terms of the action of a relatively few *kinds* of force" (p. 52). The gods are not capricious; spiritual agencies are at work behind observed events, and there is a basic modicum of regularity in their behavior. Like "atoms, molecules, and waves, then, the gods serve to introduce unity into diversity, simplicity into complexity, order into disorder, regularity into anomaly" (p. 52).

While I would argue toward the same conclusions, I would do so along different lines. For in stressing resemblances, the author has laid himself open to the criticism directed at earlier comparisons or contrasts of this kind (e.g., by Evans-Pritchard, 1934, and Beattie, 1970:260), namely, that he has compared the religious thought of simple societies with the scientific thought of complex ones instead of comparing the latter with the technical thinking of traditional societies. It was on this aspect of what one might call protoscientific rather than prescientific thought that Malinowski, and after him Lévi-Strauss, laid much stress. Note also that by "science" Horton usually refers to modes of thought rather than to an activity, an organization, or a body of knowledge. The semantic leeway that surrounds the concept "science" allows considerable latitude in many of the discussions about its growth.

I would suggest that we may compare entities of the modern scientific kind not only with specifically religious concepts but also with a more generalized kind of element (air, fire, water, etc.) based upon perceived objects or processes but also used more generally to break down the surface structure of the physical world. The generalization of these elements, which is a way of analyzing the life of the world, takes elaborate form in early literate civilizations. The reason is, I believe, related to the influence of graphic arrangements on their systems of classification,[3] but such elaborations are based upon simpler forerunners. Take, for example, the account of creation (or procreation) found in the myth of the LoDagaa of West Africa (Goody, 1972). In the second part of the Black Bagre (pp. 230-31) man goes to the sky to visit God. When he arrives there, God says that

> our ancestor
> should come forward.
> When he came,
> [God] took some earth,
> and pressed it together.
> When this was done,
> he spoke again
> and called a young girl,
> a slender girl,
> to come there too.
> She came over,
> and when she had done so,
> he told her
> to take a pot.
> She took it,
> and stood up with it.
> Then he told her
> to look for okra
> to bring to him.
> He chose a piece,

put it in his mouth,
chewed it to bits,
spat them out
into the pot.

Here we have a "symbolic" representation of procreation, the sap of
the okra being sticky and white like semen and the pot being a
receptacle resembling the vagina. As a result of this bringing-
together of the elements that go to make up humankind, a child is
born, and the man and woman who observed the act of creation
quarrel over the ownership of the child. But this is not the only part
of the narrative in which an account of procreation is given. Later
on the girl goes into the woods and sees snakes at play. She then goes
back to tell her husband how pleasurable intercourse can be. In a
sense a difference is being pointed out between the (first) spiritual
act of creation and the (continuing) animal act of procreation, the
first having to do with the supernatural, the latter with the natural.
However, I am not primarily concerned with the degree of understanding of natural processes but with the fact that the human body
is seen as compounded of elements, of earth and water (or semen)
and (elsewhere) of blood. So, in this society (and in its verbal
constructs) we find not only supernatural entities but also, in a
shadowy way, more natural elements, including fire and air, blood
and water. It did not need the elaborations of Taoist, Mohist, or
Greek to introduce us to these basic notions. Such elementary ideas,
like the kernel of the wave theories, which Joseph Needham links
with developments in Chinese science, and the essence of those
atomistic ideas linked with the West, are probably universally
present.[4] The basis for such general notions of science exists much
more widely in human societies than many of our current dichotomies allow, whether these dichotomies are viewed in a developmental
way (*from* magic *to* science) or not.

   Indeed, what lies behind Joseph Needham's idea of this change
turns out to be a more sophisticated version of the simple dichotomy
between primitive and advanced that we have been trying to qualify.
He sees two kinds of thinking emerging from "primitive thought,"[5]
namely, the causal account of natural phenomena associated with
the Greeks and the "coordinative or associative thinking" typical of
the Chinese, which attempted "to systematize the universe of things
and events into a pattern of structure, by which all the mutual
influences of its parts were conditioned" (p. 285). In the scientific or

protoscientific ideas of the Chinese, this conceptualization depended upon two fundamental principles or forces in the universe, first, the Yin and the Yang, the negative and positive projections of man's own sexual experience, and, second, the five "elements" of which all process and all substance were composed (p. 279). For, he concludes, "once a system of categorisations such as the five-element system is established, then anything can by no means be the cause of anything else" (p. 284).

In writing of the concept of Yin and Yang, Needham himself suggests that we could be dealing with ideas of such simplicity that "they might easily have arisen independently in several civilisations" (p. 277). Such "independent invention" must surely have occurred, both with the dualistic divisions and with the concept of elements; indeed, in their more general form such ideas seem intrinsic to human thought, to the use of language itself. I have already suggested that the notion of elements is present in embryonic form in LoDagaa mythology and in similar verbal forms. Other writers have found, indeed pursued, dualisms in many parts of the globe among a variety of peoples, where they have invariably succeeded in discovering at least some "opposition" between right and left, male and female; while, even for purely oral societies, some authors have erected much more elaborate schemes, which appear to display all the features of the "coordinative or associative thinking" thought to be characteristic of the Chinese.

I would therefore extend Horton's analysis further than he does himself; for the comparison between science and religion overlooks the comparison between science and protoscience (or simple technology), and this starting point tends in turn to distort the differences between simple and complex societies. The result is seen in the second part of Horton's discussion, where he deals with the differences rather than the similarities. Here he adopts Popper's (or Merton's) distinction between what he calls the "closed" and "open" predicaments, which are defined in the following words: "in traditional cultures there is no developed awareness of alternatives to the established body of theoretical tenets; whereas in scientifically oriented cultures, such an awareness is highly developed" (1967: 155); it is "the awareness of alternatives which is crucial for the take-off into science." Closure is associated with lack of awareness of alternatives and anxiety about threats to the system; openness, with the opposite.

Horton attempts to link these general characteristics with the more specific features of traditional thought. While I would accept most of these statements as pointing to certain differences between two broad groups of societies, the West and the rest, the dichotomies need to be treated as variables, both as regards the societies and as regards their characteristics. A dichotomization of this kind is often a useful preliminary for descriptive purposes; [6] once we accept it as such, we can go further and attempt to elucidate the possible mechanisms that bring about the differences, a step that usually involves modifying or even rejecting the original dichotomy. Without in any way insisting upon a single-factor theory, I want to try to show how these differences can be partly explained (rather than simply described) by looking at the possible effects of changes in the mode of communication.

Horton isolates two major features of the difference between closed and open systems, the first of which has four aspects, the second three. These characteristics can be summarized as follows:

1. The absence of alternatives, which is indicated by:
    a) a magical versus nonmagical attitude to words. In traditional thought, words, ideas, and reality are intrinsically bound up; in science, words and reality vary independently.
    b) ideas-bound-to-occasions against ideas-bound-to-ideas. In the scientific situation, the thinker can "get outside" his own system, because it is not bound to occasions, to reality.
    c) unreflective versus reflective thinking. In traditional thought there is no reflection upon the rules of thinking, hence there can be no Logic (rules) or Epistemology (grounds for knowing) in the limited sense.
    d) mixed versus segregated motives. While traditional thought deals with explanation and prediction, it is also influenced by other factors, e.g., emotional needs, especially for personal relations of a surrogate kind. This personalization of theory gets eliminated only with the application of the rules of the game.
2. Anxiety about threats to the system, which is indicated by:
    a) protective versus destructive attitudes toward established theory. In traditional thought, failures are excused by processes of "secondary elaboration" which protect beliefs; the questioning of basic beliefs, on divination, for example, is a blocked path "because the thinkers are victims of the closed predicament" (p. 168). Contrast the scientific attitude. It is above all his "*essential scepticism* toward established beliefs" that distinguishes the scientist from the traditional

thinker (p. 168, my italics). Having said this, Horton intro-
duces a caveat by referring not only to Kuhn's discussion of
normal science but also to the "magical" attitude of the
modern layman toward theories invented by scientists.

b) protective versus destructive attitudes to the category system.
Following Douglas' analysis, he sees "taboo" as related to
events and actions which seriously defy the established lines
of classification in the particular culture. Taboo is the
equivalent of secondary elaboration, a defensive measure.

c) the passage of time: bad or good? Horton relates the "widespread attempt to annul the passage of time" (p. 178) to the
closed predicament; for scientists, the future is in their
bones, but traditional societies lack any idea of Progress.

Let us examine these features from a different angle and ask what
it is that lies behind the closed situation. Is the absence of awareness
of alternatives due simply to the fact that traditional societies were
not presented with other choices until Europe intervened? Or are we
dealing with closure of a more inherent sort, a feature of the
traditional mind? I doubt whether Horton would ask us to accept
the latter proposition, which is essentially circular. What about the
first? Here we seem to be offered a view of African societies which
ignores historical complexity. The Kalahari, of whom he writes,
after all, have been in contact with Europeans for a number of
centuries, and many other African societies have been influenced by
Islam for a much longer period. Quite apart from these northern
imports, there was certainly much traffic in ritual, much exchange
of religious ideas and theories, among the "indigenous" societies
themselves. Some might claim that central beliefs in the efficacy of
witchcraft and the powers of diviners remained unquestioned by
such contact, being common to all these societies; but even this very
general statement is open to query; certainly the forms of divination
and the intensity of witchcraft changed under both internal and
external pressures.[7] The religious systems of simple societies are
indeed open and very far from closed. The well-established mobility
of cult is incompatible with the complete closure of thought, closure
and openness being in any case variables rather than binary
oppositions. Horton has himself pointed to the true situation in
nonliterate societies: if traditional cultures see ideas as bound to
occasions—if, for example, general statements arise in the context
of healing rather than as abstract programs about what we believe—
then, when the contexts change (because of famine, invasion, or

disease) or when individual attitudes change (because of the recognition that the remedy has not worked), the ideas and practices will themselves change. They seem more likely to do so here than in societies where ideas, religious or scientific, are written down in scholarly treatises or in Holy Writ.

This observation raises the question of the relationship between modes of thought and modes for the production and reproduction of thought that lies at the heart of the unexplained but not inexplicable differences that so many writers have noted. As we have said, Horton argues that traditional and scientific thought differ in the "essential scepticism" of the latter toward scientific beliefs. I have remarked elsewhere that many observers have described Africans as being skeptical, especially about witchcraft, divination, and similar matters.[8] What seems to be the *essential* difference, however, is not so much the skeptical attitude in itself but the accumulation (or reproduction) of skepticism. Members of oral (i.e., "traditional") societies find it difficult to develop a line of skeptical thinking about, say, the nature of matter or man's relationship to God simply because a continuing critical tradition can hardly exist when skeptical thoughts are *not* written down, *not* communicated across time and space, *not* made available for men to contemplate in privacy as well as to hear in performance.

In many cases it is "oral" and "literate" that need to be opposed rather than "traditional" and "modern." Awareness of alternatives is clearly more likely to characterize literate societies, where books and libraries give an individual access to knowledge from different cultures and from different ages, either in the form of descriptive accounts or utopian schemes. But it is not simply the awareness of being exposed to a wider range of influences. Such openness would be largely mechanical and would be available to the inhabitants of a city like Kano, with its variety of trans-Saharan travelers, as much as to the inhabitants of eighteenth-century Boston or Birmingham. It is rather that the *form* in which the alternatives are presented makes one aware of the differences, forces one to consider contradiction, makes one conscious of the rules or argument, forces one to develop such "logic." And the form is determined by the literary or written mode. Why? Because when an utterance is put in writing it can be inspected in much greater detail, in its parts as well as in its whole, backwards as well as forwards, out of context as well as in its setting; in other words, it can be subjected to a quite different type of scrutiny and critique than is possible with purely verbal communication. Speech is no longer tied to an "occasion"; it becomes timeless. Nor is it attached to a person; on paper, it becomes more abstract, more depersonalized.

In giving this summary account of some of the implications of writing or, at any rate, of extensive literacy, I have deliberately used words with which others have spelled out the traditional/modern dichotomy. Horton speaks of the differences between personal and impersonal theories; and while he is referring to a rather different aspect of the problem (personal gods as against impersonal forces), the points are related. Again he speaks of thought being tied to occasions (hence in a sense less abstract or less abstracted), an idea which can also be discussed more concretely in terms of systems for communicating signs and symbols. Writing makes speech "objective" by turning it into an object of visual as well as aural inspection; it is the shift of the receptor from ear to eye, of the producer from voice to hand.

Here, I suggest, lies the answer, in part at least, to the emergence of logic and philosophy. Watt and I have elsewhere suggested that logic, in its formal sense, is closely tied to writing: the formalization of propositions, abstracted from the flow of speech and given letters (or numbers), leads to the syllogism. Symbolic logic and algebra, let alone the calculus, are inconceivable without the prior existence of writing. More generally, a concern with the rules of argument or the grounds for knowledge seems to arise, though less directly, out of the formalization of communication (and hence of "statement" and "belief") which is intrinsic to writing. Philosophic discourse is a formalization of just the kind one would expect with literacy. "Traditional" societies are marked not so much by the absence of reflective thinking as by the absence of the proper tools for constructive rumination.

Let me now turn to the second category of contrasting aspects, those related to anxiety about threats to the system. As Horton appreciates, traditional thinkers are not the only people who find change threatening; so too, Kuhn claims, does "normal science" (1962:81). It is certainly true that growth, progress, and change are more characteristic of "modern" societies, but they are not absent from other cultures. Nor, as we have seen, is skepticism. With regard to time concepts, we find a difference of emphasis which can reasonably be related to differences in technology, in procedures for the measurement of time (Goody 1968). Indeed, too much weight is often placed upon differences between cyclical and linear approaches to time. For example, the concept of chronology is linear rather than circular; it needs numbered series starting with a fixed base, which means that some form of graphic record is a pre-requisite.

Note that in talking of anxiety about change, Horton is not referring to observed reactions to threats but rather what are hypothesized as possible defenses against such threats. My own limited observations have not revealed major difficulties of this kind on the individual level; people accommodate the airplane flying overhead into some classificatory scheme, as Worsley (1955) pointed out in the context of Groote Eyland totemism, without finding themselves threatened because it cuts across their distinction be-tween birds that fly in the air and machines that move on the ground. I make this point because Horton sees one of the main distinguishing features of African thought as the "closure" of the systems of classification. Here he follows Mary Douglas' discussion of taboo as a reaction to events that seriously defy the established lines of classification.

In support of this theory, incest is seen as flagrantly defying the established category system because it treats the mother, for ex-ample, as a wife and is therefore subject to taboo. Equally, twins are dangerous because multiple births confuse the animal and the human world; the human corpse is polluting because it falls between the living and the dead, just as feces and menstrual blood occupy the no-man's-land between animate and inanimate. But what does this mean?

Let us take incest. The argument is difficult to follow, for several reasons. Societies in West Africa often classify potential wives as "sisters" (this is indeed a feature of permitted cousin marriage and a Hawaiian terminology); nevertheless, men find no difficulty in sleeping with some and not others. Equally, some "mothers" are accessible as sexual partners, just as, in our society, some "mothers" are "superior" to childbirth. If we look at systems of classification from the actor's standpoint, there is little problem in coping with overlapping categories; the Venn diagram is as relevant a model as the Table. Moreover, the whole discussion seems to rest upon a simplistic view of the relationship between linguistic acts and other social behavior. In addition, what is at issue here is the question of "taboo" as a category requiring explanation, either in Douglas' or in Horton's terms. Neither classificatory closure nor taboo seems very satisfactory as defining characteristics of traditional thought.

Another aspect of thought with which Horton deals is the contrast between the magical and nonmagical use of the word.[9] The author

himself points out—for he is very sensitive to questions of similarity and difference—that the outlook behind magic (at least in
the sense of the dominance of the word, its entailment with ideas
and action) is an intellectual possibility even in a scientifically
oriented culture (e.g., in the dominance of mind over matter). I
would go further and say that even the problem of classification (a
mode of bringing data under control which is intrinsic to the whole
range of sciences) is not far removed from the magical use of words
in spells. Today the magic of the (printed) word has in a sense
replaced the magic of the (spoken) word. Nevertheless, there
certainly is some truth in Horton's contention concerning the shift
away from word magic. What truth there is, I suggest, turns once
again on the effect of separation, of objectification, which writing
has on words; for words assume a different relationship to action
and to object when they are on paper than when they are spoken.
They are no longer bound up directly with "reality"; the written
word becomes a separate "thing," abstracted to some extent from
the flow of speech, shedding its close entailment with action, with
power over matter.

I suggest that many of the differences that Horton characterizes
as distinctive of open and closed systems of thought can be related to
differences in the systems of communication and, specifically, to the
presence or absence of writing. But this does not mean that we are
dealing with a simple dichotomy, for systems of communication
differ in many particular respects (for example, ideographic from
phonetic scripts). There is no single "opposition" but rather a
succession of changes over time, each influencing the system of
thought in specific ways. I do not maintain that this process is
unidirectional let alone monocausal; thought feeds back on communication; creed and class influence the kind and extent of literacy
that prevails. In drawing attention to the significance of this factor,
I attempt to avoid the conceptual slush into which one flounders
when such differences are attributed either to "culture" (who denies
it, but what does it mean?) or to vague, descriptive divisions such as
open and closed, which themselves need explaining rather than
serve to explain.

The above discussion has attempted to show that it is not so much
skepticism itself that distinguishes postscientific thought as the
accumulated skepticism that writing makes possible; it is a question
of establishing a tradition of critical discussion. It is now possible to
see why science, in the sense we usually think of this activity, occurred

only when writing made its appearance and why it made its most striking advances when literacy became widespread. In one of his essays (1963, chap. 5, esp. pp. 148–52), Karl Popper traces the origin of "the tradition of critical discussion [which] represents the only practical way of expanding our knowledge" to the Greek philosophers between Thales and Plato, the men who, as he sees it, encouraged critical discussion both between schools and within individual schools. Kuhn, on the other hand, sees these forms of activity as having no resemblance to science.

> Rather it is the tradition of claims, counterclaims, and debates over fundamentals which, except perhaps during the Middle Ages, have characterized philosophy and much of social science ever since. Already by the Hellenistic period mathematics, astronomy, statics and the geometric parts of optics had abandoned this mode of discourse in favour of puzzle solving. Other sciences, in increasing numbers, have undergone the same transition since. In a sense . . . it is precisely the abandonment of critical discourse that marks the transition to a science. Once a field has made that transition, critical discourse recurs only at moments of crisis when the bases of the field are again in jeopardy [1970:6–7]

Let us leave aside the discussion about the distinction between critical discourse and puzzle-solving, between innovative and normal science, with Kuhn's implication of incompatibility (an implication Popper would strenuously deny). Thales' thought is not science as we know it. But it is an essential preliminary to the kind of problem-solving involved in science, and it is significant that this kind of critical discourse is seen as emerging in one of the first literate societies.

This point relates to another of the concepts that have been much discussed by philosophers and anthropologists, namely, rationality (see, e.g., Wilson, 1970). As with skepticism, rationality is often seen as one of the differentiating features of the "modern mind," of the scientific view. This is not a debate we find very promising. For, as with logicality, the argument is conducted in terms of an opposition between rationality and irrationality (with the occasional introduction of the nonrational as a third term), and rationality is seen as adhering to certain operations rather than to others. The usual way of avoiding the radical dichotomy is by resort to diffuse relativism (all societies are rational). However, if we look more closely, a third possibility emerges. Take Wartofsky's definition of rationality. Science is "concept-ordered," but the use of concepts is intelligent, not yet rational: "rational practice entails ... the self-conscious or reflective use of concepts; i.e., the critical attitude towards scientific practice and thought, which constitutes not simply scientific knowledge alone (which is its necessary condition), but the *self-knowledge* of science, the critical examination of its own conceptual foundations" (Wartofsky 1967:151). Rationality in this sense implies metaphysics, which is "the practice of rationality in its most theoretical form" (p. 153); "a rational theoretical science is continuous with the tradition of metaphysical theory-construction" (p. 154); metaphysics is a "heuristic for science." Whether or not we agree with Wartofsky's point, it seems clear that the kind of reflective use of concepts required by his definition of rationality is greatly facilitated by the process of giving speech permanent embodiment and thus creating the conditions for an extension of reflective examination.

Since my theme has been the relationship among processes of communication, the development of a critical tradition, and the growth of knowledge (including the emergence of science), I want to conclude by offering an illustration of the way in which literate techniques operate as an analytic tool, promoting criticism leading to the growth of knowledge. My example is taken from a book on this subject, edited to Lakatos and Musgrave (1970), which discusses Thomas Kuhn's *The Structure of Scientific Revolutions* (1962). For Kuhn, a scientific revolution consists of a change in paradigm, a gestalt-switch, from one set of assumptions and models to another. Otherwise, science (normal science) proceeds to work within one paradigm by solving the puzzles offered by it. The very boundaries of a paradigm are a condition of growth of a subject, a development from a preparadigmatic stage, since, by limiting the scope of inquiry, they create specialist areas of concentration, based on positive results. Contrast this approach to that of Popper, who sees criticisms as lying at the heart of the scientific enterprise, which is a state of "revolution in permanence." The difference between the two views is essentially between science as a closed community and as an open society.

For any discussion of Kuhn's contribution to the history of science, some agreement on the word "paradigm" is essential. Yet in his book, as Margaret Masterman points out in a favorable essay, he has used the word in some twenty-one different ways, which she attempts to reduce to three major clusters of meaning (1970:65): (1)

metaphysical paradigms, associated with a set of beliefs; (2) *socio-logical paradigms*, a universally recognized scientific achievement; and (3) *artifact or construct paradigms*, which turn problems into puzzles.

In his reply to criticisms, Kuhn acknowledges the ambiguity of his usage and suggests a substitution of *disciplinary matrix* for cluster (2), above (p. 271), and *exemplars or problem-solution paradigms* for (3), though he sees (3) as contained in (2) (p. 272). In other words, the author explicitly qualifies his earlier use of the term paradigm and hence can no longer talk of a pre- or post-paradigm period when describing the maturation of a scientific specialty. His footnote on page 272 explains this somewhat radical modification, which waters down the whole concept in the process of clarifying it.

Let us suppose (I will complicate the assumption later) that Kuhn's reformulation, which makes a "revolutionary" statement seem to fall well within the bounds of "normal" science, was due to Masterman's criticism. How was that criticism developed from the standpoint of technique? Her first footnote explains the circum-stances of its composition.

> This paper is a later version of an earlier paper which I had been asked to read when there was to have been a panel dis-cussion of T. S. Kuhn's work in this Colloquium; and which I was prevented from writing by getting severe infective hepa-titis. This new version is therefore dedicated to the doctors, nurses and staff of Block 8, Norwich Hospital, who allowed a Kuhn subject index to be made on a hospital bed [p. 59].

In other words, the detection of ambiguity or inconsistency leading to a reformulation of the argument was effected by reference to a box of filing cards which kept track of different usages of one key word in the author's argument. It was effected by a purely literary technique, which permitted a more systematic exploration of a written text than was possible by the more casual techniques of visual inspection usually undertaken by critics of a written text and which form the basis of the kind of criticism offered by Watkins or Feyerabend in the same volume.

My point here is that, by putting speech down onto paper, one creates the possibility of what is almost a different kind of critical examination. Imagine (though it is a fanciful task) Kuhn's book as an oral discourse. No listener, I suggest, could ever spot the twenty-one different usages of the word "paradigm." The argument would flow from one usage to another without anyone's being able to perceive any discrepancy. Inconsistency, even contradiction, tends to get swallowed up in the flow of speech (*parole*), the spate of words, the flood of argument, from which it is virtually impossible for even the most acute mind to make his mental card index of different usages and then compare them one with another.

I am not suggesting that the differences (or shades) of usage were deliberately manipulated to confuse the reader and to carry the argument. Kuhn's acceptance of the criticism shows that he recognizes what he did not earlier perceive, that his new concept (new in this context) was largely unanalyzed. It was a kind of self-deception. My point is that the oral mode makes this kind of self-deception easier to carry out and less easy to detect. The process of (constructive) criticism, whether by the speaker or by another, is inhibited, made more difficult.

Equally, the more deliberate deception of the orator is perhaps less easy to overcome than the unintentional ambiguities of the writer, whose inconsistencies stand out by themselves. By means of rhetoric, through the gift of gab, the "tricks" of the demagogue are able to sway an audience in a more direct way than is the written word. What is at issue here is in part the *immediacy* of the face-to-face contact, the visual gesture and tones of voice, that marks oral communication. It is the play seen, the symphony heard, rather than the drama read, the score studied. But, more than this, the oral form is intrinsically more persuasive because it is less open to criticism (though not, of course, immune from it).

The balance of my argument has been a delicate one. In the first place, I have attempted to set aside radical dichotomies; in the second, I reject diffuse relativism. The third course involves a more difficult task, that of specifying particular mechanisms. In the present paper I have tried to analyze some aspects of the processes of communication in order to try to elucidate what others have tried to explain by means of those dichotomies. This is not a great-divide theory. It sees some changes as more important than others, but it attempts to relate specific differences to specific changes.

The effort to compare and contrast the thought ways of "traditional" and "modern," literate and preliterate, societies may seem of marginal interest to the more recent history of knowledge. So it is from many standpoints. But from the most general of these, it serves to define the problem we are dealing with. For example, the development of science in western Europe in the seventeenth century is sometimes seen as resting upon views about (1) the lawfulness of nature, which permits comprehension, and (2) man and nature as antagonists and the outcome of the ideology of the control of nature as "growth." If we are to understand the particular contributions of Western (or any other) science to the development of human thought, then we must be a good deal more precise about the matrix from which it was emerging, about the preexisting conditions and the nature of "prescientific thought." Thus the attempt to gain precision leads us inevitably into an examination of the ways of thinking of earlier times and of other cultures, as well as of the manner in which these ways of thinking were related to particular modes of communication between man and man, man and God, man and nature. All of these were influenced by major events, such as the development of scripts, the shift to alphabetic literacy, and the invention of the printing press. I repeat that I am not proposing a single-factor theory; the social structure behind the communicative acts is often of prime importance. Nevertheless, it is not accidental that major steps in the development of what we now call "science" followed the introduction of major changes in the channels of communication in Babylonia (writing), in ancient Greece (the alphabet), and in western Europe (printing).

REFERENCES

Beattie, J. H. M. 1970. "On Understanding Ritual." In B. R. Wilson, ed., *Rationality*. Oxford.

Cassirer, E. 1953. *An Essay on Man*. New York.

Cole, M., and Scribner, S. 1974. *Culture and Thought*. New York.

Douglas, M. 1966. *Purity and Danger*. London.

Evans-Pritchard, E. E. 1934. "Lévy-Bruhl's Theory of Primitive Mentality." *Bulletin of the Faculty of Arts* (Alexandria) 2:1–36.

Goody, J. 1968. "Time: Social Organisation." *International Encyclopedia of the Social Sciences* 16:30–42.

———. 1972. *The Myth of the Bagre*. Oxford.

———. 1975a. "Literacy and Classification: On Turning the Tables." In R. K. Jain, ed., *Text and Context*. London.

———. 1975b. "Religion, Social Change and the Sociology of Conversion." In J. Goody, ed., *Changing Social Structure in Ghana*. London.

———. *Intellectuals in Non-literate Societies*. In press.

——— and Watt, I. P. 1963. "The Consequences of Literacy." *Comparative Studies in Society and History* 5:304–45.

Horton, R. 1967. "African Traditional Thought and Western Science." *Africa* 37:50-71, 155-87.

—— and Finnegan, R. 1973. *Modes of Thought*. London.

Kuhn, T. 1962. *The Structure of Scientific Revolutions*. Chicago.

——. 1970. "Logic of Discovery or Psychology of Research?" In I. Lakatos and A. Musgrave, eds., *Criticism and the Growth of Knowledge*.

Lakatos, I., and Musgrave, A., eds. 1970. *Criticism and the Growth of Knowledge*. Cambridge.

Lévi-Strauss, C. 1962. *La Pensée sauvage*. Paris.

Lévy-Bruhl, L. 1910. *Les Fonctions mentales dans les sociétés inférieures*. Paris.

Masterman, M. 1970. "The Nature of a Paradigm." In I. Lakatos and A. Musgrave, eds.. *Criticism and the Growth of Knowledge*.

Needham, J. 1956. *Science and Civilisation in China*. Vol. 2: *History of Scientific Thought*. Cambridge.

Popper, K. 1963. *Conjectures and Refutations*. London.

Todorov, T. 1973. "Le Discours de la magie." *L'Homme* 13:38-65.

Tambiah, S. J. 1968. "The Magical Power of Words." *Man* 3: 175-208.

Wartofsky, M. 1967. "Metaphysics As a Heuristic for Science." In R. S. Cohen and M. W. Wartofsky, eds., *Boston Studies in the Philosophy of Science*, vol. 3. New York.

Wilson, B. R., ed. 1970. *Rationality*. Oxford.

Worsley, P. M. 1955. "Totemism in a Changing Society." *American Anthropologist* 57:851-61.

Joseph Ben-David

11

Organization, Social Control, and Cognitive Change in Science

Sociologists of science have studied mainly the behavior of scientists, both as performers of a social role which implies certain values and norms and as members of a profession. They have had little to say about the relationship between social conditions and the cognitive contents of science. Methodologically and theoretically, the sociology of science has been closer to the sociology of professions and organizations than to the sociology of knowledge.

This state of affairs has been found disappointing by many, and they have criticized it as a shortcoming which should be corrected. Others have rejected this criticism, doubting that an important and systematic relationship exists between social structure and the substantive contents of science.[1]

Most of this debate has been conducted on an exhortatory and programmatic level where debates can never be resolved. The problem is not whether there is a relationship at all between the contents and the social conditions of science, since the existence of some relationships has never been denied, but what kind of relationship there is and what importance it has for the growth of science or for various aspects of social life that one might be interested in exploring.

"Social conditions" is obviously a mixed category, which includes everything from the relationship between nations to the organization

I am deeply indebted to Robert Merton for his comments on an earlier draft of this paper, to Stephen Toulmin for discussions of some of its themes, and to the Ford Foundation for its support of my research.

244

and social atmosphere of a single laboratory. In this paper I shall deal with the effects of a limited range of such conditions, namely, the effects of the way scientific research and teaching are organized and of the way scientific contributions are recognized and evaluated. These effects will be explored through the review of two historical turning points in science, namely, the emergence of modern science in the seventeenth century and the emergence of modern scientific disciplines at the end of the eighteenth and early nineteenth centuries.

The Significance of the Seventeenth-Century Academies of Science

The first case which I propose to consider is the often debated question of what conditions gave rise to modern science. Starting with Robert K. Merton, sociologists of science have considered the events leading to the establishment of the Royal Society of London as the most important step in the transition from medieval and Renaissance to modern science.[2] This importance has been called into question by Thomas Kuhn in a review article.[3] He argues that the sociologists' concentration on England as the place where modern science chiefly emerged is a mistake, since British supremacy in science at the end of the seventeenth century was due exclusively to Newton. Had Newton not been an Englishman, Britain would not have been considered the leading scientific power in the seventeenth century, and no one would have paid any attention to the social conditions prevailing in that country as "the main clues to the rise of modern science."

He then goes on to argue that intellectually Newton was not representative of English science. He belonged rather to the Continental tradition stemming from the abstract mathematical approach of Greek science, which was relatively independent of observation and experiment. The English tradition in the seventeenth and eighteenth centuries was nonmathematical, paid little attention to the Greek and medieval tradition, and depended mainly on instruments, observations, and experiments. This second tradition had little effect on "scientific theory or conceptual structure" until the middle of the eighteenth century. Only at the end of that century were the tools of the Continental mathematical tradition applied to the products of the English empirical movement, and only then did the modern scientific role, which combines mathematical thinking with experimental skill, emerge.

I shall not try to discuss the debatable proposition that Newton belonged wholly to the Continental tradition. But there appear to have been good reasons for concentrating on British social conditions in order to discover "the main clues to the rise of modern science"—clues quite independent of Newton. In the seventeenth century there existed, all over Europe, a scientific movement which strove for recognition as a new kind of philosophic endeavor. For this movement the foundation of the Royal Society was an event of supreme importance. It was the first decisive victory in the fight for public recognition of science as an autonomous intellectual inquiry, free from the control of theology or philosophic doctrine. In France, members of this movement recommended the imitation of the new English institution; scientists everywhere had used it as a center of correspondence and recognition before anyone knew of Newton.[4] Thus the establishment of the Royal Society in 1660 (when Newton was eighteen) was an important event in the history of science quite apart from the glory bestowed on it by Newton's membership more than a decade later (1671).

But of course the question is not whether the foundation of the Royal Society was regarded as an important event by contemporaries but whether we can regard it as the beginning of the scientist's role in the modern sense.

Kuhn's definition of this role is based on scientific "tradition." He includes in this term a variety of things, but its crucial aspect seems to be the general (metaphysical) view of nature underlying scientific craftsmanship. Therefore, Kuhn dates the beginning of the modern scientific role from the time when the rise of a mathematical theory which could be effectively applied to the products of empirical observation and experiment pushed into the background the differences between the preconceived notions of scientists steeped in different philosophic traditions. "Role" is conceived of here as the cognitive and technical contents of what the incumbent of the role knows and does. When those contents change, the role changes.

On the other hand, sociologists who have investigated the beginnings of the scientific role have been interested in the normative, or moral, aspect of the scientist's behavior. For them, the question was not how scientists actually worked but how scientists demarcated themselves from other intellectuals, by what norms they wanted to judge one another's work, and how they wanted to be perceived and judged by the larger society. The scientists of the seventeenth (or the eighteenth) century did not invent the importance of either observation or mathematics or even the independence of these from religion and philosophic doctrine. Many ancient and medieval scholars were well aware of all this and acted—within limits—accordingly.

The innovation of the seventeenth century was the insistence that the kind of inquiry that could be judged by empirical and mathematical criteria should be made the contents of a separate intellectual role and that there should be a separate institutional structure for the evaluation of those who performed this role. The extent to which there existed a consistent view of the world and a well-established tradition of intellectual craftsmanship to make the establishment of a separate role and separate institutions for this kind of inquiry worthwhile and feasible was a question about which there were serious doubts at the time.[5] It can be argued that the belief in the superiority of the empirical-mathematical method was a utopian faith throughout the seventeenth century and in much of the eighteenth. Before Newton it could claim little evidence in its favor, and afterwards it had to rely on a small number of cases (Newton, Huygens, etc.) for a very long time. But the faith arose, and was maintained in the absence of crucial evidence, as a result of the overwhelming problems which beset intellectual life. The theological and philosophic disputes of the time created an impasse where no debate could be resolved. There was an urgent need for a reliable method for adjudicating intellectual disputes and evaluating intellectual merit. This need prompted the members of the Oxford experimental philosophy club and subsequently the members of the Royal Society to regard their experimental and mathematical interests and methods as patently superior to those of the contemporary guilds and groups of theologians, philosophers, physicians, and lawyers. They possessed a method which made for uncoerced consensus and therefore promised a cumulative growth of knowledge, at least in the field of natural philosophy. They did so at the price of abandoning the philosophic search for all-encompassing knowledge. But that search seemed to have led nowhere; moreover, there was a growing expectation, arising from Baconian philosophy, that the search for comprehensive knowledge, now to be abandoned by the individual, would be retrieved in the long run by the cumulative work of generations. Against this background the price to be paid did not seem excessive.[6] Thus the new role of the scientist as a philosopher applying mathematical and empirical, preferably experimental, methods to the study of nature arose in the seventeenth century, although in actual fact there were very few people who could combine the mathematical with the experimental method.

The situation which prevailed in late-seventeenth- and early-eighteenth-century natural science can be compared to that which exists today in much of social science. The success of social science is still not convincing enough to justify in all eyes the separation of the role of the social scientist from that of the ideologist, the journalist, or the practical man reflecting on his experience. It is often pointed out that some of the latter have shown a better grasp of the workings of society than the social scientists have. Or it is demonstrated that this or that social scientist has actually engaged in ideology and that, in fact, the criteria according to which he defines himself as a scientist, rather than as an ideologist committed to a political program, are far from unequivocal. Moreover, every now and then theories arise, such as Marxism or psychoanalysis, which manage to mix scientific rationality and self-fulfilling prophecy (the parallel to magic in relation to natural science) in such ingenious ways that the demarcation between social science and ideology becomes temporarily blurred. Yet people can still be identified as social scientists by their belief in the possibility of the eventual success of a science of society; by their insistence on judging one another's work on the basis of such criteria as empirical evidence, statistical inference, and logical reasoning; and by the fact that, though they constantly become involved with ideologies, they eventually are prodded, by interacting with other scientists, into extricating themselves from such involvements.[7] Thus, in spite of the diversity of the intellectual traditions of social science, a community of social scientists exists, held together by a common belief in the possibility of an objectively testable knowledge of society, by a common value that the attainment of such knowledge is socially desirable, and by a common morality (which is often transgressed but never with good conscience) of submission to being judged by the norms of the currently defined methods of scientific work. Similarly, natural scientists in the seventeenth and eighteenth centuries defined themselves as different from the general philosophers, theologians, and magicians, from whom—according to the contents of their work—they were barely separable, and from craftsmen and empirical practitioners, whose skills and insights were often superior to those of the scientists.[8]

The Impact of Scientific Academies on Eighteenth-Century Science

It has to be seen now how this—intellectually perhaps premature—institutionalization of science influenced its development. The purpose of the new roles and organizations was, as I have pointed out, to establish and maintain the norm that scientific truth must be based on strict (preferably mathematical) logic and be supported by empirical evidence. According to the scientistic utopian belief, research, once this approach was adopted, would lead from one discovery to another, and science would be sustained by its sheer intellectual momentum and the utility of its discoveries.[9] With the appearance of the great discoveries of Newton, it appeared for a while that the utopian program would be fulfilled. But these great events were followed by disappointment. There were few discoveries and continued intellectual confusion. The hope that science would lead to a continuous orderly advance of consensual knowledge and that its distinctness as an experimental-mathematical enterprise would be preserved was far from assured. In order to maintain science as a distinct consensual enterprise—which was its main attraction—there was needed a social mechanism to promptly and justly decide which discoveries, however small, were acceptable by the standards of science and which were not. Since the belief in science was based on the assumption that experimental and mathematical methods were superior to other types of thought, only the existence of such a mechanism could ensure that science would be judged on its own merits; namely, that it would be given credit for its own achievements and would not be charged with the failures of quacks and other nonscientists.

But such a mechanism was needed for the maintenance of consensus not only at a time when science was particularly threatened by lack of significant advances and lack of theoretical consensus. The problem of judgment and recognition had to be taken care of by social means even at the best times of science. Although the methods of experiment and mathematical proof are in a way self-administering, in practice scientists, more than workers in other intellectual fields, require an institutional system of reward allocation. Scientists, like philosophers and scholars, must publish their findings in order to fulfill any social function. Furthermore, only through publication and recognition of authorship can they establish rights to their own intellectual property. In general philosophy and humanistic scholarship, things are relatively easy. Philosophers and scholars can appeal to a wide public, and they need not fear that their competitors will anticipate them or steal their creations. In these fields, style is so much part of the message that plagiarism requires actual copying and can easily betray itself.

Not so in science. Because of the technical nature of the contributions, evaluation of scientific work cannot be solicited from the general public (and, if solicited, it would be irrelevant and of little value). Therefore, only one's own colleagues can serve as a proper audience and as a legitimate source of recognition. This makes plagiarism a very likely possibility. Scientific results, because they are specific and are independent of writing style, are easy to steal. Moreover, because of the frequency of genuinely independent simultaneous discovery, it is difficult to detect plagiarism or, in the case of genuine multiple discovery, to assign property rights.

Therefore, problems of recognition, evaluation, and adjudication of priorities were major issues for the newly established scientific community, as they are even today, when that community is much better established.[10] As a result, the evaluation of contributions became the major function of the official academies. Originally they were designed as institutions for cooperation in research, and, in the case of the Paris Academy of Sciences, even for cooperative research. But the state of the art, in which experiments could be performed in a workshop far simpler than a modern kitchen, called for little cooperation in research; and after a period of trial and error, the academies, especially the Paris Academy of Sciences, became in practice organizations for the public and official recognition of the contributions of individual scientists.[11]

There is ample evidence that in the practice of the academies "the scientific method" served as a set of procedural norms of judgment. Because of the diversity and immaturity of scientific theory, the debates of the day turned frequently on questions which were not and could not be empirically investigated. Here are a few among many examples:

> Mariotte, Frenicle, Buot, Claude Perrault, and Huygens could not agree upon the nature of gravitation. DuVerney and Perrault failed to interpret similar anatomical evidence on the function of the ear in the same fashion. DuClos' explanation of the increase of weight in calcination and his treatment of the process of coagulation did not bring about any consensus either. To decide by a majority vote which position was correct was absurd, for all the scientists firmly believed that truth was determined by nature and not by the will of men. In practice, the most that the company could assert as being true was that portion of evidence about which there was no disagreement.
>
> Generally, it was the undigested observation of some phenomenon that was thereby considered as true "positively." For the rest, the greatest service the Academy could perform was to publish the opinion of each of its members, no matter how many contradictions might appear.

The better part of wisdom, if the Academy was to have a long and useful existence, was to resist the temptation to judge where judgment was premature. Fontenelle, who grasped the realities of the life of the Academy better than any of his contemporaries, became an eloquent spokesman for this philosophical position. While discussing academic disagreements over the circulation of sap in plants, he remarked that "The academy was the natural judge between these two views. But since a large part of wisdom consists in making no judgment, it declared that the subject was not yet sufficiently clear. It is necessary to wait until there is a fairly large number of experiments and facts before extracting a generalization. There is a common tendency to rush to formulate general principles, and the mind runs toward systems. But we must not always trust in the merit of this order."[12]

This account shows how significant for the development of science was the emergence of the new role and the new institutional structure, devoted to the cultivation of norms of scientific evaluation on the basis of experiment and mathematics. Even though the research practices of individual scientists did not always fit the norms, since they rushed "to formulate general principles" prematurely, the evaluation of their work by the official representatives of the scientific community, the Academy, was based on strict observance of those norms. The norms were necessary to maintain the moral cohesion and the motivation of the scientific community. They enabled the community to exist and to function over a long period of time, even in the absence of outstanding achievements and a unified tradition. Without these institutionally enforced norms the unity of the scientific enterprise might have been in jeopardy.

This was the importance of the social structures which arose in the seventeenth century for the cognitive development of science in the following century. The social control exercised by the academies of science ensured the maintenance of the unity of the scientific endeavor. It discouraged doctrinal approaches which threatened scientific consensus, and it treated with hostility doctrines, such as Mesmerism, which seemed to be inconsistent with good experimental procedure. On the other hand, it rewarded contributions based on experimentally testable knowledge. This had a selective influence on the development of science, and it probably created a predisposition for the favorable reception of the new mathematical-experimental tradition, which seemed to have succeeded in creating theories in which all concepts were linked to empirical observations.

This was, of course, an indirect influence on the cognitive development of science. Yet it was a crucial one, since without it the scientific effort might easily have lost its purpose and direction.

The importance of the institutions created in the seventeenth century in maintaining the unity and purpose of science explains why sociologists of science have been more interested in the changes which occurred in science in the seventeenth century than in those that occurred in the eighteenth. These seventeenth-century changes, such as the programmatic creation of the new social role of the natural philosopher, and of the new organization of the scientific academy, were easily discernible social events. These were not trivial things from the point of view of the growth of science, in spite of the apparent lack of success of the new organizations in creating the kind of science and the kind of scientists that the founders of the scientific movement envisioned. Their importance lies in the fact that they influenced the volume and the location of research and, indirectly, by withholding recognition from the metaphysical elements of theories, its cognitive direction as well.

The Sociologists' Neglect of the Eighteenth-Century Revolution in Science

One can also understand why sociologists neglected the changes in science which occurred in the late-eighteenth and early-nineteenth centuries. Ostensibly, the emergence of new physical and chemical theories, which succeeded in combining experiment with mathematics, had no effect on the social structure of science. In contrast to the seventeenth-century British scientists, who at every point emphasized the difference between themselves and their philosophic predecessors, the scientific innovators of the eighteenth century claimed only to have carried to new heights the enterprise which had begun in the seventeenth century. They were quite content to be, not revolutionaries, but worthy heirs of their predecessors.

Nor did they initiate new organizations, as had their predecessors more than a hundred years before. They were pleased to take their place in the academies and other institutions which had been emerging throughout the seventeenth and eighteenth centuries, and all they wanted was to extend the influence of these institutions to increasingly wider circles of society. The revolutionary changes in French scientific institutions at the end of the eighteenth and the beginning of the nineteenth centuries resulted more from the political than from the scientific changes of the period.[13] Thus one can speak of the rise of a new kind of role in the seventeenth century but not of one at the end of the eighteenth or at the beginning of the nineteenth century. The cognitive change in science which occurred in the latter centuries gave rise to some organizational developments but not to changes in the institutional definition of either science or the scientists' role.

From a sociological point of view, the situation was the reverse of that in the seventeenth century. Then groups of scientists, supported by other believers in the utopian potentiality of science, chose an organization which they (wrongly) believed could actually generate and then propagate the kind of science they dreamed of. However, that science did not exist, and so the new organizations could not create it. This became clear very soon, when, though the institutional conditions were present, the discoveries did not follow as predicted. In contrast, at the end of the eighteenth century, the science capable of rapid development was there, but the motivation to create new organizations for training researchers and to exploit the opportunities inherent in the state of science were relatively weak. The innovations in scientific training and education made in 1795-98, such as the attempt to make the Ecole Polytechnique into an advanced scientific school, to make science an important part of upper-secondary education, and to introduce research into the new schools of medicine, were initiated by scientists and scientistic intellectuals. But it was the latter rather than the former who were really interested in education. The scientists themselves maintained, throughout the revolutionary period, a relatively high degree of consensus and tried to support one another and to preserve the Academy of Sciences. Therefore, when Napoleon—who loathed intellectuals but liked scientists—suppressed the educational reforms favoring science, he encountered little opposition to this among scientists. The scientists were quite satisfied with the resurrected old Academy as the first class of the Institute, with increased support for their personal work, and with the extension of opportunities for the employment of scientists in some of the specialized institutions of higher education or in noneducational capacities; they did not worry too much about science education in general or about the organization of research in particular.[14] All this would seem to indicate that the emergence of new physical and chemical theories at the end of the eighteenth century had neither direct social causes nor direct social effects. The discoveries changed science but did not change the social definition of the role of the scientist.

The Effect of the Eighteenth-Century Scientific Revolution on the Uses and Organization of Science

However, the discoveries were connected—indirectly—with social conditions at both ends of the causal chain. Even the discoveries of Lavoisier and Laplace were perhaps not entirely unrelated to the social control over science exercised by the Paris Academy of Sciences. As I have pointed out above (p. 251), the insistence of that academy on upholding the ideal of perfect overlap between (preferably mathematical) theory and (preferably experimental) empirical evidence prepared the ground for the triumphant acceptance of these discoveries and probably enhanced their immediate effect.

There was also a reverse effect of the new theories on the organization of science. In order to understand this effect, we have to see what the social significance of the new discoveries was and what kind of social opportunities they created. From the point of view of the scientistic utopia of the seventeenth and eighteenth centuries, Lavoisier and Laplace were a kind of fulfillment. The entire eighteenth century awaited the reappearance of a scientific hero to carry on the work of Newton, and these two seemed to answer the expectation. Of course, like Newton, Lavoisier and Laplace failed to realize exactly the Baconian utopia foreseen by the founders of the scientistic movement in the seventeenth century. No method emerged for teaching mediocre minds how to be creative, nor did science contribute to technology except in a marginal way. Still, the results bore a respectably close resemblance to what was originally envisioned, since scientists made some well-advertised contributions to technology, and there were now theories and methods capable of generating relatively long-term programs of significant research. With the emergence of such programs, science became organizable.

The most immediate social opportunities inherent in this development were educational. Possessing a body of consensual and theoretically organized knowledge, science, especially physics, could be used as an educational discipline. Teachers of science could now claim as much authority for their knowledge as teachers of Latin or Greek grammar had always claimed for theirs. They could also claim authority to direct the research of disciples who wanted to become scientists, since the fruitful directions of research could be derived from existing authoritative knowledge, and those who mastered the field could discern and determine those directions. Therefore, research could be organized as a school where a master directed his student apprentices in carrying out a program of research conceived by him.

These opportunities, inherent in the new kind of scientific theory, were immediately recognized in France, where most of the major advances had taken place. However, as I have pointed out, except for the few transitional years between the Terror and the Empire, no need was felt in France to take advantage of these opportunities. That they were recognized is shown by the educational reforms of the mid-1790s and by the creation of the Society of Arcueil, but no significant group in society had sufficient motivation to exploit them.[15] People were satisfied with classical education, and scientists who had no reason to be dissatisfied with either their scientific or their social attainments did not pay too much attention to missed educational opportunities.

The situation was somewhat different in Germany. Not that the attitudes toward science were more favorable there than in France. They were in fact much less favorable. But the attitude toward intellectuals and education was different. While Napoleon despised the philosophers and their educational schemes, the civil servants of defeated Prussia sought alliance with their philosophers. This led to the foundation of the University of Berlin in 1810 as a new type of institution, where teachers were expected to be creative scholars. The intention was to make the University of Berlin the center of all German intellectual life. Its actual effect was to induce the other German states to reform their universities as well. The existence of more than twenty German-language universities competing with one another for scholarly fame gave rise to a veritable market for scholars. As a result, the universities, which were originally designed only for producing future professionals—namely, high-school teachers, doctors, lawyers, and theologians—became to some extent training institutions in research.[16] This research impetus got its start in the humanities, especially in the classical languages, which were the most important teaching subjects for high-school (*Gymnasium*) teachers. Intensive special courses, "seminars," given to these future teachers for the purpose of increasing their proficiency in their field of teaching, became in fact schools of research when led by great scholars.[17] In the same manner, teaching laboratories in chemistry (established mainly for the training of pharmacists) and physiology (created for training doctors) were turned into research laboratories where a few of the abler students conducted original research under the guidance of a professor.[18]

This development of laboratory research at the universities occurred by default, since, as we have pointed out, experimental sciences were regarded as subjects barely worthy of the universities. Once it occurred, however, the opportunities for exploiting the potentialities inherent in the emerging scientific disciplines through research organized in schools became apparent. The competition between the universities of the different German states impelled the states to support the experimental fields which showed striking achievements, regardless of the educational philosophies held by the bulk of the academic profession or by the administrators and the rulers upon whom the universities depended. Starting about 1825, with the foundation of Liebig's laboratory at Giessen, the German universities became in less than two decades the undisputed centers of world science, surpassing in their scientific productivity both France and Britain.

The Social Functions of Nineteenth-Century Science

These developments changed the social functions of science radically. Intellectually, eighteenth-century science represented mainly the spirit of free and critical inquiry, subject only to logic and empirical evidence. Now, in the nineteenth century, it symbolized the triumph of comprehensive theoretical systems. The new physical and chemical theories had an air of perfection, or near perfection, about them. They could be interpreted as the beginning of an era of a logically complete system of experimental philosophy in the physical sciences. The task of the future appeared as a matter of filling in details and of extending the system to the biological and the social sciences. According to this view, the model of all science was classical physics.[19] Any inquiry which did not live up to this model or was not visibly advancing toward it, either because of insufficient overlap between observation and theory or because of imperfections of either theory or method, was suspect and considered inferior.

The change was even more dramatic in the educational functions of science. As noted above, there was little education and virtually no systematic training in science during the eighteenth century. What influence the scientific approach had on education was mainly limited to casting doubt on the value of the content and method of the prevailing education. In the nineteenth century, by contrast, the advanced study of science became one of the principal realizations of the new university ideal of integration of research and training.

Training for research had many similarities to indoctrination. The student was brought up in a tradition of theories, methods, and exemplary cases of discoveries codified in textbooks, considered as constituting a coherent and closed system. He was assigned research topics which arose out of that tradition, and he was supposed to treat his research problems as "puzzles" to be solved by the theories and methods available within that tradition; in this way, he would contribute to its further perfection.[20]

This gave rise to another radical departure from the eighteenth-century situation, when scientific achievements could bring honor but seldom income to the scientist. Now, in the nineteenth century, his achievements often conferred on him more or less well-paying teaching positions and, especially in Germany, monopolistic powers over productive research resources.[21] This created a vested interest in blurring the distinction between the procedural rules of science and the actual research traditions of a particular group within science. Since these particular traditions were thought to be adhering strictly to the procedural rules, there seemed to be no need for a superior authority, situated outside the research group or school, to judge whether the achievements of its members lived up to the standards of science. This tendency to identify a discipline with a research school had particularly insidious results in Germany, where the teaching laboratory and the university institute were the principal resources available for research and could be obtained only through the recognition of a specialty as a discipline and the establishment of a separate chair for it. The result was an eagerness on the part of certain schools to monopolize disciplines, as well as an effort to turn research schools into recognized independent disciplines.

This development introduced a bias into scientific thinking. Discoveries which did not fit into one of the existing disciplines or did not promise to become "systematic" teaching disciplines (that is, relatively comprehensive and logically well structured) were either relegated to an inferior category of "narrow" specialities (the administrative corollary of which was that a person in such a field could not be made into a full professor—he was not *ordinierbar* [*ordinarius* = full professor]) or were actually attacked and ridiculed. Many examples of such attitudes can be cited, such as the total rejection of Semmelweiss's excellent work on the causes and prevention of puerperal fever; the nonrecognition of the discoveries of Mendel; and the hurdles placed in the way of bacteriologists, physiological chemists, and physical chemists, which made it very difficult for them to become established at the universities.[22] Even people like Otto Hahn and Lisa Meitner, whose excellence and the importance of whose work were beyond doubt and dispute, had difficulty in overcoming the hurdles of disciplinary boundaries which were so conspicuous a feature of the German universities.[23]

Disciplinary Dogmatism, Monopoly, and Social Control in Nineteenth-Century Science

This disciplinary exclusiveness and rigidity became a hallmark of science education and training for research. Thanks to institutional differences, the actual policies toward innovations were more liberal in some countries than in Germany; this was especially true in the United States. However, the philosophy of disciplinary science had spread all over the world, and it dominated, in particular, the teaching of science.[24]

At first sight this disciplinary dogmatism of nineteenth-century science appears to constitute a change in the norms of scientific judgment. In the seventeenth and eighteenth centuries the academies evaluated scientific contributions according to formal criteria of mathematical and empirical inquiry which were relatively unbiased toward different theories. With the emergence of the new disciplines this general model gave way to specific disciplinary models containing more or less elaborate theories and unstated metaphysical assumptions about the nature of matter, light, electricity, living organisms, etc. This development seems to have introduced into scientific judgment a bias which had not been there before. The disciplinary models now seemed to dominate scientific thought; there appeared to be no visible control over them by a central supradisciplinary authority, such as had been exercised by the Paris Academy of Sciences in the eighteenth century.

That this is only part of the picture will, however, become obvious if, instead of concentrating on the rejection of discoveries which did not fit the preconceptions of one or another particular scientific discipline, we ask the question: In how many cases did rejection result in the actual suppression of the innovations? It seems that this occurred very rarely. The two most well-known cases are those of Semmelweiss and Mendel, whose innovations, rejected by scientific authorities, were forgotten and so had to be rediscovered. Only in the case of Semmelweiss was there actual suppression, in the sense that the rejection of his discovery was unsuccessfully contested.[25]

Mendel did not accept the erroneous opinion of the leading scientific authority, but he did not fight it, either. Nägeli was probably prejudiced by his disciplinary orthodoxy against Mendel—who was a nonphysiologist—and so did not trouble to understand Mendel properly. But Mendel, who was somewhat of an amateur, was quite happy to follow the suggestions of Nägeli and turn to other investigations rather than follow up his own insights, especially since his further experiments (with hawkweeds) did not conform to his theory. Therefore, this was hardly a case of suppression.

As a matter of fact, what is surprising in the sociology of nineteenth-century science is not the prevalence of local attempts at suppression but the fact that they so rarely succeeded and that at no point was there any doubt among those with different prejudices that the contest of views could be resolved by accepted scientific procedures and that consensus would eventually be reestablished. No school managed to establish a monopoly over even a single discipline in science. When Laplacean physics ruled in France, there were physicists elsewhere, like Faraday and Oersted, who followed lines of inquiry not indicated by the French tradition. Again, the sway of a narrowly conceived theory of cellular pathology in Germany could not prevent the rise of bacteriology in France and eventually also in Germany. Some of the most important discoveries of the age, such as the evolutionary theory of Darwin, arose entirely outside any disciplinary framework or research tradition. Finally, by the end of the century, discoveries which did not fit into any existing discipline, such as those in physiological chemistry, biochemistry, and physical chemistry, became increasingly numerous. They were all received with skepticism and they were often fought over, but with few exceptions their importance was recognized and prejudice was overcome with no significant delay. Intellectually, the "market" for scientific ideas worked reasonably well—much better than most other social institutions. This is not to say that productive resources, such as laboratories, institutes, and research funds, were placed immediately at the disposal of recognized innovations. That allocation depended also on other conditions: positively, on such conditions as the existence of an outside, nonscientific market for the innovation (e.g., bacteriology) and the availability of resources still unassigned to other purposes (a condition which, at the end of the nineteenth century, was much more characteristic of the new, still rapidly developing systems of the United States and Japan than it was of Europe);[26] or, negatively, on the fact that the direction of research institutes was monopolized by those who occupied chairs (a condition which, as we have seen, characterized German science).

Furthermore, while disciplinary monopolies undoubtedly retarded the granting of autonomy and adequate resources to new fields, they do not seem to have oppressed the innovative spirit. Thus most of the new fields originated in Germany and Austria, where the disciplinary monopolies were the strongest. Scientists from these countries were among the pioneers, or were the pioneers, of the theory that disease is caused by infection, of Mendelian genetics, of biochemistry, and of physical chemistry, although all these innovations were discriminated against, fought over, and in one case actually suppressed by the academic authorities. It should be noted, too, that the rise of the neo-Newtonian research school of Laplace was accompanied by the acceptance of the un-Newtonian wave theory of light by Arago, one of Laplace's outstanding disciples.[27] It appears that the disciplinary organization of teaching and research not only did not discourage innovation but perhaps was actually conducive to it. The necessity to make rational sense of an entire field and to map out its borders not only focused attention on certain problems but also must have exposed the logically weak points and limitations of the existing tradition. To adventurous minds this could be a challenge and a way of lifting themselves above the existing tradition. In addition, mastery of the tradition saved the student from useless efforts to rediscover things that had already been discovered. This made it possible for him to choose the unsolved problems, which presented a real challenge. Thus what may well have been blinkers for the mediocre served probably as eye-openers for students with original minds.

It appears, therefore, that a distinction must be made between the effects of disciplinary traditions and the effects of disciplinary monopoly. Indoctrination in the former does not seem to have diminished dissent and independence of thought. In fact, it may have produced more originality and independence. But disciplinary monopolies were detrimental to the development and diffusion of innovations. Unchecked, such monopolies could have led to the long-term deterioration of science (they probably did have this effect in Germany). The reason that this did not happen was that, in spite of appearance, the social control of science through the recognition, publication, and rewarding of contributions, established and institutionalized in the academies of the seventeenth and eighteenth centuries, was never entirely transferred to the organizations of teaching and research. The academies continued to exist. While the Paris Academy of Sciences and the Berlin Academy lost some of their importance, the Royal Society of London regained much of its central standing in world science. Eventually the establishment of the Nobel prizes in 1901 created a new institution of world-wide allocation of rewards for science as a whole. Even more important were the new disciplinary and interdisciplinary journals and scientific societies which began to appear at the end of the eighteenth century and the national and international scientific conferences.[28] Some of the latter, such as the International Chemical Conference of Karlsruhe in 1860 or the Solvay Conference in physics in Brussels in 1911, settled questions of central importance in their fields.[29]

Hence, what happened, in the transition from the eighteenth to the nineteenth century, was that the organization of science became both more differentiated and more decentralized. The new functions of organizing research and of training for research were taken up by university-based research schools, while the control functions were shared by the academies, scientific journals, societies, and conferences. Because of the consolidation of national scientific communities and the absence of a central worldwide elite, located in one place, international conferences, such as the two just mentioned, occasionally assumed the function of making authoritative decisions and formulating new consensus in almost exactly the way this had been done in the eighteenth century. But these were exceptions. In general, the formal judicial procedure of the academies was replaced by the impersonal working of market-like mechanisms based on all these various organizations. The individual scientist who happened to be rejected by a disciplinary authority had several courts of appeal. He could submit his paper to several journals, present it as a book to the general scientific community, as Darwin did, or demonstrate it by impressive, highly visible experiments, as did Pasteur and Koch. These appeals were all made to organizations and publics which were separate from organizations of teaching and research and were often interdisciplinary in scope and international in their membership. These organizations and publics were relatively free of bias, and they applied the same universalistic norms of judgment as the eighteenth-century academies had. Prejudices and theories going beyond the evidence were disregarded, and well-supported empirical findings of significance were usually recognized even if they did not fit into any of the established fields or even if their theoretical underpinning was less than what was usually required within the established disciplinary traditions.[30]

Conclusion: Science as an Intellectual and Moral Endeavor

This story stops about the end of the nineteenth century. Much has changed since then in science as well as in its organization, but some of the generalizations that can be made on the basis of this material, about the social structures and mechanisms involved in and influencing scientific change, are still valid today.

One of these generalizations concerns the continuity or discontinuity of both the scientific role and the institutions of science. The cognitive contents of science have undergone great changes since the seventeenth century. Several of these changes were of fundamental significance, or, as some prefer to say, they were "revolutionary." But none of the so-called revolutions was accompanied by anything like the social and philosophical movement of the sixteenth and seventeenth centuries. There were no philosophical sects, no semi-conspiratorial international networks, no prolonged battles against the central institutions of learning, and no relentless campaigning for recognition of the institutional independence of a new philosophy like the one that accompanied the scientific revolution which began with the publication of Copernicus' work and ended with the foundation of the Royal Society in London. The institutional aim of that revolution—namely, the establishment of science as a distinct intellectual activity, to be controlled only by its own norms—was accomplished in the seventeenth century. After that, fundamentally significant ("revolutionary") discoveries could be made with no further institutional revolution.

The second conclusion concerns the kind of influence exercised by social structure—in this case the influence on the cognitive contents of science exercised by two kinds of mechanisms: those by which scientific research is evaluated and recognized, on the one hand, and, on the other, those by which scientific research is organized and supported. As we have seen, both kinds had a selective influence, recognizing or supporting some kinds of research and denying recognition to others. Of particular interest here is the effect of research organizations. As we have noted, these constituted potential monopolies which interfered with the development of certain innovations. However, further consideration has to be given to the way this interference occurred. One possibility would have been the kind of effect emphasized by most sociologists of knowledge, who postulate that the emergence of distinct schools of thought ("paradigms," etc.), particularly if reinforced by vested interests, tends to prejudice, shape, and limit human thought, making it resistant to innovations. The other kind of influence would have been simple and straightforward monopolistic practice to insure the interests of a particular group in research resources and appointments.

Although it is impossible to say that the former effect was absent, there is no evidence that it was stronger than what one would expect on the ground of common-sense knowledge about the limited flexibility of the human mind and its dependence on the tradition it has acquired. In any event, the effect was neither universal nor, probably, unambiguous. Innovations and discoveries which broke through the boundaries of existing paradigms continued to be made in the nineteenth-century setting of strict disciplinary traditions bolstered by monopolistic or oligopolistic teaching and research organizations, and they were probably made with as great a frequency as ever or anywhere (or, perhaps, with even greater frequency). Moreover, they were made in the absence of internal crises within the tradition. There was no crisis in physics to prompt Arago to formulate his wave theory, nor was there one in biology to stimulate Pasteur to revolutionize important parts of the field.

Therefore, even though many people probably identified with the scientific tradition in which they were brought up, in the same way that people identify with their religion, there is no evidence that this presented a problem for science. Most people are not innovators in either science or religion, and the few who are original thinkers do not seem to be hindered by having been brought up within a given tradition. In fact, such upbringing is probably an important source of their innovativeness. The difference between science and religion is not that the one is innovative while the other is traditional. Both can be either. The differences reside in the fact that in science there are better criteria than in religion to distinguish the valid from the misleading innovations and, above all, in the fact that social control in science has been inimical to monopoly, whereas in religion its main function has been to strengthen monopoly.

The main condition which prevented the monopolization of science by any one scientific doctrine has been the separation of the social-control mechanisms for recognizing and evaluating research from the organizations for research and teaching in science. The reasons for this separation lie in the fact that, as has been shown in this paper, modern science has never been content to be either a pastime of private individuals in pursuit of esoteric knowledge or the handmaiden of technology. Since the very inception of the scientific movement in the seventeenth century, scientists have claimed universal recognition and authority for science as the manifestation of a superior type of public knowledge. They have maintained this claim successfully—in spite of the esoteric nature of science, which makes it accessible to only small numbers of experts in each field—because of the existence of institutional mechanisms which have maintained the unity of the scientific endeavor and have vouched for its integrity by authoritative control of what should be admitted into science and what should be rejected from it. This is essentially a judicial function. It is not enough that it be done competently; it must also be done publicly, according to norms and criteria which can be understood by everybody (including those unable to appreciate the substance of scientific contributions).[31]

Scientists who perform this function are like judges in a court. They must be careful and circumspect and must insist on impersonal rules of procedure which cannot be challenged. This is not to say that they always live up to these requirements; but, if they do not, they are likely to be found out, to be exposed and criticized for the exercise of bias. Therefore, on this level there is a tendency to adhere to strictly universalistic rules of procedure and to eliminate from influence any extraneous interests or personal and philosophic prejudices. Of course, what is regarded as universally acceptable procedure will not be independent from the views prevailing in different scientific fields. But as far as evaluation of contributions is concerned, it is difficult, as we have seen, to reject something as nonscientific except on universally accepted grounds. This liberal tendency is reinforced by the fact that the allocation of scientific recognition is usually a supranational and, at least to some extent, a supradisciplinary process; the effect of any particular bias is thus minimized.

These judicial decisions are very different from the decisions which research workers have to make. The latter have to guess what is a live and promising question to be solved and what is likely to be a dead end. These questions cannot be decided on the basis of the strictly universalistic norms adopted in the evaluation of finished research. The difference is like that between judging well-processed evidence, presented in court, and deciding which of several clues to follow in a criminal investigation. Based on insufficient knowledge, the decision cannot be perfectly universalistic. Even the best hunch, as long as it is unsupported by evidence, cannot be judged by "preestablished impersonal criteria." One can also not expect at this stage either "disinterestedness" or "skepticism" on the part of the investigator. To the contrary, he is expected to be committed to and involved with his ideas; otherwise he would be unwilling to risk his time, effort, and occasionally also his money on the exploration of a mere hunch. This involvement and lack of objectivity are not contrary to the norms of scientific evaluation; for those norms apply only to the evaluation of results to be made public, while hunches are private and are not intended, and usually are not even allowed, to be published.

Recently several authors have interpreted this relatively normless behavior as a contradiction of the established sociological view which considers science an institution regulated by norms. They consider the normative variability of scientists' behavior with respect to their own research an indication that this behavior may be determined by value commitments and group involvements rather than by the logic of inquiry or the norms of scientific conduct. Whether this is a fruitful hypothesis for investigation remains to be seen.[32] But certainly there is no contradiction between this relatively normless behavior and the institutional view of science. As I have shown, social control in science is a function analytically and empirically distinct from research. The effectiveness of the social control, as well as its distinctiveness, is probably one of the main conditions which make it possible for the individual investigator to use his imagination and intuition freely. Because he will eventually be judged by fairly strict and impartial norms, he can be allowed practically as much individual freedom as he wishes.

This is another way of saying that science, as science has been understood for the past 300 years, is a social endeavor and that scientists, in addition to being physicists, chemists, or economists, are also members of a moral community. As Edward Shils has pointed out, one of the characteristics of this community is that in principle it subjects "every single element in the [scientific] tradition ... to critical appraisal."[33] The institutions and processes concerned with this appraisal have been an important part of the history of science. They have a logic and a structure of their own that interact with but are not determined by the cognitive contents of science and the organizations of research.

Talcott Parsons

12 Some Considerations on the Growth of the American System of Higher Education and Research

Few would contest that by the usual standards of academic excellence the American system of higher education has, particularly during the present century, achieved a rather notable position, not merely of quantitative development but of qualitative level. It clearly differs, of course, from most European systems in that most of its institutions of higher education do not conform to a single national "plateau" standard; rather, there is an immense range, from a considerable number of institutions of an academic quality which compares favorably with the best in any country, through a bewildering variety of differing and, in terms of academic standards, lower-level institutions, until we get to the level of local community colleges, many of which have, perhaps unfairly, been referred to as slightly glorified secondary schools. Considering these qualitative differences, Raymond Boudon is probably correct in saying that the proportion of American students to population, in what is a rough and only approximately definable elite sector, is not very much different from that found in a number of European countries since the end of World War II. [1]

Nevertheless, there is a certain paradox in this development. The development we have in mind took off in the aftermath of the Civil War, just over a century ago, and gathered strength in two subsequent phases, namely, in the period which, starting in the 1890s, lasted until about the 1930s, and in the period following the end of World War II. The author happened to be an exchange student in Germany in the interim between the second and third phases, namely, in 1925. He well remembers a social occasion in the fall of 1925 in Heidelberg in which his dancing partner was curious about why he, an American, should have come to study in Germany. When I explained my interest in learning about German culture and science, she said, condescendingly, "Oh, I understand—bei Ihnen gibt es wohl keine Wissenschaft." Even in 1925 this was scarcely a fair or competent judgment of the American academic scene, but it was much closer to being the truth then than it was later.

At any rate, as far as I personally was concerned, going to Germany rather than to an American graduate school in my own field—and this on top of a year in England at the London School of Economics—was probably an index of a certain "elitist" American attitude not uncommon at the time. This is to say that I had the usual view that European intellectual culture was superior to our own and that, in preparing myself for what at the time was a very vaguely defined career, I thought that extensive contact with that culture would be advantageous to me, not only for the specific benefit which I could derive from the studies, but also for the positive valuation attached to a European education.

This high evaluation of European culture stood at the time, as it has not ceased to do, in rather sharp contrast with the corresponding stereotypes about the "materialism" of American society and culture. It seems a special kind of paradox that this peculiarly materialistic culture, allegedly dominated by the pursuit of self-interest and profit, should have proved to be the place in which a distinguished university system grew up. Clearly, the roots of that system go back in certain respects to well before the Civil War, but there was a notable flowering in the period immediately following that war. Perhaps the appointment of Charles W. Eliot as president of Harvard in 1869 is as good a landmark as any. There were academic revivals throughout the older established universities—at Yale, Columbia, Princeton, and Pennsylvania—and in the notable new foundations, such as the Johns Hopkins University, Cornell, and the University of Chicago. The University of Michigan and the University of California, first at Berkeley, then at Los Angeles, and then Stanford University, also became important institutions.

This development rested on twin pillars. One was the land-grant policy, which was first enacted in the course of the Civil War and was overwhelmingly oriented to the training of young people in the practical arts of agriculture and mechanics. The other was the presence, even in the publicly supported institutions, of the "tradition" of liberal education. I think, for example, of the history of the University of Michigan, which early established a liberal-arts college, around which its distinguished complex of graduate and research institutions eventually grew up.

This development of American higher education also comprised a bewildering combination of public and private institutions and institutions with a variety of emphases. Eventually, however, a dominant type emerged.[2] This was the "full" university, centered on a faculty of arts and sciences, which in most cases had joint responsibility for teaching programs in a graduate school, on the one hand, and an undergraduate college, on the other. It became clear relatively early, however, that members of the faculties of such institutions would be expected to devote themselves to research objectives as a major function. This institutionalization of research as a primary academic function can be said to have gathered force in the early years of the present century. Finally, these universities did not confine themselves to the more purely academic functions at either the graduate or the undergraduate level but became, rather, the focal centers of a ring of schools of applied professional training, of which the three primary subcategories were law, medicine, and engineering; but the range substantially broadened in the course of the present century to include, for example, schools of business and public administration, education, and social welfare.

There is a certain sense in which this organization built on the traditions of European university organization. The preeminence, however, of the faculty of arts and sciences, and its relatively pure academic functions, was by and large an American development, not shared especially by the Continental institutions.[3] That the professional schools were included in the university complex we consider to be a notable feature of the development of this complex.[4] It should be noted, too, that faculties of arts and sciences usually came to include instruction and research in the whole range of intellectual disciplines, extending from mathematics and physics through the other natural sciences, the social sciences, and the humanities, and from time to time new disciplines were added to the traditional lists. Thus, economics became an established academic discipline in Great Britain in the late-nineteenth century and in this country at about the same time; sociology had a more tenuous hold in the beginning but has since become established; and psychology has experienced a phenomenal growth. An interesting case on the borderline of the social sciences and the humanities is linguistics, which became an established discipline only in quite recent years.

This upsurge of high-quality academic institutions, in which the development of universities, just sketched, was combined with a notable upgrading of a group of high-standard liberal-arts colleges which did not have graduate or professional schools, provided a base for the development of the larger system of higher education. Compared especially to European systems, the American had the additional feature of a much broader spread at somewhat varying levels of quality. The gradations have been continuous; that is, there has been no sharp break between elite and nonelite institutions. The hierarchy, furthermore, has not been a simple pyramid; for example, an undergraduate education in one of the better liberal-arts colleges has been fully equivalent to that offered in the undergraduate college of many major universities, though the liberal-arts colleges have not provided opportunity for graduate or professional study. Apart from this, however, there has been an enormous spread, also, with respect to the principal types of institutions. This has had a double significance for the system as a whole. In the first place, it has provided openings for some kind of higher education for an unusually large and rapidly increasing proportion of the relevant age cohorts. The American system has finally reached a stage where, even with recent cutbacks, more than 50 percent of the graduates of secondary schools go on to some kind of formal education beyond secondary school. The result has been a much broader educated base here than in most other countries.

The other particularly important advantage has been that the very extensive system of higher education has provided a job market for the people trained in the more central universities, notably in their graduate schools of arts and sciences. This market has been far more extensive here than in most European systems and has contributed to a general process of upgrading the academic standards of the system as a whole.

It would seem from these considerations that Boudon's point, which was made with special reference to the French system, is almost doubly relevant to the American.[5] There has been, that is to say, an immense quantitative increase, not merely in absolute but in relative sizes of institutions of higher education and in percentage involvements of the respective age cohorts. This has undoubtedly accentuated the phenomenon which Boudon stressed for the European systems, namely, the relative devaluation of the privilege of acquiring a higher education beyond the secondary school. To be a "college graduate" in the United States in the present generation confers nothing like the relative distinction it did when the grandparents of the recent graduates were young.

A particularly dramatic analysis of the way this situation has worked out has been presented in Neil Smelser's recently published monograph on public higher education in California.[6] California, in its policy for public education, tried to drive a "troika" of three "horses," namely, the university, the state colleges, and the community colleges. Smelser demonstrates vividly some of the strains which appeared when mere mortals attempted to manage this complex system.[7] For a time, however, it catered to virtually every interest. Thus the university sector, notably in the Berkeley and Los Angeles campuses, attained a very high level of academic distinction, particularly in research. The state colleges opened educational opportunity to a much wider sector of the age cohort than could have been admitted to the university. Finally, some higher education has been offered on a very large scale to still other sectors of the population through the community-college program.

How is one to explain this relatively sudden development of American institutions of higher learning, especially in view of the cliché that America is overwhelmingly materialistic? One very popular line of explanation must be rejected at the very start, as Max Weber, Merton, and other scholars have rejected it.[8] This is the notion that the development of knowledge, particularly in the sciences, which can be technologically applied, occurred in the first instance as a purely economic investment on the part of the business interests who expected to benefit from the technological results. After a fashion, this explanation fits with the establishment of the land-grant policy by the American Congress, and it fits in at certain later points as well; but it notably fails to fit with the high prestige that came to be accorded to "liberal education" and to pure rather than applied research.

The explanation I would like to outline is a different one—a multiple-factor explanation. It has to do with the fact that we have been dealing with a process of differentiation and other concomitant aspects of developmental change which cannot be reduced to a single set of paramount factors. We would like to suggest that there were two sets of factors in addition to the obvious economic interests. One of these lies in our own cultural background and can be focused in particular on the influence of Puritanism or the Protestant-ethic tradition.[9] The other lies in the high prestige of European models of concern with culture.

The first of these two factors derives from an indigenous condition whose influence has already been subjected to an important analysis by Robert Merton, building on hints from Max Weber's work, and carried on in different respects by S. N. Eisenstadt and Joseph Ben-David.[10] It holds that a predisposition for rational intellectual culture was strongly present in the heritage of ascetic Protestantism which the founding fathers of the Colonial era brought to the shores of North America, notably to New England; but one should not forget that similar considerations were also important to the founders of Virginia.[11]

The second factor relates to the drive for upward mobility or success which has so strongly characterized American society almost from the beginning. Unquestionably, intellectual culture had very high prestige in Europe during the period of American history with which we are concerned. The very fact that American society was undergoing a new development of prosperity and economic productivity greatly enhanced the mutual attention Europeans and Americans paid to each other across the Atlantic. One manifestation of this attraction was intermarriage between wealthy American and aristocratic European families. Another important manifestation lay in American concern for the arts in the European style, which led to the foundation of a number of American museums, private collections, symphony orchestras, and the like by wealthy patrons. Finally, a third important manifestation was the large number of young Americans who went to Europe near the turn of the century to study, especially, though by no means exclusively, in the universities of Germany.

The first point, then, is to challenge the notion that the basic American cultural heritage, specifically that aspect of it relevant to the normative order, has been as materialistic as has so frequently been alleged. If Weber's position is historically correct, even to a moderate degree, the concern for economic productivity (with its many concomitants—notably profit) and the concern for morality and, indeed, for cognitive understanding have been by no means antithetical, or even totally unrelated, to each other. On the contrary, all of these features have common roots in a long cultural tradition of the West, certain directions of which reached a kind of culmination in Puritan England in the seventeenth century, producing an ethos which was deeply ingrained in the early settlers of English-speaking North America.

This ethos was in certain respects the common background of the achievements of the "Anglo-Saxons" in economic productivity, in science and philosophy, and in certain aspects of the rational analysis of normative order, notably in the context of law. I think I should add that certain very central components of the modern pattern of individualism were also involved in this complex.[12]

The most important considerations on this point are that the primary cultural heritage of American society which centered on movements to the left of Anglican Protestantism throughout the Colonial period, and well down into the period of independence, was far from being, in the simple stereotypical sense, predominantly "materialistic." It seems to me open to grave doubt that even today this is the dominant meaning of institutionalized American orientations. I have long felt that the famous Protestant ethic, far from being dead, constitutes a continuing substratum of our national culture. I think Tiryakian makes a particularly important point in his contention that the Protestant ethic has been so pervasively institutionalized that it has come to form a kind of matrix that has selectively shaped the attitudes of the adherents of the other principal religious traditions that entered on the American scene in large numbers at rather late stages, namely, the tradition of Roman Catholicism, which does not greatly antedate the middle of the nineteenth century, and the tradition of Judaism, which, on anything like a mass basis, did not enter until near the end of the nineteenth century.[13]

The Protestant ethic in this sense could motivate—and, in my opinion, in historical fact has notably contributed to—both economic development and cognitive development. The record of British science in the crucial seventeenth century, including the foundation of the Royal Society, as analyzed in Merton's classic study, shows that as early as the first part of the American Colonial period the potentialities of the Protestant ethic for the promotion of science were already strong.[14] In this respect, then, there was not—as the common sense of today's intellectuals would often have it—a basic conflict between "materialistic" concern with economic productivity and "idealistic" dedication to intellectual productivity, particularly in the sciences and in the relevant branches of philosophy. Rather, both potentialities were built into the primary cultural heritage and have developed in response to differing circumstances in the environment of the cultural heritage.

One of the difficulties obscuring this point lies in the tendency to confuse the relationship between materialism and idealism with what, in this context, seems to be a secondary, though extremely important, distinction between concern for collective interest, on the one hand, and the pursuit of individual self-interest on the other. The relationship between the materialism-nonmaterialism dichotomy and the collectivism-individualism dichotomy clearly goes back to the Puritan heritage. Robert Bellah, in particular, stresses the extent to which the early Puritan settlers placed emphasis on the collective conception.[15] He quotes at length, for example, from the sermon delivered by John Winthrop on the evening before the landing in Massachusetts Bay in 1630. Quite clearly, Winthrop's emphasis was on the goal of setting up a truly Christian commonwealth on those barren shores, a conception which was otherwise phrased as establishing the "city on the hill."[16]

However, it is also well known that, certainly by the time of its Puritan phase, as distinguished from the original Calvinism, ascetic Protestantism had come to incorporate a very important individualistic component. In both England and the United States this component became increasingly prominent, certainly by the generation of the founding fathers of the republic if not before. The philosophical father of this aspect was John Locke, the primary ideologist, as it were, of the Glorious Revolution of 1688 in England and a major figure in the background of many intellectuals, both American and European.[17] One need perhaps mention only Thomas Jefferson and Benjamin Franklin among the founding fathers. Franklin is particularly important in this connection because of his role in creating a favorable cultural atmosphere for the pursuit of scientific interests. It might be remembered that Franklin was the most important founder of the American Philosophical Society, the oldest learned society in the United States.

It seems to me that the special salience of the syndrome of economic individualism—that is, the version of Utilitarian derivatives, which stressed and indeed glorified the rational pursuit of economic self-interest—is not in any simple sense attributable either to the Puritan tradition or to Locke's secularized version of it but rather to circumstances which developed in England and the United

States mainly in the nineteenth century. Seen in this light, economic individualism can quite correctly be said to have served as the groundwork of the predominant ideology of what, following Alfred Marshall, we may call the "free enterprise" system—to avoid to some extent the connotations of the term "capitalism."[18]

With reference to the central problem of this essay, however, I should continue to insist that the development of economic individualism was not as such the central meaning of this kind of individualistic stance but was rather an ideologically exaggerated branch of the main cultural tradition. That this branch should not be permitted to stand alone seems to be made clear not only by its historical connections with the more collective emphasis but by the fact that certain of the cultural movements with which we are primarily concerned, though they are clearly individualistic in a certain emphasis, do not involve in quite the classical economic sense the rational pursuit of self-interest. This seems to be preeminently true of the commitment of motivation and careers to intellectual enterprises. This was an endemic feature of what I still think it is legitimate to consider a part of the main American cultural-normative tradition. Indeed, it is my view that the predominant trend has been toward a synthesis of the individualistic and the collective components. It seems to me that there has been a kind of a natural, ready-made synthesis, at least until very recently, in Great Britain. Most British economists and much ideology on the non-socialist side have strongly stressed the "rational pursuit of self-interest" in the best Utilitarian tradition,[19] but this emphasis has been strongly counteracted by a tradition of concern for the national collective welfare, even though the form it takes be imperialism, to say nothing of the welfare-state developments of more recent times. It seems probable that the tendency to bifurcation along these lines has in the American case been encouraged by lack of a nationalistic-aristocratic tradition of the British variety. In the absence of such a tradition, it has been easier to maximize the appeal to self-interest and to contribute to the ascendancy of this syndrome in a quasi-official ideological context.

Certain tendencies to redress the balance have, at least, been conspicuous—in an intellectually limited sphere, to be sure—in the social sciences; we may note, for example, the development of the concept "institutionalized individualism."[20]

I shall return to this issue, but I should first like to introduce a hypothesis as to the nature of the process of social change out of which the American university system developed. As in other cases, a primary reference point for the beginning of analysis lies in the concept of a process of structural differentiation.[21] The differentiation I have in mind in the present case is not primarily one which has occurred within the traditional rubrics of distribution of collective organizations in the society, but somewhat cuts across them. I think the keynote is the differentiation between the two primary aspects of the instrumental-rational orientation, historically rooted in the Protestant ethic, which have just been discussed. What happened was a gradual process of differentiation of the more intellectual and cognitive orientational contexts from that of economic productivity. Business firms tended to become more and more definitely specialized as profit-oriented economic organizations. At the same time there grew up a societal "investment"—which was partly but by no means exclusively or predominantly financial—in the development of what we may call "cognitive production." This built on the general urge toward the universalization of education, which had started nearly a generation before the Civil War at the level of public elementary education and had then not only spread to increasingly larger proportions of the relevant age cohorts but had undergone a process of upgrading of educational quality to progressively higher levels.

It is mainly as a culminating stage in this upgrading process that the expansion of higher education, which is our primary concern in this paper, is to be seen historically. The structure of the system of economic enterprise has been such that a major development in these directions had to be, in the first instance, organizationally independent of economic enterprise. However important in-service training in industrial firms and industrial research organizations may have been, they could not become the main organizational sponsors and the main symbolic legitimizers of the complex of higher education and research.

Parallel considerations apply in a very interesting way to government. Unlike the situation in most of Europe, the main system of higher education here has received mixed government and private support and supervision. If anything, in the crucial phase of development of the university system, the private institutions tended to take the lead; but in the more recent period of growth, especially in the last fifteen years or so, massive support from public authority has been of central importance, in the first instance at the state level and secondarily at the local or community level, especially in the larger cities. It is very notable that, with minor exceptions, such as the three military academies, there is no such thing as a national university in the United States, in the sense of one established and basically controlled by the federal government. It is of course true that the federal government has intervened massively since World War II in the financial support of research and has gradually extended support for training programs in the sciences and the professions, such as medicine and engineering. By and large, however, the federal government has carefully avoided an openly directive role and has relied heavily on panels drawn from outside the government for evaluating proposals for research grants and training programs.

The circumstances in which government involvement in higher education and research developed favored a relatively decentralized system, one in which the teaching and research institutions, and the professional groups whose primary social location was within these institutions, enjoyed a considerable degree of autonomy. This means that there is a parallel between the process which led to the differentiation of the economic from the cognitive-intellectual concerns of the society, on the one hand, and the process which led to the differentiation of both from incorporation in the sphere of governmental function, on the other. At the same time, contrary to the tendency of many left-oriented interpreters to see government control around every corner of the winding way of academic development, these processes have not resulted in what is in any simple sense a government-sponsored or controlled system.

My contention, then, is that what has occurred in this country has been the development of what is, relatively speaking, a highly autonomous system. It is notable, of course, that the primary center of gravity of the research function has come to be located in the universities, not in organizationally separate research institutions on the model, say, of the Soviet Academy of Sciences. I have repeated this formula in print on a number of occasions,[22] but I think it has to be repeated once again in the present context. The most convenient reference is to the frequently expressed opinion of Daniel Bell, who belongs in a somewhat different sociological tradition from either Shils or myself, that the universities have come to be the most important sector of the American social structure. Bell goes on to say that the underlying reason for this is the development and mobilization of a new but crucially important resource in the operations of the society, namely, "theoretical knowledge."[23] I would here stress the term "theoretical." The important contributions of the educational system have mainly not been based in the old-fashioned practical-empiricist tradition but in the more theoretically oriented disciplines and subsectors of disciplines.

Our hypothesis was that the emergence of the higher-level cognitive complex in this context was the outcome of a process of differentiation—a process of differentiation occurring by and large between the two primary factors or orientational aspects of the underlying "rational" cultural tradition, namely, the one which was economically oriented, and the other which was cognitively oriented.

I agree with David Landes, in his analysis of the Industrial Revolution, that an essential component of such a process of differentiation is an impressive and quantitatively large payoff in advantage to those who have a "consumer's" interest in the process.[24] In the famous case of the British textile industry, which was the leader in the early Industrial Revolution, it was the massive cheapening of commercially acceptable cotton goods which constituted this payoff.

I would like to suggest that, for the development of the system of higher education, the payoff took the primary form of enhancement of prestige; this linked in with both the individual and the collective versions of the success orientation of American society. Prestige consisted, in this case, of the capacity of American groups to identify with the European models which were most important at the time and then to emulate and possibly even surpass them. In other words, a relatively massive increase in the availability of high-quality cognitive output was an essential condition of this process of differentiation, and the domestic consumers of this output were, on the whole, the prestige-hungry groups in the upper reaches of American society. They had become acutely conscious of the sense in which America's cultural status had come to be defined as inferior to that of the principal European nations, and they were, shall we say, desperately anxious at least to catch up, if not to excel. This consideration applied at the individual level and, in the relatively early stages, was particularly exemplified by the young American scholars who undertook, often at considerable personal sacrifice, studies at European universities in the late-nineteenth and early-twentieth centuries. At the collective level it was exemplified by the willingness of a notable generation of academic administrators to mobilize financial backing, much of which came from the business community, for the establishment of facilities for higher education in which the research component came to be more and more strongly emphasized. Such figures as Eliot and Gilman and, in a slightly later generation, Harper and Nicholas Murray Butler, and also Andrew White at Cornell, were prototypes of this orientation.

I have the impression that these people were in a way representative of the business elite who, from the point of view of their personal careers, had not opted for a business role. Eliot is a striking example; he was the scion of a prominent Boston merchant family, who, instead of entering the family business, opted to become a scientist and, at the time of his appointment—at the age of thirty-five—to the presidency of Harvard, was an assistant professor of chemistry at MIT. The fascination of European culture was highly manifest in that generation of American upper-class young people. The James family was an interesting combination in that Henry moved permanently to England and became a prominent English literary figure, whereas William studied abroad, more in Germany than in England, and returned to the United States to become a leader in the development of American psychology and philosophy. Perhaps even the career of Henry Adams is relevant; although he never settled into an American academic career, the author of *Mont-Saint-Michel and Chartres* was surely one of the preeminent Americans of his generation to be deeply immersed in European high culture. My suggestion is, therefore, that without this reinforcement from the upper business groups and the willingness of some rather maverick members of those groups to devote their careers to this development, it probably could not have succeeded on anything like the scale that it did. In a certain sense it was a recapitulation of the involvement in European culture of a notable group of the founding fathers, among whom we have mentioned Franklin and Jefferson, both of whom undertook extremely important diplomatic missions in Europe in connection with the movement for American independence. Jacksonian Populism diminished this sensitivity of American society to aristocratically based European cultural influences, but the generation of the post–Civil War period revived that sensitivity at a crucial time from the point of view of the development of higher education and research.

This discussion of the process of differentiation suggests the relevance of three components of the paradigm of progressive social change with which I have worked.[25] These are adaptive upgrading, inclusion, and value-generalization.

Adaptive upgrading refers to the meeting of the needs of what is, at the level of prestige and influence, analogous to a market demand. In the case of the Industrial Revolution it was quite literally a market demand; in the case of the system of higher education, however, it seems to have been a hunger for the prestige which was derivable from some kind of identification with the standards of high European culture. As I have noted above, this hunger applied not only to the cognitive fields, but also to the arts, though perhaps, in American conditions, it was a little easier to institutionalize it in the predominantly cognitive fields of the sciences. This hunger was felt by the members of an increasingly affluent class, who in various ways were willing and able to provide financial support for the kinds of developments we have been talking about. On the liberal-education and research level, then, government involvement came a good deal later, and at a time when the more practical technological payoff had become more prominent.

It is also interesting to observe the relation that developed between people identified with more or less established local "patriciates"—as in Boston, New York, Philadelphia, and Baltimore—and some of the big "tycoons" of the new industrial development—the Rockefellers, Carnegies, and Mellons—who were, by comparison, *parvenus* and who had trouble in gaining full social acceptance even in the United States, to say nothing of European society. We suggest that their susceptibility to financial appeals for nonprofit causes, notably in the cultural area of the intellectual disciplines and the arts, was related to their *parvenu* status. After all, the Rockefellers and Carnegie established the first really large American philanthropic foundations, both of which have played a notable role in the development of the American academic system. The munificent gift of John D. Rockefeller, Sr., which made possible the founding of the University of Chicago is an outstanding symbol of this tendency. It is interesting that the Mellons, though they have supported such institutions as the Carnegie-Mellon Institute of Technology in Pittsburgh, have been more concerned with art. The fact that the late Andrew Mellon established the National Gallery of Art in Washington and donated to it his immensely impressive private collection of European paintings is a symbol of the adoption of the life-style of the higher reaches of European society by some American business leaders.

It is exceedingly important to note that in both the more definitely cognitive fields and in the arts there was a very strong emphasis on quality. The American academic founders of the new phase, men like Eliot, Gilman, White, and Harper, had an eye for academic excellence and tried to attract persons of great intellectual distinction to their faculties. Similar is Andrew Mellon's choice of Bernard Berenson and Sir Joseph—later Lord—Duveen as mediators in the transfer of ownership of important European art to the United States. We could multiply examples.

The American emphasis on quality in both the cognitive domain and the arts seems to be an example of the far from perfect but still impressive integration of cultural values with the prestige values which helped to motivate financial support. If we take the case of art, which provides a less controversial example than science, we can say that classical masterpieces of Renaissance or Dutch art are the ones which have commanded the highest prices where anything approaching a free market for such masterpieces has existed. The British National Gallery's acquisition of the famous *Cartoon* of Leonardo Da Vinci and the New York Metropolitan Museum's acquisition of Rembrandt's *Aristotle* at what were reported to be extremely high prices are cases in point.

Correspondingly, American standards of academic excellence have largely been modeled on the best of Europe, and the influx of European scholars, not unconnected with political disturbances in Europe, has contributed in a major way to this excellence.[26] Einstein's arrival of course somewhat preceded the migration forced by the Nazi movement, but in the physical sciences a very substantial number of European migrants were at least in a partial sense exiles, and to a lesser degree this was the case in other intellectual fields.

My suggestion is, therefore, that the initial payoff, outside the academic system itself, came from those socially elite elements who for complex reasons had a deep interest in identifying with and emulating the higher European cultural achievements. In the early stages of the expansion of the academic system this was a sufficiently extensive market to support the earlier take-off phases. In the later phases, however, other considerations have certainly played a role.

It may be of interest that I first met Edward Shils when I had a visiting appointment at the University of Chicago for the summer quarter of 1937. He organized an informal discussion group on matters of sociological theory during that quarter. As it happened, I was then engaged in reading the galley proofs of *The Structure of Social Action,* which appeared in the late fall of the same year.[27]

Whatever other merits *The Structure of Social Action* may or may not have had, it did constitute a major operation of international communication in theoretical sociology, above all through the prominence given in it to the work of Durkheim and Max Weber. It seems to me that the influence of both of these figures on American sociology had up to that time been minimal. One might almost put it that Durkheim had been badly misinterpreted, first, by social psychologists, as the group-mind theorist, and, second, by the anthropologists, as the armchair anthropologist. An extensive sympathetic account of the theoretical nature of his contributions had not really been provided by anyone in the English language. Weber, on the other hand, was virtually unknown in the English-speaking world; and, where he was known, it was in a narrow historical sense for his essay on *The Protestant Ethic and the Spirit of Capitalism.*[28] I think that it is correct to say that as a comparative sociologist he was virtually unknown in the mid-1930s, though Shils, as one of a few, had obviously thoroughly familiarized himself with Weber's work at that time.[29] Since that summer I have always considered Shils to be a major partner with myself in developing and communicating sociological theory at the high intellectual level of these two founders of the theoretical discipline and in subsequently being concerned with problems which had been to a very large extent shaped by their work. I think it fair to say that this use of certain European models had a major transformative effect on American sociological thinking and contributed importantly to raising the levels of theoretical sophistication in our discipline. In all probability I would not have undertaken my part of the venture had I not, as late as the mid-1920s, undertaken European study. And of the two countries in which I did study, namely, England and Germany, by far the more profound intellectual influences stemmed from the German experience, notably from the work of Max Weber. Though Weber had died five years before I went to Germany, Heidelberg, where I studied, had been his home for many years, and his intellectual influence was clearly dominant in the relevant part of the Heidelberg academic community.

In connection with the sociology of sociology, it will be remembered that in many places a major rationale for paying attention to this discipline was that it could form an intellectual groundwork for the field of social welfare and the emerging profession of social work. It seems to me a notable fact about the University of Chicago that these two sets of interests did not fuse there at all; instead, a sharp division took place in the face of the very notable development of social work in Chicago, connected above all with the name of Jane Addams. In the long run the University of Chicago department of sociology refused to have any close association with the social-work contingent in the pre-Weber/ Durkheim phases of the development of sociology itself. It is perhaps worth noting also that when sociology finally came to Harvard as a recognized discipline, it for all practical purposes replaced a modified program in the field of social work known as "social ethics." At Columbia, too, sociology was in its earlier days closely affiliated with social work, but by the time of Robert MacIver an essential separation had taken place; and in the influential phase of Columbia sociology just terminated, in which the dominant figures have been Robert Merton and Paul Lazersfeld, only very tenuous relations to social work existed, in spite of the fact that certain theoretical ideas influential in the social-work field had been originated largely by Merton and were further developed and popularized by certain of his students.[30]

As a final note, it may be remarked that Shils in the Chicago sociological community stood out in his graduate-student and early staff years as a kind of maverick, certainly in part because of his strong interest in Europe sociology; for the Chicago tradition had been overwhelmingly American in its intellectual background, in spite of its early emphasis on the work of Georg Simmel.[31]

Perhaps the considerations that I have sketchily presented and developed in this paper present at least the beginnings of an explanation of a very important institutional development in American society which the dominant ethos of American social science, which gives such heavy weight to economic considerations, has been unable, it seems to me, to explain satisfactorily. As Gerald Platt and I especially stressed in our recent book, *The American University,* and as I further developed in my contribution to the recent book edited by Smelser and Almond on higher education in California, there has never been any serious question of an organizational separation of the natural sciences—which, after all, have been the source of by far the most important technological payoffs—from the social sciences and the humanities. It is one of the primary features of what we have called the academic "bundle" that in the core arts and sciences sector of university organization, in spite of certain organizational variations, the whole range of intellectual disciplines —natural sciences, social sciences, and humanities—has been included.[32] If technological payoff had been as decisive a factor in the development of academic institutions as some have contended, it is hard to see why the natural sciences would not far more frequently have separated themselves off from the other disciplines in separate faculties—if not in separate institutions. We think the persistence of this aspect of what we have called the "bundle" is important evidence in favor of the kind of explanation of the process of institutionalization of a university system which I have put forward above. By and large, the sources of this spectrum of intellectual disciplines have been deeply embedded in the European model of intellectual culture which has played such an important role in the American development.

One particularly interesting case may be noted. Several American academic institutions have been primarily concerned with training in technological fields; these are the so-called "engineering schools." One of the most eminent of these is the Massachusetts Institute of Technology. On the hypothesis that technological payoff is the big factor in academic development, it seems to me that what has happened at MIT would be exceedingly difficult to explain. In the first place, MIT evolved broadly from a training school for applied engineers into one of the most distinguished institutions in the basic natural sciences underlying engineering. Its physicists, chemists, and, for example, microbiologists have been among the most famous in the relatively "pure" aspects of these disciplines. However, MIT did not remain a school of engineering and theoretical natural science; for more than a generation now, it has been progressively expanding into other fields. It is well known that it has one of the most distinguished departments of economics in the world, and it has supported distinguished work in various other social-science fields, such as the study of organizations and international relations. It has not established an independent department of sociology, but a great deal of important sociological work goes on at MIT. Its more recently established and perhaps most prestigious competitor, the California Institute of Technology, has followed a similar path and has recently been engaged in a definite campaign to strengthen its work in social science. Somewhat similar things are true of Carnegie-Mellon in Pittsburgh and other institutions which started as more or less specialized engineering schools.

When I have spoken of prestige, especially the prestige of certain sectors of European intellectual culture, I have definitely meant not to use this concept as indicating a crassly "materialistic" interest in the successful establishment of academic work in various fields. My own position is the direct contrary of this, since I contend that the economic importance of these cultural complexes has been a reflection of their levels of excellence and achievement in predominantly noneconomic contexts. At the extreme of the "pure" intellectual disciplines, the question of strictly economic applicability has been on the whole quite subordinate.[33]

Notes

Preface

1. See Edward Shils, "The Intellectuals and the Powers: Some Perspectives for Comparative Analysis" (first published in 1958), in Edward Shils, *The Intellectuals and the Powers, and Other Essays* (Chicago: University of Chicago Press, 1972), pp. 3-22. See also Shils, "Ideology" (1968), ibid., pp. 23-41; Clifford Geertz, "Ideology as a Cultural System," in Clifford Geertz, *The Interpretation of Cultures* (New York: Basic Books, 1973), pp. 193-233; Raymond Aron, *The Opium of the Intellectuals* (London: Secker & Warburg, 1957); and Talcott Parsons, "Belief Systems and the Social System: The Problem of the 'Role of Ideas,'" in Talcott Parsons, *The Social System* (Glencoe, Ill.: The Free Press, 1951), pp. 326-83.

2. Shils, "Mass Society and Its Culture" (1960), in *The Intellectuals and the Powers*, pp. 229-47, and "Privacy and Power" (1967), in Edward Shils, *Center and Periphery: Essays in Macrosociology* (Chicago: University of Chicago Press, 1975), pp. 317-44.

3. In addition to the items mentioned in note 1, above, see Shils, "Ideology and Civility" (1958) in *The Intellectuals and the Powers*, pp. 42-70.

4. Several of the relevant papers are collected in *The Intellectuals and the Powers* and *Center and Periphery*. See also Shils, *The Intellectual between Tradition and Modernity: The Indian Situation* (The Hague: Mouton, 1961), and "Intellectuals and Their Discontents," *American Scholar* 45 (Spring 1976): 181-203.

5. Edward Shils, "The Calling of Sociology," in *Theories of Society*, edited by Talcott Parsons, Edward Shils, Kaspar D. Naegele, and Jesse R. Pitts (New York: The Free Press of Glencoe, 1961), pp. 1405-48. See also Shils, "Tradition, Ecology, and Institution in the History of Sociology," pp. 33-98 in Gerald Holton, *The Twentieth-Century Sciences: Studies in the Biography of Ideas* (New York: Norton, 1972).

6. Shils, "Center and Periphery" (1961), "Charisma, Order, and Status" (1965), and "The Concentration and Dispersion of Charisma: Their Bearing on Economic Policy in Underdeveloped Countries" (1964), all in *Center and Periphery*, pp. 3-16, 256-75, 405-21.

7. Shils, "Mass Society and Its Culture" (1957) and "Daydreams and Nightmares" (1957) in *The Intellectuals and the Powers*, pp. 229-47, 248-64, and

"The Theory of Mass Society" (1962) in *Center and Periphery*, pp. 91-107.

8. See "The Scientific Community: Thoughts after Hamburg" (1954) in *The Intellectuals and the Powers*, pp. 204-12.

9. Some of these papers have been republished in *The Intellectuals and the Powers*.

1. Aron: The End of Ideology

1. Both sides of the case are assembled in Chaim I. Waxman, ed., *The End of Ideology Debate* (New York, 1968).

2. Karl Linneback, ed., *Karl und Marie von Clausewitz: Ein Lebensbild in Briefen und Tageblättern*, 2d ed. (Berlin, 1917), p. 455.

2. Lipset: The End of Ideology

1. The relevant writings of this group include: Raymond Aron, "Fin de l'âge idéologique?" in Theodor W. Adorno and Walter Dirks, eds., *Sociologica* (Frankfurt: Europäisch Verlagsanstalt, 1955), pp. 219-33, in English in Aron, *The Opium of the Intellectuals*, trans. Terence Kilmartin (New York: W. W. Norton, 1962), pp. 305-24; "Nations and Ideologies," *Encounter* 4 (January 1955): 23-33; "The End of Ideology and the Renaissance of Ideas," in *The Industrial Society* (New York: Praeger, 1967), pp. 92-183. Daniel Bell, *Marxism-Leninism: A Doctrine on the Defensive: The "End of Ideology" in the Soviet Union* (New York: Columbia University Research Institute on Communist Affairs, 1955); *The End of Ideology*, rev. ed. (New York: Collier Books, 1962); Bell and Henry D. Aiken, "Ideology—A Debate," *Commentary* 37 (October 1964): 69-76; "Ideology and Soviet Politics," *Slavic Review* 24 (December 1965): 591-603; *The Coming of Post-Industrial Society* (New York: Basic Books, 1973). S. M. Lipset, "The State of Democratic Politics," *Canadian Forum* 35 (November 1955): 170-71; "Socialism—Left and Right—East and West," *Confluence* 7 (Summer 1958): 173-92; "The End of Ideology?" in *Political Man* (Garden City: Doubleday, 1960), pp. 403-17; "The Changing Class Structure and Contemporary European Politics," *Daedalus* 93 (Winter 1964): 271-303, reprinted in revised form in Lipset, *Revolution and Counterrevolution*, rev. ed. (Garden City: Doubleday-Anchor Books, 1970), pp. 267-304; "Some Further Comments on 'The End of Ideology,'" *American Political Science Review* 60 (1966): 17-19. Edward Shils, "The End of Ideology?" *Encounter* 5 (November 1955): 52-58; "Ideology and Civility: On the Politics of the Intellectuals," *Sewanee Review* 66 (July-September 1958): 450-80; "The Concept and Function of Ideology," in the *International Encyclopedia of the Social Sciences*, edited by David L. Sills, 17 vols. (New York: Macmillan and Free Press, 1968), 7:66-76. The latter two articles are reprinted in slightly revised form in Shils, *The Intellectuals and the Powers and Other Essays* (Chicago: University of Chicago Press, 1972).

2. "We're All Totalitarians," *Times Literary Supplement* (London), 5 May 1972, p. 507.

3. Kenneth Keniston, "Revolution or Counterrevolution?" in R. J. Lifton and E. Olson, eds., *Explorations in Psycho-history: The Wellfleet Papers* (New York: Simon & Schuster, 1974), pp. 293-94.

4. L. N. Moskvichov, *The End of Ideology Theory: Illusions and Reality* (Moscow: Progress Publishers, 1974), pp. 8, 11-12.

5. Ibid., pp. 181-82.

6. Criticisms of the "end-of-ideology" school include: Henry D. Aiken, "The Revolt against Ideology," *Commentary* 37 (April 1964): 29-39; Norman Birnbaum, "The Sociological Study of Ideology (1940-1960)," *Current Sociology* 9 (1960), esp.

pp. 115–17; William Connolly, *Political Science and Ideology* (New York: Atherton Press, 1967), esp. pp. 51–53; R. Alan Haber, "The End of Ideology as Ideology," *Our Generation*, November, 1966, pp. 51–68; Nigel Harris, *Beliefs in Society: The Problem of Ideology* (London: C. A. Watts, 1968), pp. 10–12; Joseph LaPalombara, "Decline of Ideology: A Dissent and an Interpretation," *American Political Science Review* 60 (March 1966): 5–16; Ralph Miliband, "Mills and Politics," in I. L. Horowitz, ed., *The New Sociology* (New York: Oxford University Press, 1964), pp. 86–87; Stephen W. Rousseas and James Farganis, "American Politics and the End of Ideology," in Horowitz, ed., *The New Sociology,* pp. 268–89; Dusky Lee Smith, "The Sunshine Boys: Toward a Sociology of Happiness," in Larry T. Reynolds and Janice M. Reynolds, eds., *The Sociology of Sociology* (New York: David McKay, 1970), pp. 371–87; C. H. Anderson, *Toward a New Sociology* (Homewood, Ill.: The Dorsey Press, 1971), p. 38; Giuseppe Di Palma, *The Study of Conflict in Western Society: A Critique of the End of Ideology* (Morristown, N.J.: General Learning Press, 1973); Dennis H. Wrong, "Reflections on the End of Ideology," *Dissent* 7 (Summer 1960): 286–91; Michael Harrington, "The Anti-Ideology Ideologues," in C. I. Waxman, ed., *The End of Ideology Debate* (New York: Funk & Wagnalls, 1968), pp. 342–51; Donald Clark Hodges, "The End of 'The End of Ideology,'" *American Journal of Economics and Sociology* 26 (April 1967): 135–46; Peter Clecak, *Radical Paradoxes* (New York: Harper & Row, 1974), pp. 238–39.

7. Friedrich Engels, "Ludwig Feuerbach and the End of Classical German Philosophy" (1886), in *K. Marx and F. Engels, On Religion* (Moscow: Foreign Languages Publishing House, 1957), p. 263.

8. Lewis Feuer, "Ethical Theories and Historical Materialism," *Science and Society* 6 (Summer 1942): 269.

9. See *From Max Weber: Essays in Sociology,* edited by H. H. Gerth and C. Wright Mills (New York: Oxford University Press, 1946), pp. 155–56. For basic conceptualization, see Max Weber, *Economy and Society,* trans. Ephraim Fischoff et al. (Totowa, N.J.: Bedminster Press, 1968) pp. 24–26, and *The Theory of Social and Economic Organization,* trans. A. M. Henderson and Talcott Parsons (New York: Oxford University Press, 1947), pp. 115–18. For a detailed discussion of these ideas applied to the analysis of contemporary social change, see S. M. Lipset, "Social Structure and Social Change," in Peter Blau, ed., *Approaches to the Study of Social Structure* (New York: Free Press, 1975), pp. 172–209.

10. William Delany, "The Role of Ideology: A Summation," in Waxman, ed., *The End of Ideology Debate,* p. 304.

11. As discussed and cited in Guenther Roth, *The Social Democrats in Imperial Germany* (Totowa, N.J.: Bedminster Press, 1963), p. 252.

12. Karl Mannheim, *Ideology and Utopia,* trans. Louis Wirth and Edward Shils (1929) (New York: Harcourt, Brace, 1949), pp. 222–36.

13. Ibid., p. 235.

14. Ibid., p. 230.

15. As quoted in Roy Pierce, "Anti-Ideological Thought in France," in M. Rejai, ed., *Decline of Ideology?* (Chicago: Aldine/Atherton, 1971), p. 287; see also Albert Camus, *Resistance, Rebellion and Death* (London: Hamish Hamilton, 1969), pp. 197–98.

16. This thesis is presented by T. H. Marshall in his now-classic essay, "Citizenship and Social Class," in his *Citizenship and Social Class and Other Essays* (Cambridge: At the University Press, 1950), pp. 1–85, reprinted in his *Class, Citizenship and Social Development* (Garden City: Doubleday, 1964), pp. 65–122.

17. Isaiah Berlin, "Political Ideas in the Twentieth Century," *Foreign Affairs* 28 (April 1950): 376–77.

18. H. Stuart Hughes, "The End of Political Ideology," *Measure* 2 (Spring 1951): 150, 151, 154–55.

19. Aron, "Fin de l'âge idéologique?" in Adorno and Dirks, eds., *Sociologica*.

20. Martin Jay, "The Frankfurt School's Critique of Karl Mannheim and the Sociology of Knowledge," *Telos*, no. 20 (Summer 1974), p. 84.

21. Theodor W. Adorno, *Prismen* (Berlin: Suhrkamp, 1955), p. 30.

22. Frankfurt Institute for Social Research, *Aspects of Sociology* (Boston: Beacon Press, 1972), pp. 199, 202–3.

23. Otto Kirchheimer, "The Transformation of the Western Party Systems," in Joseph LaPalombara and Myron Weiner, eds., *Political Parties and Political Development* (Princeton: Princeton University Press, 1966), pp. 184, 190.

24. Otto Kirchheimer, "Germany: The Vanishing Opposition," in Robert Dahl, ed., *Political Oppositions in Western Democracies* (New Haven: Yale University Press, 1966), p. 247. See also Otto Kirchheimer, "The Waning of Opposition in Parliamentary Regimes," *Social Research* 24 (Summer 1957): 128–56. In a note to his article in the Dahl volume, Kirchheimer remarks that these points have been discussed by a number of others, including Herbert Tingsten, Manfred Friedrich, Karl Bracher, and Lipset. See his "Germany . . . ," p. 247.

25. Lucien Goldmann, "Understanding Marcuse," *Partisan Review* 38 (1971): 258.

26. Herbert Marcuse, *One-Dimensional Man* (Boston: Beacon Press, 1964), pp. xii–xiii.

27. Leo Rosten, *A Trumpet for Reason* (Garden City: Doubleday, 1970), pp. 64–65.

28. This interview, published in *Le Monde* for 11 April 1968, is cited in "Upsurge of the Youth Movement in Capitalist Countries," *World Marxist Review* 11 (July 1968): 8.

29. Herbert Marcuse, *An Essay on Liberation* (Boston: Beacon Press, 1969), p. 56.

30. Barrington Moore, Jr., *Political Power and Social Theory* (Cambridge, Mass.: Harvard University Press, 1958), p. 183.

31. T. B. Bottomore, *Classes in Modern Society* (London: Ampersand, 1955), pp. 52–53.

32. T. B. Bottomore, *Classes in Modern Society*, 2d rev. ed. (New York: Pantheon Books, 1966), pp. 95–96.

33. Bottomore, *Classes in Modern Society*, 1st ed., p. 52.

34. T. B. Bottomore, *Critics of Society: Radical Thought in North America* (London: Allen & Unwin, 1967), p. 19.

35. T. B. Bottomore, "Conservative Man," *New York Review of Books* 15 (October 8, 1970): 20.

36. Bottomore, *Classes in Modern Society*, 1st ed., pp. 46–48.

37. Ibid., pp. 53–55.

38. Bottomore, "Conservative Man," p. 21.

39. Quoted, ibid., p. 22. The quote is from S. M. Lipset and Philip Altbach, "Student Politics and Higher Education in the United States," in S. M. Lipset, ed., *Student Politics* (New York: Basic Books, 1967), p. 244.

40. Bottomore, *Critics of Society*, p. 133.

41. T. B. Bottomore, "The Prospect for Radicalism," in Bernard Landis and Edward S. Tauber, eds., *In the Name of Life: Essays in Honor of Erich Fromm* (New York: Holt, Rinehart & Winston, 1971), p. 319.

42. S. M. Lipset, *Rebellion in the University* (Boston: Little, Brown, 1972), p. 195.

43. Quoted in Beverly Stephen, "Veterans of the Student Revolution," San Francisco *Chronicle*, 31 October 1973.

44. Joseph R. Gusfield, *Utopian Myths and Movements in Modern Societies* (Morristown, N.J.: General Learning Press, 1973), p. 1.

45. See, especially, his book, *The Uncommitted* (New York: Harcourt, Brace, 1965), and his articles, "Alienation and the Decline of Utopia," *American Scholar* 29 (Spring 1960): 1–10, and "American Students and the 'Political Revival,'" *American Scholar* 32 (Winter 1963): 40–64. Both articles are included in his collection of essays, *Youth and Dissent* (New York: Harcourt, Brace, Jovanovich, 1971), in which Keniston allows his readers to share his changes in evaluations as the years progressed.

46. Kenneth Keniston, "Revolution or Counterrevolution?," pp. 293–94.

47. See discussion and citations, pp. 30–32 of this paper.

48. For representative literature presenting different variants of the thesis, not cited elsewhere in this article, see Herbert Tingsten, "Stability and Vitality in Swedish Democracy," *Political Quarterly* 26 (April–June 1955): 140–51; Lewis Feuer, *Psychoanalysis and Ethics* (Springfield, Ill.: Charles L. Thomas, 1955), pp. 126–30; Stein Rokkan, *Sammenlignende Poliiskisosilogi* (Bergen: Chr. Michelsens Instittutt, 1958); Ralf Dahrendorf, *Class and Class Conflict in Industrial Society* (Stanford: Stanford University Press, 1959), esp. pp. 241–318; Gunnar Myrdal, *Beyond the Welfare State* (New Haven: Yale University Press, 1960); George Lichtheim, *The New Europe* (New York: Praeger, 1963), esp. pp. 175–215; Robert E. Lane, "The Politics of Consensus in an Age of Affluence," *American Political Science Review* 59 (1965): 874–95; Robert E. Lane, "The Decline of Politics and Ideology in a Knowledgeable Society," *American Sociological Review* 31 (1966): 649–62; Robert Tucker, "The Deradicalization of Marxist Movements," *American Political Science Review* 61 (1967): 343–58; Mark Abrams, "Social Trends and Electoral Behavior," *British Journal of Sociology* 13 (1962): 228–41; Manfred Friedrich, *Opposition ohne Alternative* (Cologne: Verlag Wissenschaft und Politik, 1962); Judith Shklar, *After Utopia: The Decline of Political Faith* (Princeton: Princeton University Press, 1957); Talcott Parsons, "An Approach to the Sociology of Knowledge," *Transactions of the Fourth World Congress of Sociology* (Louvain: International Sociological Association, 1959), 4:25–49; Thomas Molnar, *The Decline of the Intellectual* (Cleveland: Meridian Books, 1961), esp. pp. 199–222; Stephen R. Graubard, ed., *A New Europe?* (Boston: Houghton Mifflin, 1964), esp. essays by Ernst B. Haas, Karl Dietrich Bracher, Ralf Dahrendorf, S. M. Lipset, Alain Touraine, Eric Weil, and Michel Crozier; David Riesman, Introduction to Stimson Bullitt, *To Be a Politician* (New York: Doubleday, 1959), esp. p. 20.

49. Quoted in Rousseas and Farganis, "American Politics and the End of Ideology," p. 284.

50. Arthur Schlesinger, Jr., "Where Does the Liberal Go from Here?" *New York Times Magazine*, 4 August 1957, pp. 7, 36.

51. Arthur Schlesinger, Jr., "Epilogue: The One against the Many," in A. M. Schlesinger, Jr., and Morton White, eds., *Paths of American Thought* (Boston: Houghton Mifflin, 1963), p. 536.

52. John Kenneth Galbraith, *The Affluent Society* (Boston: Houghton Mifflin, 1958), pp. 97, 119.

53. Shils, "The End of Ideology?," p. 57.

54. Shils, *The Intellectuals and the Powers*, p. 55.

55. Aron, *The Opium of the Intellectuals*, p. 323.

56. Aron, *The Industrial Society*, p. 169.

57. Ibid., p. 161.

58. Lipset, *Political Man*, pp. 407-8.

59. Lipset, *Revolution and Counterrevolution*, pp. 268-70. Talcott Parsons also extrapolated from Marshall's analysis with particular relevance to the situation of Blacks in America. See his *Politics and Social Structure* (New York: Free Press, 1969), pp. 252, 257-59, 261, 277.

60. Lipset, *Political Man*, p. 343.

61. Bell, *The End of Ideology*, p. 404.

62. C. Wright Mills, *Power, Politics and People* (New York: Ballantine Books, 1963), p. 256.

63. Ibid., pp. 256-57.

64. John Kenneth Galbraith, *The New Industrial State* (New York: Signet Books, 1968), pp. 330-31.

65. T. B. Bottomore, *Elites and Society* (London: C. A. Watts, 1964), p. 70.

66. Bell, *The End of Ideology*, p. 405.

67. Bell, *The Coming of Post-Industrial Society*, pp. 477-78.

68. S. M. Lipset and Richard Dobson, "The Intellectual as Critic and Rebel: With Special Reference to the United States and the Soviet Union," *Daedalus* 101 (Summer 1972): 137-98; S. M. Lipset, "Academia and Politics in America," in T. J. Nossiter et al., eds., *Imagination and Precision in the Social Sciences* (London: Faber, 1972), pp. 211-89; E. C. Ladd, Jr., and S. M. Lipset, *The Divided Academy: Professors and Politics* (New York: McGraw-Hill, 1975), esp. 125-48; S. M. Lipset and Asoke Basu, "Intellectual Types and Political Roles," in Lewis Coser, ed., *The Idea of Social Structure* (New York: Harcourt, Brace, 1975), pp. 433-70.

69. From Max Weber, *Essays in Sociology*, p. 155.

70. Mannheim, *Ideology and Utopia*, pp. 230-31.

71. Ibid., pp. 232-33.

72. Karl Mannheim, *Man and Society in an Age of Reconstruction*, trans. Edward Shils (New York: Harcourt, Brace, 1950), p. 110.

73. James C. Davies, *Ideology: Its Causes and a Partial Cure* (Morristown, N.J.: General Learning Press, 1974), p. 3.

74. Rousseas and Farganis, "American Politics and the End of Ideology," p. 274.

75. Lipset, *Revolution and Counterrevolution*, p. 303.

76. Hughes, "The End of Political Ideology," p. 158.

77. Moskvichov, *The End of Ideology Theory*, p. 28.

78. Franz Schurmann, "System, Contradictions, and Revolutions in America," in Roderick Ayn and Norman Miller, eds., *The New American Revolution* (New York: Free Press, 1971), p. 61.

79. Moskvichov, *The End of Ideology Theory*, pp. 62-66.

80. Alvin W. Gouldner, "Toward a Radical Reconstruction of Sociology," *Social Policy* 1 (May-June 1970): 21.

81. Shils, *The Intellectuals and the Powers*, pp. 40-41.

82. M. Rejai, W. L. Mason, and D. C. Beller, "Empirical Relevance of the Hypothesis of Decline," in Rejai, ed., *Decline of Ideology*, pp. 274-75. See also Paul R. Abramson, "Social Class and Political Change in Western Europe," *Comparative Political Studies* 4 (July 1971), esp. pp. 146-47, and David R. Schweitzer, *Status Frustration and Conservatism in Comparative Perspective: The Swiss Case* (Beverly Hills: Sage Publications, 1974), pp. 17-21.

83. John Clayton Thomas, *The Decline of Ideology in Western Political Parties: A Study of Changing Policy Orientations* (Beverly Hills: Sage Publications, 1974), p. 13.

84. Ibid., p. 26.

85. Ibid., p. 44.

86. Ibid., pp. 45-46.

87. Rejai, Mason, and Beller, "Empirical Relevance of the Hypothesis of Decline," in Rejai, ed., *Decline of Ideology*, p. 275.

88. Lipset, "Social Structure and Social Change."

89. Thomas, *The Decline of Ideology in Western Political Parties: A Study of Changing Policy Orientations*, p. 49.

90. Richard Rose and Derek W. Urwin, "Persistence and Change in Western Party Systems since 1945," *Political Studies* 18 (September 1970): 295.

91. Richard Simpson, "System and Humanism in Social Science," *Science* 173 (May 1971): 664.

3. Eisenstadt: The Sociological Tradition

1. E. Shils, "Tradition," *Comparative Studies in Society and History* 13 (April 1971): 122-59; idem, "Intellectuals, Tradition, and the Traditions of Intellectuals: Some Preliminary Considerations," *Daedalus* 101 (Spring 1972): 21-34.

2. On the distinction between "great" and "little" traditions, see R. Redfield, *Peasant Society and Culture* (Chicago: University of Chicago Press, 1956), pp. 67-104.

3. T. Kuhn, *The Structure of Scientific Revolutions*, 2d ed. (Chicago: University of Chicago Press, 1970). P. K. Feyerabend, "Against Method: Outline of an Anarchistic Theory of Knowledge," in M. Radner and S. Winokur, eds., *Analysis of Theories and Methods of Physics and Psychology*, Minnesota Studies in Philosophy of Science, vol. 4 (Minneapolis: University of Minnesota Press, 1970), pp. 17-130. Among Mannheim's works, see, e.g., K. Mannheim, *Ideology and Utopia* (New York: Harcourt, Brace, Jovanovich, 1936); idem, *Essays on the Sociology of Knowledge* (New York: Oxford University Press, 1952). Finally, see the essays collected in R. K. Merton, *The Sociology of Science* (Chicago: University of Chicago Press, 1974).

4. J. Ben-David and R. Collins, "Social Factors in the Origins of New Science," *American Sociological Review* 31 (August 1966): 451-65.

5. E. Shils, "The Calling of Sociology," in T. Parsons, E. Shils, K. D. Naegele, and J. R. Pitts, eds., *Theories of Society*, 2 vols. (New York: Free Press, 1961), 2:1405-8; idem, "The Trend of Sociological Research," paper read at the 8th International Congress of Sociology, Evian, 1966; idem, "Tradition, Ecology, and Institution in the History of Sociology," *Daedalus* 99 (Fall 1970): 760-825.

6. E. A. Tiryakian, "Introduction to the Sociology of Sociology," in E. A. Tiryakian, ed., *The Phenomenon of Sociology* (New York: Appleton-Century-Crofts, 1971), esp. pp. 6-9.

7. Studies of the development of sociology out of philosophy are, of course, so numerous that few can be mentioned here. For some of the earlier analyses, which also contain very useful information about the relations of sociology to the development of history, jurisprudence, etc., see the surveys on the development of sociology in different countries in volume 1 of the *Encyclopaedia of the Social Sciences* (New York: Macmillan, 1930), pp. 231-320. See also H. Becker and H. E. Barnes, *Social Thought from Lore to Science*, 3 vols. (New York: Dover, 1961), esp. vol. 2, and T. Parsons, "Unity and Diversity in the Modern Intellectual Disciplines: The Role of the

Social Sciences," *Daedalus* 94 (1965): 39-65. Among the more recent surveys, see F. Jonas, *Geschichte der Soziologie*, 4 vols. (Munich: Rohwolt, 1968); S. Landshut, *Kritik der Soziologie* (Munich and Leipzig: Dunker & Humblot, 1929); E. Topitsch, *Sozialphilosophie zwischen Ideologie und Wissenschaft* (Neuwied and Berlin: Luchterhand, 1966); I. Zeitlin, *Ideology and the Development of Sociological Theory* (Englewood Cliffs, N.J.: Prentice-Hall, 1968). See also A. Salomon, *In Praise of Enlightenment: Essays in the History of Ideas* (Cleveland and New York: World, 1963), esp. chaps. 5 and 6; A. Pizzorno, "Una Crisi Che Non Importa Superare ...," in P. Rossi, ed., *Ricerca Sociologica e Ruolo del Sociologo* (Bologna: Il Mulino, 1972), pp. 327-57; R. Aron, *De la condition historique du sociologue* (Paris: Gallimard, 1971); and G. Gurvitch, "Brève esquisse de l'histoire de la sociologie," in G. Gurvitch, ed., *Traité de sociologie* (Paris: Presses Universitaires de France, 1958), pp. 28-65.

8. On the tradition of social reform as related to the development of sociology in different countries, see P. Abrams, *The Origins of British Sociology: 1834-1914* (Chicago: University of Chicago Press, 1968) pp. 8-153; R. C. Hinkle and G. J. Hinkle, *The Development of Modern Sociology: Its Nature and Growth in the United States* (New York: Doubleday, 1954), chap. 1; L. Bramson, "The Rise of American Sociology," in E. A. Tiryakian, ed., *The Phenomenon of Sociology*, pp. 65-80; A. Oberschall, "The Institutionalization of American Sociology," in A. Oberschall, ed., *The Establishment of Empirical Sociology: Studies in Continuity, Discontinuity, and Institutionalization* (New York: Harper & Row, 1972), pp. 187-251; A. Oberschall, *Empirical Social Research in Germany, 1848-1914* (Paris and The Hague: Mouton, 1965); and T. N. Clark, *Prophets and Patrons: The French University and the Emergence of the Social Sciences* (Cambridge, Mass.: Harvard University Press, 1973), chap. 3.

9. On these philosophical and ideological alignments of sociologists, see, among others, the items cited in note 7; and see also R. A. Nisbet, "The French Revolution and the Rise of Sociology in France," in E. A. Tiryakian, ed., *The Phenomenon of Sociology*, pp. 27-36; A. Giddens, "Four Myths in the History of Social Thought," *Economy and Society* 4 (November 1972): 357-86; idem, *Capitalism and Modern Social Theory: An Analysis of the Writings of Marx, Durkheim, and Max Weber* (London: Cambridge University Press, 1971), pt. 1; A. Salomon, *In Praise of Enlightenment;* F. Jonas, *Geschichte der Soziologie;* S. Landshut, *Kritik der Soziologie;* G. Gurvitch, "Brève esquisse"; R. Fletcher, *The Making of Sociology,* 2 vols. (London: Michael Joseph, 1971), vol. 7; and H. Schwendinger and J. R. Schwendinger, *The Sociologists of the Chair: A Radical Analysis of the Formative Years of North American Sociology, 1883-1922* (New York: Basic Books, 1974).

10. On de Tocqueville, see, among others, A. Salomon, *In Praise of Enlightenment,* esp. chap. 5, pp. 261-328; I. M. Zeitlin, "Liberty, Equality and Revolution" in *Alexis de Tocqueville* (Boston: Little, Brown, 1971). On Lorenz von Stein, see L. von Stein, *Staat und Gesellschaft* (Zurich: Rascher, 1934); and for a discussion, see, among others, S. Landshut, *Kritik der Soziologie.*

11. The literature on all these scholars is, of course, too immense to list it all. For one of the best analyses see R. Aron, *Main Currents in Sociological Thought,* 2 vols. (Middlesex, Eng.: Penguin Books, 1970), 2:21-107, 259-71.

On Weber, see, among others, O. Stammer, ed., *Max Weber and Sociology Today* (Oxford: Blackwell, 1971); R. Bendix, *Max Weber: An Intellectual Portrait* (New York: Doubleday, 1960), chap. 14; A. Mitzman, *Sociology and Estrangement: Three*

Sociologists of Imperial Germany (New York: Knopf, 1973), pp. 39–131; A. Giddens, *Politics and Sociology in the Thought of Max Weber* (London: Macmillan, 1972); S. H. Hughes, *Consciousness and Society* (New York: Vintage, 1958), pp. 78–82 and chap. 7; and F. Jonas, *Geschichte der Soziologie*, vol. 3.

On Simmel, see Donald N. Levine, introduction, in Donald N. Levine, ed., *Georg Simmel on Individuality and Social Forms* (Chicago: University of Chicago Press, 1971).

On Hobhouse, see P. Abrams, *The Origins of British Sociology*, pp. 101–57, 247–60; and for a brief survey, see the article by M. Ginsberg on Hobhouse in *The International Encyclopaedia of the Social Sciences*, 17 vols. (New York: Macmillan, 1968), 6:487–99.

12. See T. N. Clark, *Prophets and Patrons*, chap. 6; S. Lukes, *Emile Durkheim—His Life and Work: A Historical and Critical Study* (London: Allan Lane, 1973); A. Giddens, ed., *Emile Durkheim: Selected Writings* (Cambridge: At the University Press, 1972), introduction, pp. 1–51. See also P. Q. Hirst, "Morphology and Pathology: Biological Analogies and Metaphors in Durkheim's 'The Rules of the Sociological Method,'" *Economy and Society* 2 (February, 1973): 1–34; R. N. Bellah, introduction, in R. N. Bellah, ed., *Emile Durkheim on Morality and Society* (Chicago: University of Chicago Press, 1973); and R. A. Nisbet, *The Sociology of Emile Durkheim* (London: Heinemann, 1975).

13. K. Mannheim, *Man and Society in an Age of Reconstruction* (New York: Harcourt, Brace, 1940); idem, *Diagnosis of Our Time* (London: Kegan Paul, 1943); and idem, *Freedom, Power, and Democratic Planning* (London: Routledge & Kegan Paul, 1961). N. Jay, *The Dialectical Imagination: A History of the Frankfurt School and the Institute of Social Research, 1923–1950* (Boston: Little, Brown, 1973). L. T. Hobhouse, *Social Development: Its Nature and Conditions* (London: Allen & Unwin, 1924). See also M. Ginsberg, article on L. T. Hobhouse, in the *Encyclopaedia of the Social Sciences* (cited in n. 14, above) and the bibliography there. M. Ginsberg, *"Reason and Unreason": Essays in Sociology and Social Philosophy* (London: London School of Economics, 1947), esp. chaps. 1, 6, 15, and 16; idem, *On Justice in Society* (London: Penguin, 1965); and J. Gould, "On Morris Ginsberg," *Jewish Journal of Sociology* 16 (December 1974): 123–33. H. Freyer, *Einleitung in die Soziologie* (Leipzig: Quelle & Meyer, 1931), esp. chap. 4; idem, *Soziologie als Wirklichkeitswissenschaft* (Leipzig: Trübner, 1930).

14. On the Hobbesian problem, see, in general, S. N. Eisenstadt, "Development of Sociological Thought," in *International Encyclopedia of the Social Sciences*, 15:23–35.

15. See, for good illustrative materials, K. Marx, *Early Writings*, ed. T. B. Bottomore and N. Rubel (Middlesex, Eng.: Penguin Books, 1965), pp. 175–85.

16. E. Durkheim, *The Division of Labor in Society* (New York: Free Press, 1964), esp. bk. 1, chap. 7; bk. 3, chap. 1; and A. Giddens, *E. Durkheim: Selected Writings*.

Some of the pertinent materials on Weber's concept of legitimation have been collected in S. N. Eisenstadt, ed., *Max Weber: On Charisma and Institution Building*, selected papers, with an introduction by S. N. Eisenstadt (Chicago: University of Chicago Press, 1968), esp. pp. 11–12, 46–47, 54–61.

17. The relation of sociology to the Aristotelian tradition has been most fully explored by E. Shils, in the "Calling of Sociology" (see n. 8, above). On the place of Hobbesian problems in sociology, see the classical statement by T. Parsons, in *The Structure of Social Action* (Glencoe, Ill.: Free Press, 1949), pp. 89–95.

18. See E. Durkheim, *The Rules of Sociological Method* (New York: Free Press, 1964), chap. 3. On Spencer, see J. D. Y. Peel, ed., *Herbert Spencer on Social Evolution* (Chicago: University of Chicago Press, 1973), pp. 17–33, and Ronald Fletcher, *The Making of Sociology*, vol. 1.

19. For a comprehensive review of conceptions of social change since antiquity, especially stressing the distinction between historical and progressive-evolutionary change, see R. A. Nisbet, *Social Change and History* (London and New York: Oxford University Press, 1969).

20. See K. Marx, *Early Writings;* idem, *Selected Writings in Sociology and Social Philosophy.*

21. See K. Marx, *Selected Writings in Sociology and Social Philosophy,* pp. 236–45, 249–63.

22. G. Simmel, *Conflict and the Web of Group Affiliations* (New York: Free Press, 1964), esp. chaps. 1–3.

23. E. Durkheim, *The Division of Labor in Society;* idem, *Suicide* (New York: Free Press, 1966).

24. S. N. Eisenstadt, ed., *Max Weber: On Charisma and Institution Building,* esp. pp. 18–27, 48–65.

25. See, on the Aristotelian ancestry of sociology, E. Shils, "The Calling of Sociology."

26. This approach is of course most fully developed in the work of Max Weber. On the purely analytical level it is implied in the ideal types of the orientations of social action, as well as in the general types of orientations to social order. Some of the materials relevant for discussions have been gathered in S. N. Eisenstadt, ed., *Max Weber: On Charisma and Institution Building,* pp. 3–6, 11–12. Most relevant are, of course, Weber's comparative studies of sociology and religion.

27. E. Shils, "The Calling of Sociology," p. 1419.

28. C. Montesquieu, *The Spirit of Laws* (New York: Hafner, 1949). See also A. Salomon, *In Praise of Enlightenment,* pp. 117–41. L. Schneider, ed., *The Scottish Moralists on Human Nature and Society* (Chicago: University of Chicago Press, 1967).

On nineteenth-century ethnology and anthropology, see E. B. Taylor, *Researches into the Early History of Mankind and the Development of Civilization* (London: Murray, 1878); idem, *Primitive Culture: Researches into the Development of Mythology, Philosophy, Religion, Art, and Custom,* 2 vols. (Gloucester, Mass.: Smith, 1958). See also H. Becker and H. E. Barnes, *Social Thought from Lore to Science,* 3 vols. (New York: Dover, 1961), 2:748–57; and M. Harris, *The Rise of Anthropological Theory: A History of Theories of Culture* (New York: Crowell, 1968), chaps. 6 and 7.

On the evolutionary schools, see H. Spencer, *The Principles of Sociology,* 3 vols. (New York: Appleton, 1925–29); J. D. Y. Peel, *Herbert Spencer on Social Evolution;* H. Becker and H. Barnes, *Social Thought from Lore to Science,* vol. 2, chaps. 15 and 18; A. Comte, *The Positive Philosophy,* 2 vols. (London: Trübner, 1853); idem, *Positive Polity* (London, 1875–77); Ronald Fletcher, *The Making of Sociology;* and F. Jonas, *Geschichte der Soziologie,* vols. 1 and 2.

For a brief survey of twentieth-century developments, see S. N. Eisenstadt, "Social Institutions: A Comparative Study," in *International Encyclopedia of the Social Sciences,* 14:421–29.

29. On the development of empirical research in sociology, see B. Lecuyer and A. R. Oberschall, "Sociology: The Early History of Social Research," *International*

Encyclopedia of the Social Sciences, 15:36–53; P. Lazarsfeld, "Notes on the History of Quantification in Sociology: Trends, Sources, and Problems," *Isis* 52 (1961): 277–333.

30. For this, see, e.g., R. Aron, "Modern Society and Sociology," in E. A. Tiryakian, ed., *The Phenomenon of Sociology,* pp. 158–70. See also T. N. Clark, *Patrons and Prophets;* R. K. Merton, "Social Conflict over Styles of Sociological Work," *Transactions of the 4th World Congress of Sociology,* International Sociological Association, 7 vols. (1961), 3:29–44; and S. N. Eisenstadt, "The Development of Sociological Thought."

31. For some of these orientations of the forerunners of sociology, see note 7, above.

32. R. K. Merton, "Social Conflict over Styles of Sociological Work"; E. Tiryakian, "Introduction to the Sociology of Sociology"; I. L. Horowitz, "Mainlines and Marginals: The Human Shape of Sociological Theory," in L. Gross, ed., *Sociological Theory: Inquiries and Paradigms* (New York, Harper & Row, 1963), pp. 328–83; P. Rossi, ed., *Ricerca, Sociologica e Ruolo del Sociologo* (see n. 10, above); B. Schöfer, ed., *Thesen zur Kritik der Soziologie* (Frankfurt a.M.: Suhrkamp, 1969); R. Robertson, "The Socio-Cultural Implications of Sociology: A Reconnaissance," in T. J. Rossiter, A. H. Hanson, and S. Rokkan, eds., *Imagination and Precision in the Social Sciences* (London: Faber & Faber, 1972), pp. 59–97. For an earlier exposition, see "Supreme Values and the Sociologist, or Our Roles and Their Loyalties," in H. Becker, *Through Values to Social Interpretation* (New York: Greenwood, 1968), chap. 6, pp. 281–305.

33. E. Shils, "The Calling of Sociology," pp. 1435–41; M. Janowitz, "Professionalization of Sociology," in *Varieties of Political Expression in Sociology* (Chicago: University of Chicago Press, 1972), pp. 105–35.

34. For the consequence of this for the self-image of the sociologist, see R. K. Merton, "Social Conflict over Styles of Sociological Work," p. 42; A. Pizzorno, "Una Crisi che non Importa Superare"; I. L. Horowitz, "Mainliners and Marginals"; B. Schöfer, ed., *Thesen zur Kritik der Soziologie;* and J. Goudsblom, *Balans van de Sociologie* (Utrecht: Spectrum, 1974), chaps. 5 and 6.

35. Illuminating in this connection is the difference between Durkheim's "imperialistic" and Simmel's "narrow" definitions of sociology. For Durkheim, see E. Durkheim, *The Rules of Sociological Method,* esp. chap. 1, and T. N. Clark, *Prophets and Patrons,* chap. 6. For Simmel, see K. H. Wolf, ed., *The Sociology of Georg Simmel* (New York: Free Press, 1950), esp. the introduction and pt. 1; and D. Levine, *Georg Simmel.* For one of the latest expositions of these problems of the limits and proper subject matter of sociology, see W. G. Runciman, *Sociology and Its Place, and Other Essays* (Cambridge, Eng.: At the University Press, 1970).

36. Some of the earlier and later debates over this problem have been brought together or summarized in the following books and collections: E. Topitsch, *Sozialphilosophie zwischen Ideologie und Wissenschaft* (Neuwied and Berlin: Luchterhand, 1966); T. Adorno et al., eds., *Der Positivismusstreit in der deutschen Soziologie* (Neuwied and Berlin: Luchterhand, 1969); W. Hochkeppel, ed., *Soziologie zwischen Theorie und Empirie* (Munich: Nymphenburger, 1970), pp. 13–48, 135–54, 179–95; A. Giddens, ed., *Positivism and Sociology* (London: Heinemann, 1974); E. Topitsch, *Logik der Sozialwissenschaften* (Cologne: Kipenhauer & Witsch, 1972), pts. 2, 4, and 8. See also the literature on the founding fathers cited in note 29 and J. Goudsblom, *Balans van de Sociologie,* esp. chaps. 1–3.

The more recent controversies about these problems are very well summarized in P.

Rossi, ed., *Ricerca*, especially by A. Martinelli, writing about the United States (pp. 177-215); B. Becalli, on England (pp. 215-33); R. Scarterrini, on France (pp. 233-59); G. E. Rusconi, on West Germany (pp. 259-85); and S. L. Bravo, on the Soviet Union (pp. 285-309).

37. T. Adorno et al., *Der Positivismusstreit in der deutschen Soziologie;* A. Giddens, ed., *Positivism and Sociology;* K. H. Wollf, "The Sociology of Knowledge and Sociological Theory," in L. Gross, ed., *Symposium on Sociological Theory,* pp. 579-87. See also the works of Gouldner and Friedrichs cited in note 48, as well as A. W. Gouldner, *For Sociology: Renewal and Critique in Sociology Today* (New York: Basic Books, 1974), esp. chaps. 5, 10, and 11, and E. Topitsch, *Sozialphilosophie zwischen Ideologie und Wissenschaft.*

38. On such later discussions, see, e.g., R. Bendix and B. Berger, "Images of Society and Problems of Concept Formation in Sociology," in L. Gross, ed., *Symposium on Sociological Theory,* pp. 92-118; see also J. A. Jackson, ed., *Role* (London: Cambridge University Press, 1972); F. Hang, *Kritik der Rollentheorie* (Frankfurt a.M.: Fisher, 1972); R. Louveau, *L'Analyse institutionelle* (Paris: Minuit, 1970); S. J. Bodenheimer, "The Ideology of Developmentalism: American Political Science's Paradigm—Surrogate for Latin American Studies," *Berkeley Journal of Sociology* 15 (1970): 95-137.

For a somewhat more general point of view, see D. Ingleby, "Ideology and the Human Sciences," *Human Context* 2 (1970): 425 ff.; V. Capecchi, "Struttura e Tecniche della Ricerca," in P. Rossi, *Ricerca Soziologica,* pp. 23-121.

39. R. Boudon, "The Sociology Crisis," *Social Science Information* 2 (1972): 109-39.

40. See R. Klima, "Theoretical Pluralism, Methodological Dissension, and the Role of the Sociologist: The West German Case," *Social Science Information* 2 (1972): 69-108; C. J. Lammers, "Mono- and Polyparadigmatic Developments in Natural and Social Sciences," Institute of Sociology, University of Leiden; R. Boudon, "The Sociology Crisis."

41. See, e.g., H. P. Dreitzel, ed., *Family, Marriage, and the Struggle of the Sexes* (New York: Macmillan, 1972). For a radical's critique of the tendency of radical sociology to cut itself off from the sociological tradition, see N. Birnbaum, "Sociology: Discontent Present and Perennial," *Social Research* 38 (1971): 732-50. For a similar critique, but from a more "liberal" point of view, see A. H. Barton, "Empirical Methods and Radical Sociology: A Liberal Critique," in J. D. Colfax and J. L. Roach, eds., *Radical Sociology* (New York and London: Basic Books, 1971), pp. 460-77.

42. Some of these arguments are to be found in the discussions about modernization. See the general analysis of the development in these fields in S. N. Eisenstadt, *Tradition, Change, and Modernity* (New York: Wiley, 1974), esp. chaps. 1 and 5; see also Pizzorno, *Una Crisi.* Some of these problems are also taken up in R. K. Merton, *On Theoretical Sociology* (New York: Free Press, 1967), pp. 1-39.

43. Some of these points have been taken up by A. Pizzorno, *Una Crisi,* and fuller illustrations can be found in F. Jonas, *Geschichte der Soziologie.*

44. On Durkheim and Weber, see T. Parsons, *The Structure of Social Action,* 2 vols. (New York: Free Press, 1968), esp. vol. 1, chap. 12, and vol. 2, chap. 18; and A. Giddens, *Politics and Sociology in the Thought of Max Weber.* On Simmel, see L. A. Coser, *Masters of Sociological Thought* (New York: Harcourt, Brace, Jovanovich, 1971), pp. 177-215. On Tönnies, see A. Mitzman, *Sociology and Estrangement,*

pp. 59–131, and D. Levine, *Georg Simmel on Individuality and Social Forms.*

45. On the controversies, particularly as related to Pareto and Mosca, see the materials in F. Jonas, *Geschichte der Soziologie,* vol. 3, and the bibliography there; and see, especially, N. Bobbio, *Saggi sulla Scienza Politica in Italia* (Bari: Latrize, 1969), esp. chaps. 3, 4, 7, 8, and 10.

46. On Sombart, see A. Mitzman, *Sociology and Estrangement,* pp. 135–264. On Mannheim, see E. Shils, "Karl Mannheim," in *International Encyclopedia of the Social Sciences,* 9:557–62. On the whole period of the twenties and thirties in Germany, see R. König, *Studien zur Soziologie* (Frankfurt a.M. and Hamburg: Fischer, 1971), pp. 9–37. Some of the major expositions of this period have been incorporated in A. Vierkandt, *Handwörterbuch der Soziologie* (Stuttgart: F. Enke, 1931). On the Frankfurt school, see M. Jay, "The Dialectical Imagination."

47. Some of the best recent expositions of many of these models and counter-models are to be found in J. H. Turner, *The Structure of Sociological Theories* (Homewood, Ill.: Dorsey, 1974). See also J. Rex, ed., *Approaches to Sociology* (London: Routledge & Kegan Paul, 1974), and N. C. Mullins and C. C. Mullins, *Theories and Theory Groups in Contemporary American Sociology* (New York: Harper & Row, 1973).

The different types of controversies that have arisen around these models are analyzed, from the point of view of our present discussions, in S. N. Eisenstadt, "Some Reflections on the Crisis in Sociology," *Sociological Inquiry* 44 (1974): 147–58.

48. From among the many works on the antinomianism of the student movement, see S. N. Lipset, *Rebellion in the University: A History of Student Activism in America* (London: Routledge & Kegan Paul, 1972); S. N. Eisenstadt, "Generational Conflict and Intellectual Antinomianism," in P. Altbach and R. S. Laufer, eds., *The New Pilgrims: Youth Protest in Transition* (New York: Mackay, 1972), and the other materials in this volume.

On radicalism and crisis in sociology, see R. W. Friedrichs, *A Sociology of Sociology* (New York: Free Press, 1970); A. W. Gouldner, *The Coming Crisis of Western Sociology* (New York and London: Basic Books, 1970); and J. D. Colfax and J. L. Roach, eds., *Radical Sociology.* For a critical review of these works, see J. Ben-David, "The State of Sociological Theory and the Sociological Community: A Review Article," *Comparative Studies in Society and History* 15 (October 1973): 448–72. Further discussion can be found in S. N. Eisenstadt, "Some Reflections on the Crisis of Sociology."

49. For some illustrations, see T. Schranger, "A Reconceptualization of Critical Theory," in J. D. Colfax and J. L. Roach, eds., *Radical Sociology,* pp. 132–48; J. Horton, "The Fetishism of Sociology," ibid., pp. 171–93; N. Birnbaum, "Sociology: Discontent Present and Perennial"; and S. J. Bodenheimer, "The Ideology of Developmentalism: American Political Science's Paradigm—Surrogate for Latin American Studies."

50. The centrality of these topics in the present sociological discussions is illustrated by the great number of works which deal with them. See, for example, the items cited in notes 36 and 49 and also J. D. Douglas, ed., *The Relevance of Sociology* (New York: Appleton-Century-Crofts, 1970). For an interesting illustration of the growing concern with some of the more marginal problems, see John O'Neill, *Sociology as a Skin Trade* (London: Heinemann, 1972).

51. See, e.g., R. Quinney, "From Repression to Liberation: Social Theory in a

Radical Age," in R. A. Scott and J. D. Douglas, eds., *Theoretical Perspectives on Deviance* (New York: Basic Books, 1972), pp. 317-42. See also the essays in W. Hochkeppel, *Soziologie zwischen Theorie und Empirie.*

52. The debates among German sociologists illustrate this tendency very well. See R. Klima, "Theoretical Pluralism, Methodological Discussion, and the Role of the Sociologist: The West German Case"; S. N. Eisenstadt, "Some Reflections on the Crisis in Sociology"; and the July-August issue of *Sociologische Gids* (1973/74), pp. 255-69.

53. On the functional model in social anthropology, see A. Kuper, *Anthropologist and Anthropology: The British School, 1922-1972* (London: Allan Lane, 1973). On sociological models, see J. Turner, *The Structure of Sociological Theory;* N. Mullins and C. Mullins, *Theories and Theory Groups;* and J. Rex, *Approaches to Sociology.*

54. For extensive reviews of the analytical and methodological approaches connected with these paradigms, see G. A. De Vos and A. A. Hippler, "Cultural Psychology: Comparative Studies of Human Behavior," in G. Lindzey and E. Aronson, eds., *The Handbook of Social Psychology,* 2d ed., 5 vols. (Reading, Mass.: Addison-Wesley, 1969), 4:323-417, and A. Inkeles and D. J. Levinson, "National Character: The Study of Model Personality and Socio-Cultural Systems," ibid., pp. 418-506.

Modernization studies have been reviewed extensively in S. N. Eisenstadt, *Tradition, Change, and Modernity,* chaps. 1 and 5.

Many studies on stratification have been collected in R. Bendix and S. M. Lipset, eds., *Class, Status, and Power,* 2d ed. (New York: Free Press, 1966), and later, with a somewhat greater orientation to problems of equality, in C. S. Heller, ed., *Structural Social Inequality* (New York: Macmillan, 1969).

For studies of status incongruence, see G. Lenski, "Status Crystallization: A Non-Vertical Dimension of Social Status," *American Sociological Review* 19 (1954): 405-13; S. Box and J. Ford, "Some Questionable Assumptions in the Theory of Status Inconsistency," *Sociological Review* 17 (1969): 187-201; and E. E. Sampson, "Status in Status Congruence," *Advances in Experimental Social Psychology* 4 (1969): 225-70.

The shift from the functionalist model in the sociology of religion is best illustrated in the changes of emphases in the study of ritual; for this, see, e.g., C. Geertz, "Ritual and Social Change: A Javanese Example," *American Anthropologist* 59 (February 1957): 34-38, and R. A. Rappaport, "Ritual, Sanctity, and Cybernetics," *American Anthropologist* 73 (1971): 59-76. For a more recent and general analytical survey, see N. D. Munn, "Symbolism in a Ritual Context: Aspects of Symbolic Action," in J. J. Honigman, *Handbook of Social and Cultural Anthropology* (Chicago: Rand McNally, 1973), pp. 579-613.

55. For some interesting hypotheses relating to the importance of such forces in the ascendancy of the functional-structural model in sociology, see H. Kuklick, "A Scientific Revolution: Sociological Theory in the U.S., 1930-1945," *Sociological Inquiry* 43 (1973): 3-22.

56. For the area of modernization, see, e.g., S. J. Bodenheimer, "The Ideology of Developmentalism"; G. Omvedt, "Modernization Theories: The Ideology of Empires," in A. R. Desai, ed., *Essays on the Modernization of Underdeveloped Societies,* 2 vols. (Bombay: Thacker, 1971), 1:119-37; A. R. Desai, "Need for Re-evaluation of the Concept," ibid., pp. 458-74; E. de Kadt and G. Williams, eds., *Sociology and Development* (London: Tavistock Publications, 1974); and the discussion in S. N. Eisenstadt, *Tradition, Change, and Modernity,* chaps. 1 and 5.

For political sociology, see, e.g., D. L. Smith, "The Sunshine Boys: Toward a Sociology of Happiness," in J. D. Colfax and J. L. Roach, eds., *Radical Sociology,* pp. 28–44; P. L. Hall, "A Symbolic Interactionist Analysis of Politics," *Sociological Inquiry* 42 (1972): 35–75; idem, "The Negotiation of Identities: Ego Rejects Alter-Casting: Or, Who Is a Liberal?" *Sociological Inquiry* 42 (1972): 93–99; R. Moss Kanter, "Symbolic Interactionism and Politics in Systemic Perspective," *Sociological Inquiry* 42 (1972): 77–92.

For the field of stratification, see, e.g., J. Stolzman and H. Gamberg, "Marxist Class Analysis versus Stratification Analysis as General Approaches to Social Inequality," *Berkeley Journal of Sociology* 18 (1973/74): 87–105.

57. See, among many others, A. Gouldner, *The Coming Crisis of Western Sociology;* R. Friedrichs, *A Sociology of Sociology;* J. D. Colfax and J. L. Roach, eds., *Radical Sociology;* and N. Birnbaum, "Sociology: Discontent Present and Perennial."

Analyses, by several experts, of the outcry about crises can be found in R. Boudon, *The Sociology Crisis;* R. Klima, "Theoretical Pluralism, Methodological Discussion, and the Role of the Sociologist: The West German Case"; P. M. Worsley, "The State of Theory and the Status of Theory," *Sociology* 8 (January 1974): 1–17; and S. N. Eisenstadt, "Some Reflections on the Crisis."

58. R. K. Merton, "Insiders and Outsiders: A Chapter in the Sociology of Knowledge," *American Journal of Sociology* 78 (1972): 9–47. For a similar point, see J. D. Douglas, "The Relevance of Sociology," in J. D. Douglas, ed., *The Relevance of Sociology,* pp. 185–233.

59. On Durkheim and Weber, see the items cited in note 44. On Mannheim see the items cited in note 46, and see also L. A. Coser, *Masters of Sociological Thought,* pp. 429–63, and E. Shils, *Karl Mannheim.*

On developments in the field of stratification, see, e.g., N. Birnbaum, "The Crisis in Marxist Sociology," in J. D. Colfax and J. L. Roach, eds., *Radical Sociology,* pp. 108–31.

In the field of health, see H. P. Dreitzel, ed., *The Social Organization of Health* (New York: Macmillan, 1971).

In the field of sex relations, see H. P. Dreitzel, ed., *Family, Marriage, and the Struggle of the Sexes.*

In the field of deviance, see I. Taylor, P. Walton, and J. Young, *The New Criminology: For a Social Theory of Deviance* (London: Routledge & Kegan Paul, 1973); P. Rock and M. McIntosh, eds., *Deviance and Social Control* (London: Tavistock Publications, 1973); and I. Taylor and L. Taylor, eds., *Politics and Deviance* (Middlesex, Eng.: Penguin, 1973).

In the field of modernization, see the discussion in S. N. Eisenstadt, *Tradition, Change, and Modernity,* p. 1, and E. de Kadt and G. Williams, eds., *Sociology and Development.*

60. See, among readers, R. Bendix and S. N. Lipset, eds., *Class, Status, and Power;* P. L. Lazarsfeld and N. Rosenberg, eds., *The Language of Social Research* (New York: Free Press, 1955); R. K. Merton et al., eds., *Reader in Bureaucracy* (New York: Free Press, 1952); and the other numerous readers published in the fifties and early sixties.

R. K. Merton, L. Broom, and L. S. Cottrell, eds., *Sociology Today* (New York: Basic Books, 1959).

G. Gurvitch, ed., *Traité de Sociologie,* 2 vols. (Paris: Presses Universitaires de France, 1958-60); R. König, ed., *Das Interview: Formen, Technik, Auswertung* and

Beobachtung und Experiment in der Sozialforschung (Cologne: Verlag für Politik und Wirtschaft, 1956 and 1957); idem, ed., *Handbuch der empirischen Sozialforschung*, 2 vols. (Stuttgart: F. Enke, 1962, 1969); G. Groeneman, W. R. Heere, and E. U. W. Veranjsse, eds., *Het Sociale Leven in Al Ziin Facetten* (Assen: Van Gorcum, 1958).

61. J. Turner, *The Structure of Sociological Theory*, and S. N. Eisenstadt, "Some Reflections on the Crisis of Sociology."

62. On the societal and political implications of sociological research, and on the related topics discussed, see, e.g., J. L. Horowitz, *Professing Sociology: Studies in the Life-Cycle of Social Science* (Chicago: Aldine, 1968), esp. pt. 3. For an earlier exposition of these problems, see P. F. Lazarsfeld, W. H. Sewell, and H. L. Wilensky, eds., *The Uses of Sociology* (New York: Basic Books, 1967). Later concerns are represented in G. Sjoberg, ed., *Ethics, Politics, and Social Research* (London: Routledge & Kegan Paul, 1967); J. D. Douglas, ed., *The Impact of Sociology: Readings in the Social Sciences* (New York: Appleton-Century-Crofts, 1970); I. Lochen, *Sociologies Dilemmas;* and almost any issue of the *American Sociologist*, but especially the supplement to vol. 6 issued in June 1971.

63. Illustrative of these tendencies are F. Ferrarotti, *Una Sociologia Alternativa* (Bari and Laterza: Italia, 1962); B. Schofer, "Thesen zur Kritik der Soziologie"; L. T. Reynolds and J. M. Reynolds, eds., *The Sociology of Sociology* (New York: Mackay, 1970), esp. chap. 2; H. S. Becker, "Whose Side Are We On?" *Social Problems* 14 (Winter 1967): 239–47; and A. Gouldner, "The Sociologist as a Partisan: Sociology and the Welfare State," *American Sociologist* 3 (May 1968): 103–16.

64. Illustration of such reexamination can be found in B. Schofer, "Thesen zur Kritik der Soziologie"; I. Lochen, *Sociologies Dilemmas;* L. Gallino, "Crisi della Sociologia Ricerca Sociologica, e el Ruolo del Sociology," in P. Rossi, *Ricerca Sociologica*, pp. 301–22; and R. Friedrichs, *A Sociology of Sociology.*

65. R. Bendix, "Sociology and the Distrust of Reason," *American Sociological Review* 35 (1970): 831–43.

66. S. M. Lipset and E. C. Ladd, "The Politics of American Sociologists," *American Journal of Sociology* 78 (July 1972): 67–104.

67. One of the latest expositions of this problem can be found in R. Pieris, "The Implantation of Sociology in Asia," *International Social Science Journal* 21 (1969): 433–45.

68. For illustrations of ideologically based criticisms, see J. D. Colfax and J. L. Roach, eds., *Radical Sociology*, pp. 45–66 and 171–93, and J. Horton, "The Fetishism of Sociology." For the general tenor of the debates, see *Sociological Inquiry*, vol. 40, no. 1 (1970), esp. A. Fasola-Bologna, "The Sociological Profession and Revolution," pp. 35–43; Martin Nicolaus, "Remarks at the American Sociological Association Convention," *American Sociologist* 4 (May 1968): 154–56; and H. J. Krysmanski and Peter Marwedel, eds., *Die Krise in der Soziologie* (Cologne: Paul Rugenstein, 1975).

69. See R. Bendix, "Sociology and Ideology," pp. 173–87, R. K. Merton, "The Precarious Foundations of Detachment in Sociology: Observations on Bendix's 'Sociology and Ideology,'" pp. 188–99, and R. Bendix, "Comment," pp. 200–201, all in E. A. Tiryakian, ed., *The Phenomenon of Sociology* (New York: Appleton-Century-Crofts, 1971).

70. See R. K. Merton, "Structural Analysis of Sociology," in R. Coser, ed., *Social Structure* (tentative title) (New York: Free Press, forthcoming).

4. Janowitz: The Journalistic Profession and the Mass Media

1. Edward A. Shils, "The Theory of Mass Society," *Diogenes* 39 (1962): 45–66.

2. There has been a vast flow of historical studies, reports, biographies, auto-biographies, and general accounts of journalism and the mass media. These materials are carefully annotated in three bibliographies: Harold D. Lasswell, Ralph D. Casey, and Bruce Lannes Smith, *Propaganda and Promotional Activities: An Annotated Bibliography* (Minneapolis: University of Minnesota Press, 1935); Bruce Lannes Smith, Harold D. Lasswell, and Ralph D. Casey, *Propaganda, Communication and Public Opinion: A Comprehensive Reference Guide* (Princeton: Princeton University Press, 1946); Bruce Lannes Smith and Chitra Smith, *International Communications and Political Opinion: A Guide to the Literature* (Princeton: Princeton University Press, 1956). More recent literature is covered in Donald A. Hansen and J. Herschel Parsons, *Mass Communications: A Research Bibliography* (Santa Barbara: Glendessary Press, 1968).

3. Walter Lippmann, *Public Opinion* (New York: Macmillan, 1922), p. 274. See also Robert E. Park, "News as a Form of Knowledge," *American Journal of Sociology* 45 (March 1940): 669–86.

4. Jeremy Tunstall breaks down "gatekeeper" into a number of more specific components: map-making, ranking (individuals, organizations, and nations are ranked in order of importance and newsworthiness), focusing, and summarizing (*The Westminster Lobby Correspondents: A Sociological Study of National Journalism* [London: Routledge & Kegan Paul, 1970], p. 13).

5. Systematic scholarship on the sociology and professional organization of journalists remains limited. Under the stimulation of Harold D. Lasswell, Leo Rosten prepared a study in depth, *The Washington Correspondents* (New York: Harcourt, Brace, 1937), which remains one of the leading references. Tunstall's *The Westminster Lobby Correspondents* deals with the equivalent group in British journalism, and he has also published a study entitled *Journalists at Work: Specialist Correspondents, the News Organizations, News Sources and Competitors-Colleagues* (London: Constable, 1971). These studies contain valuable material on the values and cultural assumptions of journalists. A sample survey of 1,225 journalists in the United States, undertaken by John Johnstone in 1971, concentrates on social demography and career patterns; see John Johnstone, *Newsmen and Newswork* (Urbana, Ill.: University of Illinois Press, forthcoming).

6. Gaye Tuchman, "Objectivity as a Strategic Ritual: An Examination of Newsmen's Notions of Objectivity," *American Journal of Sociology* 77 (January 1972): 660–79.

7. Vince Blasi, "The Newsman's Privilege: An Empirical Study," *Michigan Law Review* 70 (December 1971): 229–84.

8. Paul H. Weaver, "The New Journalism and the Old—Thoughts after Watergate," *Public Interest* 35 (Spring 1974): 67–88.

9. Johnstone, *Newsmen and Newswork*.

10. The discussion of the career lines of journalists is based on the findings of Johnstone, ibid.

11. Lippmann, *Public Opinion*, p. 271.

12. Ibid., p. 274.

13. Commission on the Freedom of the Press, *A Free and Responsible Press* (Chicago: University of Chicago Press, 1947).

14. United States National Advisory Commission on Civil Disorders, *Report* (Washington, D.C.: U.S. Government Printing Office, 1968).

15. "The News Media and the Disorders," ibid., pp. 201-20.

16. Harold Wilensky, "The Professionalization of Everyone?" *American Journal of Sociology* 70 (September 1964): 137-58.

17. Harold D. Lasswell, "The Person: Subject and Object of Propaganda," *Annals of the American Academy of Political and Social Science* 179 (May 1935): 187-93.

18. Edward A. Shils, "Daydreams and Nightmares: Reflections on the Criticism of Mass Culture," *Sewanee Review* 65 (Autumn 1957): 586-608.

19. For an overview of research trends, see Morris Janowitz, "The Study of Mass Communication," *International Encyclopedia of the Social Sciences*, 17 vols. (New York: Macmillan and the Free Press, 1968), 3:41-53.

20. Harold D. Lasswell, *Propaganda Techniques in the World War* (New York: Knopf, 1927), and his *World Politics and Personal Insecurity* (New York: McGraw-Hill, 1935).

21. Elihu Katz and Paul Lazarsfeld, *Personal Influence: The Part Played by People in the Flow of Mass Communication* (Glencoe, Ill.: Free Press, 1955); Bernard Berelson, "The State of Communications Research," *Public Opinion Quarterly* 23 (1959): 1-6; Joseph Klapper, *The Effects of Mass Communication* (Glencoe, Ill.: Free Press, 1960).

22. The Surgeon General's Scientific Advisory Committee on Television and Social Behavior, *Television and Growing Up: The Impact of Televised Violence* (Washington, D.C.: U.S. Government Printing Office, 1972).

23. For an overview of these issues, see Jay G. Blumler and Jack McLeod, "Communication and Voter Turnout in Britain," in *Sociological Theory and Survey Research*, edited by Timothy Leggatt (London: Sage Publications, 1974), pp. 265-312. See also Morris Janowitz and Dwaine Marvick, *Competitive Pressure and Campaign Consent* (Ann Arbor, Mich.: University of Michigan Press, 1956), and Kurt Lang and Gladys Lang, "Mass Media and Voting," in *American Voting Behavior*, edited by Arthur J. Brodbeck (Glencoe, Ill.: Free Press, 1959).

24. Commission on the Freedom of the Press, *A Free and Responsible Press*, p. 100.

25. John Wale, *Journalism and Government* (London: Macmillan, 1972).

26. Morris Janowitz, "Content Analysis and the Study of the Symbolic Environment," in *Politics, Personality and Social Science in the Twentieth Century*, edited by Arnold A. Rogow (Chicago: University of Chicago Press, 1969), pp. 155-70.

27. Commission on the Freedom of the Press, *A Free and Responsible Press*, p. 139.

28. A. J. Liebling, *Mink and Red Herring: The Wayward Pressman's Casebook* (New York: Doubleday, 1949).

29. H. Phillip Levy, *The Press Council: History, Procedure and Case* (London: Macmillan, 1967).

30. Ibid., p. 26.

31. John E. Polich, "Newspaper Support of Press Councils," *Journalism Quarterly* 51 (Summer 1974): 199-212.

32. L. Erwin Atwood and Kenneth Starck, "Effects of Community Press Councils: Real and Imagined," *Journalism Quarterly* 49 (Summer 1972): 230-38.

33. Johnstone, *Newsmen and Newswork.*

34. Herbert Gans, "The Famine in American Mass Communications Research: Comments on Hirsch, Tuchman and Gecas," *American Journal of Sociology* 77 (January 1972): 697-705.

5. Johnson: Economics and the Radical Challenge

1. The Econometric Society was established only in the 1930s, and few among its supporters were genuine econometricians, even if one uses that term conventionally but inappropriately to include mathematical economic theorists. The emphasis laid by Alfred Marshall, in particular, on the importance of the study of economic history had the unfortunate long-run effect in Britain of producing, through the influence of his star pupil, John Clapham, the separation of economic history from economics, to the loss of both: economic history lost its contact with economic theory, and economics lost its historical perspective, except in the crude form of awareness of the Marxist tradition. Economic history has only recently been revolutionized, under the banner of "cliometrics" (econometrics applied to history); significantly, this revolution has been carried out in the United States, where economic history has remained a constituent course in an economics degree at both the undergraduate and the graduate level.

2. It is ironic to recall, in view of the antimathematical cast of recent "radical" student criticism of economics, that in the immediate post-World War II period many Marxist student-economists saw mathematics and statistics as the tools by means of which the superiority of Marxist scientific economics over orthodox economics would be demonstrated and validated.

3. There is a fascinating history to be written of the internal battle at Chicago between the Cowles Commission and the National Bureau tradition, represented by Milton Friedman, and its probable connection with the development of Friedman's methodology of "positive economics," the eventual movement of the Cowles Commission from Chicago to Yale, and the more or less sustained resistance of the Chicago Department of Economics to the increasing emphasis on mathematical economic theory that rapidly conquered other centers of graduate work in economics.

4. For somewhat different reasons, not worth entering into here, the field of international economics has recently been reformulated in the language of Euclidean geometry, in terms of "the proofs of the theorems of comparative advantage."

5. It should be noticed that there remains a fundamental difference between graduate work and research leading to the Ph.D. in economics and other social sciences, on the one hand, and the equivalent activity in the natural sciences, on the other; for the problem and the method employed to solve it in the natural sciences are understood and accepted to be the property of the thesis director, while in economics, whatever the contribution of the thesis director or thesis committee may have been, the thesis itself is credited to the intellectual work of the student candidate. This difference has the advantage of maintaining the individual intellectual independence of the student and the disadvantage of creating considerable ambiguity in the assessment of the genuine originality and maintainable competence of the individual recipient of the Ph.D.

6. Actually, research quickly revealed that popular concern about poverty and

economic research devoted to it have had a history of long cycles, correlated with phases of prolonged cyclical depression; it would have been possible (though no one to my knowledge did so) to push economic history to the prediction that poverty as a conservative concern would be succeeded by income and wealth distribution as a radical concern.

7. Among the economists, Milton Friedman, the leading Republican-monetarist, and James Tobin, the leading Democrat-Keynesian, agreed in advocating the negative income tax; economists differed most sharply with noneconomists over the recommendation by the latter of minimum-wage laws to eliminate poverty.

8. Report has it that the attempt to seize the microphone was foiled by Professor Fritz Machlup, a past president with a long history of participation in the American Association of University Professors and in civil rights activities, who seized the microphone himself and refused to relinquish it.

9. Note, in the Appendix account of the 1969 business meeting, the rewording of the motion censoring the State Department for refusing a visa to a Marxist. This type of reworking has been the characteristic fate of "radical" motions at subsequent annual business meetings; and a unanimous vote in favor of a motion that no one should be discriminated against for any irrelevant reason is scant comfort to the Women's Liberation Movement.

10. See the Statement by Gordon Tullock, Exhibit II in the Appendix.

11. The "radical" statement presented at the 1969 business meeting (see Exhibit I in the Appendix) presents not even a caricature of what economists actually do, since a caricature posits an original existential subject.

12. At the final stage of decision, the nominating committee joins the executive committee, which automatically accepts all nominations except that of the president-elect; occasionally the joint vote has reversed the nominating committee's candidate for that office. See the next note.

13. The retiring president becomes ex officio chairman of the nominating committee. This makes for a certain periodicity in the alternation of the presidency among leaders of different schools, notably between Harvard and its east-coast satellites and the University of Chicago–Columbia University axis, with the California complex also becoming a claimant in recent years. Other rivalries and coalitions are also evident, especially in the elevation of three former members of the Austrian School to the presidency in close but not immediate succession.

14. The role of serendipity in institutional response to radical minority pressure is exemplified by the 1974 meetings of the American Economic Association, which occurred after this paper was sent to the editor. The meetings occurred in San Francisco, near the scene of a sequence of recent events at the State University, San Jose, involving "political fixing." As a result of the tiresome length of the business meetings held after the presidential address, the executive had decided to change the timing of the business meeting to 4:00 P.M. on the second day, with any carryover of business to be handled by resuming the business meeting after the presidential address that evening. Predictably, attendance was sparse, and a radical group was able to command a majority in favor of committing the Association to the establishment of a committee on political discrimination, despite a speech by Professor Fritz Machlup pointing out, on the basis of his long and active participation in the work of the American Association of University Professors, the heavy timecost of such work and the amount of legal knowledge required. The proposed committee is charged with the obligation to investigate allegations of political discrimination in hiring as well as in firing. What this could imply is indicated by

another resolution by the same two junior members of the Association, ruled out of order as conflicting with the Association's constitution, resolving "that the American Economic Association urges economics departments to take immediate measures to attract and hire permanent (tenure track) economists working in the Marxian economic paradigm." The interesting point to the present author was that the appointive and elective officers of the Association saw no connection between the decision to shift the time of the meeting in order to avoid wasting members' time and the commitment of the Association to an expensive activity that might result in guaranteeing professional recognition and status on the basis of political affiliation rather than academic competence.

15. The Association is not obliged to publish all of the papers presented on even its own program, and it has been increasingly forced by cost conditions to limit and ration space in the *Proceedings* issue of the *American Economic Review*.

6. Bendix: Province and Metropolis

1. Figures are based on W. H. Bruford, *Germany in the Eighteenth Century* (London: Cambridge University Press, 1959), pp. 333–36. Bruford's classification simplifies a much greater complex of jurisdictions, but it is sufficient for my purposes. The following sketch of the "Holy Roman Empire" is derived from Klaus Epstein, *The Genesis of German Conservatism* (Princeton: Princeton University Press, 1966), pp. 238–44, and Karl Biedermann, *Deutschland im Achtzehnten Jahrhundert*, 3 vols. (Leipzig: J. J. Weber, 1880), 1:14–71. My interpretation is much indebted to the study by Mack Walker, cited below.

2. I have adopted Mack Walker's term "home town," which refers to the German *Kleinstadt*, but have made it into one word to distinguish it from the American "home town," which has quite different connotations.

In an estimate for 1800, Walker calculates that, in a total German population of about 28 million (including Prussia and German-speaking Austria), two-thirds were rural and one-third urban. Not size, but the existence of some rights of self-government is the distinguishing characteristic of the "urban community." Some 7 percent of the total lived in about three dozen "large" towns (population above 15,000), while 25 percent lived in the 4,000-odd hometowns (population ranging from 750 to between 10,000 and 15,000 inhabitants). This comes to a total hometown population of some 7 million for all German territories under the Empire. However, there was much regional variation, with a greater frequency of hometowns in the western and southern parts of Germany and a lesser frequency in Prussia and Hannover. See Mack Walker, *German Home Towns: Community, State and General Estate, 1648–1871* (Ithaca: Cornell University Press, 1971), pp. 27–33.

3. Ibid., pp. 16–17.

4. See the analysis of the thought of Justus Möser in Epstein, *The Genesis of German Conservatism*, chap. 6.

5. Walker, *German Home Towns*, pp. 108–33.

6. Biedermann, *Deutschland im Achtzehnten Jahrhundert*, 1:100–102. For the electoral state of Mainz, the author gives a ratio of 1 official for every 250 inhabitants, or close to 1,000 officials for a population of 244,000, not counting court personnel and the clergy. In the ducal residence of Saxony-Weimar, the civil servants, military, and court personnel made up a fifth of the town's adult male population in 1699 and a quarter in 1820. See Hans Eberhardt, *Goethes Umwelt* (Weimar: Hermann Böhlau, 1951), pp. 26–27.

7. *Bürger* and *Bürgertum*, or *Bürgerstand*, refer to the towns' practice of allowing

or denying new residents the *Bürgerrecht,* or right of the citizen, on the basis of a community judgment of their financial and moral standing. The terms also convey the sense of being below the aristocracy but above artisans or peasants, not to speak of personal servants. For reasons indicated below, these German terms came to be associated with a level of education, and this association is missing from "middle class" or "bourgeoisie." The term *Bürger* also evokes connotations of financial and moral standing that have been transferred from the context of a small self-governing community to the larger society.

8. Membership in the Paulskirche is tabulated in Gerhard Schilfert, *Sieg und Niederlage des demokratischen Wahlrechts in der deutschen Revolution* (Berlin: Rütten & Loenig, 1952), p. 406. The author classifies the first group as a "civil-service intelligentsia" (*beamtete Intelligenz*) as distinguished from the "free intelligentsia."

9. Even in Prussia it was an uphill struggle. For a description of Prussian officialdom in the eighteenth century which emphasizes corruption, nepotism, indolence, and all the other negative attributes of bureaucracy, see Hans Rosenberg, *Bureaucracy, Aristocracy, and Autocracy* (Cambridge, Mass.: Harvard University Press, 1958), chaps. 2-4. However, Rosenberg also shows the emergence of "public law" and the merit system.

10. Figures on student enrollment in the eighteenth century are rather complete. The high point of student enrollments occurred in 1735-40, with about 8,500 students. That figure declined to about 6,000 in 1795 and to less than that in the war years that followed. Thus there was a marked decline in enrollment in the second half of the century, to a level of roughly 31 students for every 100,000 inhabitants. Eulenburg attributes the decline to three factors: the gradual increase in economic activities, the greater attraction of a military career for members of the nobility, and the improvement of secondary education, together with the prolongation of academic studies. See Franz Eulenburg, *Die Frequenz der deutschen Universitäten,* Abhandlungen der philologisch-historischen Klasse der Königl. Sächsischen Gesellschaft der Wissenschaften, no. 24 (Leipzig: B. G. Teubner, 1904), pp. 131-39 and passim.

11. Johann Wolfgang von Goethe, "Literarischer Sansculottismus (1795)," *Sämtliche Werke,* 27 vols. (Zurich: Artemis Verlag, 1950—), 14:182-83 (all translations in this paper are mine, unless otherwise noted).

12. Biedermann, *Deutschland im Achtzehnten Jahrhundert,* 1:144-45.

13. Data in the preceding paragraphs are derived from Johannes Goldfriedrich, *Geschichte des deutschen Buchhandels,* 3 vols. (Leipzig: Verlag des Börsenvereins der Deutschen Buchhändler, 1909), vol. 3, chaps. 5 and 9, and Joachim Kirchner, *Das Deutsche Zeitschriftenwesen,* 2 vols. (Wiesbaden: Otto Harrassowitz, 1958), 1:115-18.

14. Goethe was a conservative who favored Germany's political fragmentation because, from a cultural standpoint, it had brought many benefits. He also felt personally indebted, for assistance and largesse, to the benevolence of "his very own" ruler. For his attitude toward Grand Duke Carl August, see No. 34b of his Venetian epigrams in *Sämtliche Werke,* 1:229. The opening line reads "Klein ist unter den Fürsten Germaniens freilich der meine . . .").

15. Quoted in Hans-Georg Hass, ed., *Sturm und Drang,* 2 vols. (Munich: C. H. Beck, 1966), 2:1545.

16. Biederman, *Deutschland im Achtzehnten Jahrhundert,* 1:285 n.

17. Quoted ibid., vol. 2, pt. 1, p. 101, from K. Fr. von Moser, *Der Herr und der Diener* (1759).

18. This description of the French fashion in Germany is indebted to Biederman, (ibid., vol. 2, pt. 1, pp. 54–176). For a modern characterization on which I have also drawn, see Adrien Fauchier-Magnan, *The Small German Courts in the Eighteenth Century* (London: Methuen, 1958), passim.

19. Frederick II was relatively permissive in matters of censorship, yet his edict of 1784 stipulated that no private individual had the right to make critical judgments concerning the activities of sovereigns and their courts or to publish news of these activities and distribute them by means of print. "A private person is also quite incapable of making such judgments, since he will be lacking in the complete understanding of circumstances and motives." Quoted in Jürgen Habermas, *Strukturwandel der Öffentlichkeit* (Neuwied: Hermann Luchterhand, 1962), p. 38.

20. Quoted from K. Fr. von Moser, *Vom Nationalgeist* (1766) in Biedermann, *Deutschland im Achtzehnten Jahrhundert,* 1:158. On the same page Biedermann also quotes an article from a *Berliner Monatsschrift* of 1787, entitled "A New Way to Immortality for Sovereigns," in which the writer "advises" the rulers of his day to prepare their people through gradual education for the self-government of a republic. Once this has been accomplished, they should resign their power voluntarily and announce the introduction of a republican constitution. This article appeared two years before the French Revolution.

21. See Hermann Wätjen, *Die erste englische Revolution und die öffentliche Meinung in Deutschland,* diss., Heidelberg (Heidelberg: Carl Winter, 1900), passim, and Franz Muncker, *Anschauungen vom englischen Staat und Volk,* Sitzungsberichte der Königlich Bayerischen Akademie der Wissenschaften (Munich: G. Franzsche Verlag, 1918), pp. 27 ff.

22. Moral weeklies were periodical publications of a predominantly didactic tone, lacking any up-to-date character or news content and using a variety of entertaining literary devices to carry their message. By using a fairly stringent definition of the type, Martens comes to an estimate of some 110 moral weeklies for the period 1720–70. Most of them had editions of a few hundred up to one thousand, and most lasted only a few months or years. However, editors and publishers often started new ventures, because, when bound into volumes, the weeklies served as books in private libraries, and this seems to have made them profitable. The majority originated in Protestant territories, and there primarily in large towns, like Hamburg, Leipzig, Berlin, Hannover, and Nüremberg; few appeared in towns with princely residences, though a good many were published in hometowns of the type discussed above. They were notably absent from the southwestern parts of Germany. See Wolfgang Martens, *Die Botschaft der Tugend* (Stuttgart: J. B. Metzler, 1968), pp. 108–23, 161–67. My discussion below is based on this latest and most comprehensive study. Martens considers the influence of English weeklies like the *Spectator* significant. That influence is minimized in Hans M. Wolff, *Die Weltanschauung der deutschen Aufklärung* (Bern: A. Francke, 1949), chap. 3.

23. The moral weeklies never portray the virtues of common people, for it was held that such people lived by time-tried rules and had neither the leisure nor the background for a life of principle derived from reason. The weeklies did not begrudge these people their due respect if they were an asset to the community. However, in the Enlightenment sense of the word, one cannot expect them to be

"virtuous." The laws of the time drew a distinction between educated commoners
(*Bildungsbürgertum*) as the "nation" and these common folk as the *Pöbel* (literally,
"rabble"). Where even very progressive writers called artisans and peasants "half-
men," who were not ready for enlightenment, the moral weeklies were not likely to be
more egalitarian.

24. Martens, *Die Botschaft der Tugend,* pp. 141-61. The quotation from the
Patriot appears on pp. 146-47. See also ibid., pp. 370-403, for a more detailed
analysis of attitudes toward the aristocracy and the lower classes as expressed in the
moral weeklies.

25. Quoted from *Der Alte Deutsche* (1730), ibid., p. 334.

26. Quoted from *Der Mensch* (1751-56), ibid., pp. 349-50.

27. Ibid., p. 353. I return to this universalist aspect of the Enlightenment below.

28. R. O. Moon, trans., [*Goethe's*] *Wilhelm Meister, Apprenticeship and Travels,*
2 vols. (London: G. T. Foulis, 1947), 1:250-51.

29. For a succinct statement of this interpretation and supporting documentation,
see Fritz Brueggemann, "Der Kampf um die Bürgerliche Welt- und Lebens-
anschauung in der deutschen Literatur des 18. Jahrhunderts," *Deutsche Viertel-
jahrschrift für Literaturwissenschaft und Geistesgeschichte* 3 (1925): 94-127. See
also the discussion in Roy Pascal, *The German Sturm und Drang* (Manchester, Eng.:
Manchester University Press, 1959), chap. 3 and passim.

30. Quoted from Hans-Egon Hass, ed., *Sturm und Drang,* 2:1537-38.

31. See ibid., p. 1539, and Friedrich Schiller, *On the Aesthetic Education of Man,*
trans. E. Wilkinson and L. Willoughby (Oxford: Clarendon Press, 1967), pp. 30-43.

32. See the letter to Duke Augustenburg in Hass, ed., *Sturm und Drang,*
2:1541-42.

33. Friedrich Schiller, *Werke,* 22 vols. (Weimar: Hermann Böhlaus Nachfolger,
1958——), 22:248. The passage occurs in a review article on the poems of G. A.
Bürger. Note how close Schiller's position is to the precept of the Hamburg *Patriot:*
"Neither too bad or pedestrian for the scholar, nor too lofty and incomprehensible for
the unlearned"—a similarity which can be noted without minimizing the difference
in cultural level.

34. See the instructive articles by Gordon Craig, "Friedrich Schiller and the
Problems of Power," in Leonard Krieger and Fritz Stern, eds., *The Responsibility of
Power: Historical Essays in Honor of Hajo Holborn* (Garden City, N.Y.: Anchor-
Doubleday, 1969), pp. 135-56, and "Friedrich Schiller and the Police," *Proceedings
of the American Philosophical Society* 112 (December 1968): 367-70. Schiller's
realism is recognized even in the Marxist view that Schiller's work represents a retreat
from politics into a timeless realm of beauty. See Georg Lukács, *Goethe und seine
Zeit* (Bern: A. Francke, 1947), pp. 106-9.

35. Schiller, *Werke,* 22:106.

36. This is not to argue the case for German idealism but to show what sense it
made to the believers. In his study of hometowns Walker has shown that it is
instructive to look at the small-town bourgeoisie, which developed in Germany for
better or worse, rather than remain preoccupied with the absence of a strong liberal
bourgeoisie. My point about the rationale of the idealist posture is similar.

37. See Goethe, *Sämtliche Werke* 2:485 (see n. 11, above) (from the *Xenien* of
Goethe and Schiller).

38. For the quotations from Humboldt and Wolf, see Friedrich Paulsen, *Geschichte des gelehrten Unterrichts,* 2d ed., 2 vols. (Leipzig: Veit, 1897), 2:200.

39. Goethe, *Sämtliche Werke*, 1:234 (Epigram 58).

40. For a characterization of this reformist conservatism within the whole range of conservative reactions, see the excellent and comprehensive study by Klaus Epstein, *The Genesis of German Conservatism*, chap. 2 and passim. Epstein emphasizes that the conservative response antedated the French Revolution. The same point may be made with regard to the whole gamut of political opinions.

41. Cf. the analysis of democratic and socialist stirrings in Germany in Fritz Valjavec, *Die Entstehung der politischen Strömungen in Deutschland, 1770–1815* (Munich: R. Oldenbourg, 1951), pp. 180–228. The full range of German responses to the Revolution has been studied a number of times. In addition to Epstein and Valjavec, see Alfred Stern, *Der Einfluss der Französischen Revolution auf das deutsche Geistesleben* (Stuttgart: J. G. Cotta, 1928), passim, which deals with the intellectual elite, and Jacques Droz, *L'Allemagne et la révolution française* (Paris, 1949), passim, which deals with the elite as well as with regional variations in response. Among the earlier studies of this topic, in addition to those by G. P. Gooch and Karl Biedermann, mention should be made of Woldemar Wenck, *Deutschland vor hundert Jahren*, 2 vols. (Leipzig: F. W. Grunow, 1887, 1890), esp. vol. 2, because of its ample use of fugitive contemporary sources.

42. See Biedermann, *Deutschland im Achtzehnten Jahrhundert*, 1:152–57.

43. Quoted in Wenck, *Deutschland vor hundert Jahren*, 1:202–4.

44. Valjavec, *Die Entstehung* ..., pp. 146–79, 244–54. See also Robert Elsasser, *Über die politischen Bildungsreisen der Deutschen nach England*, Heidelberger Abhandlungen zur mittleren und neueren Geschichte, no. 51 (Heidelberg: Carl Winter, 1917), chap. 4.

45. See the instructive article by Rudolf Stadelmann, "Deutschland und die westeuropäischen Revolution," *Deutschland und Westeuropa* (Schloss Laupheim: Steiner, 1948), p. 22. For a more differentiated analysis of this political consensus, see Rudolf Vierhaus, "Politisches Bewusstsein in Deutschland vor 1789," *Der Staat* 6 (1967): 175–96.

46. Quoted in Vierhaus, "Politisches Bewusstsein in Deutschland vor 1789," p. 184.

47. Both statements by Struensee are quoted in Epstein, *The Genesis of German Conservatism*, pp. 391–92.

48. J. P. Eckermann, *Gespräche mit Goethe* (Wiesbaden: Insel Verlag, 1955), pp. 493–94. The conversation is dated 4 January 1824.

49. See the conversation of 27 April 1825, ibid., pp. 518–19.

7. Geertz: Centers, Kings, and Charisma

1. For an excellent general review of the issue, see S. N. Eisenstadt's introduction to his collection of Weber's charisma papers, *Max Weber on Charisma and Institution Building* (Chicago, 1968), pp. ix–lvi. For the psychologization of "legitimacy," see H. Pitkin, *Wittgenstein and Justice* (Berkeley and Los Angeles, 1972); for "inner-worldly asceticism," D. McClelland, *The Achieving Society* (Princeton, 1961); for "rationalization," A. Mitzman, *The Iron Cage* (New York, 1970). All this ambiguity and even confusion of interpretation are, it should be said, not without warrant in Weber's own equivocalness.

2. For some examples, see "Philosophers and Kings: Studies in Leadership," *Daedalus*, Summer, 1968.

3. P. Rieff, *The Triumph of the Therapeutic* (New York, 1966).

4. E. Shils, "Charisma, Order, and Status," *American Sociological Review,* April, 1965; "The Dispersion and Concentration of Charisma," in W. J. Hanna, ed., *Independent Black Africa* (New York, 1964); "Centre and Periphery," in *The Logic of Personal Knowledge: Essays Presented to Michael Polanyi* (London, 1961).

5. E. Kantorowicz, *The King's Two Bodies: A Study in Medieval Political Theology* (Princeton, 1957); R. E. Giesey, *The Royal Funeral Ceremony in Renaissance France* (Geneva, 1960); R. Strong, *Splendor at Court: Renaissance Spectacle and the Theater of Power* (Boston, 1973); M. Walzer, *The Revolution of the Saints* (Cambridge, Mass., 1965); M. Walzer, *Regicide and Revolution* (Cambridge, Eng., 1974); S. Anglo, *Spectacle, Pageantry, and Early Tudor Policy* (Oxford, 1969); D. M. Bergeron, *English Civic Pageantry, 1558–1642* (London, 1971); F. A. Yates, *The Valois Tapestries* (London, 1959); E. Straub, *Repraesentatio Maiestatis oder Churbayerische Freudenfeste* (Munich, 1969); G. R. Kernodle, *From Art to Theatre* (Chicago, 1944). For a recent popular book on the American presidency in this vein, see M. Novak, *Choosing Our King* (New York, 1974). Anthropological studies, especially those done in Africa, have of course been sensitive to such issues for a long time (for an example: E. E. Evans-Pritchard, *The Divine Kingship of the Shilluk of the Nilotic Sudan* [Cambridge, Eng., 1948]) and both E. Cassirer's *Myth of the State* (New Haven, 1946) and M. Bloch's *Les rois thaumaturges* (Paris, 1961) have to be mentioned, along with Kantorowicz, as seminal. The internal quotation is from N. Ward, as given in the OED under "Numinous."

6. There are a number of descriptions of Elizabeth's London progress (or "entry"), of which the fullest is Bergeron, *English Civic Pageantry,* pp. 11–23. See also R. Withington, *English Pageantry: An Historical Outline,* 2 vols. (Cambridge, Mass., 1918), 1:199–202; and Anglo, *Spectacle, Pageantry,* pp. 344–59. The text quotation is from Anglo, p. 345. The city was resplendent too: "The houses on the way were all decorated; there being on both sides of the street, from Blackfriars to St. Paul's, wooden barricades on which merchants and artisans of every trade leant in long black gowns lined with hoods of red and black cloth ... with all their ensigns, banners, and standards" (quotation from the Venetian ambassador to London, in Bergeron, p. 14). For Mary and Philip's 1554 entry, see Anglo, pp. 324–43, and Withington, p. 189.

7. Quoted in Bergeron, *English Civic Pageantry,* p. 17. The queen is supposed to have replied: "I have taken notice of your good meaning toward mee, and will endeavour to Answere your severall expectations" (ibid., p. 18).

8. Anglo, *Spectacle, Pageantry,* p. 349.

9. Bergeron, *English Civic Pageantry,* p. 15.

10. The quotation is given in Anglo, *Spectacle, Pageantry,* p. 350.

11. Grafton, quoted ibid., p. 352. He was not unprescient: Deborah ruled for forty years, Elizabeth for forty-five.

12. The quotation is from Strong, *Splendor at Court,* p. 84.

13. For Elizabeth's progresses outside London, see Bergeron, *English Civic Pageantry,* pp. 25 ff.; Withington, *English Pageantry,* pp. 204 ff.

14. Strong, *Splendor at Court,* p. 84. The progress was, of course, an all-European phenomenon. Emperor Charles V, for example, made ten to the Low Countries, nine to Germany, seven to Italy, six to Spain, four to France, two to England, and two to Africa, as he reminded his audience at his abdication (ibid., p. 83). Nor was it confined to the sixteenth century: for fifteenth-century Tudor ones, see Anglo,

Spectacle, Pageantry, pp. 21 ff.; for seventeenth-century Stuart ones, see Bergeron, *English Civic Pageantry,* pp. 65 ff., and Strong, *Splendor at Court,* pp. 213 ff.

15. Yates, *The Valois Tapestries,* p. 92.

16. Bergeron, *English Civic Pageantry,* p. 21.

17. Java was Hindu from about the fourth century to about the fifteenth, when it became at least nominally Islamized. Bali remains Hindu until today. Much of what follows here is based on my own work, including a forthcoming study of the traditional Hindu state in Bali, *Negara: The Theatre State in Nineteenth-Century Bali.* For Hindu Java generally, see N. J. Krom, *Hindoe-Javaansche Geschiedenis,* 2d ed. (The Hague, 1931).

18. T. Pigeaud, *Java in the 14th Century: A Study in Cultural History,* 5 vols. (The Hague, 1963), 1:3 (Javanese); 3:3 (English). The chain actually continues downward through animals and demons.

19. Ibid., 1:90 (Jav.); 3:135 (Eng.). I have made alterations in the translation for clarity. Even then, "sacred powers" and "The Supreme Nothingness" (i.e., Siva-Buddha) remain weak renderings of difficult religious conceptions, a matter not pursuable here. For an even more differentiated hierarchy, see the *Nawantaya* text, ibid., 3:119–28.

20. Ibid. (despite its title, the work is essentially a text, translation, and commentary of the *Negarakertagama*). Of the poem's 1,330 lines, no less than 570 are specifically devoted to descriptions of royal progresses, and the bulk of the rest are ancillary to those. Literally, Negarakertagama means "manual for the cosmic ordering of the state," which is what it is really about rather than, as has so often been assumed, the history of Majapahit. It was written in 1365 by a Buddhist cleric, resident in the court of King Hayam Wuruk (r. 1350–89).

21. *Negarakertagama,* canto 12, stanza 6. I have again reconstructed Pigeaud's English, this time more seriously, to convey better what I take to be the sense of the passage. On the mandala concept in Indonesia, where it means at once "sacred circle," "holy region," and "religious community," as well as being a symbol of the universe as such, see J. Gonda, *Sanskrit in Indonesia* (Nagpur, 1952), pp. 5, 131, 218, 227; Pigeaud, *Java,* 4:485–86. On this sort of imagery in traditional Asian states generally, see P. Wheatley, *The Pivot of the Four Quarters* (Chicago, 1971).

22. Cantos 1–7. The royal family is also praised, as the first circle outward from the king. "Daymaker" is, of course, a metonym for the sun, identified with Siva-Buddha, "The Supreme Non-Entity" in Indic Indonesia.

23. Cantos 8–12. There is much controversy here over details (cf. W. F. Stutterheim, *De Kraton van Majapahit* [The Hague, 1948]; H. Kern, *Het Oud-Javaansche Lofdicht Negarakertagama van Prapanca* [The Hague, 1919]), and not all of them are clear. The pattern has in any case been simplified here (it really is a 16-8-4-point system about a center, and of course it is cosmological, not exactly geographical). "Ranking commoners" is an interpolation of mine on the basis of knowledge of later examples. "Junior king" does not indicate a dauphin but refers to the second-ranking line in the realm. This "double-king" system is general in Indonesian Indic states but is too complex to go into here. See my *Negara* for a full discussion.

24. Cantos 13–16.

25. Canto 92.

26. On the exaggeration of the size of Majapahit, see, with caution, C. C. Berg, "De Sadèng oorlog en de mythe van Groot Majapahit," *Indonesie* 5 (1951): 385–422.

See also my "Politics Past, Politics Present: Some Notes on the Uses of Anthropology in Understanding the New States," in C. Geertz, *The Interpretation of Cultures* (New York, 1973), pp. 327–41.

27. Canto 17. Other minor progresses, for special purposes, are also mentioned for the 1360s; see cantos 61 and 70.

28. Cantos 13–18. The directional system was integrated with a color symbolism, the four primary colors—red, white, black, and yellow—being disposed about a variegated center. The five days of the week, five periods of the day, and five life-cycle stages, as well as plants, gods, and a number of other natural and social symbolic forms, were fused into the same pattern, which was thus extremely elaborate, a picture of the whole cosmos.

29. Cantos 13–38, 55–60. Four or five stops are described in detail; but there must have been ten or fifteen times that many.

30. Canto 17, stanza 3. Again I have altered the translation; in particular I have rendered *negara* as "capital" rather than "town." For the multiple meanings of this word, see my *Negara*.

31. W. B. Harris, *Morocco That Was* (Boston, 1921). The following discussion is confined to the period of the Alawite dynasty, that is, from the seventeenth to twentieth centuries (it still continues), with most of the material coming from the eighteenth and nineteenth centuries. Again, I have depended heavily on my own research (see C. Geertz, *Islam Observed: Religious Development in Morocco and Indonesia* [New Haven, 1968]), and on that of my students, Lawrence Rosen, Paul Rabinow, and Dale Eickelman, all of whom have community studies of contemporary Morocco in the process of appearing. A collective study of a mid-Atlas town by Rosen, Rabinow, H. Geertz, and myself is in preparation.

32. The best study of the traditional Moroccan state is E. Aubin, *Morocco of Today* (London, 1906). The term "tribe" is difficult of application in Morocco, where social groups lack stability and definition. See J. Berque, "Qu'est-ce qu'une 'tribu' nord-africaine?" in *Eventail de l'histoire vivante: Hommage à Lucien Febvre* (Paris, 1953).

33. See A. Bel, *La Religion Musulmane en Berbérie*, (Paris, 1938), vol. 1; E. Gellner, *Saints of the Atlas* (Chicago, 1969); C. Geertz, *Islam Observed*. Many of the ulemas and marabouts were also sharifs. On Moroccan sharifs in general, see E. Lévi-Provençal, *Les Historiens des Chorfa* (Paris, 1922).

34. On *baraka*, see E. Westermarck, *Ritual and Belief in Morocco*, 2 vols. (London, 1926); C. Geertz, *Islam Observed*.

35. On Mulay Ismail's truly astounding mobility, see O. V. Houdas, *Le Maroc de 1631–1812 par Ezziani* (Amsterdam, 1969), pp. 24–55; text reference at p. 46. On Mulay Hasan, see S. Bonsal, *Morocco As It Is* (New York and London, 1893), pp. 47 ff.; cf. Harris, *Morocco That Was*, pp. 1 ff.

36. S. Schaar, *Conflict and Change in Nineteenth-Century Morocco* (diss., Princeton University, 1964), p. 72. The constant mobility also shaped, and similarly, the nature of the court: "The very life that the greater part of the members of the [court] must lead, uproots them and cuts them off from any contact with their tribe or their native town, and attaches them, to the exclusion of all other ties, to the institution on which they are dependent. The bulk of the [court] ... centres around the Sultan, and becomes nomadic like him. Their life is passed under canvas, or else, at unequal intervals, in one of the imperial cities—constant change, in fact, and no ties anywhere. The horizon narrows, everything outside disappears, and the members of

the [court] have no eye for anything but this powerful mechanism, mistress of their lives and their fortune" (Aubin, *Morocco of Today,* p. 183).

37. W. B. Harris, *Tafilet* (London, 1895), pp. 240–43; F. Weisgerber, *Au Seuil du Maroc modern* (Rabat, 1947), pp. 46–60 (where one can also find a plan of the camp). On the move it was no less impressive; for a vivid description, complete with snake charmers, acrobats, lepers, and men opening their heads with hatchets, see Harris, *Morocco That Was,* pp. 54–60. The harkas were multitribal enterprises, the core of which was composed of the so-called military—*jaysh*—tribes, who served the court as soldiers in return for land and other privileges. One can't resist one more proverb here: *f-l-ḥarka, baraka:* "There is blessing in movement."

38. Schaar, *Conflict and Change in Morocco,* p. 73. The violence mostly consisted of burning settlements and cutting off the heads of particularly recalcitrant opponents (which, salted by the Jews, were then displayed over the entrance to the king's tent or palace). Mediation, which was more common, was conducted by royal officials or, often, various sorts of religious figures, specialized for the task. Schaar (ibid., p. 75) remarks that kings, or anyway wise ones, took care not to be overly harsh: "The ideal was to hit the enemy lightly, collect tribute payments, establish a firm administration in their midst, and move on to the next target."

39. Material on the Tafilalt mehalla can be found in Harris, *Tafilet,* pp. 213 ff.; R. Lebel, *Les Voyageurs français du Maroc* (Paris, 1936), pp. 215–20; R. Cruchet, *La Conquête pacifique du Maroc et du Tafilalet,* 2d ed. (Paris, 1934), pp. 223–41; G. Maxwell, *Lords of the Atlas* (New York, 1966), pp. 31–50; F. Linarès, "Voyage au Tafilalet," *Bulletin de l'Institut de la Hygiène du Maroc,* nos. 3–4 (1932). Cf. R. Dunn, *Morocco's Crisis of Conquest: The Southeast, 1881–1912* (in press), who stresses the king's desire to stabilize the Tafilalt against French incursion as a motive for the trip. Ten women of the royal harem also accompanied the king, and Cruchet (p. 223) estimates about 10,000 hangers-on, merchants, "et autres parasites qui sont la rançon d'une troupe, n'est pas une sinécure," as well.

40. Maxwell, *Lords of the Atlas,* pp. 39–40.

41. Harris, *Tafilet,* p. 333.

42. Harris, *Morocco That Was,* pp. 13–14; for a fuller description, see Harris, *Tafilet,* pp. 345–51.

43. For the argument concerning the ritual destruction of the monarchy, see Walzer, *Regicide and Revolution.* With Walzer's argument that the trials and executions of Charles and Louis were symbolic acts designed to kill not just kings but kingship, I am in agreement; concerning his further argument that they altered the whole landscape of English and French political life permanently and utterly—that is, that these rituals were availing—I am less convinced. The other wing of this sort of argument is, of course, that democracy makes the anthropomorphization of power impossible: "Die Repräsentation [i.e., of "majesty"] verlangt eine Hierarchie, die der Gleichheit des demokratischen Staates widerspricht, in der jeder Bürger Soverain ist und Majestas hat. So aber alle Könige sind, da kann keiner mehr als König auftreten, und die Repräsentation wird unmöglich" (Straub, *Repraesentatio Maiestatis,* p. 10 [see n. 5, above]). But along with a number of other people, from Tocqueville to Talmon, I am not persuaded of this either.

44. For a description of some of the *siba* activities at the end of the Protectorate, see E. Burke, *Moroccan Political Responses to French Penetration, 1900–1912* (diss., Princeton University, 1970). On *ratu adil,* see Sartono Kartodirdjo, *Protest Movements in Rural Java* (Singapore, 1973).

45. Novak, *Choosing Our King*, pp. 211, 224–28, and 205–8 (see n. 5, above). I have omitted, without indication, so as not to clutter the page with ellipses, large segments of these passages, and have repunctuated, reparagraphed, and even run some sentences together, both in the interests of brevity and to eliminate as many as possible of Novak's personal comments, some of which are extremely shrewd, others mere alternative clichés. Thus, though all the words are his (or those he is quoting), and nothing has been done to alter the meaning, these excerpts are better regarded as précis than as true quotations. For a similarly vivid view of 1972 presidential-campaign theatrics from another part of the forest, see H. Thompson, *Fear and Loathing on the Campaign Trail, '72* (San Francisco, 1973).

8. Bellow: Writers and Literature in American Society

1. John Ruskin, *Sesame and Lilies* (London: George Allen & Unwin, 1871), p. 49.
2. John Huizinga, *America*, trans. Herbert H. Rowen (New York: Harper & Row, 1972), p. 302.
3. Owen Barfield, *Unancestral Voice* (London: Faber & Faber, 1965), p. 21.
4. Harold Rosenberg, "The Herd of Independent Minds" in *Discovering the Present* (Chicago: University of Chicago Press, 1973), p. 16.
5. Edward Shils, "The Rights, Powers, and Responsibilities of Intellectuals," cited from an unpublished background paper given at Aspen Institute Humanistic Studies conference in 1973.
6. Wyndham Lewis, *The Writer and the Absolute* (London: Methuen, 1952), p. 6.

9. Clark and Clark: Patrons, Publishers, and Prizes

1. "Writer's estate" is used as a general term to designate the social, economic, and cultural situation of the writer and, most particularly, the social and economic structures that support literary creativity.
2. The following is a representative statement: "Often [writers and intellectuals] have been highly vocal rather than directly influential; but always society has respected them as an honored minority, like the holy men of India" (John Ardagh, *The New French Revolution* [New York: Harper & Row, 1968], p. 354, contrasting the situation in Britain—although he suggests that the prestige of French intellectuals is declining, moving closer to the British case). Saul Bellow, elsewhere in this volume, stresses the deference shown to writers in France, a point which Gertrude Stein makes even more definitively:

> But really what they do do is to respect art and letters, if you are a writer you have privileges . . . and it is pleasant having those privileges. I always remember coming in from the country to my garage where I usually kept my car and the garage was full more than full, it was the moment of the automobile salon, but said I what can I do, well said the man in charge I'll see and then he came back and said in a low voice, there is a corner and in this corner I have put the car of Monsieur the academician and next to it I will put yours the others can stay outside and it is quite true even in a garage an academician and a woman of letters takes precedence even of millionaires or politicians, they do, it is quite incredible but they do, the police treat artists and writers respectfully too.
> (*Paris France* [New York: Liveright, 1970], p. 21)

3. On a scale of 100, "auteur de romans d'avant-garde" ranked 55.7 in France as compared to 57.0 for "author" in the United States, 64.6 in Belgium, 66 in Poland, 70.6 in Israel, and 71.0 in Italy. (French score from P. Clark and T. N. Clark, "Stratification and Culture: The Position and Roles of Intellectual and Other Elites

in France and the United States," draft paper, 1974. Other scores from Donald J. Treiman, *Occupational Prestige in Comparative Perspective* [New York: Seminar Press, forthcoming].)

4. Herbert R. Lottman refers to "the popular belief that the average Frenchman is a cultural *maven,*" in "The French: They are Hooked on La Télé," *New York Times,* 20 April 1975, section 2.

5. According to the United Nations *Statistical Annual,* France in 1972 published 48 new titles per 100,000 inhabitants, compared to 19 in the United States, 50 in Belgium, and 64 in West Germany.

In the most thorough comparative study of reading habits, the French, who averaged 7 minutes per day in reading books, did not differ greatly from the United States or West German sample, each of which averaged 5 minutes per day. The Belgians led the French, with 14 minutes; and the high was attained by the Russians, who spent 29 minutes a day in reading books. See Alexander Szalai et al., eds., *The Use of Time* (The Hague: Mouton, 1972), p. 580.

6. Consider this statement: "La gloire aussi bien que les sinécures attendent l'écrivain à Paris. Cette fascination s'exerce même au-delà des frontières: de Bruxelles, de Suisse, d'Italie, d'Angleterre, de New York, affluent les littérateurs. Ils croient ne pouvoir vivre nulle part mieux, plus *efficacement* qu'à Paris" (François Nourissier, "Le Monde du livre," in B. Pingaud, ed., *Ecrivains d'aujourd'hui* [Paris: Grasset, 1960], p. 33).

7. See Table 2 in the Appendix, below, for a summary of different sources of support in the two countries. We are currently investigating these in greater detail. See P. Clark, "Styles of Subsidy: Support for Literature in France and the United States" (unpublished).

8. A study of 623 French *gens de lettres* from 1300 to 1830 showed that 26 per cent came from the nobility, 30 per cent from the *magistrature,* and 23 per cent from the liberal professions. The percentage of noble origin declined from 50 in the period 1330-1500 to 16 in 1776-1825. See Alfred Odin, *Genèse des Grands hommes: Gens de lettres français modernes* (1895), cited in Alain Girard, *La Réussite sociale en France* (Paris: Presses universitaires de France, 1961), p. 287. A 1960 sample of 170 French writers showed only seven (14 per cent) of working-class or peasant origins, and only thirteen (8 per cent) from the petty bourgeoisie (Nourissier, "Le Monde du livre," p. 43).

9. See Howard M. Vollmer and Daniel L. Mills, eds., *Professionalization* (Englewood Cliffs, N. J.: Prentice-Hall, 1966).

10. See Table 1 in the Appendix to this article.

11. See the discussion in J. L. Price, *Culture and Society in the Dutch Republic* (New York: Scribner's, 1974), chap. 5.

12. Thus the duc de la Rochefoucauld received a pension of 8,600 livres in 1659—not as a writer but as an aristocrat (J. R. Charbonnet, ed., *Maximes* [Paris: Larousse, 1934], p. 4). For comparative purposes, peasants earned 100-200 livres annually; the upper nobility, 50,000-250,000 livres. See Pierre Goubert, *L'Ancien régime, I* (Paris: Colin, 1969), p. 162.

13. Purely public goods are shared by many persons, whereas purely private goods are enjoyed solely by their owners. Though most goods fall in between, they may be ranked along this continuum from public to private. Cf. T. N. Clark, "Centralization Encourages Public Goods," Comparative Study of Community Decision-Making, Research Report no. 39 (1972).

14. This type of exchange analysis is explicitly linked to institutionalization of new

norms and values in more detail in T. N. Clark, "Structural Functionalism, Exchange Theory, and the New Political Economy," *Sociological Inquiry* 42 (1972): 275-98.

15. See Reinhard Bendix, "Province and Metropolis," in this volume.

16. G. Avenel, *Les Revenus d'un intellectuel de 1200 à 1913* (Paris: Flammarion, 1913), p. 297.

17. To modern eyes this dismissal seems all the more untoward in view of the fact that the dismissed historiographer, Pelisson, was a "real" historian. On Molière, see Antoine Adam, *Histoire de la littérature française du XVIIᵉ siècle*, 5 vols. (Paris: del Duca, 1962), 3:10-11, 235-36; for Racine and Boileau, see ibid., 4:265.

18. In 1746 Voltaire was given this same post by Louis XV, when it carried an annual income of 1,600 livres. Voltaire sold it three years later (while keeping the title) for 30,000 livres. Jacques Donvez, *De quoi vivait Voltaire* (Paris: Les Deux-Rives, 1949), p. 106. On Racine, see "Chronologie," *Europe*, no. 453 (January 1967).

19. Quoted by Georges Couton, *Corneille* (Paris: Hatier, 1958), p. 93.

20. Not until 1945 did Great Britain have a national agency to subsidize the arts. On patronage in England see Michael Foss, *The Age of Patronage: The Arts in England, 1660-1750* (Ithaca, N.Y.: Cornell University Press, 1971), and John S. Harris, *Government Patronage of the Arts in Great Britain* (Chicago: University of Chicago Press, 1970), chap. 11.

21. Cited by Donvez, *De quoi vivait Voltaire*, p. 7.

22. See André Billy, *L'Abbé Prévost* (Paris: Flammarion, 1969).

23. In 1765 Catherine the Great purchased Diderot's library for the generous price of 15,000 livres, left him the use of it, provided a pension of 750 livres, and subsequently made Diderot custodian of his own library of 1,000 livres a year, paid in advance for fifty years. See Jacques Proust, *Diderot et l'Encyclopédie* (Paris: Colin, 1967), pp. 105-10.

24. Robert Darnton, "The High Enlightenment and the Low-Life of Literature in Pre-Revolutionary France," *Past and Present*, no. 51 (May 1971), pp. 81-115.

25. Writing was never considered incompatible with noble status and did not provoke loss of aristocratic privileges (*déroger*), whereas painting was acceptable only if untainted by commercial dealings. See Marcel Reinhard, "Elite et noblesse dans la seconde moitié du XVIIIᵉ siècle," *Revue d'histoire moderne et contemporaine* 3 (1956): 23. Even today the ideal of the amateur writer is not entirely out of date. André Malraux's view of the writer as an "adventurer" is often cited as an obstacle to the development of professional norms.

26. According to Avenel (*Les Revenus d'un intellectuel*, pp. 293-95), Corneille's critic was one Gaillard. A century later Diderot would confirm that "l'honneur [était] la portion la plus précieuse des émoluments de l'auteur" (Proust, *Diderot et l'Encyclopédie*, p. 89, n. 34).

27. David T. Pottinger, *The French Book Trade in the Ancien Régime* (Cambridge, Mass.: Harvard University Press, 1958), chap. 11.

28. Royalties in the modern sense of a percentage of sales (also termed *droits d'auteur*) did not become the rule until after 1850 (Avenel, *Les Revenus*, p. 322). Subsequent legislation in the nineteenth century extended the period of copyright. (At present it is good for fifty years after the author's death.)

29. See Madeleine Varin d'Ainvelle, *La Presse en France* (Paris: Presses universitaires de France, 1965), pp. 201-2; Albert J. George, *The Development of French Romanticism: The Impact of the Industrial Revolution on Literature* (Syracuse,

N.Y.: Syracuse University Press, 1955), chap. 6; and Dr. Véron, *Mémoires d'un Bourgeois de Paris*, 2 vols. (1857) (Paris: Guy LePrat, 1945).

30. Total production of books increased from between 500 and 600 works annually at the end of the eighteenth century to a high of 14,000 titles at the end of the nineteenth (21,500 in 1970) (R. Estivals, "Bibliologie et Prospective," in J. Cain et al., eds., *Le Livre français* [Paris: Imprimerie Nationale, 1972]).

31. See George, *The Development of French Romanticism*, pp. 64 ff.; André Maurois, *Prométhée, ou la vie de Balzac* (Paris: Hachette, 1965), pp. 212, 368; Véron, *Mémoires*, 1:60-61; and F. W. J. Hemmings, *Zola* (Oxford: Clarendon Press, 1966), pp. 125-26.

32. Pierre Labracherie, *La Vie quotidienne de la Bohème littéraire au xixᵉ siècle* (Paris: Hachette, 1967), pp. 105-6, 113; Benjamin Bart, *Flaubert* (Syracuse, N.Y.: Syracuse University Press, 1965), p. 362. These figures may be compared with other incomes in the nineteenth century: 5,000 francs for a professor in Paris in 1850 to 14,500 francs in 1880; 700 francs for a primary school teacher in 1880; 700-800 francs for a miner in 1858-68. Before his great success with *L'Assommoir* Zola was earning 15,000 francs a year from his literary journalism, while as a débutant in Paris in the 1860s his income had totaled only about 6,000 francs (of which 2,400 francs were for his work at Hachette, the publisher). See Terry Nichols Clark, *Prophets and Patrons: The French University and the Emergence of the Social Sciences* (Cambridge, Mass.: Harvard University Press, 1973), p. 46; Paul Louis, *La Condition ouvrière en France depuis cent ans* (Paris: Presses Universitaires de France, 1950; Hemmings, *Zola*, p. 125; Armand Lanoux, *Bonjour Monsieur Zola* (Paris: Hachette, 1962), p. 68.

33. Emile Zola, "Un prix de Rome littéraire" (1877), reprinted in *Le Roman expérimental* (Paris: Garnier-Flammarion, 1971), pp. 321, 324.

34. Labracherie, *La Vie quotidienne*, p. 69; Maurois, *Prométhée*, p. 602; idem, *Olympio* (New York: Harper & Row, 1956), pp. 74, 134-36.

35. Véron, *Mémoires*, 2:14-15; M. L. Pailleron, *François Buloz et ses amis: La Vie littéraire sous Louis-Philippe* (Paris: Calmann-Lévy, 1919), p. 380; Hemmings, *Zola*, p. 126; Bart, *Flaubert*, p. 729.

36. See Pierre Bourdieu, "Champ intellectuel et projet créateur," *Les Temps modernes* (November 1966); Nourissier, "Le Monde du livre," pp. 29-45; Robert Laffont, *Editeur* (Paris: Robert Laffont, 1974).

37. Despite their size, virtually no American publishers conduct any market research. Lewis Coser discusses this and related matters in "Publishers As Gatekeepers of Ideas," a paper presented to the International Sociological Association, Toronto, August 1974.

38. "Les matières politiques ou morales ne seront traitées dans l'Académie que conformément à l'autorité du Prince, à l'état du Gouvernement et aux lois du royaume" (Statute 22, l'Académie française, *Règlements de 1635*). The *Annuaire de l'Académie française* (1974) notes that "on s'étonne aujourd'hui que le plus grand poète vivant ne siège point sous la coupole, mais l'Académie ne pouvait passer outre à un veto du pouvoir" (p. 28). Presumably the reference is to Saint-John Perse, Nobel laureate.

39. Emile Cassirer, *Les Cinq Cents Immortels* (Paris: Henri Jouve, 1906), pp. 210-12.

40. *Annuaire de l'Académie française* (1974), p. 18.

41. Choucri Cardahi, *Regards sous la Coupole* (Paris: Mame, 1966), p. 24 (on

Zola's futile attempts) and p. 35: "L'idéal de l'Académie fut d'être la représentation de l'esprit française" (quoting Gaston Boissier, former secrétaire perpétuel). Cf. Paul Valéry, "Fonction et mystère de l'Académie," in *Trois siècles de l'Académie française* (Paris: Firmin-Didot, 1936), pp. 508-17; Valéry also stresses the attraction for politicians (p. 512).

42. Octave Feuillet, the first novelist elected as such, examined this prejudice in his reception speech in 1862, cited by Paul Bourget, "Le Roman à l'Académie," in *Trois siècles*, pp. 213 ff. Marivaux, Voltaire, and Victor Hugo were members, but each had been admitted for works other than novels. Charles Nodier explained to Balzac the objection to the bohemian: "L'Acádémie... s'évanouit à l'idée d'une lettre de change qui peut envoyer à Clichy. Elle est sans coeur ni pitié pour l'homme de génie qui est pauvre ou dont les affaires vont mal... Ainsi, ayez une position... et vous êtes élu" (*Lettres à l'Etrangère*, cited by Maurois, *Prométhée*, p. 477).

43. In 1848 Alfred de Musset received a prize as consolation for his failure to be elected to the Académie. However, the prize was something of an insult, since it was destined for "un artiste pauvre, dont le talent, déjà remarqué, mérite d'être encouragé" (G. Barrier, "Chronologie," in A. de Musset, *La Confession d'un enfant du siècle*, ed. G. Barrier [Paris: Gallimard-Folio, 1973], p. 327). Musset was eventually elected in 1852.

44. Of these five prizes, two were in history and philology and one was shared with the Académie des Beaux Arts, so only two remained solely for literature. Of these two, one (the Prix Montyon) was restricted to "la littérature utile." However, "literature" was defined broadly enough to include most prose works, and "la littérature utile" was not restricted to how-to-fix-it manuals. Balzac hoped to win the Prix Montyon in 1836 for his novel *Le Médecin de campagne;* it went to de Tocqueville's *De la démocratie en Amérique.* For lists of all prizes and winners through 1895, see Comte de Franqueville, *Le Premier siècle de l'Institut de France* (Paris: J. Rothschild, 1895), vol. 2. Current prizes (not amounts) are found in the *Guide des Prix littéraires* (Paris: Cercle de la Librairie, 1965). Amounts for 1974 are from a personal communication from the secretary of the Académie française.

45. The Académie française has always been in the midst of sociopolitical debates. In 1879 Monseigneur Dupanloup resigned in protest against the election of Renan (positivism and clericalism were not harmonious); Anatole France, an ardent Dreyfusard, ceased attending meetings because of the silent and not so silent reprobation of his colleagues. In 1975, Pierre Emmanuel, known for his poetry about and activity in the Resistance, resigned in protest against the election of Félicien Marceau, who had been imprisoned for collaboration with the Germans during World War II.

46. See Rémy Ponton, "Programme esthétique et accumulation de capital symbolique," *Revue française de sociologie* 14 (April-June 1973): 202-20. The pension of course ceased in 1870.

47. Labracherie, *La Vie quotidienne,* p. 111 (on Baudelaire); Bart, *Flaubert,* pp. 727-35. As Flaubert's case shows, pensions were given by the government, usually through the ministry of the interior or the ministry of education. Flaubert's pension came through the latter, Hugo's, during the Restoration, from the former. In a letter to Flaubert, Maupassant states that some 600 pensions were at that time awarded by the government, probably basing his assertion on private information to which he had access as an employee of the ministry. Benjamin Bart notes that such a list, if it existed, may well have been destroyed; research by a number of scholars in the

archives of the ministry of education has failed to uncover any lists (personal communication, B. Bart, 1975). Sainte-Beuve at one time was on the lists of both the ministry of the interior and the ministry for foreign affairs; the latter piece of information was especially elusive, since the subsidies granted by the foreign affairs ministry did not have to be approved by the Chamber of Deputies and so could more easily remain secret.

48. Maurice Regard, *Sainte-Beuve: L'Homme et l'oeuvre* (Paris: Hatier, 1959), p. 105; Ponton, "Programme esthétique" (on Leconte de Lisle, Coppée, Heredia); Barrier, "Chronologie," p. 325 (on Musset).

49. See Roger Fayolle, *La Critique* (Paris: Colin, 1964), for changes in critical attitudes from the seventeenth to the nineteenth century.

50. According to the *Guide des Prix littéraires,* in 1965 the Société had 54 literary prizes to award, totaling about $3,000. Since many legacies have diminished in value over time, a number of prizes have recently been combined. By 1971 the Société had 36 prizes to award, considerably fewer than the 143 prizes totaling $65,000 awarded by the Académie française in 1974.

51. See Edouard Montagne, *Histoire de la Société des Gens de Lettres* (Paris: Librairie Mondaine, n.d.), passim. The distinction between protective and professional associations is made in A. M. Carr-Saunders and P. A. Wilson, *The Professions* (1933) (London: Frank Cass, 1964), p. 271.

52. As reported in 1882 in the journal, *Le Bien public,* cited in George Ravon, *L'Académie Goncourt en dix couverts* (Paris: Edouard Aubanel, 1943), p. 30.

53. Cited by André Billy, *Vie des frères Goncourt,* 3 vols. (Monaco: Editions de l'Imprimerie nationale, 1956), 3:166.

54. Léon Daudet, *Souvenirs littéraires* (Paris: Grasset, 1968), pp. 368-69. Daudet here echoes the criticisms contained in one of the novels of his father, Alphonse Daudet, *L'Immortel* (1888), a satire on the Académie française.

55. See Robert Escarpit, *La Révolution du livre* (Paris: UNESCO, 1965), pp. 79-81, 127-33, for figures on average printings; and, on the effects of the Goncourt, see Jean-François Revel, "The Literary Prize System," *Times Literary Supplement* (London), 29 September 1969, p. 1081; Armand Lanoux, "Une Académie la tête en bas," *Les Nouvelles littéraires,* 20 November 1969; Nourissier, "Le Monde du livre" (see n. 6, above); and the survey of prizewinners, "Que devez-vous au Goncourt?" *Les Nouvelles littéraires,* 23 November 1967.

56. Neither the Interallié nor the Renaudot offers monetary awards, and the original Goncourt prize of 5,000 francs had shrunk to 50 francs (about $10) by the 1960s. Some 622 literary prizes are awarded in France, but most provide more glory than cash. Cash awards (outside those of the Académie française) totaled only about 350,000 francs ($81,000) in 1965, but they were complemented by travel, wine, jewelry, and even a Christmas wreath. These nonmonetary awards of course reinforce the symbolic nature of the prizes, a key aspect of the prize system.

57. The publicity surrounding the prizes and the elections to the Académie Goncourt and, especially, to the Académie française very likely contributes to, even as it betokens, the newsworthiness of literary activities in France. Comparison of *Time Magazine* and *L'Express* in 1973-74 showed that *L'Express* gave, on the average, twice as much coverage to literary activities as *Time.*

58. One group of leftist critics in 1968, dissatisfied with the interrelations between prize committees and the market, innovated to the extent of founding a new prize, the Prix Littérature, "pour déjouer toute colonisation économique et dogmatique de la vie

littéraire." There is even a prize for "the worst, the silliest, the most boring, or the most disappointing work of the year"—the Prix Nana.

One cannot but speculate on the cultural and institutional sources of this respect for literary prizes. One thinks immediately of the continual use of rankings and prizes throughout the traditional French educational system, the search for order and classificatory precision (sometimes labeled Cartesianism), the respect for technical expertise, and the reliance on commissions of experts for numerous decisions.

59. Revel, "The Literary Prize System." For an account written at the request of the Académie Goncourt and using its archives, see Jacques Robichon, *Le Défi des Goncourt* (Paris: Denoël, 1975); this work also contains Edmond Goncourt's will, the statutes of the Académie, a list of prizewinners through 1974 (including final votes and losers), and a list of the recipients of the recently established short-story and historical-narrative prizes.

The opposition to the prize system in general and to the Goncourt in particular (for variability of standards, timidity of choice, and prominence of extraliterary criteria) has become particularly strident in recent years. In addition to the bombings which marked the 1975 prize season, more temperate critiques of the prize system and its effects on French publishing are found in Roger Gouze, *Les Bêtes à Goncourt* (Paris: Hachette, 1973); Robert Laffont, *Editeur* (Paris: Robert Laffont, 1974), pp. 175–93; and André Gouillou, *Le Book Business* (Paris: Téma-Editions, 1975), pp. 109 ff.

60. The "literary system" englobes the institutions and individuals concerned in the creation, production, diffusion, and reception of literary products. See P. Clark, "The Comparative Method: Sociology and the Study of Literature," *Yearbook of Comparative and General Literature* 23 (1974): 5–13.

10. Goody: Literacy, Criticism, and the Growth of Knowledge

1. See, specifically, J. Goody and I. P. Watt, "The Consequences of Literacy," *Comparative Studies in Society and History* 5 (1963): 304–45.

2. I am indebted to E. A. Havelock, *Preface to Plato* (Cambridge, Mass.: Harvard University Press, 1963), and to David Olson, "The Bias of Language in Speech and Writing," in H. Fisher and R. Diez-Gurerro, eds., *Language and Logic in Personality and Society* (New York, 1976).

3. See my paper, "Literacy and Classification: On Turning the Tables," in R. K. Jain, ed., *Text and Context* (London, 1975).

4. I am much indebted to discussions with D. Gjertsen, Department of Philosophy, University of Ghana.

5. Needham's view of primitive thought owes much to Lévy-Bruhl, a fact that influences his interpretation of the Chinese achievement: "The selection of 'causes' at random from this undifferentiated magma of phenomena was called by Lévy-Bruhl the 'law of participation' in that the whole of the environment experienced by the primitive mind is laid under contribution, i.e. participates, in its explanations, without regard either for true causal connection or for the principle of contradiction" (Needham 1956:284).

6. I do not myself see how the suggestions that Watt and I put forward concerning the consequences of literacy can be considered a "great-divide theory," since we treat "literacy" as a variable. Moreover, it is clearly only one of many changes in the *mode* of communication which might influence the *content* of communication. Since I am referring to Ruth Finnegan's article in the volume on *Modes of Thought* (1973) that

she edited with Robin Horton, I should add that Horton's article takes a somewhat different position than the one I have commented upon here.

7. See my "Religion, Social Change and the Sociology of Conversion" in J. Goody, ed., *Changing Social Structure in Ghana* (London, 1975).

8. See my *Intellectuals in Non-literate Societies* (in press).

9. For a more recent discussion, see S. J. Tambiah, "The Magical Power of Words," *Man* 3 (1968): 175-208, and T. Todorov, "Le Discours de la magie," *L'Homme* 13 (1973): 38-65.

11. Ben-David: Social Control and Cognitive Change in Science

1. For a summary of this controversy, see Diana Crane, *Invisible Colleges* (Chicago: University of Chicago Press, 1972), pp. 8-11.

2. Robert K. Merton, *Science, Technology, and Society* (New York: Howard Fertie, 1970).

3. Thomas S. Kuhn, "Scientific Growth: Reflections on Ben-David's 'Scientific Role,'" *Minerva* 10 (January 1972): 173-74.

4. See Thomas Sprat, *The History of the Royal Society of London for the Improving of Natural Knowledge* (London, 1667). Sprat speaks of the Royal Society as the "general *Banck* and Freeport of the world [in the new learning]" (p. 64); about England as "the Head of a *Philosophical League*, above all other countries in Europe" (p. 113); and about French recognition of England as the country which has *"Real Philosophy"* (p. 126). For a discussion showing that the existence of a "Philosophical League" and the recognition of English leadership following the foundation of the Royal Society were not merely an expression of patriotic bias on Sprat's part, see Harcourt Brown, *Scientific Organizations of Seventeenth-Century France (1620-1680)* (Baltimore: Williams & Wilkins, 1934), pp. 15-60.

5. The criticisms of and doubts about the Royal Society are summarized in R. F. Jones, *Ancients and Moderns: A Study of the Rise of the Scientific Movement in Seventeenth-Century England*, 2d ed. (Berkeley and Los Angeles: University of California Press, 1965), pp. 237-72.

6. Sprat, *History of the Royal Society*, pp. 22-58.

7. One of the most interesting documents showing a sociologist's attempt to make a basically Marxist position amenable to judgment by the accepted criteria of the scientific community is Karl Mannheim's *Ideology and Utopia* (New York: Harcourt, Brace, 1936), pp. 155-64. For a discussion of the relationship between science and ideology, see Edward Shils, *The Intellectuals and the Powers, and Other Essays* (Chicago: University of Chicago Press, 1972), pp. 37-38.

8. For discussions of the ambiguous relationship between science and these other modes of thought and the difficulty of demarcating one from the other, see Alan Debus, *Science and Education in the Seventeenth Century: The Webster-Ward Debate* (London and New York: MacDonald and American Elsevier, 1970), pp. 1-57; P. M. Rattansi, "The Social Interpretation of Science in the Seventeenth Century," in Peter Mathias, ed., *Science and Society* (Cambridge: At the University Press, 1972), pp. 1-32.

9. Margery Purver, *The Royal Society: Concept and Creation* (Cambridge, Mass.: MIT Press, 1967), pp. 60-61, 77, 80-81; Roger Hahn, *Anatomy of a Scientific Institution: The Paris Academy of Sciences, 1666-1804* (Berkeley: University of California Press, 1971), pp. 11-12, 24-36; Keith Michael Baker, *Condorcet: From*

Natural Philosophy to Social Mathematics (Chicago: University of Chicago Press, 1975), p. 93.

10. Robert K. Merton, "Priorities in Scientific Discovery: A Chapter in the Sociology of Science," *American Sociological Review* 22 (1957): 645-59; Warren O. Hagstrom, *The Scientific Community* (New York: Basic Books, 1965), pp. 69-104.

11. Hahn, *Anatomy of a Scientific Institution,* pp. 22-23, 26-34.

12. Ibid., pp. 32-33. Hahn uses the apposite term "phenomenological positivism" to describe this policy. For a similar policy, adopted earlier by the Royal Society, see Sprat, *History of the Royal Society,* pp. 106-9. But there this method was part of the original design of the Society. See also Stephen G. Brush, "The Royal Society's First Rejection of the Kinetic Theory of Gases (1821): John Herapath versus Humphrey Davy," *Notes and Records of the Royal Society of London* 18 (December 1963): 161-80, for an example of a recourse to the principles of scientific method as a judicial-moral argument in a case in which substantive scientific opinion was divided.

13. See Hahn, *Anatomy of a Scientific Institution,* pp. 278-85, for the background of the French reforms of higher education after 1794; and see René König, *Vom Wesen der deutschen Universität* (Darmstadt: Wissenschaftliche Buchgesellschaft, 1970), pp. 27-40, for the antecedents of the establishment of the University of Berlin and the reform of higher education in Prussia during the first decade of the nineteenth century.

14. Hahn, *Anatomy of a Scientific Institution,* pp. 245-46, 288-312.

15. The Society of Arcueil (1807-22) was a group of physicists and chemists, led by Berthollet and Laplace, who shared common interests and worked on related problems. See Maurice Crosland, *The Society of Arcueil* (Cambridge, Mass.: Harvard University Press, 1967), pp. 232-428; Robert Fox, "Scientific Enterprise and the Patronage of Science in France, 1800-1870," *Minerva* 11 (1973): 442-73.

16. Joseph Ben-David and Awraham Zloczower, "Universities and Academic Systems in Modern Society," *European Journal of Sociology* 3 (1962): 45-84.

17. Friedrich Paulsen, *Geschichte des gelehrten Unterrichts auf den deutschen Schulen und Universitäten,* 2 vols. (Leipzig: Von Veit, 1892), 2:269-74.

18. For the importance of the training of pharmacists, see Bernard Gustin, "The Chemical Profession in Germany, 1790-1867" (Ph.D. diss., University of Chicago, 1975).

19. For the emergence of such a view, resulting from the spectacular advances in classical mechanics during the second half of the eighteenth century, see L. Pearce Williams, *The Origins of Field Theory* (New York: Random House, 1966), pp. 30-31. See also E. J. Dijksterhuis, *The Mechanization of the World Picture* (London: Oxford University Press, 1969), pp. 499-501.

20. This is still the prevailing tradition in science teaching; see Thomas S. Kuhn, *The Structure of Scientific Revolutions* (Chicago: University of Chicago Press, 1962), pp. 10-22.

21. For the monopolization of research resources by heads of institutions, see Awraham Zloczower, "Konjunktur in der Forschung," in F. Pfetsch and A. Zloczower, *Innovation und Widerstände in der Wissenschaft* (Düsseldorf: Bertelsmann, 1973).

22. For the case of Semmelweiss, see Bernard J. Stern, "Resistance to Medical Change," in his *Historical Sociology* (New York: Citadel Press, 1959), pp. 363-65. On Mendel, see Hugo Iltis, *Life of Mendel* (London: Allen & Unwin, 1932), pp. 191-204. On biochemistry, see Robert Kohler, "The Background to Edward Büchner's Discovery of Cell-Free Fermentation," *Journal of the History of Biology* 4

(1971): 57-58; Awraham Zloczower, "Konjunctur in der Forschung," on the difficulties that bacteriology as a discipline encountered at German universities; and James Richard Bartholomew, "The Acculturation of Science in Japan: Kitasato Shibasaburo and the Japanese Bacteriological Community, 1885-1920 (Ph.D. diss., Stanford University, 1971), pp. 170-71.

23. For the hurdles against cooperation between the chemist Otto Hahn and the physicist Lisa Meitner, see Otto Hahn, *Scientific Autobiography* (New York: Scribner's, 1966), pp. 50-72.

24. Kuhn, *The Structure of Scientific Revolutions*, pp. 10-22.

25. On Semmelweiss and Mendel, see note 22, above.

26. Bartholomew, "The Acculturation of Science in Japan," pp. 185-91.

27. Crosland, *The Society of Arcueil*, pp. 126, 427, 458-59.

28. For the rise of journals, see D. McKie, "The Scientific Periodical from 1665 to 1798," in A. Ferguson, ed., *Natural Philosophy through the Eighteenth Century and Allied Topics* (commemoration number to mark the sesquicentennial of the founding of the *Philosophical Magazine*) (London: Taylor & Francis, 1948), p. 127.

29. See Armin Hermann, *The Genesis of Quantum Theory* (Cambridge, Mass.: MIT Press, 1971), pp. 139-43, on the Solvay Conference.

30. A conspicuous case of appeal to a larger public has been described by Brush in "The Royal Society's First Rejection of the Kinetic Theory of Gases." John Herapath actually took his debate with the Royal Society to the columns of the London *Times*. This brought him some recognition and sympathy; however, his somewhat faulty exposition of the kinetic theory did not arouse much interest.

31. The importance of the public nature of scientific knowledge has been stressed by John Ziman, *Public Knowledge: An Essay Concerning the Social Dimension of Science* (London: Cambridge University Press, 1968); see also Baker, *Condorcet*, p. 78.

32. I. Mitroff, "Norms and Counternorms in a Select Group of the Apollo Moon Scientists," *American Sociological Review* 39 (1974): 575-96. See also S. G. Brush, "Should the History of Science Be Rated 'X'?" *Science* 183 (22 March 1974): 1164-72.

33. "The Scientific Community: Thoughts after Hamburg," in Edward Shils, *The Intellectuals and the Powers, and Other Essays*, p. 209 (this essay was originally published in the May 1954 issue of the *Bulletin of the Atomic Scientists*).

12. Parsons: Growth of American Higher Education and Research

1. Raymond Boudon, "Crise universitaire et participation," *Economies et sociétés* 4 (September 1970): 1670-1704.

2. See Laurence R. Veysey, *The Emergence of the American University* (Chicago: University of Chicago Press, 1965).

3. See Joseph Ben-David, *American Higher Education: Directions Old and New* (New York: McGraw-Hill, 1972).

4. On certain considerations involving this development, see Talcott Parsons and Gerald M. Platt, *The American University* (Cambridge, Mass.: Harvard University Press, 1973); and Talcott Parsons, "The University 'Bundle': A Study of the Balance between Differentiation and Integration," in Neil J. Smelser and Gabriel Almond, eds., *Public Higher Education in California: Growth, Structural Change, and Conflict* (Berkeley, Calif.: University of California Press, 1974).

5. Boudon, "Crise universitaire et participation."

6. Neil J. Smelser, "Growth, Structural Change, and Conflict in California Public

Higher Education, 1950-1970," in Smelser and Almond, eds., *Public Higher Education in California*, pp. 9-141.

7. Ibid.

8. Max Weber, "Science as a Vocation," in H. H. Gerth and C. Wright Mills, eds., *From Max Weber: Essays in Sociology* (New York: Oxford University Press, 1946), pp. 129-56; and Max Weber, *The Protestant Ethic and the Spirit of Capitalism*, trans. T. Parsons (New York: Scribner's, 1930). See also Robert K. Merton, *Science, Technology, and Society in Seventeenth Century England* (New York: H. Fertig, 1970).

9. See the extremely interesting analysis of this by Edward A. Tiryakian, "Neither Marx nor Durkheim—Perhaps Weber," *American Journal of Sociology* 81 (1975): 1-33.

10. Merton, *Science, Technology, and Society*. Weber, *The Protestant Ethic and the Spirit of Capitalism*; see also the introduction to this volume by T. Parsons, pp. 13-31. S. N. Eisenstadt, ed., *The Protestant Ethic and Modernization: A Comparative View* (New York: Basic Books, 1968). Joseph Ben-David, *The Scientist's Role in Society: A Comparative Study* (Englewood Cliffs, N.J.: Prentice-Hall, 1971).

11. See Perry Miller, *Errand into the Wilderness* (Cambridge, Mass.: Harvard University Press, 1964).

12. As has been true of so many major contributions in the social sciences, Weber's analysis of the relation between the Protestant ethic and not only capitalism but other paramount features of modern "industrial" society has been the subject of extensive controversy, in the course of which many gross misinterpretations of his work have been made. We are now fortunate that three particularly competent and well-balanced surveys of literature on what has come to be called "the Protestant-ethic problem" are available in published form in English. The first of these is the one written by Dr. David Little in a bibliographical appendix to his notable study *Religion, Order, and Law* (New York: Harper Torchbooks, 1969). A second is the introduction by S. N. Eisenstadt to the volume entitled *Max Weber on Charisma and Institution Building* (Chicago: University of Chicago Press, 1968), pp. ix-lvi. The third one, by Benjamin Nelson, is Chapter 2, "Weber's Protestant Ethic: Its Origins, Wanderings and Foreseeable Futures," in Charles Y. Glock and Philip Hammond, eds., *Beyond the Classics?* (New York: Harper & Row, 1973). I would like to add another contribution to this list. This is the paper by Tiryakian, "Neither Marx nor Durkheim—Perhaps Weber." This paper is not, however, a survey of the literature, but the latter part of it on Weber contains an extremely insightful discussion of the Protestant-ethic problem in its relevance to the understanding of American society.

13. Tiryakian, "Neither Marx nor Durkheim—Perhaps Weber."

14. Merton, *Science, Technology, and Society*.

15. See Robert Bellah, *The Broken Covenant* (forthcoming).

16. Cf. Miller, *Errand into the Wilderness*.

17. John Locke, *The Second Treatise of Civil Government: An Essay Concerning the True Original Extent and End of Civil Government, and A Letter Concerning Toleration* (1690), edited with a revised introduction, by J. W. Gough (New York: McMillan, 1956).

18. Alfred Marshall, *Principles of Economics*, 8th ed. (London: Macmillan, 1925).

19. See Elie Halévy, *The Growth of Philosophic Radicalism*, trans. Mary Morris (New York: Macmillan, 1928); first published in French as *La Formation du*

radicalisme philosophique, 3 vols. (Paris: F. Alcan, 1901-4). See also Lionel Robbins, *An Essay on the Nature and Significance of Economic Science,* 2d ed. (London: Macmillan, 1935).

20. Though Bellah emphasizes his intention to stress this concept in his introduction to *The Broken Covenant,* the actual text of the book, as I have seen it, in fact fails to fulfill this promise. It seems to me a particularly crucial one for the appraisal of the issues with which Bellah is concerned.

21. For the case of the Industrial Revolution, for example, see Neil J. Smelser, *Social Change in the Industrial Revolution* (London: Routledge & Kegan Paul, 1959), and David S. Landes, *The Unbound Prometheus: Technological Change and Industrial Development in Western Europe from 1750 to the Present* (London: Cambridge University Press, 1972).

22. See Parsons and Platt, *The American University,* esp. chap. 2, pp. 33-102.

23. See Daniel Bell, *The Coming of Post-Industrial Society* (New York: Basic Books, 1973).

24. Landes, *The Unbound Prometheus.*

25. Cf. Talcott Parsons, "Comparative Studies and Evolutionary Change," in Ivan Vallier, ed., *Comparative Methods in Sociology* (Berkeley, Calif.: University of California Press, 1971), pp. 97-139.

26. See Donald Fleming and Bernard Bailyn, eds., *The Intellectual Migration: Europe and America, 1930-1960* (Cambridge, Mass.: Harvard University Press, 1969).

27. Talcott Parsons, *The Structure of Social Action* (New York: McGraw-Hill, 1937).

28. Weber, *The Protestant Ethic.*

29. Edward A. Shils, *The Intellectuals and the Powers, and Other Essays* (Chicago: University of Chicago Press, 1972).

30. Cf. Robert K. Merton, "Social Structure and Anomie," in *Social Theory and Social Structure,* rev. ed. (New York: Free Press, 1957), pp. 131-60; also see, for example, Richard A. Cloward and Lloyd E. Ohlin, *Delinquency and Opportunity: A Theory of Delinquent Gangs* (New York: Free Press of Glencoe, 1961).

31. English translations of a number of Simmel's essays appeared in the *American Journal of Sociology* in the years 1896-1906. Many of these essays and others have been reprinted in English in the following volumes: Robert E. Park and Ernest W. Burgess, eds., *Introduction to the Science of Sociology,* 2d ed. (Chicago: University of Chicago Press, 1924); Edgar F. Borgatta and Henry J. Meyer, eds., *Sociological Theory: Present Day Sociology from the Past* (New York: Knopf, 1956); and Kurt H. Wolff, ed., *Georg Simmel, 1858-1918: A Collection of Essays, with Translations and a Bibliography* (Columbus: Ohio State University Press, 1959).

32. Cf. Parsons, "The University Bundle," in Smelser and Almond, eds., *Public Higher Education in California.*

33. There is a famous story which may or may not be apocryphal—this hardly matters—that concerns the mood of the Harvard department of mathematics a generation and more ago where on some festive occasion a toast is said to have been drunk to the discipline of mathematics, and the toast ran, "To mathematics! May she never have any practical applications." It seems to me that this incident, whether it actually happened or not, may serve as a symbol of the kind of explanation I wish to put forward of the very big development of institutionalization in the academic world.

Contributors

RAYMOND ARON
Collège de France

SAUL BELLOW
The University of Chicago

JOSEPH BEN-DAVID
The Hebrew University

REINHARD BENDIX
The University of California at Berkeley

PRISCILLA P. CLARK
The University of Illinois at Chicago Circle

TERRY NICHOLS CLARK
The University of Chicago

S. N. EISENSTADT
The Hebrew University

CLIFFORD GEERTZ
The Institute for Advanced Study, Princeton

JACK GOODY
Cambridge University

MORRIS JANOWITZ
The University of Chicago

HARRY G. JOHNSON
The University of Chicago

SEYMOUR MARTIN LIPSET
Stanford University

TALCOTT PARSONS
Harvard University

DATE DUE